# CRUSADE AGAINST DRINK IN VICTORIAN ENGLAND

# Crusade against Drink in Victorian England

Lilian Lewis Shiman

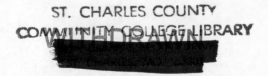
St. Martin's Press   New York

First published in the United States of America in 1988

Printed in Hong Kong

ISBN 0–312–17777–1

Library of Congress Cataloging-in-Publication Data
Shiman, Lilian Lewis.
Crusade against drink in Victorian England.
Includes index.
1. Temperance—England—History.   2. Temperance
societies—England—History.   I. Title.
HV5446.S55   1988      363.4′1′0942      85–26081
ISBN 0–312–17777–1

To my husband, Paul L. Shiman

# Contents

# Preface

My interest in the temperance movement was first aroused when I was a graduate student at the University of Wisconsin. It was at the suggestion of Professor John F. C. Harrison that I started my research in this field and I am grateful for the initial help and guidance he gave me. I should also like to acknowledge the assistance I received from the Department of History at the University of Wisconsin with their award of a Martha L. Edwards scholarship which made possible my first research trip to England.

I should like to express my appreciation to the Bunting Institute of Harvard University which supported this work for two years with an independent research fellowship.

The material for this work could not have been gathered without the help of many individuals both in England and the United States. To Muriel Daniels and her staff at the British Temperance League's headquarters in Sheffield go my warmest thanks. They were generous both with their time and their knowledge. To J. B. Harrison and K. Underwood of the Church of England Council for Social Aid (successor of the CETS), to the late Philip Mallendar of the Yorkshire Band of Hope Union, to T. Garth Waite of the United Kingdom Alliance, to Joanna Dawson of Harrogate and to Mark Hayler, son of Guy Hayler, I owe a debt of gratitude for their help and patience.

I should like to acknowledge a considerable obligation to the teetotallers of Birstall. Alderman Stone and his wife, who were instrumental in introducing me both to temperance materials and to individual teetotallers of the area, were very helpful, as were all the individuals who allowed me to interview them. They gave me their time and knowledge of their experiences with the temperance movement. Printed words cannot express the personal attachment many of these lifelong teetotallers have to the temperance reformation.

To the administration and colleagues at Nichols College I owe a special thanks. The help and support I received from them was important in bringing this work to its fruition.

One of the great joys in bringing this book to publication is the pleasure of my children Daniel, Philip and Elizabeth in it. Their large contribution has been the ungrudging acceptance of a mother often buried away in her 'temperance writings', which became a natural part of their lives. But I am sure they will understand that I dedicate this book to my husband Paul, whose help and encouragement enabled me to keep going during difficult times. His critical eye has helped me immeasurably in my writings. Needless to say, I accept full responsibilities for any mistakes that any reader may find.

LILIAN LEWIS SHIMAN

**Note.** 'Teetotalism', 'teetotal', etc., was created in Preston in 1834–5. In the nineteenth century it was usual to spell 'teetotaler' with one 'l'; even in the official evidence of the Royal Commission on Liquor Licensing it was spelt with one 'l'. Only rarely do we find it with two 'l's.

*Round about, round about, applety pie*
*Daddy loves ale and so do I*
*Mammy gets up, and fills us a cup*
*And Daddy and me we sup it all up.*
   *Sup it all up*
   *Sup it all up*

(old Yorkshire ditty)


*My drink is water bright*
*Water bright, water bright*
*My drink is water bright*
*From the crystal spring.*

(popular Band of Hope song)

# Introduction

It is no historical accident that the temperance movement arose in the nineteenth century. It was one of many social reforming causes such as anti-slavery, evangelical religion, factory reform and public education – which were contemporaneous and overlapping; many members of one were also members of others. Anti-slavery had little direct effect on the domestic affairs of England, and evangelical religion aimed to change the lives of all social classes, but the temperance movement, along with others, was concerned with the welfare of the emerging working classes, attempting to mitigate the social dislocation caused by the industrialisation of Britain.

There was a great deal of drinking in eighteenth-century England, the heyday of gin, but no temperance movement arose to fight it. Not that there was no opposition then to excessive drinking; many individuals were horrified at the amount of drunkenness, especially among the lower classes – Hogarth's drawings can be seen as an indictment of the drinking habits of his age – but no movement or organisation arose to counter the evil. Drinking was firmly fixed in traditional social and cultural practices in England. At every formal dinner the health of the monarch and other notables was toasted with great ceremony and only alcoholic beverages could be used. On informal occasions too there was drink on every table; the upper classes had their table and fortified wines, while the lower classes drank mainly beer and cider. In entertaining friends or relatives virtually everyone, of every class, would serve some kind of alcoholic beverage. Many of the upper classes frequented private clubs, where they could drink socially with their associates, while the working classes made the public houses the centres of their social lives; there they would hold meetings and dances and partake in all kinds of recreational activities. John Dunlop, in his book *The Philosophy of Artificial and Compulsory Drinking Usage in Great Britain and Ireland*, revealed to the general public many of the current trade practices and claimed that the working classes had many more drinking customs than did the middle and upper classes, although all commercial agreements were sealed with drink.

Prior to the nineteenth century, then, all classes drank, often to

1

excess, but only a few worried about it. It was a man's right to get drunk if he wanted to. Drunkenness carried no social stigma; to be 'as drunk as a lord' was a common English expression. Both Pitt the Younger and Fox, it was said, drank excessively, but no one thought the less of them for it.

In the nineteenth century, however, a change occurred and intemperance began to be perceived as a problem. In fact all drinking was seen in a different context than formerly. The 'work discipline' concept brought into being by industrialisation transformed drunkenness from a personal state of excess sociability into an anti-social vice. Drinking caused absenteeism and instability among the working classes: Saint Monday, once an accepted 'hangover' day, was no longer sanctioned. Drinking decreased the efficiency of the working classes and was therefore undesirable, according to a growing number of anti-drink supporters.

E. P. Thompson, in his book *The Making of the English Working Class* (London, 1963), has shown the role Methodism played in moulding the workers to the strict work discipline that the new factories demanded. Temperance, it can be said, supplemented the work of the Methodists. But it did more than help create efficient workers; it played an important role in organising the social lives of many workers. Life in the new manufacturing centres was very difficult and there were few agencies to help the immigrant worker adjust to his new situation. The temperance societies provided a supportive framework which assisted many people who had been uprooted, psychologically as well as physically, to adapt from traditional modes of behaviour to newer, more viable patterns attuned to their existing circumstances.

The nineteenth-century working-class family unit met many obstacles in trying to preserve its integrity. Frequently whole families had only one small room with the minimum of facilities for a home, and some of the very poor families had to share even this meagre situation with others. It is not difficult to understand why many living in this condition preferred to spend their time away from home, in drinking houses, where they were assured of the warmth and comfort that was lacking in their own abodes.

The difficulties of these workers were often increased by the lack of communication between the various levels of society in the industrial areas. Even at work, employees had little personal contact with their employers, especially as the factories got bigger.

'We hardly know the number of people we employ, and deal with them not as units but in hundreds – as hands not men', said George Melly, a Member of Parliament for Liverpool and a former official in that city.

The separation between the classes was intensified by the formation of varying life-styles based on widely differing economic situations. So distinct were these patterns of living that when members of different classes had any social contact, they were often incapable of communicating with one another. The poor and the ignorant found themselves alone and helpless in a world of ever-recurring trade cycles and increasing poverty. The slums became their permanent fate and their only escape was the momentary oblivion produced by intoxication. As a popular saying had it: 'Drink is the quickest way out of Manchester.'

Not all working-class men were willing to allow outside circumstances to control their lives. Thoughout the nineteenth century a substantial number sought ways to advance themselves and their fellows through individual and group action. A small minority were able to create their own success; they were the heroes of the age. The majority, however, unable to carry the load alone, sought to form and maintain associations that would be mutually supportive. Particularly in the new industrial towns, where the religious and secular establishments were unable to provide leadership in the development of stable working-class communities, did such voluntary associations proliferate. Some were only temporary phenomena, but a considerable number proved to be durable, lasting for many decades. Methodist chapels, for example, frequently became the centres of religiously linked communities that provided all manner of support for their members. Trade unions and trade clubs gave more than economic assistance. Likewise the temperance movement did more than fight intemperance. It became an important vehicle for fulfilling the social and, eventually, the religious needs of its members. The temperance societies that survived the century – with life if not with vigour – were those that were sufficiently firm in their temperance principles to be flexible enough to absorb the ever-changing modes of popular culture and to utilise them within the temperance context. The anti-drink cause had to change its focus and activities as the world around it changed.

The temperance movement in England in the nineteenth century went through four major phases. At the beginning, in the early years of the 1830s, temperance was a traditional middle-class movement with clergymen and upper-class reformers providing leadership for the largely middle-class membership who, out of Christian charity, were helping their lesser brethren fight intemperance. Few working-class leaders or groups were prominent at this time.

The second phase can be dated from the mid 1830s to the late 1840s, when working-class teetotallers dominated the movement. Teetotal temperance at this time provided a psychological 'place' for its members and gave them a sense of personal worth. The movement became one of the many major self-help agencies that the working-class created and supported in the 1840s. At this time the temperance movement became a vehicle for individual self-improvement that was so clearly beloved by many reformers of this period. It was at this time that the teetotal movement produced most of its best-known working-class leaders, some of whom, by the end of the nineteenth century, had become successful economically, politically and socially.

From the late 1850s to the mid 1870s the moral suasion temperance movement was dormant while attention was focused on experiments to curb the sale of drink through legislative action. Attempts were made to introduce prohibition, both nationally and locally, in the 1860s and 1870s, but these attempts failed.

Meanwhile, intemperance in England appeared to increase and the churches and other institutions felt the need to take a more effective stand. Moral suasion temperance revived, therefore, when gospel temperance appeared on the scene in the mid 1870s. Linking the anti-drink reform with religion, it once again stressed personal abstention. At the same time the political fervour had not completely died and local governments became increasingly involved with the 'drinking question' as numerous battles over the issuing and conditions of licences for local drinking houses were fought between temperance reformers and the drinking interests. These battles led to a new community action on the licensing issues both locally and nationally.

This third phase of the anti-drink movement, the 1880s and 1890s, came at a time when many of the old teetotallers were firmly established in local political circles, holding offices of both status and power. The political influence of the temperance reformers was recognised officially by the Liberal Party in 1891 when it made local prohibition a part of its Newcastle Programme.

The fourth and last period for the temperance movement came with its rejection by both the electorate and the churches. When the Newcastle Programme was defeated in the election of 1895, its temperance clauses were blamed for the defeat. On the religious side the churches refused to insist on teetotalism as a condition of membership in their denominational temperance societies and would condemn only intemperance, not moderate drinking. Furthermore, the Church of England refused to allow non-alcoholic wine at the sacramental table, a change many teetotallers had striven for. With this double blow the temperance movement turned inward. It created local teetotal communities that were safe from the drink-infested world. From the middle of the 1890s to the outbreak of the war in 1914, these increasingly isolated groups, clustered around their local temperance halls, remained as the last vestige of the great crusade against drink.

# Part One

# An Unpopular Cause – Visionaries and Fanatics

# 1 The Temperance Reformation

When the temperance reformation came to England in the late 1820s it did not come directly to London, but was first established, almost prophetically, in the north, where the cause was to find much of its sustenance and vigour throughout the nineteenth century. It did not take long, however, for it to spread throughout the country and to find support among many individuals who were committed to other reforming causes. These early champions of the temperance cause saw it as only one part of a larger movement to reform the manners and culture of English society. 'Every day's experience tends more to confirm me in my opinion that the temperance cause lies at the foundation of all social and political reform', said Richard Cobden, the anti-Corn Law leader. Two other well-known reformers, Lord Shaftesbury and Earl Stanhope, were also active in the early temperance cause.

In the first years of the movement, in the early 1830s, the aim of temperance reformers was 'to produce a great change on public opinion and practice'.[1] It was their object to 'awaken public attention to the incalculable and increasing evils of intemperance'.[2] In effect, what they sought was a reformation in the drinking practices of all classes. Mostly of middle-class background, the reformers wanted their own class to set an example for the 'lower orders' and, with this end in mind, they concentrated on publicising temperance principles among the middle classes. 'While other societies spread the broad light of heaven over whole hemispheres, Temperance Societies concentrate for a moment to burn up a single abomination',[3] proclaimed Professor Edgar, a leader in the movement. That single abomination was, of course, intemperance, and for the temperance societies there was just one objective: to reduce intemperance.

The first English temperance reformers did not regard alcoholic drink itself as evil or its consumption as wrong; they drank wines and fermented beverages quite freely and condemned only the excessive use of distilled spirits. The temperance societies which these reformers organised were likewise not rigid about the drinking habits of their members and usually allowed even those who drank spirits to join if they wished. Drunkenness was what the reformers aimed to discourage, not social drinking. Because the majority of these early temperance advocates believed controlled, moderate drinking to be best they were later known as the 'moderation' or 'anti-spirits' movement, to distinguish them from the later teetotal dominated movement.

A person joining the early temperance movement would need to make few, if any, personal sacrifices, although a considerable minority voluntarily gave up all alcoholic drink as an example for others. This was done from personal choice, not because of any institutional demand of the movement. Founded on Christian charity, these early abstainers took their position from St Paul's command: 'It is good neither to eat flesh nor to drink wine, nor anything whereby thy brother stumbleth, or is offended or is made weak.'[4] Thus self-denial was one tenet of the early temperance movement, but only for those who chose it. Coercion was shunned. 'To *command* to abstain is antichristian – to abstain may be a noble exercise of Christian liberty', wrote Edgar, a professor of divinity as well as a well-known temperance lecturer.[5] Consequently the signing of the pledge was a voluntary act, not an essential qualification for membership in the movement; all were encouraged to sign it as a public affirmation of their position on intemperance.

The early temperance supporters were not concerned with reclaiming those who were already drunkards. They restricted their activities to preventing drinkers from reaching that condition: the drunkard had already put himself beyond the interest of supporters of moderation by his demonstrated weakness in allowing himself to reach such a state. 'Drunkards we hold to be almost irreclaimable . . . it is rather too late for men to become members, when they have become drunkards',[6] said William Collins, a noted temperance advocate, at a public meeting. The *Temperance Penny Magazine*, the journal of the British and Foreign Temperance Society, went further than Collins in its rejection of the intemperate. An article in the magazine insisted on the drunkard's being held responsible for his own condition. He is not a 'passive being' acted upon by intoxicating beverages, the article proclaimed; the drunkard forms his own character. The idea that his character '*would be formed for him and not by him*' is a socialist dogma 'not expressing the true principles of the gospel'. Drunkenness, the article claimed, springs not from the distilled spirit or fermented liquors but from 'the depraved propensities of the drunkard himself'.[7] Following this line of reasoning further, the article stated: 'if the drunkard had not bought the seller would not have sold.'[8] And so these reformers did not stigmatise the vendors of intoxicating drink – they had a legitimate trade. Far from condemning the seller, many societies had wine merchants and brewers on their subscription lists: the secretary of the Penrith Temperance Society was a brewer.[9]

In an effort to 'lay before the moderate and respectable and the influential classes such a clear and unvarnished statement of the mischiefs arising from convivial habits, solitary indulgence, long-established customs',[10] temperance societies held public meetings in towns all over the country. The tone of these meetings was such that only the most respectable and concerned citizens would attend. They would be addressed by some eminent authority whose personal and professional qualifications were beyond reproach. Typical was one held by the Leeds Temperance Society, as recorded in its minutes for 9 March 1831. At this meeting the speaker 'was particularly eloquent and kept up the attention and delight of a large audience consisting of ladies and gentlemen of respectability and influence until 10 o'clock'.[11]

The early temperance reformers introduced very few innovations in the established techniques of English reforming movements; they were content to copy methods originated by other reformers. These moderationists were careful to avoid shocking the sensibilities of the public. The major tool used to spread the movement was the local temperance society, set up in every town where there were enough supporters to sustain one. In the first year of the reformation, 1830, twenty societies were 'planted', with a total membership of 2000 to 3000.[12] The north of England was a particularly fertile area for these associations. In Manchester the temperance society boasted a membership of 1200 to 1500 and the neighbouring town of Blackburn claimed a membership of 600 for its very prosperous temperance society.[13] The Blackburn reformers were asked not only to support the anti-spirit pledge but to avoid all inns and other places that sold spirits, except 'when necessary for refreshment in travelling, or transacting business when from home'.[14] In Bradford the founding society of the movement maintained its 'peculiar prominence' as a leader of the reform. It was fortunate from the start in having the constant support of many of the prominent men of the town, among them ministers, clergymen, doctors and merchants. It was a merchant, the Scotsman Henry Forbes, who introduced the cause of temperance into England. While on a business trip to Glasgow he attended a meeting of a temperance society already established there, and joined the movement. On his return to Bradford he decided to start a temperance society, the first in England. From the beginning many manufacturers and merchants were staunch supporters of the movement. They regarded temperance as an important aid to any social improvement of the working classes.[15]

The medical profession was a target for much temperance propaganda. It was hoped that if the doctors could be alerted to the dangers of intemperance they would be persuaded to desist from recommending spirits as medicine except where absolutely necessary. Medical declarations were drawn up testifying to the dangers of intemperance and doctors were solicited for their support of these documents.[16]

In London and many southern towns the movement was not quite so fortunate in its initial reception as it was in the north. Twice Scotsman William Collins went to London to set up a temperance society and twice he failed. He managed to organise societies in other towns, but could not attract enough interest in the capital to set up and sustain a regular organisation. Not until 1831, after nineteent provincial societies were set up, was the London Temperance Society inaugurated.[17] Then, a few months later in June 1831, after a highly successful public meeting in Exeter Hall, London, attended by many men prominent in English ruling circles, it was decided to change the name of this society to the British and Foreign Temperance Society and make it into a national body[18] – the only one representing the entire moderation movement. Despite its rather slow start, this society could soon boast of having the Bishop of London as its patron, and five other bishops as vice-presidents.[19]

Attracting many churchmen to its board was quite an achievement for the London society. The reformers were always anxious to ally with the forces of religion but the attitude of the churches towards the anti-spirit movement was an ambivalent one, usually determined by local conditions and individuals. Both the Church of England and the non-conformist churches were sympathetic to moderation principles, but they would not take up temperance work in any official way. Instead they left to the individual ministers and clergymen the decision whether and to what degree to support the movement. When the first temperance society was formed in England in 1830, nine of its thirty-two officers were dissenting ministers and their first agent was a Baptist minister.[20]

Along with the temperance societies, agents were an indispensable means of spreading the principles of the reform. The agents of the moderation societies were well-educated, respectable men with close church connections, established or non-conformist. Many were ordained ministers, with Baptists predominating. They were hired by both local and national societies to travel in the local areas, giving lectures and organising societies. The best-known agent of the moderation movement was the Rev. James Jackson of Hebden Bridge, Yorkshire, a Baptist minister who had worked for the British and Foreign Temperance Society before transferring to the Bradford Temperance Society. He became a well-known figure in northern temperance circles, making tours through Yorkshire and Lancashire, contacting individuals and groups who could aid the cause.[21] Through his efforts the prestige and influence of the Bradford society were greatly increased. Whenever he set up a new society, he encouraged it to become an auxiliary of the Bradford Temperance Society, which was then regarded as the 'mother' organisation.[22]

Other agents of the movement were also anxious to extend the influence of their own associations. Those employed by the British and Foreign Society, in particular, wanted to enrol affiliates all over the country and so strengthen the London-based society's claim to being a national organisation. By 1834 nine agents were employed by this national group, most however for a limited term. Three of them worked voluntarily, giving their services out of love of the movement.[23]

The professional activities of the British and Foreign Temperance Society, like those of many other anti-spirit groups, were severely circumscribed by its lack of funds. The temperance movement was never successful in acquiring the large sums of money that other reforming societies managed to attract,[24] and so had to utilise the services of unpaid advocates wherever possible. Fortunately for the temperance reformation, there were many dedicated reformers willing and able to spend their own time and

money in furthering the cause. Like the professional agents, many
of these men were from religious, middle-class backgrounds.
William Collins, for example, an extremely active temperance
worker, was an elder of the Presbyterian Church and Dr
Beaumont, a president and lecturer of the Bradford society, was
the son and brother of non-conformist ministers. The only reward
these men received was the knowledge that they were helping
their less fortunate brothers in a Christian spirit. Often their work
entailed personal as well as economic sacrifice but, in their
judgement, the cause was well worth it.[25]

One group of middle-class Englishmen that firmly supported
the temperance reformation throughout the nineteenth century
was composed of members of the Society of Friends. Stimulated
by their social concern for the unfortunate, they were often
instrumental in introducing the principles of the movement to
areas that would otherwise have been untouched by the reform.[26]
Their widely accepted reputation for charity as well as for
everyday honesty and goodness made them excellent allies in
getting the support of other 'respectable' groups. They did not
restrict their work to activities with the middle class, but tried to
heighten awareness of the evils of intemperance among the lower
classes.[27] They also provided a large share of the funds used by
temperance societies and independent temperance agents.[28]

Like all contemporary reform movements, the temperance
cause exploited fully the value of the printed word, publishing
tracts, journals, essays and books for the edification of the public.
Lectures that had succeeded in stimulating interest in the cause
when delivered were later published as tracts, which were either
distributed free or sold for a penny or two. Temperance journals
served as a connecting link between the scattered parts of the
movement and as a means of propagandising temperance views
among the uncommitted public. There was close cooperation
among the various societies throughout England, with exchanges
of literature and speakers the rule rather than the exception. This
helped promote a feeling of a cohesive movement among its
individual parts.[29]

It was not long, however, before this spirit of cohesiveness was
torn asunder by the appearance of teetotalism. A more extreme
form of temperance, teetotalism meant total abstinence. The
teetotallers believed that the moderation movement was
incapable of bringing about any signficant reduction in the role of

alcoholic beverages in English life. The Beer Act of 1830, which permitted unlimited beer houses, had been introduced as a temperance measure. But the results had not substantiated the moderationists' predictions that drunkenness would decline with free trade in beer;[30] instead, along with a great increase in the number of beer houses, there was a sharp rise in intemperance.[31] The teetotallers realised that, in some parts of the country, beer was just as much a problem as spirits. Whereas gin was the most popular drink of the lower classes and the chief cause of intemperance in London, in the north country beer was the favoured beverage and the main source of drunkenness.[32] The teetotallers, mostly of lower-class northern origin, were well aware of this fact.

For a short while the total abstainers and the moderationists managed to exist side by side in the same temperance organisations, but the teetotallers soon saw to it that pledges of total abstinence were adopted as the basis of membership in most parts of the movement. By the end of the 1830s the moderation movement was dying[33] and for the next three decades temperance became synonymous with total abstinence in English reforming circles. No large moderation society was able to survive the attacks of the teetotallers, who were determined to make the movement strictly teetotal. The moderationists did not give up their organisations without a fight and some very bitter battles wrecked many a society.[34] But, at the same time, the moderationists were aware of the lack of progress they had made in their fight against intemperance.

In evaluating the work of the early temperance movement one can ask if the moderation phase of temperance was the failure the teetotallers later claimed it to have been. Was it so ineffectual? Was nothing accomplished? In fact it was strikingly successful in publicising the evils of intemperance. So well did it do this job that never again was the problem of excessive drinking completely ignored. Many of the changes in the licensing laws, along with a public awareness of the iniquities of uncontrolled drinking, can be counted among the achievements of the anti-spirit movement. It managed to arouse so much interest that a parliamentary committee to investigate drunkenness was set up in 1834. Although this committee achieved little in the way of legislative curbs on the sale of alcoholic beverages, it did publish the evidence and the conclusions of its investigations, thus revealing

to the public much that had been hidden in the depths of many
an industrial slum. For the first time the government had
systematically set about collecting information on what was later
to be called the 'National Evil'.[35]

Along with this accumulation of knowledge, the moderationists
were responsible for persuading numerous citizens to take up the
cause of temperance. A minority, but a significant minority, of the
people who had worked for the moderation principle stayed on to
fight intemperance with the total abstinence principle when the
teetotallers took over. They were committed enough to the
reformation to ignore the changed attitude of the 'respectable
classes' towards temperance when the lower-class teetotallers
predominated. Moderationists could also claim credit for the
establishment of a number of precedents that were adopted by
their successors. Local and national societies, for example,
remained an important aspect of the movement; and when the
teetotallers found it necessary to set up their own societies, they
were all patterned on the moderation models. Agents and
lecturers were similarly parts of the old movement that the
newcomers retained, though in a somewhat changed form.

Nevertheless, in spite of so many successes, the early
temperance movement failed to achieve its goal of reduced
intemperance. After years of temperance agitation, Englishmen,
especially the lower classes, were drinking more than ever. The
Beer Act of 1830 was successful only in showing that beer could
intoxicate almost as easily as gin, and that the substitution of
fermented drinks for distilled spirits was not a step forward in the
fight against drunkenness. Moderation, clearly, was not enough
to reduce excessive drinking among the lower classes of England.

The moderationists also failed to rouse the churches to
militancy against intemperance. It was the absence of any official
support from the churches that hampered temperance in
becoming a central issue for social reformers in the first half of the
nineteenth century. Forty years later, when the churches officially
came to the rescue, the problem of excessive drinking received
wide publicity. Then a number of Royal Commissions and Select
Committees were appointed by the government to investigate the
problem of intemperance and its related issues.

The moderationists were also unsuccessful in their attempts to
communicate with the segment of the population most afflicted
with excessive drinking. The reformers had little first-hand

knowledge of the evil they were trying to fight; nor did they attempt to go below the surface of the problem to seek a solution. Attending lectures may have increased their members' knowledge of the effect of alcohol on the body, or the role of alcohol in the Bible, but it did not stimulate them to become personally involved in the battle against drunkenness. Neither did it encourage them to take part in house-to-house visitations or tract-distribution, methods that the teetotallers found invaluable in making personal contact with those who needed help.[36]

Furthermore, there was a class difference between the reformers and the subjects of the reformation, and many of the latter were distrustful of the middle-class temperance workers. In York a temperance historian, when discussing this issue, wrote that the weakness of the moderation society in his city lay in its social basis; 'the effect of its being organized by the great and noble was calculated to create prejudice among the very classes which it was intended to reach and benefit.'[37] He pointed out another problem for the anti-spirit movement: 'The drink of the rich was safeguarded; whilst that of the poor and squalid and miserable was proscribed . . . they gave nothing up, they evinced no practical sympathy – they touched not his case so much as with their little finger.'[38]

But apart from the class differences and the lack of personal contact, the moderation societies suffered from another major defect: they were against something they could not define. When does moderate drinking become excessive drinking? When does a socially acceptable activity change into a socially repugnant evil? These were questions they could not answer. The later teetotallers avoided these questions by proclaiming that *all* drinking of alcoholic beverages was wrong; the first glass was as bad as, if not worse than, the third or fourth or fifth. Indeed, the moderate drinker was believed by the teetotallers to be worse than the drunkard because he drank knowing what he was doing, choosing to do it freely, without the compelling force that the drunkard experienced. Furthermore the moderate drinker was, according to the teetotallers, a greater danger to society as a bad example to weaker men, leading them to believe that, if others could drink without harm, so could they. Here was the major difference between the two groups: for the early moderationists it was the uncontrolled appetite that was evil, while for the teetotallers the appetite itself was wrong.

# 2 The Teetotal Lifeboat

## FROM MODERATION TO TEETOTALISM

As we have seen, from the start of the temperance movement there had been at least a few members committed to the principle of personal abstinence,[1] but it was not until 1832 that teetotalism became a collective principle and a basis for membership in a temperance group. In that year seven workingmen of Preston, under the leadership of Joseph Livesey, joined in signing a total abstinence pledge that renounced the use of all intoxicating beverages.[2] Livesey, who was later revered by teetotallers as the father of teetotalism, was a self-educated handloom weaver of poor family who was active in many reforming causes. He was also an ardent Anti-Corn Law leaguer. He published a weekly journal, *The Struggle*, and later the *Moral Reformer*. All his social work was motivated by a strong love of humanity which was apparent in his writings as well as in his personal works. Although the other six signatories of this first teetotal pledge were unimportant in the later movement, Livesey maintained his attachment to the temperance cause throughout his life.

By this joint act of seven Lancashire working men, the teetotal movement was born, and it spread quickly throughout the country. The teetotallers believed that only complete prohibition of the consumption of all intoxicating drinks would eliminate drunkenness, by preventing the development of any appetite, moderate or excessive, for intoxicants. Furthermore, they claimed that the drunkard's craving for alcoholic beverages could only be permanently eliminated by a strict lifetime adhesion to total abstinence principles. Teetotalism was, in one widely circulated temperance drawing, the lifeboat that rescued the passengers on the floundering ship of moderation sailing in the Sea of Intemperance.[3]

At first it was hoped that the movement could remain intact, with both moderationists and teetotallers working together in the national and local societies, but this proved to be impossible. The fundamental spirit of teetotalism was so different from that of the traditional reform of the moderationists that any accommodation of the old principles by the new teetotallers was doomed to failure.

Teetotalism signalled more than just a change in the degree of abstention imposed on its members; it was the start of a new religion, the 'holy cause of teetotalism' as it was called in one temperance journal,[4] with the pledge as creed, the temperance advocates and agents as missionaries, and reformed drunkards as the saved. This analogy with religion is not an abstract one; the teetotallers deliberately adopted the style, language and methods of some of the non-conformist denominations in their proselytising. Many consciously modelled themselves on the itinerant preachers of the Primitive Methodist Connexion, parading through the streets singing temperance hymns[5] and organising outdoor meetings on public grounds to reach those who would not enter their halls.[6] One early teetotal advocate told of his trip to Preston, 'the Jerusalem of teetotalism',[7] which he called 'My Pilgrim's Progress'. Because of this trip, he claimed, he became 'invested with a sort of halo – a glamour – which seemed to lift me up' above the other teetotallers.[8] It is not surprising, therefore, to find that many of the religious authorities were unhappy with this state of affairs and accused the teetotallers of being infidels in the Christian world.

The pledge was often called the 'cornerstone' of the movement; through it the individual was admitted to the fellowship of the reformers. Exceptions were made for Quakers and other groups who could not sign for religious reasons. But anyone else could become a member of a temperance organisation only by signing the pledge.[9] For some 'reclaimed characters', as reformed drunkards were sometimes called, taking the pledge was like being baptised; it completely changed a man spiritually.[10] In many instances, in fact, the life of the recently pledged drunkard changed far more dramatically than that of the newly baptised member of the Christian church; there was a complete separation from his old life, both physically and psychologically. Long-standing friendships and haunts had to be forgotten, along with the blandishments of former drinking companions. New habits had to be established. Because of the severity of the break, some reformed drunkards made the pledge their psychological crutch, upon which they leaned when facing moments of temptation. One working man expressed the sentiments of many other former drunkards when, conceding that the pledge itself did not give one strength, he yet insisted on signing it so that 'I shall have an answer to give when they want me to drink.'[11] Other working men

might mock him for signing it, but they would understand why he
would not want to break it once he had signed.

Unhappily for the temperance movement, not all pledges were
honoured. 'The painful proportion of pledgebreakers was always
a source of much anxiety' to the early teetotallers, wrote the son of
a temperance pioneer.[12] The editor of a well-known teetotal
journal, *The Temperance Advocate*, complained that it was common
practice for drunkards 'to sign the pledge one week and break it
the next'.[13] In some towns, if a man was known to have broken his
pledge, an officer of the local temperance society would visit him
to seek his repentance and the renewal of his pledge. If this failed,
his name, with those of other reprobates, was solemnly read out
at the next public temperance meeting, so all should know who
had been faithless. Then the names were officially struck from the
list of members. The original teetotal society at Preston, among
others, followed this procedure.[14]

In contrast to the many who believed in the value of the pledge,
there were those who felt it should not be necessary for a man to
sign a promise; he should have enough self-control to resist
temptation without such an artifical aid.[15] One temperance
supporter, the Rev. Newman Hall, put forth a common view when
he said 'Surely my abstaining and saying in general society that I
abstain on principle and urging others is all that we mean by a
pledge.'[16] Similarly, another temperance sympathiser, the artist
George Cruikshank, refused to sign the pledge because he was
'pledged to the Almighty on the faith and honour of a
gentleman'.[17]

Opposition to the pledge was sometimes motivated by religious
sentiment. There was a fear among some religious leaders that the
pledge would take the place of the baptismal vow. 'The
temperance pledge is dangerous as it is a pledge to man and might
supersede the solemn pledge of all Christians to renounce all sin',
complained one critic.[18] The Church of England never officially
approved the pledge and later, in its own temperance society, had
instead a 'declaration'. The Roman Catholic Church likewise had
its doubts and only encouraged the pledge if it was administered
by a priest and if it was understood that it was not an oath or a vow
but a 'solemn resolution – a promise made to man'.[19] But for many
laymen the pledge became the focus for much of their anti-teetotal
hostility.

No doubt some of the aversion towards the pledge found among the non-temperance public was caused by the bitter and ugly fights within the movement over the various forms of the pledge. These fights, occurring chiefly in the late 1830s and early 1840s, were responsible, according to at least one prominent temperance worker, for the negative image of the cause among the more respectable segments of the population. The movement was rent apart by the formation of parties around the different pledges. So strongly and fanatically did some groups battle over this issue that they almost destroyed the movement. Each group claimed their pledge was the only legitimate one for the temperance cause and the acceptance of any other was wrong. The battles over the pledges were accompanied by much personal rancour and long-lasting bitterness. (Tales of the fights and the schisms were circulated widely among the non-temperance public, much to the detriment of the cause.)

Although total abstinence was quickly adopted by an increasing majority of temperance reformers in the north, there were many moderationists, especially in the south of England, who did not want to make the leap from a limited prohibition to one that covered all intoxicating drinks. It seemed an extreme move to those who saw no harm in taking a glass of wine with friends. Changing the pledge was more than adding a further prohibition to the lives of the temperance reformers, it was, in many instances, the start of a new life-style. When a man signed the moderation or anti-spirit pledge, he agreed not to drink ardent spirits, but at the dinner table could, like all other diners, partake in wine or ale without any conflict. He would, of course, have to refuse the customary after-dinner brandy but this was no great matter and such a refusal was often put down to a mild eccentricity by his non-temperance colleagues. With the teetotal pledge of personal abstinence, the social difficulties became greater. Because English social customs in the nineteenth century were closely tied to alcoholic beverages, the teetotaller was set somewhat apart from his drinking colleagues by being unable to partake in some of them. The total abstainer would not drink wine, ale or brandy nor would he drink the customary toasts in intoxicating beverages. Nevertheless an accommodation could be found by recognising the teetotaller as a special case. His personal restrictions on his own diet did not have to affect others. Non-teetotallers dining with him could dine and drink as customary, even at the teetotaller's home. Such a situation, in which the teetotaller offered drink to others, was roundly condemned by the more ardent teetotallers, who could see little hope for the elimination of social customs involving drink if those customs were supported by the teetotallers themselves.

In order to combat this evil of social drinking, the long pledge was introduced. This pledge contained all the prohibitions of the short pledge, as the simple pledge of personal abstinence was called, but added a promise not to give alcoholic beverages to others. In its more extreme form it even forbade the giving and taking of alcoholic sacramental wine (a serious problem for a minister of religion) as well as medically prescribed intoxicating stimulants. For the socially prominent, the long pledge was a disaster. No one would want to dine at a house where no wines were served, specially in the first half of the nineteenth century, when there were few substitutes for ale and wine at the table.

Unfortunately for the temperance movement, the battle of pledges was put into a north versus south framework. The traditional distrust between the northerners and the southerners in England manifested itself in the temperance movement, with the teetotallers of the north believing the southerners to be lukewarm in their commitment to teetotal principles, as evidenced by their adoption of the short pledge. (It was not unusual to refer to the short pledge as the south pledge.) The southerners, on the other hand, believed the northerners to be fanatics willing to wreck the movement rather than support any compromise. To them this was demonstrated by the innumerable pledge fights in the northern societies. The geographical split between the two sections of the English temperance movement was further widened by an institutional division. The northerners, unwilling to be organised by a London-based society, set up their own 'national' organisation, which they called the British Association for the Prevention of Intemperance. Originally a short pledge society, the British Association (as it was popularly called) quickly adopted the long pledge. (The other permanent national society, the London-based National Temperance Society, was only established after years of fighting in the capital city over pledges.)

One of the major mistakes the anti-spirit movement had made, according to many teetotallers, was to allow membership in its societies without personal commitment to the cause. They felt it was essential for all supporters of the movement to be fully identified with it. It was not enough to attend a weekly meeting for an hour or two, or to have one's name on an 'ornamental' board of organisational officers. All must be workers in the teetotal cause, to which they officially bound themselves when they signed the pledge. For Joseph Livesey a true teetotaller was one 'that never feels happy unless he is planning and working to confer the same blessings on others'.[20] Livesey felt that all teetotallers should take their message personally to the public through street meetings, home visitations and tract distribution. For this father of teetotalism, every member should be an advocate; but this was the ideal, not the reality, and the teetotal movement, like the anti-spirit cause, had to have a class of agents and advocates as standard-bearers for the temperance reformation. Men went forth from Preston and other centres of teetotalism to alert the whole of England to the dangers of drink. In the initial years the teetotal agents often travelled in pairs: 'we adopted the apostolic modes', wrote one of the early workers.[21] At every opportunity they distributed the tracts which they carried with them and in whatever circumstances they found themselves, they searched for ways to disseminate information about the movement.[22]

These teetotal workers were very different from those who laboured for the moderation societies. While the moderation agent was a member of the middle classes with a strong religious affiliation, the teetotallers were mostly drawn from non-religious, working-class backgrounds. They saw themselves as destroyers of an evil source of degradation and misery among the working classes and, protected by their 'temperance armour', they went forth to do battle with the demon drink. Many were reformed drunkards, aggressive and abrasive, caring little for current notions of respectability.[23] Their own past intemperance made them effective in their work among drunkards.[24] Some of these uneducated and often illiterate agents adopted names calculated to appeal to the type of people they were hoping to reach. Thomas Swindlehurst called himself 'The King of Reformed Drunkards', James Hocking was known as the 'Birmingham Blacksmith', while Thomas Worsnop gloried in the appellation 'Eccentric Advocate'. All were colourful and crude characters, their speech as rough and ragged as their clothes. They frequently made a nuisance of themselves. The non-temperance public had numerous derogatory nicknames for them and, because of them, as one pioneer complained, often thought all teetotallers 'low bred and ill mannered'. Public dislike was sometimes overt: at least one teetotal advocate was killed by bullies hired by a local publican to beat him up, and many others were attacked.[25]

The respectable gentlemen of the temperance movement were not particularly happy with the activities of these vulgar teetotallers, but they were not averse to using their services to their own advantage. In many towns it was a common practice for the local society to hire the services of a teetotal 'character' to attract a crowd before the gentlemen of the sponsoring society arrived, so that there would be a ready-made audience to greet them. This procedure was deplored by some advocates, who felt they were doing the work while the 'gentlemen' were getting the credit. Such class tension within the temperance movement was well illustrated by an incident involving Tom Worsnop, a crude, uneducated, reformed drunkard who was very effective in getting publicity for the temperance movement. The gentlemen of the Driffield Temperance Society hired Worsnop two weeks prior to their 'grand festival' to drum up interest in temperance and in the festival. As usual, the 'Eccentric Advocate' came with his rattle, bright flag and unorthodox appearance. When the start of the festival was at hand and Worsnop's labours were done, the gentlemen of the society were anxious for him to leave town immediately. His biographer put it bluntly: 'It was not intended that Tom should remain over the festival as his flag and rattle and general style of doing things was considered a little below the character in which the committee wished the festival to come off.'[26]

In the early days of teetotalism, when the system of agencies was not so institutionalised as it later became, much was done on a trial and error basis. The majority of the first teetotal agents and advocates were 'self-employed' itinerant workers who took up the banner of temperance on their own initiative. Completely dependent on their own talents and energies for their livelihood, they travelled around the country, living on the money they collected from whatever audiences they could attract. Sometimes one was hired by an individual or a society to do a particular job. When the job ended, he had to find something else. A small minority built up a national reputation that enabled them to secure a very comfortable standard of living but such a position was not easily gained and the majority of self-employed advocates remained poor.[28]

In its first decades the movement as a whole suffered from the circulation of stories about the exploits of self-proclaimed temperance advocates.[29] One of these men appeared in the market-place of a Yorkshire town, claiming, according to one newspaper report, 'to be the propounder of a system of temperance which he imagines he has a divine commission to establish'. He supported the drinking of wine but forbade the partaking of any beverage made from grain. 'God was angry with Beer and Spirit drinkers', he said, and had sent 'several years of wet weather as a punishment for the destroying of grain'.[30] Later, as the movement progressed and settled down to a more protracted fight than originally anticipated (the forces of drink being more entrenched in the people's lives than had been realised), the organisations that employed agents had to set some standards for employment.

One of the radical innovations the teetotallers introduced into the temperance movement, when they took control of it, was a concern for the drunkard. Unlike the moderationists, who said 'Drunkards we hold to be almost irreclaimable',[31] the teetotallers believed that 'while a man retains his faculties he may be a subject of reformation and therefore in *no instance* should we give any man up'.[32] Consequently, they made the reclamation of drunkards a major goal of the movement, on a par with the original aim of eliminating intemperance.[33] Reformed characters who took the pledge were given a special place in most teetotal temperance societies.[34] 'Temperance Trophies' they were called by one teetotal journalist, who saw them as symbols of the movement's success.[35] But the temperance cause gained more from reformed drunkards than badges of success. From the ranks of these men it obtained its most dedicated workers; they were the 'bulwark' of the temperance cause, according to one temperance writer.[36]

Reaching the intemperate was the first and most critical task of the temperance societies. A common method of making this contact was for the societies to hold free teas specially for drunkards. In return for free tea and food the imbibers were expected to listen to the experiences of former drunkards who had reformed, as well as to temperance messages from the sponsoring society. So effective were the addresses by former inebriates that they were utilised in public temperance meetings all over the country. They were cheap and entertaining and made it unnecessary to recruit high-priced talent to draw in an audience: there was an abundance of men who, for the privilege of standing on the platform, were willing to pour out their hearts, describing their own experiences in a highly dramatic fashion.[37] 'His confessions of wickedness were sometimes of such a startling character as to cause a shudder in the hearers of his shocking revelations', said one teetotaller in describing the speech of a reformed drunkard.[38] So happy were these men to tell the stories of their past degradation that some advertised their availability in temperance journals. All this prompted one temperance paper to deplore the behaviour of the reformed drunkard who, the journal claimed, 'will parade his doings in drink as though they were virtues of the highest order, and his getting on in the world as the climax of virtue'.[39]

As a means of preventing backsliding, newly pledged men were encouraged to form groups that would give them companionship without drink. But these groups were more than an aid against temptation. Former associations (usually involving drink) and the support structure that was often part of the relationship had to be replaced with teetotal alternatives. One way of doing this was to organise teetotal associations in which the members had more than their teetotalism to bind them together. Teetotallers of the same trade, for example, formed social groups, as did teetotallers working at the same mill or factory.[40] Such groups not only strengthened the resolution of the individual in times of temptation but also offered him a positive alternative by helping him develop new habits that would indirectly as well as directly reinforce his new teetotal principles.

Not everyone saw the ex-drunkard as a hero to be applauded. Some members of the public viewed the role of the former inebriate in the temperance proceedings with misgiving. The Rev. James Fawcett of Leeds found it 'revolting to see men proclaimed in handbills, parading themselves on platforms as reformed drunkards'.[41] Some critics felt that the change in the reclaimed drunkard was a superficial one and not the 'thorough spiritual change of heart and life' that would make it a real reformation.[42] The intemperate had some failing in their characters that had originally allowed them to fall into a state of continual inebriation, argued some critics, adding that teetotalism did not cure this weakness. Instead it was changed into an excess of temperance spirit; extreme drunkenness and degradation became extreme teetotalism and respectability. 'The poor fellow fancies that his character is so much improved, that he is far more righteous than many of his neighbours', wrote one critic about the reformed drunkard.[43] In his view, and that of many others, the defect in the drunkard's character remained.[44]

The teetotallers, with their new principles, aims and methods, caused the existing temperance movement to undergo a radical change. The middle-class moderation reform had little in common with the aggressive, working-class-oriented teetotal movement. The innovative methods brought by the teetotallers attracted new kinds of workers, who in turn introduced goals more in keeping with their own social and economic status. So different were the two forms of temperance seen to be, that strong criticism was directed against the teetotallers for taking control of the old temperance movement. In 1836, at a debate between the teetotallers and the moderationists in Leeds, the latter complained that the teetotallers were like lodgers who come into the home and then take it over, dispossessing the original owners.[45] To this criticism the teetotallers replied that it was they who had done most of the work in the old temperance societies and had kept many of them alive.[46]

Unfortunately for the teetotal movement, the greater portion of middle-class reformers of the moderation society were so unhappy with the working-class teetotallers that they withdrew their earlier support for temperance reformation. The teetotallers were forcing a change not only in the principles but also in the style of the movement: orderly educational lectures by well-known authorities were replaced by emotional meetings addressed by former drunkards.[47]

Where the existing temperance society was able to resist the pressures of the extreme teetotallers, a separate working-class teetotal society was sometimes formed. In Bradford and York there were distinct societies for working-class teetotallers and middle-class reformers. A few other towns also had two societies, but this duality could flourish only where there was enough sentiment and money for two groups in one town.[48] More typically, the moderationists were given the choice of joining the teetotallers or leaving the movement altogether, and the majority left.

While there were some prominent moderationists, such as Thomas Beaumont and John Dunlop, who were quickly convinced of the need for the new teetotal doctrine, others, such as John Edgar, the Ulster Professor of Theology, and William Collins, the Glasgow printer, could not support total abstinence as a basis for the movement. Edgar was reported by the *Liverpool Mercury* in 1841 to have said that 'he entertained the most confirmed abhorrence of teetotalism as insulting to God and disgraceful to man'.[49] Another moderationist who vehemently opposed the new principles wrote in a moderation journal that because of teetotalism the cause of temperance 'is identified with the cause of socialism, infidelity and many secret associations, whose object is to change all our political and religious institutions . . .'[50] Many teetotal leaders greatly regretted the inability of the old leaders to join the mainstream of the temperance movement.

One distinct group which did not remain in the movement after it became teetotal was that of the brewers and wine merchants. There had been an element of self-interest in their support for moderation principles; restrictions on spirit-drinking would increase the consumption of beer and wine and consequently their profits would rise. A Leeds teetotaller, writing of his early experiences, told of addressing a temperance meeting in the mid-1830s where the audience included brewers, maltsters and wine merchants. They had assembled to hear an anti-spirit lecture and, when they discovered that the speaker was a teetotaller, the meeting disintegrated in uproar.[51] A brewer who was the treasurer of the temperance society in Penrith would not let teetotallers speak at meetings sponsored by the society.[52]

Not all the temperance work of the brewers and wine merchants was done for selfish reasons. Many were genuinely distressed at the number of drunkards and, like the majority of moderation supporters, they saw the difference between moderate and excessive drinking as the critical issue. One licensed victualler in Tewkesbury, himself a total abstainer, was the only person in town to let a teetotal advocate have a room in which to give a temperance lecture.[53] In 1859, when the Bradford Temperance Society was in a bad financial state and the temperance hall was threatened with foreclosure, it was a brewer, a Mr Leah, who paid the mortgage in full, along with other debts outstanding against the hall.[54] There were some brewers and maltsters who became so convinced of the value of teetotal temperance that they gave up their connection with brewing. One of the most active teetotal families in England was founded by John Andrews, a maltster who gave up his profession and became a full-time temperance worker. He started and ran a temperance hotel in Leeds, where his son John junior became chairman of the local temperance society.[55] Many other temperance societies owed their existence to the labours of this family. Nevertheless, most of the brewers, as one would expect, rejected teetotal principles and eventually left the temperance movement.

Complete loyalty to the temperance cause, whether anti-spirit or teetotal, was to be found among a number of men and women who had originally joined because of their own first-hand experience of the effects of intemperance on family life. The Rev. Francis Beardsall, for example, came from an innkeeping family. His father had squandered the family fortune on drink and had eventually died of his excessive drinking.[56] William Bell, another well-known temperance worker, grew up with a hatred of drink after seeing his home and his mother destroyed by his father's intemperance.[57] On the distaff side there was Catherine Booth, the wife of the founder of the Salvation Army. It was said that she induced her husband to sign the pledge.[58] Her father was for many years a pledged teetotaller until one day he broke his pledge and started drinking. Becoming a drunkard, he lost his job and wrecked his home, quickly descending into poverty and ill health.[59] His story of self-destruction through an uncontrollable appetite for drink was one that was repeated many times over among working men and others in the nineteenth century.

## WORKING-CLASS TEETOTALISM: A SELF-HELP MOVEMENT

The decline in middle-class membership of the temperance movement when the teetotallers took over was partly offset by the new working-class element that for the first time became an important part of the movement. There had been some working-class people in the moderation societies but they had rarely had any effective role to play. With the coming of the teetotallers the movement became the home of many talented, aggressive, mobile workers, seeking to improve their lowly status through the exercise of their own talents. Teetotalism, to these men, was a form of self-control, the practice of which was essential if they were to make their way up the ladder of English society.

Teetotallers 'made me feel that a man's position and success did not, after all, depend so much on his birth and parentage than on his own efforts and perseverance', wrote Thomas Whittaker, echoing the sentiments of many self-made teetotallers.[60] Typically these men were ambitious and of a flexible disposition, able to adjust to new situations and circumstances and thus take advantage of any opportunities offered them in bettering their position. Some of them believed that their future success lay with the temperance movement, but the majority, while remaining loyal members of the teetotal movement, achieved success in other spheres of life.[61]

Because the life of a teetotaller was often a lonely and difficult one, abstainers setting themselves apart from other working men, great self-discipline had to be exercised to resist the temptation to break the pledge. It was not an uncommon sport for workmates to try to bet that total abstainers, knowingly or unknowingly, could be made to break their pledge.[62] In addition, the traditional lower-class entertainments were all intimately connected with drink, either being held in a public house or otherwise involving drinking customs; the teetotaller had to replace them with new ways of spending leisure time and money. Only the most dedicated men could maintain their principles in the face of these difficulties. Such men could apply the same ambition and self-control to other aspects of their lives and utilise these abilities to better themselves. It is not surprising, therefore, to find that many ambitious temperance advocates who were successful in temperance work or other fields had spent their youth in mutual improvement schemes, some setting up educational institutions and others political clubs. The story of the teetotaller who started life at the very bottom of the ladder as an itinerant handloom weaver, usually unemployed, and rose to be mayor of Chester and its first teetotal sheriff, was one duplicated by other temperance colleagues. He expressed the view of many teetotal working men when he wrote: 'Self dependence is a noble virtue, to be cultivated and encouraged. Self-help is, of all help, the best because it brings with it manly satisfaction of difficulties subdued.'[63]

Teetotal societies of an informal kind could be organised very easily. Half a dozen teetotallers could get together and decide to form a teetotal association without reference to any other group. Consequently, the number of working-class teetotal groups that were formed in the 1830s, 1840s and 1850s can be only roughly estimated. Joseph Livesey thought that there must have been at least forty of them in London alone at any given time.[64] Some may have been simply working men's teetotal societies, but there were others which joined the principles of total abstinence to political and economic or religious principles. Most disappeared as quietly as they were formed, leaving no evidence of their existence except in the memories of former members.

In Bradford a working-class teetotal society claimed a membership of 2000, 500 of whom were said to be reclaimed drunkards.[65] At first, they rented a room which they called the Victoria Temperance Room in the centre of the town, but unfortunately there was a great deal of hostility directed against them and they were evicted.[66] This made them decide to build their own hall as soon as possible.

Like many other working-class temperance halls, that of the Bradford Long Pledge Association, as this working-class teetotal society was called, played an important role in the wider working-class activities of the town. The teetotallers used part of the building to house an educational institute where lessons in arithmetic, bookkeeping and singing, as well as special classes for women, were held.[67] With the financial help of local philanthropists, the long pledgers were able to open a library for the use of all who would pay sixpence a quarter. Unfortunately the school income paid less than half the school's expenses, and though dissolution was repeatedly staved off by holding teas, concerts and other entertainments, the educational institute was finally closed early in 1858 after only eighteen months of operation.[68]

Even though the educational institute had been given up, the hall continued to house another school. A ragged school, supported solely by one Quaker teetotaller, John Priestman, was held there. The woolcombers also used the hall for their meetings, as did the Rechabites, a working men's teetotal benefit society.[69] Political meetings organised by the Chartists and the Radical Reform Association were also held in the hall and it was the meeting place for secularists, phrenologists and phonographists.[70]

In 1846, when the Long Pledge Hall opened, it was, in fact, the only public building in Bradford, apart from the Bradford

Temperance Hall, the other temperance building.[71] In most northern industrial towns of the mid-nineteenth century there was a great lack of public halls which could be rented for working-class meetings. Public houses in many towns supplied rooms for smaller meetings, but their rental usually involved an expectation that members would drink up 'for the good of the house'. Sometimes a 'wet rent' was levied, with a stipulated amount of drink to be bought by the organisation using the rooms.

The Bradford teetotallers were not the only working-class group to have a hall of their own. In Woodhead near Leeds, a village of 6000 inhabitants and seventeen licensed houses, the teetotallers in conjunction with other working-class groups promoted and established an improvement society in 1841. After ten years of successful existence they were able to buy a new Temperance Hall and Mechanics Institute at a cost of £900. Only £100 of this was paid by the working classes. This building had eight large classrooms and a spacious lecture hall where reading and writing were taught. The building was used for teetotal meetings as well as a Sunday School and other self-improving activities.[72]

Other temperance groups formed self-help organisations, but many of them appear to have been founded a decade or so after the Bradford and Woodhead groups. In Keighley a mutual improvement class was formed 'in connection with' the Temperance Society in October 1861.[73] The previous year, 1860, had seen the formation of a Temperance Cooperative Society in the southern town of Brighton. This group charged an entrance fee of one shilling and invited all working men 'to improve their social position'.[74] In 1862 the mechanics of Manchester and Salford formed their own temperance society which they called the Manchester and Salford Mechanics Teetotal Association.[75]

The Chartist fervour of the 1840s did not leave the temperance movement untouched. There were teetotal Chartist groups spread all over England. Hull, Sheffield, Oldham, Chesterfield, Manchester, Manningham, Northampton, Preston, Ashton-under-Lyme, Kettering and Leicester were named as having such organisations.[76] In Leeds there was a Total Abstinence Charter Association which held its first tea party on 1 January 1841, and in the same town the teetotallers and the Chartists joined together to organise the Hunslet Union Sunday School.[77] Henry Vincent, a well-known Chartist and temperance advocate, travelled around the country lecturing on teetotal Chartism and helping set up local organisations. In 1845 the Scottish Temperance League hired Vincent to lecture the Scottish workers on temperance.[78]

In the metropolitan area there was an East London Chartist Association, which made its members pledge themselves not only to total abstinence but also 'to cause the People's Charter to become the law of the land'.[79] This group collected money to start a library of 'useful books' so that their members 'may spend their leisure hours profitably and set a good example'.[80] Although the members were interested in improving themselves, the major aim of the Association was mutual aid. Members were to help one another in seeking employment and were asked to trade with one another whenever possible. The secretary was to keep a list of the occupations and trades of all members, which was to be read aloud before the gathered membership at the monthly meetings.[81] The motto of the East London Chartist Temperance Association was 'Do unto others as ye would they should do unto you'.[82] In order to reduce the possibilities of hostilities being aroused, no topics dealing with matters of theology were allowed to be discussed. A prospective member must have been a teetotaller for at least one week before he was admitted to the society 'in order to try the principle and prevent a relapse'.[83]

Like many other working-class groups at the time, the East London Chartist Temperance Association sponsored lectures on topics of 'interest and value' to its membership. One of these talks was on the subject of 'the necessity of the working classes abstaining from all intoxicating drinks in order to assist themselves in obtaining their political rights'.[84]

Although there was much talk about teetotal Chartism in the period when Chartism was popular among the working class, one well-known Leeds temperance advocate, active in temperance circles at the time, believed that the number of teetotal Chartist societies was not as great as their publicity warranted.[85] Nevertheless, in some minds the two were linked. One middle-class organiser of a teetotal society was told 'you will make chartists of the lower classes'.[86] This emphasis on self-help schemes, which gave leadership roles and experience to many uneducated and often crude, albeit talented, working-class men, was too radical to be supported by many members of the 'respectable' classes, who saw themselves as leaders and not followers of the lower orders. This type of activity caused many middle-class people to look with hostility on any temperance society.

## TEETOTALISM AND THE PUBLIC

Besides trying to overcome the hostility of the anti-spirit members of the movement, the teetotallers also had to contend with a general public that liked neither them nor their doctrines. One source of much anti-teetotal feelings stemmed from the popular belief in the nourishing qualities of ale: Disraeli called ale 'liquid bread'. Many working men felt they could not do heavy work without drink; it was even claimed that the men that drank the most were the best workers. A teetotal labour leader disagreed: 'Good workmen often drink because their exceptional skill provides them with the means. It is the abuse of their natural strength and energy that enables them to drink, not their drinking habits that make them energetic.'[87] The reformer Sir Edward Chadwick took note of the working men's view of the efficacy of beer and commented, 'Strong beer overexcited men, and as the excitement was for a short period, a repetition of the stimulus was requisite.'[88] Sir Edward told of a meeting of some labourers who had begun to understand the true role of such stimulants: they told a witness that 'they had been offered porter in the morning, but they declined, and assigned as a reason . . . that it made them work their hearts out.'[89] The *Spectator* also entered the controversy with an editorial that claimed alcohol, 'if not a nutriment, is a whip, enabling men to get more out of themselves, at a price, than they otherwise would'.[90] To combat the belief in the value of ale and similar beverages to the physical strength of a working man, the teetotallers held a meeting in Exeter Hall, in 1848, at which a number of working-class teetotallers demonstrated 'the practicability and efficiency of Total Abstinence from strong drinks in connection with the successful performance of heavy labour'.[91]

To fight popular belief in the nutritious qualities of ale, Joseph Livesey devised a 'scientific' discourse called the 'Malt Lecture'. He and other teetotallers went around the country giving it at temperance galas and festivals, where it was often the highpoint of the activities, especially if Livesey himself delivered it. Basically, it was a crude analysis of sixpenny-worth of ale; the lecture claimed to prove that it contained only one halfpenny worth of nourishment.[92] The finale was always dramatic. Taking samples of different alcoholic liquids, along with some of the ale used in the preceding demonstration, the lecturer arranged them in saucers around a table, each type of beverage in its own dish. Then he set them alight. This proved, according to the teetotallers, that the substance they all had in common was alcohol, an inflammable ingredient.

But the Malt Lecture and teetotal demonstrations were not successful in changing Englishmen's minds about their 'national' beverage. Some of the failure must, however, be attributed to the prevailing view of a healthy appearance. The most admired physique at this time, the sign of good health, was that of a ruddy-complected fat man – the fatter the better. In fact, the physical appearance of a heavy drinker was close to the ideal. Unfortunately most teetotallers were thin. Consequently, whenever there was a temperance parade the local societies tried to get a fat teetotaller to head it. 'Slender Billy' of Preston was very much in demand as a parade leader. This teetotaller weighed twenty-four stone (336 pounds). As one old temperance worker recalled: 'Billy's tremendous figure was a wonderful sight. His "corporation" so filled the eyes of the people that they did not see the thin ones there.'[93] Another teetotaller wrote of this same Billy: 'He was the finest speciman of a teetotaller Preston had ever seen, tall, robust, "built like a castle".'[94] The closest rival Billy had in the movement was Thomas Swindlehurst, the self-proclaimed 'King of the Reformed Drunkards', who tipped the scales at a mere eighteen stone (252 pounds).

The popular belief in the need for alcohol in maintaining good health is not surprising when we find that the medical profession itself held similar views. Nineteenth-century doctors were dependent on alcoholic beverages for many of their cures. They used them as stimulants and as medicine with dietary properties. 'A glass of brandy' was a common prescription and for a considerable length of time it was fully accepted that alcohol was an effective medicine in the fight against cholera and influenza.[95] One abstaining clergyman complained that when some patients told their doctors they were going teetotal, the latter would try to persuade them that it would be detrimental to their health.[96] More than one teetotaller gave up his abstaining principles when his doctor told him to take spirits for the sake of his health.[97]

Publicans advertised their wares as 'Pale Ales strongly recommended by several eminent physicians'.[98]

It was difficult for teetotallers to repudiate medical claims for the use of alcoholic beverages because no one actually knew what their effect was on the human body. In the absence of any scientific data on the subject, doctors, along with many others, naturally preferred to stick to the old customs, feeling that it was up to their critics to prove them wrong. Eventually this was done. But it was not the English teetotallers who produced the evidence that downgraded alcohol as a health-giving ingredient. It was two French medical professors, Drs Lallemand and Perrin; together with Mr Dury, a distinguished chemist, they published in 1860 the results of research which showed that alcohol goes through the body without changing, indicating that it is neither nourishing nor heat-producing.[99] The teetotallers were quick to see the value of this work and gave it wide circulation among English doctors. But progress was slow. The habits of many generations were not to be put aside so easily.

The popular feeling regarding the efficacy of alcoholic beverages was further reinforced by the attitude of English insurance companies. At first these companies were reluctant to insure teetotallers at all, believing them to be very bad risks. Some of the more progressive companies would insure the abstainer only if he paid an extra premium. This situation so irked teetotallers that a number of them joined together in 1841 to set up their own insurance company, which they called the United Kingdom Temperance and General Provincial Institute.[100] One of the very valuable but unforeseen services this company was to render to the movement was the accumulation of statistics favourable to teetotalism; it provided the raw material for many later teetotal arguments. Abstainers, it was found, were better health risks than any kind of drinker, moderate or immoderate.[101] When this became known, the company, later followed by some non-temperance insurance companies, lowered the premiums for total abstainers; in the eyes of many abstainers, this was a vindication of teetotal principles.

Teetotallers, with their abnormal dietary restrictions – abnormal, that is, for the nineteenth century – were often considered to be eccentric. Many 'persons of cultivation and refinement' were 'averse to exposing themselves to a charge of singularity, eccentricity or censoriousness', commented one abstainer when discussing this problem.[102] If the prohibition of alcohol had been their only eccentricity no doubt their reputations would not have been so poor, but it was not unusual to find teetotallers supporting other health 'causes'. Many men joined the temperance movement because of their views on health rather than for moral reasons, and many such men were also active in movements that promoted other dietary beliefs. Abstainers were prominent in the ranks of various vegetarian organisations,[103] which often combined a prohibition on the eating of meat with prohibitions on alcohol and tobacco. Such groups manifested the growing mid-nineteenth-century concern about diet, some of this interest being stimulated by a 'physical puritanism' that was becoming popular among the labour aristocracy, who saw their bodies as their sole 'capital'.[104]

The use of tobacco was also a controversial subject among teetotallers. One extreme view of the effects of tobacco was printed in a teetotal journal in 1847: 'smoking induces drinking, drinking induces intoxication, intoxication induces bile, bile induces jaundice, jaundice leads to dropsy, dropsy terminates in death.'[105] It was not uncommon for temperance societies to ban speakers who used tobacco. Such an action by the Andover Temperance Society in 1862 sparked a great controversy among teetotallers, with many letters on both sides written to a temperance journal, *The Temperance Advocate*. In some of these letters tobacco was held responsible for many evils of contemporary society. One teetotaller felt that the weed shattered the nervous system: 'Tobacco does mainly fill our lunatic asylums.'[106] Because some teetotallers smoked, the issue was hotly debated. Some societies did not admit as members those who used tobacco, adding an anti-smoking clause to their pledge.[107]

With their cultivated sensitivity to the problem of physical health, many abstainers were interested in a variety of health schemes. Hydropathy in particular attracted many teetotallers and was well advertised in temperance journals. At one point it was proposed that a failing hydropathic establishment be bought by teetotallers and run by them for the benefit of the movement.[108] This suggestion never became a reality but individual teetotallers continued to patronise such establishments and sometimes had some pecuniary interest in them. Joseph Livesey was a great believer in 'water inside and outside the body',[109] and was forever trying to promote various hydropathic resorts in his temperance writings.[110]

Much of the displeasure shown by the public towards the temperance reformation can be traced to the fanaticism of the agents and advocates. Frequently, the reformers were accused, not without reason, of interfering in matters which were none of their business. So ardent were many teetotallers in furthering their cause that they became oblivious to the sensitivities of others.[111] Particularly in the initial years of the movement, when the zeal of its converts was white hot, we find the lower-class workers so completely immersed in the teetotal cause that they lose their perspective on all other matters.[112] They believed they were spreading a message that would save thousands, or even millions, from a drunkard's grave, and they were too filled with their mission to care about the ways and manners of polite society. On being called extreme, one teetotaller answered that the fishermen of Galilee were 'extreme men . . . The martyrs were "extreme" and their extremity was ever to the endurance of death for their principles.'[113] Later on, however, these teetotallers came to deplore the coldness of the middle classes and sought ways to draw into the movement the 'respectable classes' they had formerly offended.[114]

No doubt much of the hostility the middle classes felt towards teetotalism was class inspired. They were not happy to see the 'inferior' classes trying to raise themselves up the social ladder, especially when they were doing so without middle-class guidance. Furthermore, in England in the 1830s and 1840s there was a fear of any and all working-class organisations. Such groups were thought to be seditious and dangerous, sources of anti-government intrigue. It took the middle classes several decades to realise that the temperance movement not only posed no threat to them but was even an aid to the established system. By giving an outlet to the ambitions of many working men, it acted as a safety valve for some of the pent-up anger and frustration the new industrial conditions generated among workers during the 1830s and 1840s, which also saw many other workers' movements such as Chartism, socialism and unionism flourish. But, aside from class antagonisms, the middle-class critics of teetotalism found aspects of the movement that disturbed them. 'Teetotallers are always talking about saving money and of material values' was a common criticism.[115] There was a good deal of truth in this, for the movement deliberately pointed out the material benefits that accrued to teetotallers. Reformed drunkards continually testified to the new-found affluence that abstinence had brought them and frequent were the lectures showing the 'pecuniary relation existing between the conditions of man and teetotalism'.[116] Teetotallers purposely promoted this type of argument for temperance because it was one to which many working men responded.[117]

One of the major stumbling blocks to a better reception of temperance doctrines by the public was the role drink played in English social life of the nineteenth century. The majority of English men and women enjoyed drinking and associated intoxicating beverages with sociability. Lord Shaftesbury was not alone in believing that a glass of wine had the 'peculiar power of stimulating good spirits and evoking social fellowship'.[118] The majority of Englishmen considered the teetotallers a dreary group of people. 'Some people will say, that where the temperance plan is adopted and particularly in the principle of entire abstinence, there is an end of cheerfulness, friendship and sociability', wrote Joseph Livesey, who wanted teetotallers to disprove this belief by non-alcoholic hospitality.[119] But the common pattern was for teetotallers to stick together. They would not entertain non-teetotallers because such people would expect something alcoholic to drink; nor would they attend the amusements of others because drink would be served there. Unfortunately for the teetotallers, the decanter was a symbol of hospitality; it was present whenever there was any visiting. Not to offer a guest a drink with some alcoholic content was considered rude and very inhospitable.[120]

Among the working classes drink was also used as a currency for payment of services. When the wife of a teetotaller died, according to a story in a temperance journal, no one volunteered to help with the funeral. It was a tradition for all females who acted as attendants at a funeral to be rewarded with rum. In this case, when everyone knew the family would not give any such recompense, no one came to help. The husband turned for aid to a temperance advocate who knew the teetotallers of the town. He was able to collect enough abstaining women willing to act as funeral attendants, who were rewarded with tea in a teetotal hotel after the funeral.[121]

If the teetotaller was viewed as eccentric or inhospitable in polite circles, among many of the poorer classes he was thought to be downright dangerous. Following current ideas of political economy, these working men thought temperance advocates were hired by the masters to get the workers to reduce their spending, to see how little they could live on. 'It was even urged that if the workers ceased to drink, in accordance with the iron law of wages, the standard of living falling, wages would fall to the new subsistence level.'[122] This argument was heard repeatedly through to the end of the century, and teetotallers were never able to answer it satisfactorily. One teetotal working man acknowledged the complaint but answered it by pointing out that his master had raised his wage when he became a teetotaller.[123]

Part of the teetotaller's difficulty in replying to the charge of being in the pay of the masters was due to the fact that many masters, particularly in the northern textile areas where teetotalism was strong, supported the movement and paid its advocates. No doubt this was sometimes done out of self-interest – the employers wanted a sober and satisfied workforce – but many also appreciated the outlet teetotalism gave to the drives and energies of the more ambitious workmen. Not a few of these masters had themselves started out as working men and through their own efforts had worked their way up into the manufacturing class. They were close enough to their own humble beginnings to identify somewhat with the ambitions of the working-class exponents of self-help. This was particularly true of employers in the West Riding textile trade and the Lancashire cotton trade, industries relatively new to their areas and flexible and open enough to accept all kinds of talented men at all levels. The belief that a man was limited only by his own talents was particularly prominent in the first half of the nineteenth century, the time of the self-made captains of industry.

But not all employers were happy to employ teetotallers, and more than one master dismissed his workers when he found they had become abstainers. Thomas Whittaker, the teetotal pioneer, and Henry Anderton, the teetotal poet, both lost their jobs when they signed the pledge.[124] Sweeny New Colliery in Oswestry, in advertising for workers, stated that no teetotallers would be hired.[125] Working men sometimes refused to co-operate with a teetotal workmate and might sabotage his work or otherwise make it difficult for him to stay.[126] Teetotalism introduced a dissonant note into a working situation that could prosper only when harmony prevailed. On the other hand, some teetotal masters would employ only total abstainers; this was particularly true when there were not many men involved and the job entailed residing in the master's house.[127]

Among the opponents of the temperance reform should be counted those who had a direct interest in the continued drinking habits of the people, those of 'the trade', as it was often called. Distillers, brewers, publicans and beer-house keepers were all anxious to discredit the teetotallers at any opportunity, and were frequently responsible for the disruptions that caused numerous temperance meetings to disband. It was a common practice for a publican to appear at a teetotal meeting to give free ale to anyone who wanted it,[128] in order to taunt the teetotallers and also to put them in the position of advising their audience to refuse a free gift. But just how much mischief can be laid to the publicans is difficult to ascertain. They were convenient scapegoats for the teetotallers. Joseph Livesey resisted this tendency; he refused to turn the publican into a public devil, preferring to see him as a man trying to make a living. The man that bought the drink was in his eyes as much responsible for the traffic in liquor as the man who sold it.[129] But Livesey's position was unusual. The majority of teetotallers, along with the prohibitionists, preferred to place all the blame for intemperance on those who lived by the liquor trade. The publican was made to appear a robber of the poor, who took the working man's money for his own personal gain.[130]

Another group of Englishmen that had an economic interest in the maintenance of the public's drinking habits was the farmers,[131] who grew the grain and hops that the brewers and distillers used in making beer and spirits. Consequently, the rural areas were considered to be hostile to temperance until proven otherwise. Temperance advocates knew that, if they tried to speak in rural areas, they would usually meet great antagonism.[132]

Some of the disfavour with which the 'respectable' classes viewed the temperance movement must be attributed to the interminable battles the teetotallers fought among themselves. The temperance reformation was continually split over what, to many outsiders, must have seemed minor issues – not only doctrines and pledges but also personalities. There was scarcely a branch of the movement that at some time or other was not subjected to some kind of schism. Temperance journals as well as temperance tracts, and even some non-temperance literature, were filled with acrimonious accusations from one side or another. Sometimes the temperance battles became so serious that they were transferred to the courts, of which one of the most famous was the Lees verses Gough lawsuit. It split the entire movement, with societies and individuals taking sides, and prompted Thomas Whittaker to write to the *British Temperance Advocate*, 'These squabbles about minor matters have nearly in several cases destroyed our cause.'[133]

However, it would be incorrect to assume that the total population of England in the mid-nineteenth century was hostile to the temperance reformation. The majority were indifferent to the reformers. The public was not interested in what the teetotallers were preaching; many did not even know what teetotalism meant. According to one journal, some who signed the pledge believed that they were only allowed to drink tea.[134]

# 3 So Many Christian Icebergs to Melt

One cannot understand the attitude of the churches towards alcoholic drink without taking into account the social context in which such drink was used. Drinking was as much a part of religious as of secular life, wrote Joseph Livesey, when pointing out that at one ordination twenty-one toasts were drunk.[1] Aside from its role in religious ceremonies,[2] intoxicating liquor was often present at many other functions of the churches. It was customary, for example, to supply home-brewed ale at the quarterly meeting dinners of the Methodists, as well as to the singers at Sunday School anniversaries.[3] Furthermore, according to E. C. Urwin, the Methodist temperance historian, 'In many churches, alcoholic stimulants were provided for the ministers before and after preaching.'[4]

It was not uncommon for bottles of wine and brandy to be given to ministers by members of their congregations as gifts in appreciation of their services, as was the custom in all walks of life in England in the early and mid-nineteenth century. Frequently a cordial or a brandy was offered to a minister as refreshment when he visited the home of a member of his congregation, and it has been claimed that it was this type of hospitality which made some ministers such drunkards that they were dismissed from their posts.[5] The Rev. Jabez Burns told of a returned church missionary who, when offered tea, coffee or cocoa with his evening meal, called them slops and went to bed without anything to eat, preferring to fast rather than have his supper without ale.[6]

In some villages it was the custom to give children intoxicating drink at church festivals. In one Yorkshire village the local temperance forces campaigned against this practice and succeeded in getting it abolished in all the local churches except the Methodist New Connection, which insisted on retaining the tradition.[7] But the Methodists were not the only denomination tolerating alcoholic beverages. After the foundation stone of a new Congregational Church was laid, the participants adjourned to the local inn, where they had their dinner and drank a number of toasts.[8] Ale was as popular then as tea is today. At the beginning

43

of the century no one questioned its use as no one today questions the use of tea. And so the churches in nineteenth-century England, reflecting the prevailing social mores, saw very little wrong in moderate drinking. However, all the churches condemned drunkenness, basing their position on the Bible, which, while referring agreeably to drinking, completely condemns intemperance: it says that the gates of heaven are closed to the drunkard. Drinking and intemperance were thus viewed as two entirely different matters by the churches. 'A drunkard is a public enemy', said John Wesley,[9] expressing a sentiment with which few people in England would have disagreed.

We have already seen that when the temperance reformation first came to England, the churches, accepting the role of social drinking, did not wholeheartedly embrace the new movement.[10] But neither did they reject it. Instead, preferring to take no stand on the temperance reformation, they left it to gain what church-connected support it could from individual ministers, whose participation in the cause was a purely personal choice. And temperance did receive a great deal of assistance from both clergymen and dissenting ministers in the early days of moderation.[11]

The coming of teetotalism, however, changed the situation between the churches and temperance completely, causing a separation of the two. This estrangement continued for over three decades, until the rise of Gospel Temperance in the 1870s. The withdrawal of the support of the churches from the movement after the total abstinence principle became dominant embittered many teetotallers, who preferred to see the churches as enemies if they refused to be friends.[12] This change in church support caused one teetotal journal to comment:

> Previous to the extension of the principle of Abstinence to *all* intoxicating liquors, a large number of clergymen in Britain supported our Societies; but since the low ground of *abstinence from ardent spirits alone* had been abandoned, *and the higher ground of abstinence from all intoxicating beverages* had been advanced to, many of them, from whom better things might have been expected, have refused us their countenance and aid.[13]

The situation between teetotalism and religion was

complicated by the fact that the churches themselves did not speak with one voice on the subject. Whereas some churches would give a cold shoulder to temperance workers,[14] others, believing the Grace of God was not for drunkards, came to identify total abstinence with religion.[15] Frequently there was disagreement on the issue of temperance among churches or chapels of the same denomination. Furthermore, the temperance reformation itself was not a unified movement with a single creed; there were great variations in the views and personalities of its leaders. Local organisations differed greatly one from another, and often the relationship between the churches (and chapels) and the individual temperance bodies would depend on local conditions.

It was not just the change of principles that turned many people of religion, along with other members of the 'respectable classes', away from the temperance cause. As we have already seen, there was an alteration in the character of the movement, with resultant change in both methods and personnel, when teetotalism became paramount. As the nature of the movement changed, so did the attitude of the religious leaders towards it. Except for certain non-conformist sects, such as the Primitive Methodists and the Bible Christians, who were active among the lower orders in society, the churches in mid-nineteenth-century England were generally very 'respectable', placing great value on their social position and the esteem in which they were held by the more 'comfortable' classes.

## THE CHURCH OF ENGLAND AND TEETOTALISM

The Church of England in particular, as the religion of the establishment, was very sensitive to deviations from accepted behaviour patterns, viewing with suspicion any new ideas that did not fit into the prevailing orthodox modes of thought and action. When teetotalism was introduced, the Church preferred to ignore the new principles rather than try to work with them.

This change of attitude towards the temperance reformation can be seen in the address of the Bishop of Ripon to the Bradford Temperance Society on the occasion of the opening of the Bradford Temperance Hall on 2 July 1838, when teetotalism had already gained a firm hold on the movement. The Bishop admitted that 'When the proposition was first made to me, I must confess, I hesitated whether I ought to preside over such a meeting as this.' He told the gathering he had come because he was sure what had been said about them by their critics could not be true; 'They supposed your object was to substitute the principles of Total Abstinence in the place of the principles of the religion of Jesus Christ'. The Bishop then told the meeting that he had decided to become a member of their temperance society and wanted everyone to know that he was basing his decision upon Christian principles.[16]

At this opening of the Temperance Hall in Bradford, the established church was represented not only by the Bishop of the diocese but also by the Rev. G. S. Bull of St James; the Rev. T. Drury, Keighley; S. Redhead, vicar of Calverley; J. Cheadle, Vicar of Bingley; J. Barber, incumbent of Wilsden; and J. Bardsley, curate of Bingley. The majority of these clergymen were, or later became, leading supporters of the temperance reformation in their parishes. The Rev. J. Barber of Wilsden, who asked in his speech at the Bradford opening that all intoxicating drinks be 'laid aside except in the Lord's Supper', was president of the Wilsden Total Abstinence Society.[17] He was well known in his parish for his charity and compassion to all and, although not a rich man, he gave generously to the poor.[18] The Rev. Barber was a former teacher of the Rev. James Bardsley, who was also a protégé of the Rev. G. S. Bull,[19] and a life-long supporter of the temperance reformation, working long and hard for it both in Yorkshire and in Lancashire, where he eventually settled.[20]

Another clergyman and president of a temperance society present at this meeting was the Rev. Theo Drury. Unlike many of the teetotal clergy, Mr Drury came from a well-to-do family and had been educated at Harrow and Cambridge. He originally came to Yorkshire because of his friendship with the Duke of Devonshire, who gave him the living at Keighley. During his twenty-six years' tenure in this post, Mr Drury devoted a great deal of his time and money to helping the working-class members of his parish. He was a strong supporter of the ten-hour movement for factory reform[21] and was instrumental in getting a Mechanics Institute organised in Keighley. A founder also of the Keighley Temperance Society, he remained faithful to the movement during both its moderation and its teetotal phases.

The Rev. G. S. Bull, who was also present at the Bradford

meeting, was another worker in the ten-hour cause, so strongly identified with this movement that he was called the 'ten-hour parson'.[22] But the Rev. Bull was active in the temperance cause as well as the movement for educational reform.[23] Like many other clerical temperance supporters of this period, he was devoted to the teetotal cause because of his concern for the working classes and the difficult conditions in the new industrial centres. Many of these clergymen saw the temperance movement as one means of helping the poorer members of society.

It is, therefore, not surprising that, in these early years of teetotalism, the greatest clerical support for temperance was to be found in the areas that were experiencing the greatest social dislocation through rapid urbanisation and industrialisation. To many clerics the temperance movement seemed to show working men a way out of their low condition. The Bishop of Norwich expressed this view in a letter written in 1837 to one of his clergymen: 'Temperance Societies are most instrumental in raising thousands and tens of thousands from degraded profligacy to virtuous and industrious habits, and converting sinners from the ways of vice to those of religion.' The Bishop asked all his parish priests to help this movement and its supporters.[24] The Diocese of Ripon, whose Bishop joined the local temperance movement, included the West Riding of Yorkshire, an area noted for its strong temperance sentiment. Particularly in Bradford and the surrounding areas, where many of the teetotal associations were organised by clerics of the established church, there was a strong tradition of temperance work in the parish churches. So many Bradford and district clergymen were involved in the movement that in 1840 they formed an association to 'extend the principles of total abstinence through the area'.[25] That same year, on Easter Sunday, members of the Bradford branches of the Rechabites, a working-class teetotal society, held a procession to Christ Church, where they heard a temperance sermon,[26] which created little surprise in the town: a teetotal society had already been formed in 1839 at this church and both church and society worked closely with the working-class members of the parish.[27]

A few miles away, in the village of Bingley, the local temperance society was completely dependent on the parish church for leadership and vitality. When the incumbent was an enthusiastic supporter of the reformation the society flourished, but when he was not it became dormant. Close by, in the village of Wibsey, the incumbent during the 1840s was also a leader in the temperance movement in his parish. He organised a meeting in the local schoolrooms to discuss setting up a parish temperance society and invited Rev. Bull to come and speak on the matter.[28]

It also happened that Church of England clerics would cooperate with dissenting ministers to organise local temperance societies. For instance, in 1834 in Haworth, another Yorkshire village, Rev. Patrick Brontë, Rev. M. Saunders and Rev. J. Winterbottom, along with other local ministers and clergymen, met to form a temperance society. Mr Saunders, the Baptist minister, was made secretary of the new society. Mr Brontë, father of the famous Brontë sisters, was the incumbent of the parish. Mr Drury of Keighley chaired the meeting and Rev. D. Taylor of Bingley came to give his support along with Rev. D. Marsh of Sutton. This society did not talk of a 'pledge', but asked its members to sign a 'declaration'.[29] Dissenters also worked with Church of England members in the Wilsden Temperance Society.[30]

Closely rivalling the West Riding in its strong temperance spirit was the county of Lancashire. The birthplace of the teetotal movement in the 1830s, it was also the home of the United Kingdom Alliance, the prohibition party, founded in 1853.[31] The diocese of Manchester was particularly active on the temperance issue, and a leader of the work there was the Rev. William Caine. This clergyman was unusual in that he was already a confirmed teetotaller by the time he was ordained, having signed the pledge and joined a juvenile teetotal association when he was eleven years old. Unfortunately for him, his first appointment was to the curacy of a parish that had strong anti-temperance sentiments. In fact, the members were so hostile to their new curate's activities that they forced him to resign,[32] and for the following ten years Mr Caine was without a parish. He spent the decade travelling up and down the country lecturing on temperance, after which he was appointed chaplain to the Salford jail. He returned to parish work as the incumbent of Christ's Church, Denton, near Manchester, where he remained vicar to the end of his days.[33] As an acknowledgement of his dedication to the movement, Rev. Caine was made president of the foremost temperance organisation in Lancashire, the Lancashire and Cheshire Band of Hope Union, a special honour in view of the fact that the Union was composed almost entirely of non-conformists. Caine was also very active in expounding temperance principles in non-temperance circles. So often did he raise the problem of intemperance when lecturing to the British Social Science Association, for instance, that he became known as the 'Apostle of Temperance to the British Social Science Association'.[34]

Also in Lancashire, in the city of Liverpool, a church teetotal society was founded at the early date of 11 November 1837. The Liverpool Church of England Total Abstinence Society had a youth branch and a senior section and appears to have been concerned mainly with working men. Unlike some other church societies, this organisation had a formal pledge card that contained a promise to abstain from all intoxicating beverages except when used medicinally 'or in a religious ordinance', and an agreement not to give or offer such drinks to others.[35] Little is known of the Society's activities. Like so many other temperance societies, it served local needs and was unconnected with any national association.

Attempts to set up national church temperance groups were made at various times by various clerics. One of these, the Church of England Temperance Society, was organised in April 1840 by the Rev. J. F. Witty of St John's Episcopal Chapel in Southwark.[36] Mr Witty established the headquarters of this group at Exeter Hall in London, but it did not survive for long. It had only meagre resources and in this period the clergy of the metropolitan area had very little interest in the temperance movement. When the group dissolved in 1841, after only six months' existence, a Church of England Total Abstinence Society replaced it.[37] However, nothing about this group's activities is reported in temperance or church records so that we do not know how long it survived or what it did.

The contributions of Church of England clerics to the early temperance cause should not be judged by the success, or lack of it, of church-related societies: far more important was the support individual clergymen gave to the movement, even though their support often cost them much in terms of professional advancement. The decades before the 1870s were a time when teetotalism was unpopular and many of those who were willing to support it publicly were penalised. One such well-known teetotal clergyman who would not be intimidated by popular hostility was the Rev. Henry Gale. Mr Gale was originally a solicitor who gave up this profession to join the church.[38] After he was ordained he threw himself into many reforming causes, including the Anti-Corn Law League. Gale caused a great scandal in Birmingham in 1852 when he addressed the annual meeting of the Birmingham branch of the Church Missionary Society and asked that the society insist that all its missionaries be total abstainers. An uproar ensued and Gale was expelled from the meeting.[39] So strong was the enmity he evoked that he was soon dismissed from his position as curate. Undeterred, he continued his temperance activities with the same intensity, eventually becoming one of the founders of the first truly national temperance society of the Church of England.[40]

One of the few church dignitaries who supported total abstinence and teetotal societies from the beginning in the 1830s was Archdeacon Jeffreys, who spent much of his time lecturing both at home and abroad on the need for temperance. In 1834, when he visited Van Diemen's Land on an inspection tour, he startled his audience by praising teetotalism and asking them to sign a pledge then and there 'for the mutual benefit and support of each other',[41] although he was not himself a teetotaller at the time and did not become one for another four years. In 1840 Jeffreys wrote a tract, 'The Religious Objection to Teetotalism', in which he showed great concern over the lack of support given by the churches to teetotal societies. He felt that men who cited the gospel as the source of their opposition were in error. Answering the objection that the Church cannot support temperance societies because they are 'Human Devices', he wrote that all human gifts come from the Lord and should be used to do His work. If men found the existing temperance societies too secular, he believed they should start their own on Christian lines.[42] Unlike many of his colleagues in the church, Archdeacon Jeffreys felt temperance societies were a 'Powerful handmaid of the gospel'; they alone went to the drunkard's rescue and helped him arrive at a condition in which he could learn about the gospel and become converted to Christianity.

Archdeacon Jeffreys' concern over the antagonism of many church members towards teetotalism was shared by Mrs Charles Wightman, the wife of a clergyman at Shrewsbury, who became involved in the temperance movement through her work among the poor of her husband's parish in the 1850s. She was reluctant to organise a temperance society, for she had a strong prejudice against teetotalism, but, having decided that only such a society could free her charges from the curse of drink, she eventually founded one.[43] Many of her husband's colleagues were unhappy with her work; one critic said that, having worked for some time in the Shrewsbury district and having seen very little drinking there, he could not understand why her work was necessary.[44] Mrs Wightman's work was unique only in that she wrote about her experiences in a book, *Haste to the Rescue* (1860) which was instrumental in arousing the church to greater involvement in the problem of temperance and which, according to at least one temperance historian, created the motivation for the formation of the Church of England Temperance Society.[45] It was also alleged that thirty clergymen were converted to teetotalism after reading it, as was W. S. Caine, who was to become a prominent 'temperance' Member of Parliament.[46]

Another clerical temperance supporter was the subject of a temperance story told at the yearly meeting of the Society of Friends in 1839. The Rector of Ludgvan in Cornwall, the Rev. H. E. Graham, allegedly had to start a total abstinence society in his parish to fill his empty church. His parishioners were mostly heavy drinkers who, because of their drinking, did not come to church. Through his efforts, many of them signed the total abstinence pledge and joined the church, becoming the basis for a solid, sober congregation.[47] When Canon Ellison, the future head of the Church of England Temperance Society was at Windsor, he found the drinking habits of the working classes there to be an impediment to their spiritual life. He too worked to combat this intemperance by means of a parish temperance association in the early 1860s.[48]

But not all clergymen were sympathetic to the temperance movement. In many parts of the country there was a strong antagonism between parish church and temperance hall. This was the situation in Woodhouse, a village near Leeds. In 1851 a Leeds clergyman wrote to the *Leeds Mercury* complaining about the errors and inadequacies of the temperance movement. The reply this letter elicited from George Lucas, one of the leaders of the teetotal group in Woodhouse, was printed and circulated as a tract.[49] Lucas accused all the churches in his village of neglecting the lower classes and called the parsons 'lily-handed, silken-fingered pensioners. The church in Woodhouse had not had any effect on the drinking habits of the working classes, nor had it attempted to help the poorer villagers in any way, wrote Lucas, alleging that strong class prejudices kept the lower classes out of the parish church in Woodhouse. Churches were only for the respectable, he wrote, and pointed out that only a quarter of the population in the village – men, women and children – had ever attended a place of worship. He added that there were few opportunities for the working classes to improve themselves in Woodhouse. They could not even get a hall to meet in until they managed to rent an old building which they called the Temperance Hall and Literary Institution. Answering a complaint often made against the teetotallers, Lucas wrote that the sort of people the teetotallers taught to read and write in their Sunday Schools would not, if there was no school on Sunday, go to church but rather to the public houses.[50]

Like many other working-class temperance reformers, the Woodhouse teetotallers did not see their work as one of reclaiming men to save souls. They agreed with the Rev. Fawcett that attendance at the churches and chapels, in Woodhouse at least, had not increased with the coming of temperance. 'Teetotalism never purported to fill churches and chapels', wrote Lucas.[51] It appears that the division between teetotallers and the religious organisations of Woodhouse was of long standing. Over a decade earlier, in April 1840, the *British Temperance Advocate* reported that the teetotallers were upset because the Wesleyan minister in Woodhouse refused to announce teetotal meetings.[52]

Many of the differences in the attitudes of the various parish churches towards the temperance movement may be traced to the differences in character and personality of their respective incumbents.[53] This variation was particularly important in the Church of England, which allowed its clergymen a great deal of independence. In theory the bishop was virtually the sole authority within the diocese but, because much of this power was not exercised, the local incumbent had the freedom to make his own decisions on matters concerning his parish.[54] Furthermore, the Church of England never took an official anti-teetotal stand and so did not bind any of its clergy to a course that would have proven distasteful to them.

It would be inaccurate, however, to depict English clergymen between 1840 and 1870 as being either for or against the temperance reformation. Like the rest of the population, the majority of clergymen were indifferent to the problem of intemperance, believing it to be none of their concern. They saw no reason to expend their time and energy on work that, in the limited fashion of the time, could not be construed as the responsibility of the church. Even after the Church of England set up its own temperance society in the 1870s, many of its clergy still believed that the drinking habits of the people were not the concern of the church.[55]

## TEETOTALISM IN THE NON-CONFORMIST CHURCHES

Among the non-conformist churches, the Wesleyan Methodists were officially the least sympathetic to teetotalism. Although Wesleyan ministers had been prominent in the moderation movement, many were unhappy when total abstinence took it over. Their opposition was directed both at the new principles and at the new type of member attracted by teetotalism.

Traditionally the Methodist Church was against distilled liquors. According to the Rules of the Methodist Society of 1743, spirits were to be avoided if at all possible, not only drinking them but also trading in them.[56] The Directions to the Band Societies (1744) stated that all who became Methodists agreed to drink no spirituous liquors.[57] Three years later, however, in 1747, the founder of Methodism wrote, 'Our religion does not lie in doing what God had not enjoined or abstaining from what He hath not forbidden. It does not lie . . . in abstaining from meats and drinks, which are all food if received with thanksgiving.'[58] But later Methodists were divided over the issue of personal abstinence, some claiming that in John Wesley's time ardent spirits were the problem, not wine and ale, and that if the founder were alive in the 1830s he would surely support the reformation. Individual Wesleyan ministers wrote tracts to support the movement, while others published works manifesting their opposition to teetotalism. In the early 1840s in particular, so many of these tracts were published that one temperance historian writes of the 'battle of the pens'.[59] At the same time, when two candidates for the Wesleyan ministry divulged to the authorities that they were teetotallers, they were informed that they must 'either change their opinions or choose another calling'.[60]

Much of the hostility the Wesleyan hierarchy showed towards the teetotallers stemmed from the fear that schismatic tendencies might appear if teetotalism was accepted by the chapels. The Wesleyans looked with disfavour on any new movement, seeing it as a source of further turmoil and defection, of the type that had plagued their church continually since the death of John Wesley. To justify their hostility the anti-teetotal Wesleyans could point to many incidents caused by dissension over teetotal doctrine. In some chapels officials who did not sign the teetotal pledge were persecuted by their congregations.[61] This was especially common in Cornwall, where many Cornish Wesleyans believed total abstinence to be an essential part of their religion.[62] More than one chapel in that county became the scene of a scandalous riot during a temperance meeting. One of the most notorious riots happened in Taunton in Somerset in 1836 when James Tearle, a veteran teetotal advocate, was addressing a crowded meeting; 'landlords and moderation people kicked up a row, broke the pews, and pulled the hat-pins out of the walls, and threw them on the platform', reported a Methodist temperance historian.[63] But it was never clearly established who was responsible for the uproar. In any event the congregation had to repair the extensive damage sustained by the chapel.

At least one teetotal advocate later admitted that some teetotallers had made themselves disagreeable to the Wesleyans.[64] E. C. Urwin, the Methodist temperance historian, wrote, 'Their sense of grim evil and desperate need makes extravagant language easy; their passion for sobriety may conduce to an unlovely and censorious attitude and demands strangely akin to Pharisaic legalism.'[65]

At first the Wesleyan authorities preferred to take no official stand on the issue of teetotalism, knowing that any specific action would lead to dissension.[66] By 1841, however, the situation needed clarification; an official attitude towards the teetotal heresy, as it was called, had to be formulated.[67] At the annual conference of that year the subject was raised and, though feelings ran high on both sides, the anti-teetotal forces won the day. The conservative Bunting party was still in control of the Wesleyan Conference and this group viewed teetotalism as a branch of working-class radicalism which would have to be put down.[68] Their victory came in the form of three resolutions that were passed by the conference:

1. That no unfermented wines be used in the administration of the Sacrament throughout the Connexion.
2. That no Wesleyan Chapel be lent for the meetings of the Temperance Society.
3. That no preacher shall go into another circuit to advocate teetotalism without the consent of the superintendent of the circuit to which he may be invited.[69]

As many Wesleyans feared, the anti-temperance resolutions had serious repercussions for their church. In 1842, 600 Cornish Wesleyan Methodists split off from the parent body and formed their own branch of the Methodist movement, which they called the Teetotal Wesleyan Methodists.[70] In Cornwall, the people were both strong Methodists and staunch teetotallers and more defections would doubtless have occurred there if the Wesleyan superintendents had not ignored many breaches of the 1841 resolutions. One Cornish superintendent allowed the use of unfermented wine in his area, for instance,[71] and some circuits were permitted to restrict their appointments to teetotal preachers. (It is interesting to note that both William Booth and Edwin Paxton Hood, two prominent leaders in the later Gospel temperance movement, were on the St Ives circuit of the Cornish teetotal Wesleyans).[72] The separation between the Teetotal Wesleyans and the main body did not last long; by 1860 all had been absorbed back into the mainstream of Methodism.[73]

In contrast to the official policy, events on the local level showed that there was a great deal of sympathy for temperance among Wesleyans, and not only in Cornwall. In 1846, Wesleyan temperance supporters in Liverpool, in defiance of the anti-teetotal resolutions, formed a Wesleyan Union of Total Abstainers, which quickly claimed ninety members, thirty of them ministers. Although the teetotal pledge was not required by this group, it was reported that twenty-five of them had signed it.[74] In the July 1849 issue, the *National Temperance Advocate* published a long statement of their motives and goals. They wanted to bring together teetotallers of the Wesleyan Connexion in prayer and action. 'The chief object of this Union is to obtain the active cooperation of those of our brethren who recognize the principles of total abstinence as a powerful auxiliary to the gospel', proclaimed the union in their statement, which concluded with the following remarks: 'The primary design in admitting

only members of the Wesleyan Society, was to secure heartfelt
union in prayer, which is the corner stone of the building, the want
of which had hindered the usefulness of other temperance
societies.'[75] A branch of this union was formed in 1849 in the
Yorkshire town of Huddersfield, where it immediately boasted
a membership of sixty-eight Methodists. These members
inaugurated temperance prayer meetings, which were held in the
vestry of one of the chapels, and in 1850 they sent a memorial to
the Wesleyan Conference asking them to reconsider their decision
on teetotalism. The conference was under constant pressure from
many sides to change their stand, but changes were not to be made
for a number of decades, and then only after a hard fight.

Another Yorkshire town where Wesleyan Methodists played a
prominent role in temperance circles was York. Here the
temperance society was actually organised and run by Wesleyan
Methodists and every Wesleyan minister but one in the first fifty
years of the society's existence was a total abstainer.[76] The
influence of this branch of non-conformism in York temperance
circles was so great that the temperance society there was
organised on the same lines as the Methodist chapels.[77] Registers
were kept of the names and addresses of every temperance
supporter, man and woman, in the city, and agents were
appointed to visit them every quarter to give them new tickets of
membership and collect contributions. These members were
under constant surveillance, and any deviation from the
standards of the society was duly noted.[78] No one was considered
a member who did not have a valid ticket of membership. In
Sheffield, too, in 1835 Methodists formed a temperance society on
Methodist chapel lines. Here the remnants of the original
declining society were incorporated into this new one.[79] With so
much direct connection between Wesleyans and the temperance
movement, it is not surprising to find that, despite the official
opposition of the Connexion, the two were often linked in the
public's mind.

In contrast to the Wesleyans, the hierarchy of the Primitive
Methodist Church gave their wholehearted support to the
temperance cause. Their founder, Hugh Bourne, was a staunch
total abstainer, as were many other influential leaders of this
denomination.[80] In many mining villages of Northumberland and
Durham the Primitive Methodists were identified completely
with teetotalism.[81] Not only were the temperance meetings held in

their chapels, but many of their leaders were active temperance advocates, preaching the gospel and teetotalism at one and the same time.[82] Some of the compatibility between the two may have been due to the fact that they drew their memberships from people of similar social backgrounds. Indeed their memberships often overlapped.[83] Both the temperance movement and the Primitive Methodist chapels asserted that they had produced many of the working-class leaders of the labour movement, a claim that was generally valid because many of these leaders were members at one time or another of both groups. Public speaking, a valuable skill for any leader, was learned both by lay preachers and by temperance advocates, the former in the chapels and the latter either in the Bands of Hope, a juvenile temperance organisation,[84] or in classes run by temperance societies.[85]

Friendship and mutual aid characterised the normal relationship between the Primitive Methodist chapels and the temperance societies; when on occasion antagonism did arise, it was usually over some local or personal issue. In the Hull circuit, for example, a candidate for the post of preacher was asked to promise 'not to lend any chapel for total abstinence meetings nor to announce them from the pulpit, nor to attend them himself and to discountenance all connection with them.[86] Another Primitive Methodist worker claimed he was forced out of his Sunday School position because of his teetotal activities,[87] but such cases were the exception, not the rule.

The Bible Christians were another Methodist offshoot that was often identified with teetotalism, but, like the Primitive Methodists, this sect never insisted on its members being personal abstainers. A historian of this sect, Thomas Shaw, doubted that the ministry of the Bible Christians was 100 per cent teetotal.[88] In 1854 its conference had to warn its circuits against insisting on having only teetotallers as their local preachers. Not until 1882, long after other churches had set up total abstinence societies, did the Bible Christians inaugurate one for their members.[89]

The Society of Friends, like the Methodists, had a tradition of temperance in the old moderation sense of the word. They believed in being temperate in all matters of diet and so were against any drinking or eating to excess. They saw nothing wrong in wines and beer and many prominent Quaker families were important brewers in the early part of the nineteenth century. The national school of the Society of Friends, at Ackworth, brewed its own beer for the consumption of its scholars.[90] Nevertheless, there was increasing pressure within the Society to have teetotalism adopted officially. Because not all Quakers felt the same way about this matter, there were fears that a schism might develop if such a stand were taken.[91] In the north and the west of England teetotalism was strong among the Friends, while in London it did not flourish, thus following the national pattern for teetotalism. In some of the teetotal areas feeling was so strong that only a personal abstainer could hold office in the sect, but this was strictly a local matter and not official policy.[92]

If members of the Society of Friends became teetotallers they did it for the sake of others and not because drinking alcohol was evil, as some teetotallers insisted. In 1837 a written address to the Society of Friends, asking them to support the temperance reformation, was signed by fifty prominent members.[93] The following year, Quaker Joseph Eaton, a nationally-known temperance supporter, published an address to the Society of Friends asking them to consider adopting total abstinence 'for the sake of others'.[94] Joseph Eaton was himself a teetotaller and secretary of the Bristol Total Abstinence Society, yet he had a 'good cellar' which he felt was so important that he singled it out in his will, directing 'my stock of wines and other descriptions of intoxicating Drinks to the Treasurer for the time being of the New Bristol General Hospital'. In that same will he left £50 to James Teare, a well-known teetotal advocate, and £15 000 each to the two national teetotal associations, the National Temperance League and the British Temperance League.[95]

In 1840, another address to the Society of Friends was published on the subject of temperance, signed by 110 Quakers, including Eaton and other prominent members,[96] which asked the Society to support total abstinence in 'that spirit of self-denial for the good of others'.[97] But progress was slow for the teetotal Friends. By 1860, all they had accomplished was a request by the Yearly Meeting to all Friends asking them to avoid misusing alcoholic beverages, and even then response to the appeals was disappointing. In 1865, in a published address to the Friends Temperance Union, Quaker Sam Bowly, a national leader in the English temperance movement, revealed his disappointment over the lack of support the temperance cause received from Friends and complained that 'we are not as united upon it as we have been upon the anti-slavery, and many other important philanthropic questions'.[98] Bowly was one of the founders of the Friends Temperance Union, which had been established in 1851 but did not flourish.[99]

Bowly was justified in his view that the Society was not united on the question of temperance. Some members resented the temperance pressure on the Society as a whole and were bitterly opposed to making teetotalism a part of the Society's work.[100] As far back as 1840, attempts were made to set up a Quaker temperance association in Sheffield, but it did not prosper.[101] In 1850 another was started in Liverpool but, like the Sheffield group, it was a purely local effort.[102] As can be expected, the Quaker brewers in particular were unhappy with the work of the teetotallers, especially in 1874, when the reformers managed to get the Yearly Meeting to ask those who manufactured intoxicating beverages to change their business if at all possible.[103] At least one Quaker brewer, preferring to keep his trade, gave up his membership in the Society when the pressure became too great.[104] But, despite the strong support for the temperance movement through the nineteenth century from individual Quakers, the Society of Friends never insisted on its members being teetotal and many refused to become abstainers.

As with many other sectarian groups, the meagre institutional success of temperance within the Society of Friends was no indication of the dedication to the cause shown by many individual Quakers. Many non-Quaker temperance agents and advocates were supported either wholly or in part by individual Friends, and there were very few local or national temperance organisations in which at least one member of the Society did not play a prominent role. In London, for example, the Metropolitan Roman Catholic Total Abstinence Association owed its existence to the cooperation between Quakers and Roman Catholics.[105] Together they worked to promote the cause, especially among the immigrant Irish in London. Father Mathew, the great Irish apostle of temperance, who was said to have pledged millions of Irishmen as well as Englishmen and Americans during his many temperance tours, was originally introduced to the movement by William Martin, a Friend, who persuaded the Roman Catholic priest to sign the teetotal pledge in April 1838.[106] In Doncaster, too, the temperance movement was indebted to the Quakers, as was acknowledged by one of the teetotal journals.[107] It is unnecessary to enumerate all the societies throughout the country

that owed all or part of their existence to the efforts of members of
the Society of Friends, but there were many of them.

The position regarding teetotalism of the Roman Catholic
Church somewhat resembled that of the Church of England. Both
insisted that personal abstinence must be adopted by the
individual of his own free will; they permitted no coercion.[108] Both
too preferred to remain silent on the matter of teetotalism if they
could do so without any loss of authority and if the issue was not
forced on them. Officially the Roman Catholic Church regarded
drunkenness as a sin, one of the seven deadly sins, but
'Drunkenness is not the sin of the drink but of the drunkard',
wrote Cardinal Manning,[109] who was eventually to stimulate his
church into taking part in the temperance reformation.[110]
'Alcohol has its lawful place and one must discriminate between
the use and abuse' was a traditional Catholic view of drink. One
Jesuit expounder of his church's attitude towards the temperance
reformation wrote, 'total abstinence is not a *sine qua non* of
perfection, nor necessarily a means to it'.[111] Temperance for
Catholics was *one* of the virtues, not a special one with an unique
value, explained Father Keating, and so the church was reluctant
to give its approval to a temperance society that focused only on
this one issue. The Roman Catholic Church also condemned
those temperance societies by whom 'temperance is converted
into a fantastic form of Deism'[112] and, in order to counteract any
attraction exerted by non-Catholic temperance societies on
Catholics, the church encouraged its members, if they wanted any
such activities, to find them within the church. And so in some
parishes there were special Catholic temperance societies, guided
by priests. The first Catholic Total Abstinence Society was
formed in 1838 by the Rev. J. Sisk, a priest at Chelsea. Inspired to
take up the temperance mission by Father Mathew's work, Sisk
does not seem to have had much success.[113] Father Mathew was
responsible for stimulating the formation of many societies
throughout England because he himself would not set up an
organisation to care for the converts to teetotalism that he pledged
at his meetings. For the most part, the influence of Father Mathew
was only temporary and, of the millions he recruited to the ways of
total abstinence, most did not remain faithful to their pledge.[114] In
1840, after a visit from the Irish priest, two priests in Bradford
tried to organise a Catholic Temperance Society among the Irish
of the parish. Although these priests showed the way by taking the

pledge themselves, and several hundreds followed, their society did not survive for long.[115]

A different situation existed in the Catholic community at Barnsley, then a rough Yorkshire mining village. Here again the Irish were the object of the ministrations of the local Roman Catholic Total Abstinence Society run by a Father J. Bighty, a local Catholic priest. Contrary to the usual situation elsewhere, Father Bighty's organisation enjoyed amicable relations with the Protestant teetotallers of the village. In December 1841, a joint meeting of both Protestant and Catholic teetotallers was held in a Protestant chapel, after which the group stayed together to have a joint tea festival, which was addressed by Father Bighty. A few weeks later, in January 1842, another joint meeting held in the Catholic chapel was so well attended that the chapel was overflowing.[116]

Some Roman Catholics belonged to the regular non-sectarian temperance societies, but the majority preferred to have their own associations. The Protestant religion was often so closely linked with the local temperance societies that it was hard for Catholics to be comfortable as members. In the Yorkshire town of Leeds, several Roman Catholic members left the Leeds Temperance Society in order to form their own Leeds Catholic Total Abstinence Association, which was reported to be 'countenanced and encouraged by the Catholic priests in the town'. Working among the Irish in Leeds and district, this organisation quickly claimed a membership of 250.[117]

One of the best-known Roman Catholic temperance workers in the mid-nineteenth century was Father Nugent. When he first came to his Liverpool parish in the 1840s he saw how much work would be needed, not only to help his parishioners, who were mostly Irish immigrants, adjust to their new conditions, but also to integrate these newcomers into the larger society.[118] He wanted to break down the barriers that separated Roman Catholics from their non-Catholic neighbours, to make his flock become part of the city. Through his work he came to believe that the intemperance of his parishioners was the greatest impediment to achieving the better life they all sought. Father Nugent therefore started a total abstinence society for them – an association that flourished for many decades. By 1878, this Catholic Total Abstinence League had six branches throughout Liverpool, mostly catering to Irish immigrants.[119] In 1872, Father Nugent,

Cardinal Manning and others founded the national Catholic teetotal society, the League of the Cross. But up until that year individual Catholic temperance efforts remained scattered and local in nature.

At the same time that the Roman Catholics established their national temperance society, the Baptists and the Congregationalists set up their own official temperance organisation, although prior to this time there had been ministers of these Protestant churches who were active in the temperance movement.[120] From the very start of the temperance reformation in England there were some ardent teetotallers in both the lay and ministerial ranks of the Baptists and the Congregationalists. The Rev. Francis Beardsall, who initiated the agitation to have only non-alcoholic wine for the sacraments, was a Baptist minister, as was the Rev. Jabez Tunnicliff, founder of the Band of Hope, the children's temperance movement. The Rev. Jabez Burns and his son Dawson Burns, the temperance advocates, were both Baptist ministers. But their efforts had to be coordinated by non-sectarian temperance organisations because their denomination would not set up a national temperance organisation for Baptists. A few local efforts were made. In 1839, a temperance society for Baptists was formed in Newcastle.[121] In 1842, the South Midland Baptist Association passed a resolution recommending that their members give support to temperance societies.[122] When Dawson Burns listed the names of abstaining ministers in the Baptist Church in 1859, he found that they accounted for only one seventh of all the ministers in that denomination.[123]

The Congregational Church was little better in its attitude towards the temperance cause. When a ministerial declaration of support for temperance was drawn up in 1847, more Congregationalist ministers signed it than those of any other denomination. But the Congregational Rev. Newman Hall said he 'lost caste' among his fellow ministers when he became a teetotaller. He was also told by 'a pious man' that he was doing the work of the devil with his teetotalism.[124]

In 1847, when the York Temperance Society presented an address to the Annual Meeting of the Congregational Union, which was meeting in York, the reception was not enthusiastic. All the union would do was 'to commend the very important subject to which the Address refers, to the attentive and prayerful consideration of their members'.[125] Like the Baptists, the

Congregational Union would not officially endorse total abstinence, preferring to remain completely neutral on the issue. Instead, like many other churches, it left the matter for the individual chapels to decide, allowing each to state its own position on temperance reformation. In 1872, when the attitudes of the churches towards teetotalism had completely changed, John Calvert, Congregational minister for Sheffield, was allowed to read a paper before the Congregational Union's autumn meeting entitled 'The Relation of the Church to the Temperance Movement'. He told the union,

> The custom used to be for Christian ministers and churches to look upon the enterprise [temperance] as an enemy, rather than a friendly ally and this grievous mistake in not heartily taking up the cause and making it her own, engendered a spirit towards the Church which led the early temperance reformers into indiscretions and excesses of speech and action, which no-one now attempts to justify.[126]

## THE TEETOTALLERS AND THE MINISTERS

Unhappy at the official indifference of the churches towards the movement, some reformers decided to take the initiative. Instead of waiting for the blessing of the central church authorities, which seemed very slow in coming, they concentrated on individual ministers. In 1848, the teetotallers organised the drawing up and signing of a ministerial declaration of support for teetotalism. Such a declaration did not require the consent of any central authority; it was for the individual ministers alone to sign.[127] Such declarations were a common feature of the temperance reformation of the nineteenth century. They were used especially in instances in which the temperance advocates wanted to arouse interest in their movement among specific segments of the population; medical declarations as well as political and religious ones were often organised.[128]

The ministerial declaration of 1848 was a national effort: temperance supporters throughout England canvassed ministers of all denominations, asking them to sign this public avowal of support for teetotalism. All those who signed were themselves pledged abstainers.[129] Altogether 583 ministers signed, 140

Independents or Congregationalists, 111 Primitive Methodists, 87 Baptists, 56 Calvinist Methodists, 47 United Presbyterians, 42 Wesleyan Association, 29 Church of England, 25 Wesleyan Methodists, 14 Unitarians and 32 other denominations.[130]

From these figures it is clear that the Wesleyans and the Church of England were giving very little support to the principles of total abstinence. This conclusion is reinforced when we compare the size of their support with the size of their national memberships, as revealed by the religious census of 1851, only three years after the declaration was signed. According to this census, in a population of almost eighteen million, five and a quarter million were Church of England members, and just over four and a half million were non-conformists.[131] Of these non-conformists, 1 385 382 were Methodists of all types, 793 142 were Independents and 567 978 were Baptists.[132] Among the Methodists, the Wesleyans were the larger group; the Primitive Methodists were only one third as numerous.[133] If we now compare the figures for the signers of the temperance declaration with those of the religious census, we find that the largest number of signers came from one of the smallest denominations – the Independents or Congregationalists.[134] The Church of England, which could claim over half of all churchgoers in England, gave very little public support to this declaration.

Along with the national campaigns waged by teetotallers to get the support of individual ministers, the local societies conducted their own efforts. In Leeds, the coolness of the city's churches towards temperance led the Committee of the Leeds Temperance Society to pass a resolution, in April 1847, allowing all religious ministers who became members of the Society to be ex-officio members of the governing committee.[135] Six months later, the Committee also proposed to have a delegation call upon all ministers in the town in order to learn 'their sentiments on the Great Principles of the Temperance Reform'.[136] This delegation was composed of two members of the society, one a Baptist minister and the other a lay temperance official, and together they visited every minister of the gospel, including the Roman Catholics, in Leeds – sixty-five visits in all. The ministers were asked their opinions of the temperance cause; their answers were noted down and later incorporated into a report, which was entered complete in the minutes of the society. The delegation also left temperance literature with each minister, asking him to read it at his leisure. The reception given to the delegates was a varied one indeed. Some ministers were openly hostile and resented the intrusion of the teetotallers, while others were happy to show their support for the cause. But, on the whole, the ministers were indifferent to the work of the teetotallers and simply preferred not to maintain any close connection with them.[137]

At the conclusion of the report were listed the six main objections of the Leeds religious establishment to the temperance movement of the day. The first two were aimed at the pledge; the ministers thought it to be 'inconsistent with the baptismal vow' and that 'the pledge did not reach the moral nature of man'. Objection was raised against ministers of the gospel making 'one vice more prominent than another'; and the claim that temperance societies were 'promoting man's temporal welfare to the neglect of the higher claims of morality and religion' was also made. The fifth objection was based on the view that ministers would be doing less good in 'promoting Temperance than in exclusive preaching of the Gospel', and finally, there was the rejection of general temperance societies because 'irreligious men were included' and 'religion as such was necessarily excluded'.[138] These criticisms were not exclusively those of the Leeds religious establishment nor were they problems of the moment. Later in the century, when churches of all denominations were setting up their own temperance organisations, they had to formulate acceptable responses to the same complaints.

The attitude of the religious bodies of England towards the temperance reformation was scarcely less ambivalent than that of the reformers towards religion and the churches. As we have seen, the rise of teetotal doctrines introduced new elements into the temperance movement. Many of the new teetotallers had no association with the religious establishment; they were self-help groups which more often than not had found the churches obstacles rather than aids to their progress, as we have seen in the case of Woodhouse.[139] But many other teetotallers were upset by the lack of Christianity in many temperance societies. These reformers believed temperance to be the handmaiden of religion and that as soon as a drunkard reformed and was on his way to becoming respectable, he should join a church or chapel. Some temperance societies liked to report how many of their reformed drunkards were also newly affiliated chapel and church members. In 1838, for example, the Birmingham Total Abstinence Society reported that on their membership rolls they had '177 individuals, once known as dissolute drunkards, terrors to their families, now not only consistent members of teetotalism, but 170 of whom are regular frequenters of places of worship'.[140]

Attempts were made also to set up Christian temperance societies. The Rev. Francis Beardsall, a Baptist minister, was so distressed by the situation in the Manchester Temperance Society that in 1841 he resigned from the society to found his own, an association to work for the 'diffusion of the Total Abstinent doctrine upon Christian principles'.[141] This move disturbed the editors of the temperance journal, *The Teetotaler*, who claimed that several advantages were gained in the separation of temperance from religion. In an editorial letter to Beardsall published in their issue of 1 May 1841, they wrote that if only Christian temperance societies were organised, people of other religions would be excluded. 'The Jew, the Mussulman, the Hindoo, and the Chinese would be incompetent to sign your pledge of Total Abstinence.'[142] This point revealed universalist ambitions, but was not a very telling argument in a society in which there were few religious non-Christians, and fewer atheists.

The second point the editors raised concerned the tendency for any religious group or movement to split on sectarian lines. It foretold the appearance of 'Protestant Teetotaler, your Catholic Teetotalers, your Church of England Teetotalers, your Wesleyan Teetotalers . . .'[143] This is what was actually to happen in the last decades of the century, when the churches did form their own temperance societies. Although the movement could then claim the greatest number of adherents in its history, its influence was somewhat dissipated because of sectarian strife.

The editors gave still a third reason for keeping temperance separate from religion: if temperance meetings were religious and not social occasions, the whole nature of the movement would alter; the change would 'banish all appearance of gaiety and mirth from their Festivals'.[144]

The York Temperance Society, though founded and supported by Wesleyans and some members of the Society of Friends, adopted a course typical of many other temperance societies with religious connections. To preserve harmony they passed a rule forbidding party politics or any 'sectarian peculiarities' in any speeches at public meetings or in any tracts published by the Committee.[145] However, many men who joined the movement were neither willing nor able to keep it separate from religion. When accused of substituting temperance for religion in their lives, such men reacted as did the *Leeds Temperance Herald* in its issue of 18 March 1837: 'The most effectual answer to those who accuse us of putting Temperance in the place of religion is to unite the two together.'[146] This is what was done in Hull in 1847, when teetotallers organised a Christian Temperance Society.[147]

Also in 1847, religion and teetotalism were combined in the building of a 'teetotal barge'. Its keel was wetted with coffee instead of the customary beer. When finished, it went down the canal to the town of Framelode, where it participated in the festivities at the foundation of a British School.[148] Its activities drew forth from the *Teetotal Times* the comment that 'one of the most pleasing facts connected with these meetings was their strictly religious character'.[149] The journal also complained that there were many unjust charges against the teetotallers of irreligion or infidelity.[150]

The cry of infidel against the teetotal movement was one that was raised at the 1847 meeting of the Northern Division of the Evangelical Alliance in Edinburgh. Some members present proposed an investigation to 'ascertain the *connexion between teetotalism and infidelity*'.[151] Distressed by this move, the owners of the *Teetotal Essayist* canvassed 100 of the 'most eminent and experienced leaders of the temperance movement, including ministers of religion and officers of societies', for their views on this subject. The Alliance's proposal also caused a great stir in many provincial societies, whose members were upset by the seemingly official acknowledgement that temperance might have any connection with infidelity. Eventually the Alliance dropped the issue and the investigation was never made.

But the agitation against the anti-religious activities of some teetotallers continued. In the 1840s many ministers of religion in the Bradford Temperance Society resigned to set up another society based on the principles of their own Protestant creed.[152] In Sheffield, similarly, a new temperance society was organised 'on Christian principles' in 1863. One of the speakers at the inaugural meeting of this group, John Unwin, said that many Christians had difficulty working with temperance people 'on account of the infidelity which prevailed among them' and were unhappy with the 'rash railing against religion and its ministers which had done so much damage to the temperance cause'.[153]

A specific problem that caused divisions among teetotallers was the Sunday activities of many temperance reformers. Joseph Livesey always insisted that Sunday morning was the best time for disseminating information about teetotalism in the streets and house to house.[154] In Leeds, for instance, this Sunday morning work was a common activity of the more earnest teetotallers, who utilised the only non-working morning of the week to propagandise their cause. But there were continual outcries against this practice. In 1839 a letter from 'a churchman' was published in the *British Temperance Advocate* complaining about temperance meetings on Sundays. 'It does not appear necessary that temperance meetings should be held on the Sabbath . . . which is specially set apart for the worship of God', he wrote.[155]

Despite the efforts of many church-oriented teetotallers, the suspicion of infidelity tarnished the whole teetotal movement. 'We were treated as heretics and shunned as irreligious', complained Thomas Whittaker, an old teetotal advocate, looking back to the early days of the movement.[156] 'Many of the clergy prayed against the temperance movement', wrote another supporter, who also complained, rather inaccurately that no clergyman at all helped the movement in the early days.[157] The issue of the relationship of temperance to the churches was not to be effectively solved until changes had occurred in the society as a whole. Not until the 1870s, under pressure of a rising public concern for the welfare of the very poor, do we find the churches willing to work officially in the cause of temperance.

## 'THE CUP THAT BITES AND STINGS' – THE SACRAMENTAL WINE ISSUE

There was one outstanding doctrinal issue between temperance and Christianity that for many teetotallers impeded any close relationship they might have desired with the churches and chapels. This was referred to by many temperance writers as 'the sacramental wine issue' and agitated them throughout the nineteenth century. Its importance derived from the apparent irreconcilability of a fundamental part of Christian belief with an even more fundamental tenet of the teetotal-dominated temperance movement. Wine, an alcoholic and intoxicating drink, was used during the celebration of the sacraments to represent the blood of Christ, and was drunk as a part of the service. Many teetotallers believed *all* intoxicating and alcoholic drinks were poisonous and should never be touched. Consequently the Christian total abstainer found himself in a serious dilemma. Furthermore, not only was wine habitually referred to and mentioned with favour in the Bible, but it played a major part in Christ's first miracle: at the marriage feast at Cana, Jesus turned water into wine. Wine was also drunk at the Last Supper, and St Paul told Timothy, the most famous of all teetotal biblical personalities, to take a little wine for the sake of his stomach. This last point was always raised by the non-teetotaller to show biblical support for the belief that wine is good for one's health.

In the early days of temperance, when moderation ruled and when a temperance leader could state that 'no member of a Temperance Society asserts that it is sinful to drink wine',[158] there was no problem over the use of wine in religious ceremonies. It was teetotalism that brought in the issues which changed the relationship between religion and temperance. In 1837 Reverend Beardsall of Manchester (who later founded a Christian temperance society, as we have seen) started the agitation to replace alcoholic wine in the sacraments with non-alcoholic grape juice. He even produced such non-fermented wine and sold it to churches and chapels.[159]

Many teetotallers managed to avoid the difficulty of taking intoxicating wines at the communion table by taking a pledge that allowed the use of wine for religious purposes; others avoided the issue by subscribing to a pledge that only forbade intoxicants as beverages.[160] Later, however, when it came to be accepted as a teetotal belief that wine is a poison, the inconsistencies of the position that allowed the use of sacramental wine could not be overlooked. If wine was a source of injury how could it represent the blood of Christ, many asked. It is not surprising that there were many attempts by teetotallers to reconcile the principles of total abstinence with biblical doctrine.

Teetotallers disturbed by this problem at first tried to show that, despite appearances, favourable references to wine-drinking in the Bible pertained only to non-intoxicating beverages. The most popular explanation went by the name of the two-wine theory. From the various words used for wine in the Bible, two, *Ayin* and *Tirosh*, were singled out as being the most important. The first, it was claimed, was the generic word for wine, while the

second meant non-intoxicating wine – i.e. grape juice. This theory
was most effectively advanced by F. R. Lees in his Prize Essay of
1844.[161]

In explaining how he came to devise the theory, Lees wrote that
he could not believe 'that the poison drink, that is dangerous and
destroys tens of thousands', could be the same as that 'used in the
Bible by the prophets or the Son of God as a useful and safe *beverage*
for Christians'.[162] He needed to find 'a way out of this dilemma'
and so arrived at the two-wine theory as the only reasonable
solution for believing Christians.[163] This interpretation claimed
that there were two types of wine in the Bible: one was bad, a
'mocker', a 'defrauder' and a 'deceiver', and the other was good,
one that 'cheers but not inebriates'. It was this latter, good wine
that Jesus made at Cana.[164]

This explanation allowed the teetotaller to accept all of the
Bible without any sophisticated theory about the variety of wines.
He simply had to distinguish references to good or bad wine. But
there remained the major difficulty of proving that there were
indeed two kinds of wine – fermented and unfermented – in the
Bible. Many pages of teetotal scholarship attempted to establish
philological grounds for this and related theories, but the results
were inconclusive. And, in reviewing Lees' book advancing this
theory in the *Church of England Temperance Chronicle*, Canon
Hopkins asked why the Church Fathers had made no mention of
any distinction between a 'poisonous' and a 'health-giving'
wine.[165] To this question Lees gave the weak answer that the
silence of the Church Fathers was an 'example of intellectual
lapse'.[166]

The absence of direct proof for the two-wine theory did not
deter its temperance supporters. Loath to relinquish such a useful
hypothesis, they claimed it was proved by the true spirit of the
Gospels. This was the position adopted by the Irish Bible
Temperance Association (Belfast), one of whose officers, the Rev.
John Pyper,[167] characterised the opposition to the two-wine
theory as a view which 'represents Jesus Himself as a Patron of the
infernal drink-system'.[168] Thus, maintained the Rev. Pyper, the
Bible would support strong drink and would encourage not only
drinking but its consequence, drunkenness.[169]

The Marriage of Cana wine question was also handled in a
'spirit of the gospels' manner by some teetotallers. In one
discussion it was claimed that, if Jesus made intoxicating wine for

a wedding at which many had already drunk freely, he would not be a prudent man. 'Was that conduct worthy of and such as might be expected from the Author of the Prayer "Lead us not into temptation, but deliver us from evil"?'[170] A similar view was taken by the Reverend Benjamin Parson, a Congregational minister in Gloucester, in his Prize Essay, *Anti-Bacchus*, published in 1840. He believed that our Lord, who is a 'God of Love and Mercy', could recommend only wines that do not intoxicate.[171] In the same year, Rev. W. J. Shrewsbury, a Wesleyan minister well known for his temperance views, took a similar stand in his lecture published under the title 'Alcohol Against the Bible and the Bible Against Alcohol': 'The Bible *approves* of nothing but what is really good and *disapproves* of nothing but what is really evil, and as whatever intoxicates is evil the Bible must be against it.'[172]

The 'spirit of the gospels' approach could only be successful among those who were already prone to believe in this interpretation. It would not convert the antagonist nor assuage the hostility many churchgoers felt towards teetotalism. And it could be used by the opponents of biblical temperance to promote the opposite interpretation. Hence some of the temperance Bible experts sought evidence in Jewish traditions and practice to support their view of the Bible.

Because the Last Supper was a Passover meal, that religious festival was the main focus of this approach. 'Herschel, a converted Jew', claimed the *Preston Temperance Advocate* in 1837, 'said the Hebrew word *Hometz*, translated usually as leaven, meant literally fermentation and that during the Passover time the Jews were forbidden to keep anything fermented in their house.'[173] A year earlier, in the same journal, Mr Noah, a Jew, told how to make unfermented wine without alcohol, such as was used by the Jews during the celebration of Passover and such as 'he supposes was used at the Last Supper and should now be used at the communion table.'[174] However, in March 1852 a correspondent wrote in the *British Temperance Advocate* that poor Jews made their own wine, while those who could afford it bought theirs from the high priest. The writer claimed to have bought some of this wine from the high priest and to have had it analysed. Having found that it contained spirit, he asked the *British Temperance Advocate* to comment. The journal replied that it was for the opponents to show that Christ used fermented, intoxicating wine, and that later Jews restricted their ban on fermentation to corn. The law, wrote the editors of the *Advocate,* 'prohibits ferment and fermented things generally'.[175] Here the argument had shifted, the two-wine people putting their opponents on the defensive, demanding that they prove that the wine Jesus used was fermented. This view, common among teetotallers, was supported by the Dean of Carlisle, one of the most ardent of the Church of England teetotallers. In 1861 he said he had no doubt whatever 'that the cup our Lord blessed when he instituted the Holy Supper, was a cup of unfermented wine'.[176]

The Established Church did not agree with this cleric, although no official stand was taken on the matter until 1888. This did not mean that there were no parish churches using unfermented wine: practice differed from diocese to diocese. If, however, a bishop forbade the use of unfermented wine in Holy Communion, as did the Bishop of Lincoln, Dr C. Wordsworth, in 1877[177] and the Bishop of Manchester in 1885,[178] then officially the whole diocese had to obey. In Manchester, when the Bishop came to conduct the service at one of his churches and found only unfermented wine available, he delayed the service until someone procured some fermented wine.[179] This incident, which angered some teetotallers,[180] is fully understandable when one realises that, for the Bishop, unfermented wine was not wine at all and could not be consecrated for use at Holy Communion.[181] He acknowledged the problem sacramental wine might pose for reformed drunkards, but believed they were exceptional cases for whom exceptional remedies should be found. He also claimed that teetotallers' fears showed a 'lack of faith in the divine presence not to believe Christ will give us strength to resist temptation when we are simply doing His will'.[182] This was the view accepted by the church.[183]

In the 1880s the sacramental wine issue was again a source of strong agitation. The British Women's Temperance Association took it up and encouraged other temperance sympathisers to try to force the churches to use unfermented wine.[184] So strong was the pressure exerted by the temperance reformers that the Lower House of the convocation of Canterbury sent an appeal on the matter to the Upper House, which elicited the reply that the agitation 'distressed many religious persons', 'unsettled the weak' and could even 'lead to schism'. The Upper House insisted that the clergy 'should conform to ancient and unbroken usage, and should discountenance all attempts to deviate from it'.[185] This position was confirmed by the Lambeth Conference of 1888, which made it official policy to which the whole church, prelates as well as parish priests, had to adhere.[186] No doubt many members of the church were relieved to have the troublesome issue settled at last, and the implementation of such a rule certainly decreased the pressure exerted on individual members of the church hierarchy. In 1913, when a petition was presented to the Archbishop of Canterbury asking him to allow exceptions to the rule of fermented wine for Holy Communion, the Archbishop replied that he was bound by the 1888 decision and could authorise no exemptions.[187]

In the nineteenth century, other churches in Great Britain were just as unyielding on the question of substituting unfermented wine in the sacraments; when the matter was raised at a meeting of the Irish Presbyterian Church and at an Irish Wesleyan Methodist Conference, it was soundly defeated – 301 votes to 20 by the former and 85 to 11 by the latter.[188]

The English Wesleyans had faced this sacramental wine issue much earlier than the Established Church. At their conference in Manchester in 1841, Dr Bunting spoke scornfully of that 'teetotal business' and 'the annoyances arising from it', asserting that 'it is a terrible thing to start a new controversy, instead of following after peace as we ought to do in these times.' The conference voted not to allow unfermented wines in the administration of the sacrament throughout the Connexion.[189] Dr Bunting was not alone in worrying about the consequences of controversy over the use of wine in church ceremonies. In 1848 an Independent minister, the Rev. A. Pickles, told a Leeds Temperance delegation that he had refrained from joining the temperance movement at his previous post because such a move would have split his church over the wine issue.[190] But for many teetotallers the problem of drinking intoxicating wine at Communion was not a major one; the amount drunk was unlikely to create any thirst for alcoholic beverages and the power of the gospel would protect them from any evil consequences.

# 4   Legal Suasion

By the end of the 1840s the temperance movement was in a state of decline. The reformers of this period were discovering the limitations of their traditional methods of moral suasion: persuading individuals that it was morally wrong to drink was proving to be a dishearteningly slow method of fighting the national curse of intemperance. Teetotalism was not sweeping the country as its original proponents had anticipated, and so, with the hope for quick reform destroyed, many supporters lost their enthusiasm for the cause and turned to other interests. Only a few of the most dedicated reformers stayed with the movement, keeping the old societies and their work alive, waiting until a new concern with the drink problem would appear and revive the whole movement. Throughout the nineteenth century the temperance reformation was to suffer from support that ebbed and flowed.[1] Around a hard core of devoted teetotallers there were large numbers of sympathisers who followed the prevailing taste in reform and were active in temperance only when it was fashionable. In many areas where the cause was only weakly established, in times of inactivity the local societies would 'fall asleep' or disappear altogether. The mortality rate for temperance societies was high.

In some cases, debts and bad management combined with the general torpor to cause temperance societies to become moribund. In 1851 the National Temperance Society was in such a desperate state due to financial troubles and poor management that it had to be reorganised.[2] The British Temperance Association, the northern teetotal organisation, while escaping such a complete overhaul, was hard put to solve its financial problems.[3] With many local societies the situation was similar. In 1854, the Bradford Temperance Society was not doing well and so had to be reorganised in the hope of becoming financially more stable. Six years later, in 1860, there was an unsuccessful attempt to dissolve this founding society.[4] The Halifax and Huddersfield temperance societies had similar troubles, which they too managed to survive. Other groups were not so fortunate and disappeared completely, some to be refounded at a later date but most to be lost and forgotten. The anti-drink movement in the 1850s and 1860s was at a critical point; it would fade away altogether or it would discover new methods and issues that would bring it back into the lives of the people. Dissatisfied with their moral suasion position, some of the more dedicated reformers looked around for new ways to eliminate intemperance. Again it was America that offered what seemed to be a solution.

On 2 June 1851, the legislature of the State of Maine passed the first prohibition law in the western world. This law forbade all traffic in liquor, both wholesale and retail, within the boundaries of the state. News of this great victory for the anti-drink forces of America swiftly crossed the Atlantic, causing great excitement among temperance reformers throughout the British Isles: this would be the new way, the more efficient way, of bringing about the temperance reformation. Drink would be eliminated from the land by law. Where there was no drink there could be no drunkards. If England would not become sober by persuasion then it would become so by force. The legal prohibitionists, making the drink manufacturers and sellers the villains of the problem of intemperance, sought legal measures to curtail the distribution of all alcoholic beverages.

To organise and coordinate the work of the prohibitionists the United Kingdom Alliance was formed in 1853 in Manchester, the home of many other middle-class reform organisations. The Alliance, as it was commonly called, was set up to agitate both inside and outside Parliament for the legal suppression of the liquor trade. It claimed to be a political party, not a temperance organisation.[5]

## MORAL SUASION VERSUS PROHIBITION

The appearance of the United Kingdom Alliance was met with some suspicion by the older groups, who feared further fragmentation of the temperance movement. Many temperance societies had not fully recovered from the moderation–teetotal battle and so were not ready to accept yet another anti-drink philosophy that was a potential source of further discord for their movement. Furthermore, there was at this time a desire to reduce the number of anti-drink organisations; unions to bring unconnected societies together were being promoted, on both the national and the local level. Thus, for some of these 'unionists' at least, the establishment of the United Kingdom Alliance was seen as a retrogressive move.

But, aside from the organisational problems, the appearance of a prohibition party presented other difficulties for the moral suasion teetotallers. To them, prohibition meant a fundamental change in method as well as in policy. It meant a change of focus from the drinker to the seller of intoxicating beverages. Self-control, the basis on which the teetotal movement was built, was of little importance to the prohibitionist. To drink or not was for him a decision to be made by law, not by the individual. Likewise, the rescuing of the drunkard from his own intemperance was of no great concern to the legal suppressionists, many of whom were not themselves teetotallers – a fact that disturbed many members of the moral suasion groups. One law, according to the prohibitionists, would sweep drunkenness from the country. Like the Preston teetotallers, their predecessors in the anti-drink movement, the prohibitionists thought they had found the one quick, simple solution to the age-old problem of intemperance.

The United Kingdom Alliance was a highly-centralised political party with all policy radiating from its headquarters in Manchester. Local temperance societies had very little influence on its programmes, and were never directly consulted on any issue. The local Alliance agents, who had contacts with the temperance movement in the areas to which they were assigned, served as channels of communication, but the agents themselves had little influence on the policy of the central organisation. Formally, the separation between the prohibitionists and the local temperance societies remained, sometimes fostered by the moral suasionists, who did not want to be too closely linked with the prohibition party.[6] There are no statistics to show how many teetotallers joined the Alliance or any other prohibitionist group. Many local societies were split on the issue, and a number of moral suasion organisations were openly hostile to the Alliance and what it represented. In a letter to his local newspaper, one teetotaller expressed the views of many suasionists when he pointed out that, if the temperance societies openly allied themselves with the prohibition movement, their public image would suffer. The public would believe that the teetotallers, amounting to no more than one-tenth of the population, wanted to force the other nine-tenths to give up all alcoholic beverages; 'hence they will regard the movement, and regard it justly, as an attempt to infringe upon individual freedom.'[7]

Many teetotallers were also unhappy with the Alliance because it refused to ask its supporters to sign the pledge. Nor did it restrict its membership to those who believed drinking to be wrong. On the contrary, the long-time president of the Alliance, Sir Wilfrid Lawson, was known to have a fine wine cellar;[8] although he himself was a teetotaller, his guests were offered the best. This situation was frequently alluded to by opponents of the movement, who were always anxious to show up any apparent inconsistencies in the positions of temperance supporters. In order to reduce bickering over the personal habits of Alliance members, many temperance societies decided that the Alliance was not a part of the temperance movement and therefore not subject to the movement's standards. This compromise allowed the moral suasion groups to cooperate with the prohibition party whenever it was in their interests to do so without making them feel they were supporting an heretical version of their own cause. The Leeds Temperance Society, for instance, took this position when the Alliance set up a branch in their town, asserting that:

> Amongst teetotalers there is a difference of opinion respecting this movement but the fact that personal abstinence is not a condition of membership is sufficient to show that there is an important difference betwixt the Constitution of the Alliance and that of the Temperance Societies.[9]

The Leeds Society then went on to stress that, unlike the Alliance, they were concerned with the abolition of drinking by moral suasion methods.[10]

Both major national moral suasion groups, the British Temperance Association and the National Temperance Society, ran into problems concerning their relationship with the prohibition movement. In 1859, the Scottish Temperance League, a well-known anti-prohibitionist moral suasion organisation with headquarters in Glasgow, asked the British Temperance Association to send delegates to their conference, a common practice for temperance groups at that time. After the British Temperance Association had agreed to the Scottish request, the pro-Alliance members of the Association's executive board managed to exert enough pressure to have the decision reversed. Such an outcry resulted that a new meeting of the executive board was called which authorised the sending of a delegation to the Scottish conference. Many British Temperance Association members expressed disatisfaction at the influence the Alliance had managed to exert on their leadership.[11]

The London-based National Temperance Society also had to resolve difficulties arising from the appearance of the organised prohibition movement. In 1861, a group calling itself the United Temperance Council invited the National Temperance Society to amalgamate with the United Kingdom Alliance. The society refused and issued the following statement in their report:

> The position of your Committee in this respect is a very simple and obvious one. While they maintain the widest toleration for every variety of view upon the questions of legislation they feel that there is equal consideration due to those who, as a matter of principle and policy, do not sympathise with the agitation for total and immediate prohibition of the liquor traffic, and they therefore regard it as of vital consequence to the interests of the Temperance cause to maintain inviolate this liberty of opinion.[12]

This rejection of the amalgamation proposal led to much bad feeling between the two groups. National Temperance Society officials believed the Alliance was actively antagonistic to them.[13] Their president, Sir Walter Trevelyan, who was also president of the Alliance, resigned from the moral suasion society in 1861 and gave all his attention to the Alliance.[14] For many years after this, relations between the two organisations remained very cool.

On the local scene, too, there were disputes over the role of prohibition in the established temperance societies. In Huddersfield the temperance movement was severely rent by battles over prohibition. When the Alliance was founded, in 1853, the Huddersfield Temperance Society decided to stay completely apart from the prohibition movement, giving it no official support. Its members felt that its constitution did not allow it to embrace legal suppression.[15] Individual members were left free to support prohibition if they wished. Unfortunately for the society, this official neutrality displeased some of the more active members. A cleavage appeared in the membership, separating moral suasionists from those who wanted to combine the traditional activities with work for prohibition. By 1864 this split became so deep that the prohibitionists broke away and formed their own Huddersfield Temperance and Prohibition Society. But even at the inaugural meeting of this new group, attended by agents of the Alliance, anti-prohibition sentiment intruded: W. R. Croft 'caused some commotion by ascending the platform and objecting to the principle of teetotalism by force'.[16] There was little friendship between the two Huddersfield temperance groups. The original society, in fact, so wanted to impress on everyone the absolute separateness of the two that, in its annual report of 1865, it warned that, 'Notwithstanding that the two societies are totally distinct, and work independently of each other, it is felt that unless this fact be clearly impressed upon the public mind, the actions of one may occasionally be attributed to the other.'[17]

A similar fate befell the temperance movement in Leeds. After an attempt by the Leeds Temperance Society to treat prohibition as a different category of reform from moral suasion and thereby exclude it from the official work of the society, the legal suppressionists managed to get a resolution passed supporting prohibition. Unhappy with this development, the supporters of an exclusively moral suasion policy claimed that prohibition was not 'a legitimate object of the society'. In 1860 they formed a new group, called the Leeds Temperance Union, for moral suasion only.[18] George Tatham, a well-known teetotaller and former officer of the Leeds Temperance Society, who was later to be mayor of Leeds, was appointed president of the new union.[19] Edward Baines, another important Leeds teetotaller, political leader and owner of the radical *Leeds Mercury*, also left the original society to join the new one. Fourteen years later, in 1874, the prohibitionists ran a candidate to oppose Baines for a seat in Parliament. Baines claimed that the introduction of this candidate split the vote and brought about his defeat.[20]

The situation in neighbouring Bradford was rather different. Relations between the Bradford society and the Alliance supporters were quite congenial, so much so that in 1863 the Alliance agent suggested an amalgamation of the prohibitionists with the moral suasion society. The Bradford society, always conscious of its historical position in the movement, rejected the proposed change,[21] but this refusal neither split the society nor had any serious repercussions on the Bradford movement.

Amicable relations between the two groups continued. This close association was due in part to the fact that the Alliance agent in Bradford was a former agent of the Bradford moral suasion society, and also to the strength of local temperance sentiment, which allowed the successful functioning of many different types of organisations. Money was donated to a variety of anti-drink groups without arousing competition among them.

If the response of local organisations to prohibition was diverse, that of individual members was equally variegated. Teetotal friends found themselves at odds with one another over the subject of legal suppression. Unfortunately for the temperance movement, a polarisation of the issue occurred over the dispute between the American orator James B. Gough and the Alliance lecturer Frederic Lees. The actual details of the case were unclear, muddled by friends and foes alike, but eventually, under the careful scrutiny of the courts, the main outlines of the dispute emerged. Gough, it appears, was completely committed to the moral suasion camp and in one publication told the English temperance supporters that the Maine law was a 'universal failure'.[22] Dr Frederic Lees, a well-known north country prohibitionist and the most contentious of reformers (he was constantly involved in law suits and non-legal disputes),[23] was angered by Gough's words. In a letter to a teetotal friend he accused the American of being intoxicated at various times. Lees, it was revealed, also resented Gough because the latter had criticised the Alliance for not being a teetotal organisation.[24] The recipient of Lees' letter made its content public and Gough brought suit for libel, for he knew his career would be finished if the temperance movement believed him to be a drinker. He won the action but the damages awarded were very small: only five guineas. This quarrel, in which Lees and the prohibitionists were ranged on one side with Gough and the moral suasionists on the other, was detrimental to the temperance movement both because it emphasised the divisions in it and because it made for bad publicity in the non-temperance press.[25]

Joseph Livesey, the grand old man of teetotalism, did not identify himself with either side but it was well known that he very much favoured moral suasion as a method of affecting the temperance reformation. While much energy was being diverted to the prohibition campaigns, he was promoting the moral suasion position through his writings and lectures. He advocated a wholehearted return to what he believed was the only method by which a real reformation of drinking habits could be achieved. An old-style reformer, he felt the people would make the right decisions if they were educated to understand the facts clearly. He believed it was far better for them to want to give up drinking than to be forced to stop.[26]

Other teetotallers doubted the efficacy of the policies of the Alliance. If prohibition were implemented and people forced to abstain, would that bring about the temperance reformation? This was a question often asked. Even the British Temperance Association, which had a long history of support for legal suppression, having promoted it long before the Alliance was founded,[27] felt prohibition would provide only a partial solution to the problem of intemperance.[28]

# THE UNITED KINGDOM ALLIANCE[29]

In spite of the hostility of a number of anti-prohibition teetotallers, and the antagonism of non-temperance anti-prohibitionists, the United Kingdom Alliance quickly established itself as the spokesman for the legal suppressionists. After only four years of existence, however, the prohibition party came to realise that the appeal of a law modelled on that of Maine was limited. Its support and influence were confined to a small group of enthusiastic temperance extremists, or so it seemed to most nineteenth-century Englishmen.

The policy of coercion, as proposed in all prohibition bills, was responsible for much of the opposition directed against the legal suppressionists. Bills that would lead to any abridgement of personal freedom were at variance with the popular sentiment of this period. As exemplified by the writings of John Stuart Mill and others, mid-nineteenth-century public philosophy was dominated by demands for the extension of personal freedom: fewer restrictive laws were wanted, not more. Expressing the ideas of many of his contemporaries, Mill called the doctrines of the Alliance 'monstrous', and described them as an 'illegitimate interference with the rightful liberty of the individual'.[30] 'Drunkenness', Mill maintained, 'is not a fit subject for legislative interference.' To drink beer or not was a matter of personal decision; this proposed legal restriction was widely resented as

interference in the individual's domestic affairs.[31] Some critics of
Alliance policy believed that support for prohibition was a matter
of social class. Both the upper classes and the working classes felt
that the middle classes were forcing their beliefs on the rest of the
country, and they objected to this.[32]

Prohibition bills were also viewed with suspicion because they
had very little support among non-voters, who made up the
majority of the English population. A law that would affect such a
large part of the unenfranchised public would have to be passed
with the utmost caution. Many voters were still mindful of the
lesson they had learned in 1855 when rioting broke out over the
passing of the unpopular Sunday trading restrictions. Not even
the most ardent prohibitionists could pretend that prohibition
had more than minority support throughout the land. Even
twenty years later, in the mid-1870s, after many energetic
campaigns to instruct the public on the virtues of prohibition,
there was little change in the country's attitude. In 1876, in a
speech before the Manchester Statistical Society, W. Stanley
Jevons, a noted opponent of the Alliance, criticised prohibition.
Like many others he believed the passing of the Permissive Bill, as
the limited prohibition bill sponsored by the Alliance was called,
would only create disorder; and that the bill would have the same
fate as Colonel Wilson Patten's Sunday Closing Act – quick
revocation.[33] Jevons showed how a quarter of the electors could
get the bill passed so that it would be a minority law.[34] He also
claimed that the work of the Alliance had led to polarisation on the
drink issue: one was either for it or against it; there was no longer
any middle ground.[35] Another critic of the Alliance complained
that the prohibitionists had managed to make themselves appear
the champions of virtue, making their enemies play the role of the
devil.[36]

The English prohibition movement was hurt by the publicity,
given the shortcomings of the original Maine law. Repealed in
1856 and reinstated in 1858, the Maine law was proving to be a
difficult measure to implement even in its birthplace. Other
criticisms of prohibition in America, even when it was operative,
were also widely publicised. Much of the information about the
American experiment was brought back to England by interested
parties and so was hardly impartial.

In 1857, surveying its position and noting its lack of progress,
the Alliance, for the first and only time in the century, allowed

itself to compromise and give support to a more realisable objective. Recognising that a Maine-type law had no chance of being accepted by the public in the near future, the Alliance adopted Local Option – or local prohibition – as its goal. Full prohibition remained the ultimate goal, but this meant more in theory than in fact.[37] To realise Local Option the Alliance submitted to Parliament a Permissive Bill which would authorise each individual district to decide whether or not liquor licences were to be issued there. Only the ratepayers, however, were to be allowed to vote, and a two-thirds majority, a minority of the adult inhabitants in any area, were to make the decision. By their vote they would determine whether in the next three years any licences were to be issued.[38]

Alliance members expected to encounter a great deal of opposition, but they were sure that they would eventually win through. They favoured an extension of the franchise, because most of the groups currently agitating for the vote were concentrated in the northern industrial towns, where the Alliance received most of its support. Their main role until the franchise was extended, however, was to keep publicising their cause and forcing people to think about the problem of drink control. Every year, as regularly as clockwork, Sir Wilfrid Lawson, who later became president of the Alliance (1879–91), introduced a Permissive Bill in the House of Commons, and just as regularly the Bill was rejected. In its first year, 1863, the Permissive Bill received the support of only 35 members while 292 voted against it.[39] Five years later it was again defeated, 341 to 81. Clearly it was not making much progress among the lawmakers of England. It was introduced ten times in all and never showed any chance of passing. Such temperance sympathisers as the Quaker John Bright would not vote for the Bill;[40] he went so far as to ask the Society of Friends 'to leave Parliament alone on liquor problems'.[41] Edward Baines, who, according to moral suasion sources,[42] was the only teetotaller in Parliament in 1860, never supported the Permissive Bill and was a strong opponent of the Alliance. Samuel Morley was another well-known temperance MP who would not vote for the Permissive Bill in the first years of its appearance. In 1869, however, Morley changed his position and voted for it.[43] Another English politican of note who changed his mind on the subject of Local Option was William Harcourt. In the 1870s he condemned prohibition, arguing that eliminating all alcohol to prevent drunkenness was the equivalent of locking everyone in jail to prevent crime. At this period he believed moral suasion to be the only answer to intemperance.[44] But, by the last decade of the century, when he was a member of the government, he had reversed his position: on 27 February 1893, in his capacity as Chancellor of the Exchequer, he introduced a bill supporting Local Option in the House of Commons.

The United Kingdom Alliance kept its basic organisation very simple. Its work outside London and Manchester was carried on by a number of full-time professional agents, who were permanently located in districts all over England. This permanent residency of agents was of great importance to the regular temperance movement of the provinces. Frequently the Alliance agent, as the only active temperance worker in a district, was able to draw together the various anti-drink factions in the area. With his financial support guaranteed by a national organisation, he was independent of the pressures of local individuals and groups and could ignore them in a way a locally employed worker could not do.

With little supervision from the head office in Manchester, Alliance agents had the widest latitude in carrying out their loosely defined duties. Men were chosen to be agents who could be depended on to carry out their duties according to the demands of the local situation. In fact the actual role of the individual agent in the local temperance movement depended very much on the personality of the man and the conditions in his area.

Because the Alliance agent was a bridge between the political and temperance forces of the town he had to be acceptable to both in order to be effective. The agents set up Alliance auxiliaries in their areas but these did not function as did the other temperance societies. They were active only when the Alliance was conducting a campaign requiring public agitation:[45] in other periods these auxiliaries usually remained dormant. They were rarely in a position to challenge the work of the agent because they were his creation and his tool, with no independent existence.

Alliance agents were often teetotallers who had previously worked in other anti-drink organisations. Henry Hibbert, for example, the well-known Bradford Alliance agent, started as a West Riding Band of Hope agent, became the employee of the Bradford Temperance Society in 1867, and five years later resigned this position to become the Bradford agent of the

Alliance, a position he held until his death.[46] In 1872 Hibbert became a vice-president of the Bradford Temperance Society. He was thus familiar with all sections of the anti-drink movement in Bradford and district.

For the majority of teetotallers, commitment to moral suasion did not preclude support for prohibition. We have noted the antagonism that sprang up between some supporters of moral suasion and those of the new prohibition philosophy, but it would be wrong to conclude that this was typical of the relationship between the two groups, especially in the later decades of the century. Once the initial hostility towards the prohibitionists had died down, there was little enmity between the two groups. On the contrary, in most towns the various anti-drink organisations worked in harmony on many different programmes. In fact the relationship became so close that by 1872 the public had come to regard the prohibition party as the spokesman for the whole temperance movement, and very few of the moral suasionists objected. Only rarely were complaints made against the growing power of the Alliance.[47]

Therefore, when Stanley Jevons told the Manchester Statistical Society that the Alliance had set back the cause of temperance because 'it absorbs and expends the resources of the temperance army on a hopeless siege',[48] he was giving a very superficial analysis of its work. Through its political activities the Alliance was often responsible for introducing influential individuals, who had previously given no thought to the liquor problem, to the anti-drink movement. Cardinal Manning, for example, first became acquainted with the temperance cause through his work with the Alliance.[49] Furthermore, the great public campaigns organised by the Alliance were responsible for introducing the issue of temperance into many localities and residences where previously it had been non-existent. Towns that could get no financial support for temperance work welcomed the well-financed activities of the prohibitionists. To the Alliance must be given much of the credit for the revival of the temperance cause in the 1870s. Legal suppression in one form or another was to be an essential goal of the temperance movement in the last three decades of the century. Even the Church of England Temperance Society, that large and very moderate reforming organisation, had its own legislative policy. If the Alliance had not been so active in stirring up anti-drink sentiment in the 1860s and early 1870s, the later temperance crusade would not have had such an impact on English society.

## THE SUNDAY CLOSING MOVEMENT

The Sunday Closing Movement was another very important component of the anti-drink agitation of the 1860s and 1870s. It brought church leaders and teetotallers together for the first time since the decline of moderation temperance. From this movement came many reformers who reintroduced the church to the temperance movement. In this capacity the Sunday Closing Movement can be said to have played an important role in the growth of temperance in the 1870s and the subsequent developments.

Although the Sunday Closing Movement was not strictly a temperance organisation, it was the teetotallers who gave it direction and vigour. They hoped that the support of the religious groups could be broadened from a simple fight against Sunday drinking to the wider problem of restricting all drinking; for them, Sunday closing was merely a step in the right direction. But not all anti-drink adherents were supporters of the Sunday Closing Movement. Some of the more extreme Alliance supporters refused to be associated with it on the grounds that their support would compromise their strict prohibition position.[50] For the same reason, many Alliance members refused to support any sort of licensing reform.

The fears of the prohibitionists regarding the objectives of the Sunday Closing Movement had some validity. The name 'Sunday Closing Movement' was a general one, including anyone who advocated some restriction of the Sunday hours of licensed premises and thus covering a wide range of views. For some Sunday Closing advocates nothing less than the complete closing of licensed establishments on Sunday was acceptable, while others wanted only a reduction in Sunday hours. No doubt some of the dissent over goals can be ascribed to differences in motivation. Much of the movement's religious support was induced by Sabbatarianism. While the temperance suporters felt they were attacking the drink evil if they closed the licensed houses on Sundays, the Sabbatarians were not concerned with drink at all but with what they believed to be unlawful activity on the Lord's Day. The Church of England, for example, though it supported the Sunday Closing Movement, also supported the opening of public houses for a short time twice every Sunday so that the working man could get ale for his dinner and his supper.[51] The differences between the temperance and the religiously motivated groups were the cause of the severe disruption of a meeting held to discuss Sunday Closing in 1867. The Rev. Dr Garnett spoke in favour of the sale of alcohol for two and one half hours on Sunday to take care of the dietary needs of the people. Unfortunately for Dr Garnett, the vocal opponents present caused so much unpleasantness that he felt constrained to walk out of the meeting.[52]

Although there were complaints later on about the indifference to Sunday Closing of temperance men,[53] they were the early workers in the movement. It was the Bolton-based teetotal organisation, the British Temperance Association, that claimed to be the first English group to support in an organised way restrictions on Sunday drinking.[54] At its annual conference in 1844, this association resolved to take up the issue of Sunday Closing and agitate for its adoption.[55] Two years later the association helped draw up petitions supporting Sunday Closing by parliamentary measures,[56] and it also sponsored an essay competition on 'Petition the Legislature to Prohibit the Sale of Intoxicating Liquors on a Sunday'.[57]

In 1853 the supporters of Sunday Closing succeeded in getting the Forbes Mackenzie Act passed, forbidding – with some rather limited exceptions – the Sunday sale of alcoholic beverages in Scotland. The passing of this act was hailed as a great victory by all supporters of Sunday Closing, though the temperance reformers acknowledged that its success was due more to the Sabbatarian spirit of the Scottish churches than to their temperance beliefs.[58] In the same year, the British Temperance Association cooperated with the National Temperance Society in persuading some Members of Parliament to sponsor a bill for Sunday Closing in England,[59] but this was only a secondary activity of the temperance reformers, and it was not until 1860s that the Sunday Closing Movement gathered enough strength to set up its own organisation.

It was in the Yorkshire town of Hull that the first Sunday Closing Association was established, on 31 August 1861.[60] Though two laymen filled the positions of chairman and secretary, a religious minister was appointed as its travelling agent. The sections of the public the new group hoped to influence preferred to work with men of religion, especially on matters related to their faith as was the issue of Sunday activities. All sympathisers with the cause of Sunday Closing were urged to form their own associations in their own towns and then to join in a union with the original Hull group.[61] Two years later, after a great deal of agitation (prompted by legislative attempts to curtail the Sunday opening hours of licensed premises),[62] the supporters of Sunday Closing measures acknowledged the necessity of forming an organisation to initiate and coordinate activities on a national scale. A conference was held at Derby in December 1863 to set up a national Sunday Closing Association. The original Hull association was to serve as the central committee, with branches to be formed whenever and wherever possible. A total of £1000 was raised at this conference to help pay for the work of the infant organisation.[63]

Sunday Closing in England was the subject of a conference held in 1866 in Manchester, at which another national organisation was created, with its headquarters in Manchester.[64] Called the Central Association for Stopping the Sale of Intoxicating Liquors on a Sunday, CASSILS for short, it was also a joint venture of religious and temperance reformers. Again religious ministers were appointed as agents,[65] but in this case the British Temperance Association gave the new organisation the full-time services of an agent who had the experience and the skills required by this new political pressure group.[66] Like the Hull-centred group, CASSILS proposed to set up auxiliaries throughout the country to carry out the work of the movement; the travelling agents were to be responsible for starting these local groups.

By 1867 the Manchester-based organisation had a Member of Parliament as its president and the Archbishops of Canterbury and of York as vice-presidents.[67] The latter positions were, no doubt, purely nominal for the prelates themselves, but important for the movement in attracting the active support of other churchmen. The association's income in 1867 was £1225, a very respectable sum for such a group.[68] Much of this financial support came from the same sources as that of the temperance movement, although some sponsors with religious motives would give only to the Sunday Closing Movement.[69] By 1868 the Manchester group absorbed the Hull group, keeping its headquarters in Manchester but changing its name to the Central Sunday Closing Association.

The attitudes of the churchmen on the issue of Sunday Closing were diverse. This was especially true of the members of the Church of England. In 1865 the Chaplain to the Bishop of London wrote to the British Temperance Association, in reply to a query from them, saying that he would not support Sunday Closing in his district.[70] The British Temperance Association also wrote to all the leaders of the non-conformist churches and to individual ministers to solicit their support for Sunday Closing. Some of the replies received, according to officers of the association, were 'queer specimens of non-compliance'.[71]

All auxiliaries of the Central Association were encouraged to canvass householders in their districts to determine the prevailing sentiments on the subject of Sunday Closing. In a printed letter sent out from its Manchester headquarters, the Central Association suggested that congregations of churches and chapels be asked to support the work of the movement and that ministers and clergymen be invited to sign memorials supporting Sunday Closing. In order to increase the pressure on Members of Parliament, the Central Association wanted its branches to encourage local men of substance to write their MPs to ask them to support any Sunday Closing measure brought up in the House of Commons.[72] During a campaign in 1874 a Sunday Closing auxiliary sent letters to all clergymen in its area asking them if they had any influence with bishops or other members of the House of Lords, to solicit help in opposing any extension in licensing hours, as was currently being proposed in the Licensing Amendment Bill.[73]

Some Sunday Closing auxiliaries were very active, especially those in areas where the temperance movement was firmly established. Bishop Ryan, the vicar of Bradford, was president of the local Sunday Closing Association, and its two vice-presidents were the Reverend Canon Melton and Angus Holden, the latter a prominent temperance reformer and officer of the Independent Order of the Good Templars.[74] The treasurer and secretary of the Bradford Sunday Closing Association were Joshua Pollard and W. S. Nichols respectively, both well known in the Bradford temperance movement.[75] In 1875, under pressure from this well-connected organisation, the mayor of Bradford had to call a public meeting to discuss the Licensing Amendment Bill which was being considered by Parliament at that time. The Bradford association also sent a memorial to all the religious leaders in th⸍

community, asking for their support for Sunday Closing: there were ninety requests and eighty-five clergymen signed; only the Unitarian minister and four out of the ten Independent ministers refused.[76]

The auxiliaries of the Sunday Closing Association frequently worked with other local anti-drink groups, sometimes on issues only obliquely connected with Sunday Closing. In Bradford, for example, the officers of the local association called a meeting of representatives of all temperance societies in the district to discuss setting up a committee 'to secure due respect for licence regulations and by other means to diminish the evils caused by the liquor traffic'.[77] When this committee was established, two officers of the Sunday Closing Association became officials of the new group and immediately started a campaign to investigate the conditions of all licensed premises in the town.[78]

Although such temperance activities stimulated opposition, some of the antipathy to the movement was rooted in anti-religious sentiments. The Sabbatarianism of the Sunday Closing Bills made them anathema particularly to the secularists, who were active in challenging and disrupting meetings organised by the association. At one such meeting held in Huddersfield on 23 February 1871 a request by a female secularist for an opportunity to speak was denied on the grounds that she was not a resident of the town; the resulting dispute reduced the meeting to 'a state of utter confusion'.[79]

Although, even after all its local activity, the movement was unable to get a bill passed closing the public houses on Sunday, it did draw into the anti-drink movement many people who otherwise would not have had any connection with the teetotallers. Many religious men, in particular, who had previously shared the common opinion that teetotallers were cranks and fanatics, came to see that the problem of drinking, on Sunday or any other day, was not solved by being ignored. Sermons were given in churches and chapels deploring drinking on Sunday, and whole congregations were asked to be active in the fight against imbibing on the Sabbath. The fact that the hierarchy of the established church was willing to be associated with the Sunday Closing Movement made it 'acceptable' to the many segments of the population who were concerned with respectability and proper behaviour.

# Part Two
# The Great Crusade

# Introduction

The mood of English society underwent a number of observable changes in the second half of the nineteenth century. After the hungry 1840s, which spawned despair and talk of bloody revolution, there came a period of peace and prosperity when for over twenty years an increasing number of Englishmen were busy establishing themselves and their families in a settled life-style and becoming part of their communities. Unfortunately this condition changed suddenly in the early 1870s, when a great depression brought doubt and uncertainty back into the lives of industrial workers.

Throughout the nineteenth century there had been a series of trade depressions. No one understood what caused the downward trend of trade or its revival, and, so long as the cycles were relatively mild and affected only a small segment of the population, there was little national interest in them. By the 1870s, however, the cycles had become more severe in their effect. Larger numbers of people found themselves controlled economically by forces they did not understand. After two decades of increasing prosperity and optimistic belief in an even better future, many families suddenly found themselves living in fear of losing everything and becoming paupers. This fear spread not only among the families actually affected by the trade system but also to those who thought they might become involved. Consequently, there was great uneasiness among the population, leading to a re-examination of the economic system and an attempt to understand its defects. A new concern for the poor appeared which pervaded all strata of English society and which was manifested in the number of missions to the poor that were organised, as well as in the interminable discussions in the newspapers on how to remedy some of the worst evils suffered by the poorer classes and bring them into 'respectable' society.

Even prior to this depression, however, there were some individuals who were aware that all was not well with the country. Henry Mayhew was one of these; in the 1850s he published a book called *London Labour and the London Poor*, which brought to the attention of many prominent Englishmen the terrible conditions of a large part of the population.[1] It was clear that while the majority were prospering as never before, a large minority were not: Disraeli's two nations were appearing. The unsuccessful in the cities were usually ill-equipped, both mentally and physically, for a life that depended for personal success on the abilities of the individual. The price of failure was just as terrible as the fruits of success were great. There was an atmosphere of despair and hopelessness among the very poor, the 'sunken tenth' of Charles Booth's studies, with the result that suicides, accidents and all kinds of crimes were common.

Avoiding any deep analysis, many mid-Victorian reformers were content to blame drink for these unpleasant occurrences. 'Pauperism is caused by drunkenness which is caused by ignorance – that is why we have higher rates', complained one MP, a former judge.[2] Drink made a convenient scapegoat for all the troubles of society. It was easily identified and, superficially at least, could be held responsible for all depravity. William Booth of the Salvation Army wrote about 'Darkest England', equating the publican 'who lived off the weakness of our poor' with the ivory raiders who 'plundered the pygmies'.[3] He conservatively calculated that there were at least three million persons, the same 'submerged tenth', who were destitute and 'sodden with drink'.[4] Charles Booth found drink to be the culprit for much poverty, causing many families of few resources to fall into destitution.[5] Drink was also responsible for trade depressions, according to one speaker at a conference in 1879, who believed that 'the enormous expenditure of money on drink is a burden that lands upon our trade; it makes competition with other countries all the more difficult.'[6]

But drunkenness was not to be found just among the impoverished. All the working classes were drinking large amounts of alcoholic beverages, with usage increasing as the prosperity of the workers rose. Even the periodic trade depressions did no more than temporarily slow down the steady rise in the rate of consumption of alcohol which characterised the last half of the nineteenth century.[7] It was often claimed that the causes for this increased drinking were the poor living conditions of many workers and the lack of drink-free amusements that made the public house the only attractive place for recreation.[8] But while these may have been responsible for some of the motivation to drink, another factor was the change in the life-style of the new industrial workers. The factory system introduced strict hours of work and harsh codes of behaviour, all enforced by fines and threats of dismissal. The worker was forced to adhere to a regulated schedule. The psychological tension generated within the individual by a full week of such unaccustomed rigidity could generally be dispelled only by weekend drinking bouts, where oblivion was sought in the cup. Some men never came home after their Saturday shift. Instead they went straight to the licensed house with their weekly wage and there began to drink, stopping only when their money ran out or when closing time came around. Some drank right through to Sunday night, taking drink home when the public houses closed. This increase in drinking at the weekend showed clearly in the police returns. On Saturdays and Sundays there was a sharp upturn in arrests for drunkenness[9] as well as a great increase in infanticide; babies were 'overlaid' when their drunken, sleeping mothers rolled over and smothered them.[10]

With drink seemingly dominating the lives of the lower classes and being held responsible for all the evils in society,[11] the time was ripe for action. This came in the form of a great crusade against drink, which drew both individuals and institutions into the anti-drink ranks and united the efforts of religious and secular workers, of political and non-political groups. This crusade led to a great revival of old anti-drink organisations as well as to the birth of new ones.

\* \* \*

After more than twenty years of decline, the moral suasion temperance movement started to revive in the 1870s. For most of the intervening years, the United Kingdom Alliance had been the standard-bearer of the anti-drink cause, often the sole active agency fighting the drink trade. Now, with the return of interest in temperance, the old societies came to life again and began to look towards a more active future. For many of the older teetotallers this revival promised to lead the movement to greater heights than ever before because it was drawing into the fold groups that had long been indifferent to the message of the teetotallers. The British Temperance League saw this revival as a time of harvest. Following a long period of germination, the temperance seeds, sown by the early teetotal advocates, were finally reaching fruition.[12]

This change in the fortunes of the temperance movement can be traced in part to a new relationship between the religious forces of England and teetotalism. With increased concern for the spiritual and material well-being of the lower classes, evangelical religion combined with temperance to form Gospel Temperance. Like numerous other terms used by the Victorians, 'Gospel Temperance' had many different meanings. In its broadest usage it meant temperance infected to any degree with religion, and this came to mean practically any segment of the moral suasion temperance cause. Thus some Englishmen regarded the Salvation Army as part of the Gospel Temperance movement: it had a temperance base to its religious structure. Likewise, even the Church of England was sometimes said to be part of the Gospel Temperance movement. But at the other end of the scale, in its narrowest interpretation, the term Gospel Temperance referred to a specific movement, one that arose in the 1870s and swept through England with a special kind of revivalist fervour that mixed religion and temperance to form a distinctive creed. Its supporters felt that a soul could not be saved while the body was being continually corrupted by intemperance. Many families who were not themselves heavy users signed the pledge in the late nineteenth century because they believed all drinking of alcoholic beverages to be unchristian.

But, whether viewed broadly or narrowly, Gospel Temperance was strongly influenced by the developments that took place in the Church of England in the 1860s and early 1870s. Responding to the rising current of temperance sentiments, all the Christian churches in England set up their own temperance organisations and, although some of them were not fully committed to the principles of total abstinence, they all ceased their direct attacks on the temperance movement as a whole, reserving criticism for those parts of it which they found objectionable.

It would be false, however, to ascribe all the increase in temperance sentiments to events in the non-temperance world. The movement itself had worked had to disseminate temperance principles, particularly among children. Having learned from past experience, the movement realised that it must offer temperance alternatives for a full social life if it were to retain the loyalties of teetotal children after they outgrew juvenile temperance activities. Those who had joined during the innumerable, short-lived spurts of temperance popularity were kept within the fold through the establishment of adult teetotal social groups. Some, such as the Rechabites, were old, established organisations, while others, such as the Independent Order of the Good Templars, were new; but all experienced rapid growth in the last three decades of the nineteenth century. The movement established so many different social and cultural groups that it was possible for many members to lead a well-rounded life with only minimal contact with the drinking world. This meant an increasing divide between the drinking and the teetotal worlds; the local temperance hall took on a new significance as the focus of this new, non-drinking life. Societies that had previously been content to hold their activities in schoolrooms, church rooms or other quasi-public facilities, found such arrangements no longer adequate and so bought, or built, their own temperance hall. Thus the 1870s saw a great increase in the number of temperance halls in towns and villages up and down the country.

Another development of these years that increased the breadth and effectiveness of temperance reform was the obvious improvement in circumstances – economic, social and political – of many of the movement's most ardent supporters. The crude, uneducated working-class teetotallers of the early years had grown in substance and had found the respectability and position in life which they had sought. With the progressively widening franchise of the nineteenth century, many of these teetotallers had become not only voters in national and local elections, but also candidates, especially for local government positions. These teetotal advocates had learnt public speaking, organisational work and other skills invaluable to any aspiring politician through their work in the temperance movement. Because of the increased participation of teetotallers in public life, the public image of the temperance movement improved considerably.

As a consequence of this accelerated development of a temperance subculture in the late nineteenth century, a large segment of the population never tasted intoxicating drink. The dream of the early teetotallers seemed to be coming true: a race free from drink was developing. Furthermore, apart from those who were dedicated to the teetotal cause, there was also a large number of Englishmen who were regarding temperance activities with sympathy. Many former Band of Hope members who did not stay in the movement nevertheless approved of anti-drink activities enough to give them their support. The temperance work within the schools was also paying dividends in a greater understanding of the problems of excessive drinking by a larger number of Englishmen. Therefore, to many temperance reformers of the 1870s and 1880s, a teetotal England at last appeared to be a possible achievement in the near future.

# 5    To The Rescue

If there was one great impediment to the success of early teetotal ambitions it was the indifference, and even hostility, shown by religious bodies towards total abstinence. Even when large numbers of ministers and members supported the temperance cause, as was the case in the Methodist churches, the official hierarchy either was uninterested in the movement or feared it as divisive. But, as we have already shown, there were many individuals who were working for changes within their churches as they spread temperance principles among their congregations. It was to the tenacious loyalty of these men that the teetotal movement owed its revival.

The Church of England was the first of the major churches to respond to the calls of its temperance members. The other churches found it impossible to remain indifferent when the Established Church was taking the initiative and proselytising among the very class that some non-conformists had considered to be their own field of labour. Even the churches that were concerned primarily with their own middle-class members[1] could not escape the new mood, which cut across class lines and involved not only the poor but also the rich, the aristocracy and the merchants. One of the most interesting aspects of Gospel Temperance was the way it managed to draw in a great variety of people, establishing a temperance fellowship that included men, women and children from all walks of life. It was a movement about which *The Times* wrote, 'The weak are helped by the strong or by the sheer force of fellowship and numbers'.[2]

## THE CHURCH OF ENGLAND TEMPERANCE SOCIETY[3]

While the old secular teetotal societies were sleeping, and the national leadership of the anti-drink movement was in the hands of the prohibitionists, who were attempting to enforce sobriety through legal enactments, much of the old teetotal work continued, but now in independent missions. Many of these missions were run by individual clergymen who combined temperance with other social and religious activities for the welfare of their poorer parishioners. Bible classes, sick funds and training in thrift were often linked with total abstinence in programmes run by these missions. Clerics like Robert Maguire and Canon Ellison, and such associates as Mrs Wightman, were finding that intemperance was the cause of much misery and anti-Christian behaviour among the lower classes.[4] Mrs Wightman's book, *Haste to the Rescue*, described her experiences in running a parish temperance society. The National Temperance League, recognising the value of this book, had 10 000 copies of it printed and distributed free to clergymen throughout the country.[5] As the wife of a clergyman, the author, unlike many temperance advocates at this time, could hardly be accused of religious infidelity without embarrassment to the church; temperance reformers exploited fully her connection with the Established Church. The Rev. Henry J. Ellison, founder and leader of the Church of England Temperance Society, credits the book with a major role in the creation of the church temperance organisation.[6]

As is to be expected, the centres of Anglican temperance work were in the same areas in which secular temperance had flourished, particularly in Lancashire, the West Riding, Derbyshire and Staffordshire.[7] London also had a number of teetotal societies attached to parish churches. In fact the beginnings of the Church of England Temperance Society can be traced back to a meeting of clergymen in a London coffee-house in 1861. All these clergymen were active in parish temperance work and had felt a need for some kind of interchange with fellow clerical temperance workers. At this meeting they formed the Church of England Total Abstinence Society, an association based on mutual cooperation but having no power or authority over its members.[8] Finding total abstinence too restrictive in their work[9] and not too popular with the public, the group changed its name to the Church of England Reformation Temperance Society in 1863. This organisation quickly appointed a travelling secretary, who visited various parts of the country to generate interest in the problem of intemperance and helped in the formation of church-related temperance organisations whenever possible.[10] He also edited a journal called the *Church of England Temperance Chronicle*, which was established in 1862 to draw the movement together.[11]

In one of the early issues of this journal the secretary reported a lack of success on the part of the church temperance movement in the north of England as compared with the south, where branches were at least functioning, if somewhat sporadically.[12] Some of this lack of interest in the north can be traced to the fact that those who were concerned with the problem of intemperance were already connected with one of the many local temperance groups. The north, as we have seen, was the centre and the bastion of the temperance movement and did not lack anti-drink organisations. Prior to the establishment of the Church of England Temperance Society, many Church of England members had joined temperance societies that had led them into non-conformist circles,[13] a fact that caused some alarm among Church of England clergymen.[14] One of them, Canon Ellison, believed that many of the working men who were prominent in the dissenting churches were reclaimed drunkards and were 'dissenters only because dissenters showed them the way to recovery from their terrible sin'.[15]

But the problem of losing members to non-conformist groups because of the latter's temperance activities can be regarded as only a minor factor in the entrance of the established church into temperance activity. There was a growing concern within the church over the prevalence of intemperance. Archdeacon Sanford, an old and faithful friend of the temperance movement,[16] was also a close friend of the Archbishop of Canterbury and introduced some of the teetotal clergy and their ideas to the prelate. This eventually resulted in the setting up of a Committee on Intemperance by the Convocation of Canterbury in 1867.[17] At the end of its investigation and deliberations this committee issued a report on the problem of intemperance. The committee believed intemperance 'intimately and vitally affects the social condition and spiritual life of our people'[18] and that the greatest direct cause of drunkenness were beer houses, which the committee accused of being responsible for much 'prostitution and other lusts'.[19] Trade and social customs were also found to be important indirect causes of intemperance – too many fairs and 'mopps' were full of drink.[20] But, even though the Report of the Committee on Intemperance strongly condemned the existing situation and pointed out how demoralising it was to the workers, very little was done. The committee could only advise, not implement.

In 1872, another Committee on Intemperance was formed, this time by the Convocation of York. Again, the pressure for this investigation came from below, from the lower parish clergy who were dealing directly with the problem of drunkenness among their own parishioners.[21] The report of this committee, substantially no different to that of the Canterbury one, did manage to stir up enough interest to get the church's own temperance society revitalised and reorganised. First of all the society was renamed the Church of England Temperance Society and placed on a much wider foundation than previously, on a dual basis. A teetotal section and a general section were set up within the one organisation, each of equal importance. The general section was made up of those who were sympathetic to the temperance cause but not desirous of becoming teetotallers. The only condition imposed on membership for the non-abstainer was that he must want to work against intemperance and aid the reformation of the use of intoxicating drinks in society. But it was the total abstainers who provided much of the vigour, if not the numbers, of the society. They were the 'shock troops' of the movement and were sometimes resented by the less enthusiastic. Herman Ausubel, in his book *In Hard Times*, tells of an eminent aristocrat who, though favourably disposed towards temperance, refused to join the Church of England Temperance Society (henceforth abbreviated to CETS) because of the violent language used by some of its organisers and leaders.[22] An example of the strong language is Canon Wilberforce's retort on being told that temperance advocates should 'use the language of moderation, forebearance and charity'; he quoted William Lloyd Garrison: 'We must needs be red-hot for we have so many Christian icebergs around us to melt and we will be as harsh as truth and as uncompromising as justice.'[23] The temperance enthusiasts of the CETS did not differ from their secular counterparts in the strength of their convictions.

However, there was one very important feature of the ideology of the CETS that set it apart from the rest of the temperance movement – the ultimate aim of the society was moderate drinking for all; total abstinence was seen as only a temporary expedient necessitated by the extraordinary conditions in nineteenth-century England.

If by Total Abstinence for many generations to come we can eventually raise a people of restored control and with no undue craving for drink, it will be the time then for our successors to inculcate the higher doctrines of Moderation which at present do not fit the case.[24]

Moderation, then, was superior to total abstinence if, and only if, all could adhere to it.

The Church of England Temperance Society was a church-controlled organisation and its structure of authority was closely tied to that of the Church. No branch could be formed without the permission of the incumbent, who was, wherever possible, to be the president of the branch. He was also to be in complete control of it.[25] No action could be taken without going through regular church channels: vicars, bishops, archbishops could not be ignored in matters that might concern them. The authority of the hierarchy of the Established Church was guarded zealously, and any attempt to encroach on it would have caused bad feeling in the church.[26] Since some church circles suffered the society only because it could not be eliminated, it behoved the latter to conform to the church's procedures.

As with many secular temperance groups, the branches of the CETS were not very stable. There was a constant appearance and disappearance of groups. A change of incumbent would mean a change in temperance activity within a parish. An incoming clergyman who was indifferent or antagonistic to the temperance movement had the power to destroy an established branch of the CETS in his parish if he so desired. But even if the vicar was an enthusiastic temperance man, if only a minority of his parishioners shared his enthusiasm he could not carry on all the local activities by himself; if there was little local concern for temperance, the branch would die.[27]

Besides having the problems common to all anti-drink organisations, the CETS had some peculiar to itself, for instance the clashes between clerical and lay members of the society. Officially the CETS was a joint venture of the laity and the clergy but the latter tended to dominate the ruling committees, both in London and in the provinces. Although the usual relationship between the two groups was an harmonious one, there were times and places where there was serious friction between the two. In the diocese of Ripon, for example, such a conflict occurred over the appointment of the organising secretary of the diocesan temperance society. When first established, the Ripon CETS had a clerical secretary, but when he resigned his position it was given to a layman. Many members of the Ripon society were not happy with this change and wanted to recover a cleric as their secretary. After much disagreeable scheming, the pro-clerical party, composed of both clerics and laymen, managed to get the lay secretary dismissed and an ordained man installed in his place.[28]

The greatest difficulty the CETS faced was one common to all temperance groups: the constant shortage of money. Although many sources of financial support were exploited, there was never enough. Much of the CETS income came from subscriptions, from individual as well as group affiliation fees. Each branch, in theory, had to pay some quota to its immediate superior, but this obligation was often neglected.[29] Donations were also received, both on the local and national level, depending on the interests and sphere of activities of the donor.

There was no set method of organising or running a CETS branch, nor was there an established programme for the individual parts of the society. The freedom that every branch enjoyed was of great importance to the vitality of the society and was responsible for the great variety of activities sponsored by the more energetic branches. The fostering of local initiative was a deliberate policy. Some of the concerns of the CETS were directly connected with the alleviation of intemperance, but others were only distantly related, often aimed at filling a social need that had no other remedy. Thrift banks, sick and benefit societies, musical bands, funeral guilds, athletic clubs and mutual improvement societies were only some of the activities of this temperance society and it was through this diversified work that the Established Church did most to serve the many physical needs of its parishioners. In many areas the CETS was the only church agency in touch with the poorer classes. Contact was also made through the variety of missions sponsored by the society. Ranging from van missions, manned by lower-class workers that could visit isolated villages, to the middle-class women's missions, which worked with specific segments of the lower classes (for example, barmaids, laundry women and so on), they encouraged a personal involvement by the more privileged members of society in the problems of the less fortunate.[30]

But of all the activities of the Church of England Temperance Society, the one that was to have the most profound influence on English life was the Police Court Mission. Like many institutions of future significance, the Police Court Missions had a rather simple beginning. Tradition has it that in 1876 a Mr F. Rainer, a printer, went to court on business and noticed how little help was given to the prisoners. He wrote a letter to the CETS suggesting that they take up this work. Soon thereafter the first missionary was appointed in London, originally to work solely with the drunken cases in the cells. His job was to convince the prisoners to give up drink and to hand them over to the branch of the CETS in their own parish[31] when they were released.[32] But the role of such missionaries expanded as the great need for help was recognised. Magistrates came to depend on them for unofficial pretrial investigations of prisoners – a natural extension of their duties, considering the fact that the great majority of cases stemmed from drinking and drunkenness.[33] Some magistrates recognised the value of the Police Court Missions to such a degree that they actually contributed to their upkeep.[34] From these origins came the work that was to become the modern probationary service.

An offshoot of the Polict Court Mission were the Prison Gate Missions, which the CETS set up to look after newly released prisoners. Located, as the name indicates, close to the prison gates, they tried to contact the newly released prisoner as he was leaving gaol. By 1900 the CETS had Prison Gate Missions in twenty dioceses.[35]

The CETS was also responsible for organising the United Kingdom Railway Temperance Society in 1882. This was a successful venture which within five years had 7497 members in eighty branches connected with various railway lines up and down the country. The main activities of this society were the holding of temperance meetings and social teas and the publication of a journal called *The Railway Signal*. Railway workers were a particular concern of temperance people because the public greatly feared that drunken railway drivers would cause serious accidents.[36]

A Women's Union was formed as an auxiliary of the CETS. Some of its branches employed their own mission ladies who worked with women and children and were especially concerned with female intemperance. Women drunkards were believed by nineteenth-century temperance reformers to be very difficult to deal with: it was an accepted dictum that only in rare cases could female inebriates be cured.[37] That did not prevent the Women's Union from setting up and running homes for female drunkards, which were organised on a strict class basis with 'drawing room' patients who paid fees receiving the same care as was to be obtained in any similar private nursing home. Fully separated from the richer clientele were the kitchen and laundry patients, who paid what they could and worked in the home for the rest of their keep, or for all of it if they could not afford to pay anything.[38]

However, not all the work of the Church of England Temperance Society originated with the society. It did not hesitate to copy the successful methods of other temperance organisations: lifeboat crews,[39] temperance examination, temperance school lecturers[40] were all projects supported by the CETS that were the progeny of other temperance organisations. The Band of Hope, one of the most successful sections of the temperance movement,[41] served as the model for the temperance youth group set up by the Established Church. Unlike the adult societies, the CETS Band of Hope did not allow the dual basis; all the children who joined had to agree to abstain from intoxicating liquor. When the boys graduated from the Band of Hope they could join the Church Lads Brigade, which was set up by the CETS to work among those too old for the Band of Hope but too young for the adult societies. The Brigade was another very successful organisation established by the CETS.[42]

Having so many branches and sections with semi-independent status, the CETS was a fountain of creativity in the field we now call social welfare. At this time, the government was not thought to be the right agency to do such work: such activity came within the province of Christian charity. Therefore, the CETS went into the field of social work with enthusiasm and some amateur recklessness. Learning by trial and error, it played an increasingly effective role in the country's welfare work of the late nineteenth century. It was from such voluntary efforts that the later state-controlled services drew much of their knowledge and expertise. But, although the CETS was a very successful organisation in terms of the amount of welfare work it handled, there was some questioning of its methods. In particular, it was felt that the organisation suffered from a 'lack of cohesion between the branches of the Society'.[43] Too much of the work was locally determined, with the result that the areas in which there was the greatest need were often unable to get support. The location of a Police Court Mission, for example, was decided according to financing – every branch supported its own missions.

While the church gave invaluable aid to the anti-drink

movement through its temperance society, the work of the society was in turn of direct importance to the church. Ever since the religious census of 1851, the church had been aware, as was the rest of England, that it was becoming a minority church, especially in the northern towns, where the population was rapidly expanding.[44] Approximately five and a quarter million Englishmen and Welshmen attended the Church of England out of a total population of almost eighteen million.[45] The results of this census, when published, led to an increase in calls for disestablishment of the church. There were many non-conformists who, on discovering that they were more numerous than the established church, called for a reinterpretation of their position *vis-à-vis* the Church of England. All this, naturally, put the church on the defensive, as it sought to justify its favoured position. It was in such justification that the church discovered the value of the CETS, citing it as an example of the concern the church felt for all people and of the way it was translating this concern into action.[46] Here the broad programme of experimentation and freedom was invaluable in promoting a favourable image of the established church. If the CETS had kept strictly to anti-drinking activities it would not have gained the favour and support of such a wide range of people as its varied activities attracted. However, it was not just the CETS that was important in the social amelioration work of the church but also its many offshoots. The Church Army was a good example.[47] Although it eventually became independent, it maintained a close relationship with its parent body, and all members of the Church Army had to sign the teetotal pledge.[48] In 1885, when the Bishop of Peterborough was asked by a non-conformist how the church could justify its claim to be the national church, he said the CETS was the answer.[49]

By the end of the century, the CETS was the largest temperance society in the United Kingdom. In 1899 it had 7000 branches, 100 Police Court Missions and between 150 000 and 200 000 subscribing members.[50] Its size was not the only virtue by which it claimed to have an influence on English life. The CETS had the ear and voice of many well-established public figures, both in and out of Parliament, who would not have associated with other sections of the temperance movement. Church bishops would plead the temperance cause in the House of Lords, which provided excellent publicity for the movement. But in evaluating the influence of this temperance society we should not look only at the most obvious of its activities. The subtle and indirect effect the CETS had on various aspects of English life should be considered. For example, when the Society held a Jubilee Bazaar in London in 1887 it was able to get a large number of titled ladies to preside over the stalls.[51] Such support was of great value to any cause, but especially to one such as teetotalism, whose origins seemed questionable to polite society.

By the end of the nineteenth century, temperance was strongly established in the Church of England. The Very Rev. Frederick Temple, Archbishop of Canterbury and an ardent teetotaller,[52] was president of the secular National Temperance League, and special temperance sermons were preached in fifty London churches.[53] Indeed, the elevation of Frederick Temple to the See of Canterbury was seen by some temperance reformers as a victory for their cause.[54]

The CETS worked with other temperance agencies when such cooperation would not compromise its established position on any temperance question. It was not unusual for a branch of the CETS to join with other local anti-drink groups to send a solicitor to the Brewster Sessions to watch over the interests of the temperance movement.[55] But the degree of cooperation between the CETS and other groups would depend very much on the local incumbent and the climate of opinion prevailing in the area. In districts where cooperation among various organisations was a tradition, one could usually find it carried on by the CETS, but where the parish church was isolated by a clannish congregation, not much communication or cooperation could be expected by other sections of the community.

Despite its anti-drink work, the CETS was not accepted as part of the temperance movement by extreme teetotallers of non-conformist or secular societies.[56] From the beginning, the dual basis of the CETS appeared to the dedicated teetotaller to be an heretical position. By accepting him as an equal in the work of the reformation, it seemed to support the moderation drinker. Much of the difference between the non-conformist teetotallers and the CETS can be traced to basically different attitudes towards drink. For many non-conformists the problem of drink was a moral one, whereas the Church of England regarded intemperance as a social issue. As we have already seen, total abstention was adopted by some CETS members not because it was the better way, but because its adoption served as an example to those who were inclined towards drunkenness.[57] Furthermore, to the chagrin of many extreme teetotallers, the church officially insisted on retaining intoxicating wines for the celebration of Holy Communion.[58] This use, according to many non-conformist teetotallers, put CETS abstainers into an ambiguous position.[59]

Even the political programme of the CETS did not escape the criticism of many segments of the anti-drink movement. Although the CETS advocated Sunday Closing of public houses, which it wanted effected by Imperial law,[60] it simultaneously supported the Sunday opening of off-licensed shops for two hours so that people could get beer for dinner and supper.[61] Unlike the rest of the temperance movement, and much to its distress, the CETS refused to give its official support to local prohibition legislation. Nor would it support a scheme drawn up and strongly advocated by the Bishop of Chester for municipal control of drink shops.[62] In a sermon at St Paul's in 1900, the Bishop of Stepney talked of the two branches of temperance – moral suasion and prohibition. He said the temperance society of the established church should follow the middle road between these branches, balancing the desire for a change of environment with that for a change of character to achieve a sober Britain.[63] He likened the liquor traffic to 'the stone that had to be rolled away before the dead Lazarus could emerge from the grave'.[64]

## THE BLUE RIBBON ARMY

While there are varying accounts of the origin of the Gospel Temperance movement, there is general agreement among temperance writers that the American Women's Whisky War of 1873 gave the movement its greatest impetus.[65] The Whisky War began when a number of determined women in Hillsboro, Ohio, distressed over the amount of drunkenness in their town, decided to do what they could to stop it. They organised prayer meetings in the streets, immediately in front of the most notorious taverns, and managed to exert enough pressure to close some of them.[66] Their successes stimulated other groups to organise in a similar fashion, and to use the force of prayer as a weapon in the fight against drink.[67]

Prior to the efforts of the women of Ohio, there already existed in New England men's organisations that worked to reclaim drunkards, but most of these were small local groups, concerned with giving support to individuals in their locality. This reform movement, as it was known, was limited to New England and was made up of local communities of ex-drunkards and men trying to give up drink, whose members sported a red ribbon as their badge. In direct imitation a similar group called the Reform Club and Blue Ribbon Association was founded in Maine by a former drunkard and this organisation emphasised the importance of religion and prayer in reforming men. Its members sported a blue ribbon in their coat lapel. (The blue ribbon was taken from a passage in the Bible which commanded the children of Israel to wear a ribbon of blue (*Numbers* 15:37–8).) This association, like many similar ones, would have remained relatively unknown outside its own locality had not a national temperance advocate, Francis Murphy, recognised its potential on the national scene and taken it over.[68]

Francis Murphy, himself a former drunkard who had been converted to Protestantism and temperance by a prison visitor while incarcerated for crimes connected with his drinking, was fast acquiring a national reputation as an effective and emotional speaker on the subject of temperance. In 1874, at the invitation of Frances Willard,[69] a leader of the women's temperance movement, Murphy went west to extend the Blue Ribbon movement not only geographically but also in scope: that is, to include, along with former drunkards, anyone who wished to sign the total abstinence pledge, whether a drinker or not.[70] Under Murphy, changes were also made in the type of meetings the Blue Ribbon movement sponsored. No longer limited to set weekly or monthly gatherings of small groups to help one another, in the American West the Blue Ribbon movement joined religion and temperance together in the revivalist tradition. Camp meetings were held that lasted for days or weeks at a time, with the emphasis on converting the drinker to total abstinence within the time-span of the meeting.[71] Both the seller and the buyer of alcoholic beverages were the objects of attention of this movement, prayers being offered up for the 'conversion' of the tavern-keeper to Gospel Temperance principles.[72] After his western mission, Murphy returned East and met with great success in New York as well as in New England. Quickly the American temperance movement was carried away by Gospel

Temperance enthusiasm and the blue ribbon was to be found on the breasts of all kinds of men and women. Blue Ribbon missions were set up, which brought together teetotallers and ex-drunkards in an effort to 'save' more of their brothers and sisters from drink.

Gospel Temperance came to England in 1877 after William Noble, an English temperance lecturer of minor fame, visited the United States for five months and was introduced to the work of Francis Murphy and his Blue Ribbon movement in New York.[73] Noble was excited by what he saw and decided to start such a movement in London. The National Standard Theatre, Shoreditch, was the first home of the Blue Ribbon movement in England but was quickly replaced by Hoxton Hall, formerly a notorious music hall that had lost its licence. W. J. Palmer, a wealthy Quaker, hired and later bought the hall for the use of the Blue Ribbon Association.[74] It was in an excellent location for such a mission, being in the middle of a densely-populated working-class area, where mission halls were sadly needed.

The relation between W. J. Palmer and William Noble continued to be a close one throughout the life of the association. Besides buying Hoxton Hall, Palmer gave the temperance mission enough financial support to relieve it of the usual fiscal worries that beset so many other mission halls at this time.[75] Collections, at least in the early days, were of only minor importance, and the mission was able to do the work it felt was of the greatest importance, rather than that which was the most profitable. This financial independence also enabled the people who ran the mission to avoid the accusations of financial mismanagement of public funds that were launched against many mission halls in the late nineteenth century.[76]

At first, Gospel Temperance meetings were held at Hoxton Hall only once a week on Sunday, one hour after regular church services so as not to compete for the same congregation. But as the mission became a permanent part of London's lower-class life, and as it sought to help establish acceptable life-styles for its members, it extended its work into areas that were only remotely connected with temperance. Like many other temperance halls throughout the country, Hoxton Hall became the centre of a myriad of activities that filled the hall almost every minute of every day. The lack of other community facilities was only partly compensated by these mission halls in the poorer areas, but attempts were made to balance educational and religious functions with those that were strictly social. Especially on Saturday evening, a popular drinking night, great efforts were made to attract an audience to social events that would entertain for the price of one penny, or even for nothing at all.[77]

In its first years, Hoxton Hall was just one of many temperance missions in London and the provinces, distinguished only by the popularity of its founder. No one was actually paid by the mission; every worker was either an unpaid volunteer or had to raise support through his own efforts.[78] Consequently, apart from the work of an occasional provincial Gospel Temperance hall, set up in direct imitation of Hoxton Hall (Central Hall, Newcastle, was one of these), the Gospel Temperance movement had little influence outside the capital city.[79]

However, in 1880 this situation changed radically. In this year, the American Richard T. Booth, a reformed drunkard and self-appointed temperance missionary, came to England; he was the catalyst that produced the phenomenal upsurge of Gospel Temperance that changed the Blue Ribbon movement in England from a local to a national one. For almost five years England was gripped by a temperance fever that rose and fell continuously like the temperature of a sick man. By the end of the 1880s, when the Blue Ribbon movement had burned itself out, over a million Englishmen had signed the pledge and had 'donned' the blue ribbon.[80] Lords and Ladies, earls and countesses wore the teetotallers' badge along with paupers in the workhouses.[81] Other temperance groups throughout England quickly picked up the idea of wearing ribbons until there was a great proliferation of these badges in all colours. The Roman Catholic teetotallers, not wanting to identify themselves with the blue ribbon, which they thought to be closely connected to the Protestant church, selected green as their colour.[82] Another temperance group favoured the white ribbon,[83] while an anti-temperance organisation sported a yellow ribbon.[84]

The coming of Richard Booth to England, unlike the advent of Francis Murphy and other later American temperance advocates, was completely unheralded. Similar in many respects to his revivalist predecessor, Dwight L. Moody, whose techniques he copied and refined,[85] Booth was little known in his own country and was to make his reputation as an evangelist entirely in England. But, unlike Moody, Booth did not return to greater triumphs in his homeland; his reputation was more fleeting, and restricted to England and New Zealand.[86] All Booth had when he came to England was a letter of introduction to William Noble, nothing more – but it proved to be enough to set the American on the road to fame. Because of it Noble gave Booth a public welcome at Hoxton Hall, which set the American's temperance campaign rolling. Many of the leading supporters of temperance in the metropolitan area were present on the platform at this meeting, thus, giving Booth the approval of the English temperance establishment.[87]

The first English mission by Booth was held in Staffordshire, a county where temperance traditionally had found ready acceptance.[88] From the start, this mission was a great success and converts were counted in the thousands. Importing methods developed by previous generations of evangelists, Booth quickly established himself in English temperance circles as a very successful missionary; he was soon besieged with invitations to hold missions in various towns through the country.[89]

Much of Booth's success can be traced to the careful preparation he insisted be carried out before his mission commenced. This work was done by local committees formed when the American agreed to come. Ideally these committees were made up of local religious ministers as well as other influential citizens, such as politicians and justices of the peace.[90] By the 1880s this was not too difficult to arrange because many old temperance supporters were now in positions of power within the local establishment. Wide publicity was gained when the committee, under instructions from Booth, asked local ministers to offer up prayers for the success of the mission at their Sunday services.[91] Even if the minister was himself unenthusiastic about the forthcoming mission, it was difficult for him to refuse to ask for God's help and guidance for its work.[92] To many laymen hearing their minister offer up such prayers gave the mission a stamp of approval and therefore made them more receptive to its advertising.[93]

Advance publicity played an important role. Each town was plastered with broadsheets telling of the forthcoming event and whetting the appetite of the public for this new 'happening'. Special daily newspapers published before and during the mission, giving reports on missions in other towns as well as the work at home, were a popular technique for rousing public interest.[94] Frequently offices were rented in a central part of the town, where paid and unpaid workers coordinated the efforts of all the groups preparing for the coming mission. Sometimes a number of minor meetings were held to 'prepare the soil' for the coming of the evangelist himself. These smaller versions of the mission were given their share of publicity and thus increased the atmosphere of excitement.[95]

The local workers for a Booth mission had to rent a large hall, the largest in the town if possible. Churches were never used because the evangelist wanted to draw in people who would not come casually to a church service. (From this the Church of England learned that there were many benefits to be gained from holding religious missions in non-religious settings.[96]) Booth also insisted that the hall he use have a very large stage. Although it was customary at the time for all local dignitaries and those connected with the mission to be seated on the platform, the American departed from English tradition by including a full-size choir among those occupying the stage, which was an essential part of his mission. Culled mostly from local church choirs, the singers were professionally trained to sing the gospel hymns written by Booth himself, as well as a selection of currently popular hymns, and they were essential in setting the emotional climate of the meeting; working together with Booth, they were responsible for bringing the passions of the audience to a climax. At the high point of the mission Booth himself called out for members of the audience to come forward and sign the pledge, while the choir sang hymns softly in the background.[97]

In traditional English practice the main speaker was always followed by another who gave a vote of thanks, but Booth insisted that he be the last to speak, thus ensuring that the emotional spell he wove around his audience would remain with them after they left the hall.[98] By this method he also avoided a problem that plagued William Noble when he held his meetings in the traditional manner. It was a common occurrence for the hall to empty right after Noble had concluded his address, thus leaving later speakers to talk to a gaping void instead of the original crowded hall.[99]

Gospel Temperance missions in the nineteenth century were found to have a pattern of development of their own. They always started very slowly and worked up to a pitch after a few days – a good evangelist could control this rising pitch of enthusiasm. One of Booth's great accomplishments was that he was able to pace the meetings so that the mission did not 'peak' too early or too late.[100] (In Liverpool, where he held a three-week mission, he experienced one of his few failures because he held his meetings in various locations, so that the mission never reached the 'crisis' point.[101]) To take advantage of this pattern, admission in the early days of the mission was free, except for a few select seats where, for a small fee, those who wanted to avoid the crowd could sit. By the end of the mission there was no free admission. If the mission had been a good one, there was no lack of paying participants because enthusiasm was now at a peak. On the last day a 'Farewell' meeting was held which was the high point of the mission. Seats for this evening were often quite expensive: sixpence and a shilling were the common prices;[102] but there was generally no absence of takers. It was common at these final meetings to make some presentation to the speakers; often valuable gifts were given to Mr and Mrs Booth by local well-wishers.[103] Another common practice was to donate the proceeds of specially designated meetings to individuals who had worked with the mission, paying for the extra services of those who had contributed to its success. Sometimes musicians and singers were the beneficiaries or again the money might go to evangelists who had assisted the main advocates.

There were many complaints in the press regarding the lack of public accounting of the funds collected by these missions. When one newspaper decried the 'extraordinary harvest now being reaped by American temperance orators',[104] a correspondent in the *Blue Ribbon Gazette* responded with figures taken from a fourteen-day mission in Manchester, which had raised £134 in its collections. Francis Murphy, the principal evangelist, received £63, which amounted, according to the correspondent, to only two guineas per lecture. But Mr Murphy also got more than £24 from admirers in Manchester. The final meeting of this Manchester mission was held for the benefit of Mr and Mrs Willson, an American couple who sang during the second week, for whom £41 was raised. This was a handsome remuneration for one week's work, especially when all expenses, including hotel bills, were paid by the mission. This mission, in keeping with the rest, does not appear to have been stingy in providing accommodations. The hotel bill for Francis Murphy, including his family and the Willsons as well, for two weeks, was almost £40.[105]

At the conclusion of every meeting both old and new teetotallers were allowed to enrol in the Blue Ribbon Army and 'don the blue', but only new teetotallers were allowed to sign the pledge. This rule was made in response to the justifiable criticism that the figures of those converted by Gospel Temperance were not accurate because many signing the pledge were already abstainers.[106]

When the entire mission was concluded, the names of those who had signed the pledge were divided among the sponsoring churches or societies: if the signer had expressed a particular religious preference, his name was given to that church.[107] All the newly pledged abstainers were visited by paid or unpaid workers sent by the mission committee.[108] There was much criticism by the general public of the temporary effect of these missions; questions were often asked about the percentage of converts that remained faithful to their new creed.[109] No one knew the answer, and the evangelists, who wanted to show the largest figures possible, preferred to give out high estimates rather than accurate statistics.

It was soon discovered that many 'respectable' people did not like to march to the front of the hall during a mission to sign the pledge publicly. To deal with this situation, Booth inaugurated pledge booths, which were set up in the middle of the town during a mission and remained open all day. Men and women could drop in and sign the pledge without any of the fanfare that greeted those who signed during a meeting.[110] The general temperance pledge, unlike former pledges, was not a controversial one.[111] It stated: 'With charity to all and malice to none, I promise by divine help, to abstain from all intoxicating liquors and beverages and to discountenance their use by others.' Usually the pledge ended with, 'The Lord help me to keep this pledge, for Jesus' sake'.[112]

Although the relationship between William Noble and Richard Booth was, publicly at least, friendly, the same could not be said about their followers in the two movements these men spawned. Booth himself was never interested in setting up any permanent mission, leaving that work to others, while Noble believed that too large an organisation could cripple their cause and, initially at least, was not concerned with extending his mission into a national movement.[113] But many of the men who helped Booth were not willing to allow the enthusiasm roused by a mission for temperance to disappear without some attempt to retain it. Immediately after the evangelist left their area they would set up permanent missions to carry on the work. It was not difficult to organise such an agency, particularly at the end of a very successful mission, when the whole spirit of the local anti-drink forces had been raised to fever pitch by the stirring oratory of Booth and his associates. These permanent missions became quite numerous and were known as the Blue Ribbon Gospel Army. Each one was fairly independent. Supported by local money and local workers, they were connected only through the pages of the *Blue Ribbon Gospel Gazette*,[114] a journal set up to publicise the activities of the Gospel Temperance movement among its own workers as well as the general public. Following a growing popular practice of this period, many of these missions were organised along 'military' lines: the head of each group was a captain, while his assistants were designated lieutenants. By 1886 there were, according to the *Gazette*, 100 individual missions in Britain and Canada affiliated with the Blue Ribbon Gospel Army.[115]

Unfortunately for the Gospel Temperance movement, competition among its different parts emerged, particularly between the Hoxton Hall mission, which belatedly decided to spread its influence and hold missions in the provinces, and the missions of the Blue Ribbon Gospel Army. This conflict came to a head in May 1883, at a conference organised by Hoxton Hall and held in Exeter Hall[116] at which the metropolitan mission proposed to set up a Central Board of Control for regulating the Gospel Temperance movement and certifying its speakers.[117] This was an attempt to reduce the number of self-appointed advocates, who, besides being incompetent in their work, were causing much public ridicule to be heaped on the movement. A Gospel Temperance mission was a potential goldmine; the unscrupulous could make considerable sums of money selling tickets to their 'missions'. One participant at the Exeter Hall conference claimed that many working men would not attend Gospel Temperance meetings because 'they believed advocates were making money'. Such accusations were met by the answer, 'if the American workers have been well paid, they only deserved to be well paid'.[118] Other Gospel Temperance supporters, unwilling to dismiss the problem with so superficial a reply, were unhappy because missions would only help where there was enough money offered to interest the advocates. Some towns could not attract the attention of any well-known evangelist because they did not have enough money to pay the heavy expenses of a mission.[119] Not only did the town have to raise enough to cover these costs; it also had to find men of substance who were willing to put up large amounts of cash as a guarantee that expenses would be paid even if the mission proved to be a financial failure.[120]

There was also continuing criticism in the press and elsewhere regarding the financial arrangements of these missions. Rarely was the public given a comprehensive accounting of the mission's financial transactions; this lack of information encouraged rumours about mismanagement of funds. Such rumours were given substance when the public learned that many evangelists went abroad to fashionable resorts, staying in expensive hotels in warmer climates during the cold English winters.[121] In 1882, Richard Booth, for example, ill in England, went to Mentone, a winter resort in the South of France popular with well-to-do English families in the nineteenth century, where he spent months in a fashionable hotel recuperating.[122] The previous year, 1881, William Noble went to South Africa for the sake of his health, and both he and Booth went to Australia and New Zealand more than once, sometimes to hold missions, but at other times just for a rest.[123]

Not all the criticism of the Blue Ribbon Army came from the non-temperance public. Many of the older teetotallers were unhappy with the new turn in their movement. They felt slighted and neglected by the attitude of the newcomers, who were, they felt, getting the rewards that should have come to the older movement. The newcomers had 'reaped where they had not sown and gathered where they had not strewn', said one veteran of the cause.[124] Joseph Livesey, the founder of teetotalism, had his doubts about the efficacy of the new form of temperance and did not like the 'spasmodic' work of the 'month's missions'. He still felt that it was important for individual teetotallers to go among the poor and work with them on an individual basis.[125] A similar complaint was made by the Rev. George W. McCree, a founder of the Baptist Temperance Association who, for his work among the poor of St Giles, a London slum parish, was called the 'Bishop of St Giles'.[126] In an article *Old Friends and New Faces*, published as a pamphlet, McCree wrote that the American speakers never cared about 'the drunken outcasts of London'.[127] This article was written in reply to speeches given at Crystal Palace by Booth and his friend and sponsor, Canon Wilberforce, which criticised the old teetotal movement for being without religion.[128]

Thomas Whittaker was another teetotal veteran who wrote a book in answer to what he thought were unjust criticisms of the older movement.[129] Writing of the new temperance evangelists, he stated:

> They create nothing, teach little and, as it seems to me, enjoy much. As to self-denial or self abnegation where are they? They come in families and travel in tribes; and if a little poorly or out of health a trip across the Atlantic, a visit to Cannes or a residence in Mentone soon put them right . . . Now it is very easy to be very pious with a full stomach and a full purse.[130]

Some of the older teetotallers agreed with Troughton of Leeds when he told the annual meeting of the British Temperance League that Gospel Temperance had been not a help but a very great hindrance to the temperance cause and that they need go no further than Leeds to prove it.[131] This was said in 1888, when the Blue Ribbon movement was already in decline and an evaluation of its influence was possible. The town of Burnley provided similar evidence. When R. T. Booth held a mission there and 800 persons took the pledge, not one of them joined the Burnley Temperance Society, as was pointed out by a Burnley teetotaller in the columns of the *British Temperance Advocate*.[132]

But the greatest censure of the Gospel Temperance movement was made on the grounds that it was superficial, that the results of the work were ephemeral. 'Easy come easy go', wrote the editor of *Onward*, the journal of the Lancashire and Cheshire Band of Hope Union.[133] This journal also complained about the divisiveness of the Gospel Temperance movement. 'A holy rivalry now exists as to which body was doing the most earnest and aggressive work against the citadel of drink', wrote the Bradford veteran, Martin Field, in its columns.[134]

However, these complaints were balanced by the general feeling among teetotallers that any movement that could bring men to teetotalism through a mixture of religion and temperance teachings should be encouraged. The benefits, the majority of teetotallers believed, fully outweighed the defects of the Gospel Temperance movement; they felt that although some of the

American and British advocates were making money, many others were doing a good job and earning their pay. They had publicised the movement and brought into the fold many individuals who would otherwise have remained untouched by temperance teachings. The extravagant language and lavish publicity of the movement attracted large numbers to its meetings; many who came out of curiosity stayed to enrol.[135]

Not all the work of the movement can be dismissed as a passing fad. Many areas, particularly rural villages and small towns that had not experienced much contact with the earlier temperance movement, were introduced by Gospel Temperance to teetotal principles.[136] Because of Gospel Temperance, the churches were under pressure to commit themselves to some part in the anti-drink fight; before the Gospel Temperance fever had abated, almost all the major churches in England had organised their own denominational temperance societies, albeit some very reluctantly.

Although complaints were often made about the proliferation of temperance organisations, the many groups were actually an asset to the movement. Without these new societies, many converts would have had no place in the movement. As we have seen from the experience of the Burnley Temperance Society, most or all of the new abstainers did not wish to affiliate with the older societies. Eventually, to bring order into the situation, most towns organised unions of local temperance societies. United Temperance Confederations were to be found in almost all large towns and even some smaller ones; their purpose was to coordinate the work of all the temperance groups in the town. It was Gospel Temperance that led to this widespread acceptance of anti-drink principles. Without Gospel Temperance, the teetotallers could hardly have aroused such anti-drink interest in the 1880s and 1890s. So powerful and widespread was this interest, that the Liberal Party had to incorporate support for local prohibition into its programme of 1895.[137] And, contrary to the Burnley experience, most temperance organisations experienced their greatest gains in the late 1870s and 1880s.[138]

Much can be made of the personalities of the evangelists who organised the missions that roused the emotions, but, without fertile soil in which to grow, the seeds they scattered would not have flourished. When Booth returned to England for a visit in 1888 and took part in public temperance events, he created no excitement; his visit was only barely reported in the columns of the old Gospel Temperance journal, the *Blue Ribbon Gospel Gazette*'s successor, *The Signal*, the one that a few years earlier had filled its pages with his doings.[139] Many other Americans and other overseas temperance advocates came to England to hold missions in the 1890s and 1900s, some at the invitation of English temperance organisations and others on their own self-appointed missions. But they did not cause any great national excitement and their missions remained local events.[140]

In trying to understand the incredible phenomenon of the 'wave of blue passing over the land', as Canon Wilberforce described it,[141] we can see that it filled widespread needs of the time. The 'Great Depression' of the 1870s left a residue of anxiety that reduced, if not ended, the optimism that had been part of the mid-Victorian spirit. Many men and women who were attracted to Gospel Temperance missions came out of a segment of society that had only recently emerged from their working-class backgrounds. The great depression threatened these people not only materially but also psychologically. Forces outside their own control could threaten and destroy them. For many workers faced with this situation escape through drink was the answer. But drink for upwardly mobile families meant an abandonment of the rigid control that had become essential for the realisation of their ambitions. Drink was the devil that was there to tempt men in times of weakness: it was the forbidden fruit that had to be publicly denied.

Gospel Temperance missions acted as a safety valve for these frustrations and anxieties. A mass release of emotion was encouraged and achieved. And at the same time that the audience was undergoing a psychological cleansing, an enjoyable evening was being had by all. The choirs of the Gospel Temperance missions also served to entertain. When a Blue Ribbon mission was being organised in Preston and a choir of 300 to 400 voices was insisted on, the expense was justified on the grounds that it was worthwhile as entertainment for the people.[143] Canon Wilberforce, when he criticised the old teetotal movement for being too entertaining, was blind to the high degree of pleasure experienced by many participants of Gospel Temperance missions, particularly when hearing such an evangelist as William Noble, whose dramatic and emotional addresses led one temperance journal to call him 'This master of pathos and humour'.[144]

## PERMANENT MISSIONS

The success of a temperance mission, in any part of the country, depended very much on the dedication of those that founded it and nursed it through its infancy. Of the few individual missions that developed out of the Gospel Temperance movement and became well known, a majority were the work of single individuals or sometimes of couples. Outstanding among these missions was one in Blackburn, called Mrs Lewis' Temperance Mission and later Mrs Lewis' Teetotal Mission. This was an outgrowth of a Blue Ribbon mission that was held in Blackburn.

Elizabeth Anne Lewis was the daughter of teetotal parents and as a girl accompanied her father when he held outdoor temperance meetings. But it was the Blue Ribbon movement that drew her into temperance work as a full-time advocate. She was recruited to labour with the Blue Ribbon Mission when it came to Blackburn and, after the mission ended, was so involved with the work that she decided to continue it. At first she continued her association with the remnants of the old mission but eventually she built up her own organisation, hiring a hall and a working-class missioner, who was to go into the slums of Blackburn and work directly with the intemperate poor.[145]

Mrs Lewis' mission was a simple organisation, with a plain structure. No army was set up and no organising board established. Mrs Lewis' Teetotal Mission resembled the older teetotal societies, those that flourished in the 1840s, much more than it did the Gospel Temperance Missions. Joseph Livesey and Father Mathew were saints to Mrs Lewis; her teetotal hall was named after Frederic Lees, the old teetotal warhorse; and Thomas Whittaker and other veteran teetotallers were invited to talk there.[146] Like the older temperance advocates, Mrs Lewis stressed the material advantages to the poor of teetotalism; she knew that new clothes, good food and decent homes were of more immediate importance and interest to the slum-dwellers than was the rather abstract notion of having their souls saved. She understood the impression made on an audience by a speaker's confessing that in thirty years of drinking he had wasted £5000.[147] Also unlike the Gospel Missions of the day, Mrs Lewis stressed the personal involvement of reformed drunkards in the work of the mission. A strong element of self-help was fostered throughout the mission. Only Mrs Lewis could have been called middle class.

The missioners she hired (there were only two: the first, Richard Killshaw, retired in 1888 when his health failed and was replaced by William E. Moss, who stayed with the mission until his death) were both from working-class families and they received only working-class pay for their work at the mission.[148] No one could accuse them of making money out of their work.

But Mrs Lewis herself was accused of just that, and not once but many times.[149] In 1890 the stories being circulated about her were so damaging that she sued a publican for libel. It proved to be a very difficult and expensive case, but she won,[150] and Charles Garret, the Methodist leader, organised a fund to raise money to pay her court expenses.[151] Over £300 was collected, which more than paid her expenses; the remainder was added to the general mission funds.[152] Mrs Lewis herself led a very simple life and so it was not difficult for her to convince the public that she was not in mission work to make money. On the contrary, her husband helped support the mission; when Mrs Lewis died, she left only a small sum of money.[153]

Unlike some other sponsors of missions at this time, Mrs Lewis was completely involved in its work. She had one great interest and that was her mission. She personally attended to its day-to-day functioning and was not above going out into the streets and accosting strangers, asking them to sign the pledge. Following the teachings of Joseph Livesey, she would spend a great deal of her time visiting the poorest people to see how she could help them. Indicative of her personal concern for the members of her mission was her reaction to the news that one of her reformed drunkards had broken his pledge. On receiving this information, she immediately put on her hat and coat and searched all the licensed houses in Blackburn until she found the erring member. She brought him home to his wife and stayed with him until all the public houses were closed. The next morning she came to take him to work and stayed with him until he had entered the factory doors. At the end of the day Mrs Lewis was again waiting for him to take him home and then on to her mission. This close association continued until Mrs Lewis felt the man was out of danger and able to resist temptation.[154] It was this personal interest in her members that gave her such a strong place in the affections of the poor around her mission. Her members knew that she acted in their own interest, like a loving but strict mother. On one of her birthdays, she was presented with an album containing the portraits of sixty-nine reformed drunkards she had helped,[155] and on another birthday the mission members presented her with a clock.[156]

Like the teetotallers of old, Mrs Lewis made reformed drunkards the trophies of her mission.[157] They had a prominent place in her meetings. An event guaranteed to draw a full house was the experience meeting, during which some of the reformed characters would talk of their former condition in the most lurid manner and tell of the benefits that had accrued from their adoption of teetotalism. For many of the local slum-dwellers, this was a cheap and exciting form of recreation, especially if one or more of the speakers was theatrically minded and could put on a good performance.

Mrs Lewis also held parades through the streets of Blackburn in which the reformed drunkards were the greatest attraction, showing off their new clothes and the general prosperity that were the rewards of their abstinence. One of the reformer's greatest goals was to get the town's most notorious drunkards to sign the pledge and walk in her procession.[158] Such publicity was invaluable to her work. In 1888 a reporter for the local newspaper wrote a series of articles, first published in the newspaper and then reprinted as a leaflet, which were very favourable, praising her work as vital in getting many working-class families to function as society wanted them to. They also provided valuable publicity, helping Mrs Lewis raise funds and secure the aid of the local authorities. In 1913, when the King and Queen came to Blackburn, Mrs Lewis was presented to them, a great civic acknowledgement of the value of her mission to the town.[159]

It was estimated that between 1000 and 2000 pledges were signed at Mrs Lewis' mission and she tried to keep in personal contact with as many of the signers as possible. When anyone signed the pledge at her mission he was immediately put to work, helping the cause and strengthening his own association with it. By such direct involvement with the mission a member was not only made a part of the teetotal community but also was kept so busy that he would have little free time to fall back into old drinking habits. Besides, Mrs Lewis found that a reformed drunkard was more effective in rescuing others than was one who had never drunk alcohol and did not understand the temptations of drink. By focusing on Mrs Lewis as the central figure and by having a working-class missionary, the mission made teetotalism a personal experience for all converts. One man was said to have walked from Fleetwood to Blackpool, where Mrs Lewis was holding a temperance mission, so that he could sign the pledge with the lady herself.[160]

An individual mission that became one of the best known in London was that of Frederick Nicholas Charrington, an 'eccentric' missionary whose exploits were debated over many a dinner table in late nineteenth-century London. Charrington was a scion of the famous English brewing family that owned Charrington and Head. Raised in a manner suitable for the heir of such a wealthy family, Charrington left his family home when he was twenty years old and went to live in the poverty-ridden East End of London. This move was unusual but was regarded as an act of youthful idealism which Charrington would abandon when he matured and felt the desire to 'settle down'. Like many nineteenth-century merchant families Charrington's was a charitable one, giving to the poor and to various missions. For many years the family supported their kinsman's work in the East End and his father donated £300 to build a mission hall for boys. Throughout his career Charrington rarely lacked funds for his projects.[161] Samuel Morley and many other wealthy men and women were willing to contribute handsomely to his schemes. His family connections were useful in many ways, opening doors to rich and influential homes that missionaries from lesser families would find firmly closed.

Frederick Charrington was not at all the usual type of missionary and his actions repeatedly brought him into conflict with the law. His overriding passion, at least in the first decades of his missionary life, was to destroy the music halls of London, which he felt were the greatest source of evil to the poor, encouraging the intemperance and thriftlessness of fathers while leading their daughters and wives into prostitution.[162] In 1876 a group of reformers organised by Charrington pitched a tent in front of a flourishing music hall and held a temperance mission there, distributing anti-drink tracts and accosting those going in and out of the hall. An uproar ensued when the publican and his men tried to remove the reformers by force. Charrington was arrested and bound over to keep the peace.[163] This outcome did not dampen Charrington's enthusiasm; on the contrary, it strengthened it. In 1880 he was again locked up for obstructing the entrance to a music hall.[164]

In 1883 he mounted an intense campaign against another London music hall. With a group of friends to aid him (at one time the reformer had thirteen fellow reformers helping him outside the one music hall),[165] Charrington handed out leaflets that showed angels and devils fighting over individuals; he also accosted those going in and out of the hall, telling them they were 'sowing the seeds of lingering pain, sowing the seeds of a maddening brain, What would the harvest be?' – lines from a currently popular revivalist hymn.[166] Even the ardent anti-drink paper, the *Alliance News*, admitted that Charrington's 'method of tract distribution is, of course, a very annoying one to the publican'.[167] Two years later, in 1885, Charrington was again in court charged with slander and libel of a music hall owner and an injunction was issued against his harrassing techniques. He was found guilty, having called Lusby's music hall 'a pit of hell'.[168]

Charrington and his anti-music hall campaign was the subject of many court cases that titillated fashionable London and made the reformer the subject of many coarse jokes. He hired a number of men to collect information to be used against music hall proprietors when they applied for renewal of their liquor licences. Eventually, however, Charrington, like many other temperance reformers of the time, decided that the best way to deal with liquor licences was to join the County Council and fight the issuing of these licences from the inside. In 1889 he was elected to the London County Council and served for six years, opposing all applications for liquor licences that came up during his term of office.[169]

For a number of years, Charrington was anxious to build a very large mission hall in Mile End Road, in the middle of the worst slums in London. In 1883 he bought a piece of land there that cost £8000 and held a stone-laying ceremony, tickets for which cost five guineas, three guineas and one guinea. Many prominent philanthropists came, including Lord Shaftesbury and George Williams (of YMCA fame). When the Assembly Hall, as it was called, was opened in 1886 it had two balconies and held 5000 people. It was not just a temperance mission hall but housed a great variety of activities, serving as a community centre for the people of the area.[170] Here Charrington organised his own band of temperance militants which he called the 'Crusaders'. They all wore a band in the form of a 'red cross done on black velvet' attached to the left arm. All the Crusaders were active in the mission, working among local indigent families. Like many other similar groups at this time, the Crusaders had their own brass band and decorative banners for parades through the streets of London.[172]

In 1890 Charrington took over a dying journal called the *Temperance World*, which had been started in 1883 when a 'great wave of temperance revival under Mr Booth' had caused the appearance of many such papers. When the tide ebbed, most of these journals were unable to continue. Charrington carried on the paper's temperance stand but added to it his own anti-music hall cause. Consequently, its columns were filled with the evil doings of music halls throughout London.

Charrington's last great temperance scheme was begun early in the twentieth century when he bought an island off the coast of Essex as a seaside resort without drink. This temperance spa was modelled on one existing in New York.[173] The Mansion House Committee, the Daily Telegraph Fund and other similar charitable agencies, sent parties of unemployed working men to the island to build its roads, sewers and other facilities.[174] The reformer built a house for himself on the island and also a convalescent home for people from his London mission. While the whole island was a sanatorium for saving the intemperate, it was also to be a retreat for upper-class inebriates, but this part of the plan does not seem to have attracted the expected support.[175]

Mrs Lewis' and Mr Charrington's works were in many ways representative of a type of mission that was common in the last two decades of the nineteenth century. In and around Manchester, for example, there were at least seven local missions that combined temperance and evangelical religion. One at Pendlebury, under F. H. Smith, worked mostly among the colliers and their families, recruiting its workers from among those they had saved.[176] In 1889 this mission was able to build a hall that cost £2000 and could claim over 6000 Blue Ribbon members in the area.[177] Like many of the other mission halls, Pendlebury did not restrict its work to saving souls through temperance; it also gave food and clothing to the needy and sent members to visit the sick.[178]

Another mission in the same vicinity was at Openshaw, organised by the owners of a large factory. Messrs Crossley Brothers were well known as donors to many charitable institutions as well as anti-drink supporters and they decided it would be worthwhile to organise a temperance mission with their own works. Bible classes for men and women, girls' meetings, women's meetings, Saturday evening workers' prayer meetings as well as Sunday evening public services run by a pastor were only a few of the events sponsored by this mission.[179] At Openshaw a White Cross Society was also organised, a group intended to 'maintain purity and respect for women'. Only males over sixteen years of age could belong and they were encouraged in 'cleanliness of habits, good taste in clothes and home comforts . . . and good literature for home reading'.[180]

The firm of Richard Haworth and Co. of Salford also opened a club/mission for workers and paid all its expenses. At first no alcoholic beverages were served but, under pressure from the workers, this rule was relaxed; later gambling was introduced. The club quickly ran downhill until the owner of the company himself signed the pledge and started a temperance society with himself as president. The anti-alcoholic drink rule was reintroduced and the club remained teetotal. It sponsored missions from outside, at one of which the owner said he 'wanted them to be sober, reliable and efficient workmen, and that unless they abstained from intoxicating liquors there was no guarantee that they would be worth their wages'. He had spent a great deal of money introducing new machines in the mills and he did not want workers affected by strong drink to run them.[181]

Other permanent missions in the area were located in Mossley and Patricroft, and a Gospel Temperance Mission held in Mossley in twelve days raised over £103. There was some visiting between these local missions, with joint events that were drink-free playing an important part in cementing the local temperance community together.

Other types of temperance missions popular in the late nineteenth century were those run by well-to-do women. Either unmarried or married but childless, these women found themselves with time on their hands and a great desire to do useful work. Starting with a personal mission, they would often go on to much larger work. Miss Robinson and Miss Weston were typical of the unmarried women. Miss Weston was introduced to temperance and mission work by a rich friend, a Miss Williams, who was at the time running her own mission.[182] Finding that the sailors of Portsmouth needed not only physical accommodations ashore but also help with their personal lives, Miss Weston organised a Sailors' Rest, a teetotal hall and institute where social and religious events were held. She bought a house for her work with her own money and there held Bible classes, religious services, temperance gatherings and social meetings of all kinds. The house became a meeting place, or just a rest place, for sailors who did not want to go to the public house, where many would spend all or most of their money on drink or, when drunk, be robbed of the remainder. Started in the 1870s, by 1905 her 'home' had branches in Devonport and Keyham and her work was so well known that she was made a Dame Grand Cross of the Order of the British Empire.[183]

Miss Robinson was another middle-class lady who worked among England's servicemen at a time when imperialism had made the life of the soldier building an empire far afield seem glamorous and exciting. In fact, many British soldiers found that life in the Queen's service meant sickness, brutality and final discharges that left them unemployed, often unemployable, paupers. There was heavy drinking in the army and intemperance was the cause of much of the harsh punishment meted out to the soldiers. The National Temperance League had sent an agent to work among them in the late 1850s, but even though a military temperance society was formed in 1861, temperance made little headway in the army.[184] In 1873, Miss Robinson was given permission to start a temperance canteen while the army was on manoeuvres on Dartmoor. From this small beginning she went on to establish all kinds of drink-free recreational facilities. She helped set up Soldiers' Homes in garrison towns, enlisting the support of army chaplains in her work. Although Miss Robinson's motivation was religious and she regarded her work as that of a Christian saving the souls as well as the bodies of the soldiers, she was careful not to be too denominational in her spiritual work. The previous work of a woman in Aldershot had been 'too religious and too sectarian to be widely appreciated by the soldiers', complained one general, who was himself a teetotaller.[185]

Although both the Soldiers' Homes and the Sailors' Rests were supported partly by temperance contributions, with the National Temperance League providing both money and agents to help in the work, neither was viewed as strictly a temperance organisation; instead they were regarded as part of the larger missionary effort, with temperance only one aspect of their work.

Similar in many ways to the work of the Misses Robinson and
Weston was that of Mrs Wightman of Shrewsbury, though the
latter worked with the lower-class members of her husband's
parish. After Mrs Wightman, the childless wife of a parish priest
of the established church, had published her book, *Haste to the
Rescue*, which had provoked such interest in temperance within the
established church, she organised a temperance working men's
hall, with reading rooms, schoolrooms and a place where friendly
societies could meet.[186] It cost over £5000; almost £2000 were paid
by the Rev. and Mrs Wightman, the greater share being the
profits from her writings. The working men themselves were also
active in raising funds, the railway engine drivers providing their
own funds. When passengers offered to buy a driver a drink, as
was the custom at the time, he would ask for a contribution to Mrs
Wightman's hall instead.[187] Eventually meals were added to the
activities of the hall and the operation became so large that it was
turned over to the Shrewsbury Coffee House Company, which
promised to maintain it as a temperance hall. Unfortunately this
company allowed smoking and other activities of which Mrs
Wightman disapproved, but she was unable to change their
position.[188] Like many of the other mission halls of the day, this
working men's hall was the community centre for the poorer
citizens, with educational activities and social events filling the
days. But, in contrast to many of the other missions, at Mrs
Wightman's hall there were very few religious exercises. Being the
wife of a clergyman, she was sensitive to the problems involved in
allowing unauthorised men and women to conduct services and
act as spiritual leaders. Sectarianism was another difficulty; when
a visitor praised the virtues of unsectarianism at her hall, Mrs
Wightman objected, saying that 'unsectarian work is spiritual
lawlessness . . . It seems to me that when non-conformists call
their work unsectarian, they want church people to ignore their
church to join with them; and in all such combinations for mission
work, the dissenting element soon absorbs the whole control.'[189]

## THE SALVATION ARMY

Of all the missions that were active in the 1870s and 1880s only
one became a permanent member of the religious establishment in
England and the United States: the Salvation Army. Its founders,

William and Catherine Booth, like many other concerned individuals at that time, worked in missions they had created and also evangelised throughout the country.

Mrs Booth, born Catherine Mumford, was the daughter of an ardent teetotaller who suddenly changed sides and became an ardent drinker. Quickly descending from comfortable working-class respectability into drunken squalor, the family was soon destitute. Catherine Booth never forgot what drinking had done to her family and was instrumental in making teetotalism an important feature of the Salvation Army.[190]

Catherine and William Booth were already veteran evangelists when they founded what was to become the Salvation Army. William Booth was an ordained minister in the Methodist New Connexion but had resigned from that church in 1861. He was never at ease in any part of the existing religious establishment, though he worked in various branches of the Methodist Church. For a time he was a minister on the St Ives circuit of the Cornish Teetotal Methodist Church[191] but soon left and set up his own missions independently.

His first mission was in Waltham, Staffordshire, where he set up the Hallelujah Band, composed of converted criminals who spoke publicly about their conversions.[192] William Booth was not primarily a temperance reformer; he did not feel that temperance was an end in itself. Instead he saw total abstinence as one means of many of saving souls, which was the real goal of the Booths. In 1864 the Booths moved to Mile End Road, London, where they started a mission called the East London Revival Society. This name was soon changed to the Christian Mission. In 1878, deciding to make their mission a more aggressive one and in keeping with the popular spirit, they reorganised it on military lines. Booth called himself a general and gave his assistants 'commissions' as officers, while the volunteer members at the bottom were designated 'soldiers'. The name of the mission was changed to the Salvation Army.

As the *Telegraph* pointed out at the time of Booth's death, in these early days the Salvation Army was one of many similar groups.[193] There were many aggressive Christian armies formed to fight the enemies of Christendom and the marching hymn 'Onward Christian Soldiers' was heard in the streets of London and the provincial towns with increasing frequency. Just as Charrington had his Crusaders and Mrs Torrington her White

Ribbon Army,[194] so the Booths had their Salvation Army, with the 'general', the dictator, running his organisation without interference from committees or ruling bodies. The uniforms and the bands were also similar to those of other 'armies' of the day; neither the street meetings nor the public 'confessions' of the converted originated with the Salvation Army. What probably made the greatest difference, the one that showed as the years passed, was the organising ability of the Booths and the superior structure they gave to their 'army'. While William Booth was the official leader, his wife Catherine, an active talented woman, was totally involved; together they established a mission with such great appeal that by 1882 they had 521 stations with 742 paid officers and 15 000 volunteer soldiers. By this time, over £18 000 was being spent on renting rooms for meetings,[195] and the Salvation Army was beginning to stand out. Its work was hurting some established interests – so much so that a Skeleton Army was organised to break up Salvation Army and temperance meetings generally.[196]

The decade of the 1880s was a hard one for many Salvationists: they were imprisoned and fined on charges that were meant to harass them, of disturbing the peace, causing a public nuisance and others. They were even imprisoned for playing music in public and thus 'disturbing the peace'.[197] The Army tried to copy the American women by having a 'Whisky War' in South London, holding meetings on Sundays in front of public houses, but they were not very successful.[198] The public was not willing to allow the Salvation Army to close its social centres on the one day out of seven they had to enjoy themselves. But failure did not deter the Salvation Army; they thrived on persecution, seeing it as a sign of success. Had they been of no consequence, no one would have bothered to organise an opposition. By the end of the 1880s the public attitude towards this Army had changed: people saw that its members worked among the very poor, reaching those that the churches and even the regular temperance organisations could not touch. The 1890s was a great decade for the Army and by the end of the century they had made their own place in the religious establishment. The Army eventually became a church, owning many buildings, which it called 'citadels', and holding its own services. Although Thomas Huxley wrote a blistering attack on the Army's fanaticism, accusing Booth of using the Salvation Army to establish himself financially,[199] the public was thankful to have such an organisation that would work among the poor in the slums.[200] In 1902, William Booth was given the sign of acceptance; he was invited to be present at the coronation of King Edward VII.[201]

Though the Salvation Army preached total abstinence and made teetotalism a condition of membership, it remained somewhat aloof from the temperance crusade and Booth refused to support prohibition wholeheartedly; he felt it was unrealistic.[202] In 1897, a spokesman for the Army claimed they supported prohibition on the ground that the interest of the publicans and the brewers demanded it; they had souls to save and, as long as they were connected with the drink trade, those souls were in jeopardy.[203] But political activity was not part of the Salvation Army's programme and so they stayed away from the anti-drink demonstrations and other political events, and refused to support the no-compensation movement that was so popular among temperance reformers in the late 1880s.[204]

# 6   Come All Ye Children

Almost from its inception there were a few members of the temperance movement who had shown an interest in training children to shun excessive drinking, and from the early 1830s juvenile divisions of established temperance organisations could be found in some parts of the country.[1] But this interest was not a general one and children's temperance groups were only a minor part of the temperance reformation in the 1830s and early 1840s. It was only after long, hard and discouraging battles against entrenched drinking habits that juvenile temperance work was given greater prominence in the movement. Gradually more and more temperance reformers came to realise that it would be far more effective to raise abstainers from childhood than to try to change drinking habits already firmly established.[2]

## THE BAND OF HOPE

The first Band of Hope was inaugurated in Leeds in 1847.[3] Used originally to denote the children's section of the Leeds Temperance Society, the name was copied by many other temperance and church organisations as the designation for their juvenile temperance groups. With such a wide and general use, the title 'Band of Hope' came to be used as a generic term for all such youth groups, regardless of their sponsorship. The Church of England had its own Bands of Hope, as did the Wesleyans, the Society of Friends and all the secular societies. Nevertheless, within the temperance movement the term 'Band of Hope' was used as the title of a specific organisation concerned with all kinds of temperance work among children of both sexes between the ages of six and twelve.

Although the Band of Hope movement forged close ties with churches and chapels of all denominations, it was itself non-denominational. It was, however, very Protestant in spirit, and because of this it had little contact with the workers of the Roman Catholic organisations. The latter preferred to control and guide their own societies. Members of the Women's Guilds of the

Roman Catholic Church were given the major responsibility for conducting juvenile temperance activities and, as if to maintain their separateness, the Roman Catholic youth temperance organisation had its own name, the Children's Guild. There was a Jewish Band of Hope in London, but it does not appear to have been copied by co-religionists elsewhere nor to have flourished.[4]

Between 1847 and 1851 there was a steady growth throughout England of all kinds of children's temperance associations. In this early period, when there was no standard organisation or programme for these bands, anyone who so desired could start his own group and call it a Band of Hope. In an article entitled 'How to Form a Band of Hope' in one of the early issues of the *Band of Hope Review*, the informal manner in which local bands could be set up and run was described: 'Invite the children to the schoolroom or your dwelling house', suggested the article; possible activities were to read the Bible, sing a temperance song and 'explain about the misery inflicted on the country through drink'. It suggests also that the children be told how difficult it is to reclaim drunkards but how easy to keep people from becoming such 'if they *never taste* anything that can intoxicate'.[5]

Bands were often organised by individual congregations of all types of churches and chapels. If the local minister was a supporter of the temperance reformation, a band was usually established at his church. Many people connected with Sunday Schools and other working-class educational ventures were also sponsors of the movement.[6] Baptists active in the Mechanics Institute and other civic activities were among the most committed of workers in the Bradford and Leeds Band of Hope movement. The founders were Jabez Tunnicliff, a Baptist minister in Leeds, and Mrs Anne Jane Carlile, an Irishwoman who had been an active prison visitor before she took up temperance work. Devoting her time to alerting the young to the dangers of drink, Mrs Carlile had been travelling around Britain, lecturing to children in Sunday Schools and chapels, but, although she asked her listeners to sign the pledge, she did not set up or encourage any permanent children's organisation. Not until she was invited to talk to the children at a meeting sponsored by the Leeds Temperance Society in 1847 and met Jabez Tunnicliff did the idea of a permanent children's temperance organisation come into being.[7] A Ladies Committee of the Leeds Temperance Society helped Mrs Carlile and Jabez Tunnicliff at this first meeting of the Band of Hope movement, and also helped organise other children's activities.

   Though the contributions of Mrs Carlile and the Leeds Ladies Committee in these early days were of great importance, women played a minor role in the full development and organisation of the movement. Frequently they acted as helpers in the local bands, but they were rarely in decision-making positions. Even though it was often admitted that women could do more effective missionary work among women and children, few women were employed by the movement in this or any other capacity. This male domination was partly due to the prevailing attitude towards the role of women of the class that gave the greatest support to the Band of Hope movement. Encouraging women, especially married women, to work was regarded as undesirable by the Band of Hope organisers; working wives were a threat to the domestic stability that was the foundation of a respectable family. Furthermore, it was important to this class that men should have the real authority. Just as women were the helpers of their husbands in the family, so were women the assistants of men in institutions outside the home. Only in the Roman Catholic children's temperance organisation were women acknowledged to be important workers.[8]

   Despite the fact that there were great advantages to be gained from their strong local identification, the isolation of the individual units from other similar youth groups posed many problems for this pioneering work. Being the first children's society, the bands had no previous models on which to base their activities; consequently, they developed their own individual methods of work, each learning through its own experience.[9] In 1851, recognising the need for some form of local association, Band of Hope workers in Bradford joined together to form a union.[10] It was so successful that others quickly followed and soon large sections of the country were blanketed by Bands of Hope, interconnected by various types of unions. Town, country, and later denominational unions were organised, particularly in the northern industrial areas.

   As the century progressed, the majority of the individual bands became increasingly dependent on the town and county unions for help in supplying both expensive equipment and the services of experienced agents to organise their programmes. Lantern slide lectures and dissolving views, both very popular with the children, required equipment that individual bands could not afford to own, but would borrow from the unions. Speakers' plans were also drawn up by the unions as an aid to the local groups. By providing outside temperance lecturers to address the children of parochial bands, the unions were instrumental in introducing new ideas and broader visions into the narrow environment of many neighbourhood groups. This part of the union work so increased in importance that, by the end of the century, one town union claimed to have 137 names on its speakers' list and to have made an average of thirty appointments a week for speakers to talk to various organisations in the area.[11]

The Lancashire and Cheshire Band of Hope Union, with its headquarters in Manchester, and Yorkshire Band of Hope Union centred in Leeds, were the strongest organisations in the Band of Hope movement in the provinces. They were often united in opposing the London Band of Hope Union, which differed from its northern associates in many ways. Almost from the beginning, the metropolitan organisation had imitated other middle-class reforming groups by having an 'ornamental' board consisting of a titled patron, a churchman as president, and sixteen vice-presidents, twelve of whom were ministers of religion.[12] The accent was on middle-class control, as in the Sunday School movement.[13] In the north the situation was quite different. Here there was no ornamental board and there was less concern with the formal structure of the movement. The working-class self-help principle was stronger in these manufacturing areas than in the middle- and upper-class circles of the metropolitan Band of Hope movement. In the first issue of the Yorkshire *Temperance Lighthouse*, Joseph Livesey wrote:

> To establish and carry on successfully a Band of Hope, straightforward, earnest efforts are all that are required. Unions and combinations are requisite to rouse the lethargy and lukewarmness of many, but any three thorough-going teetotalers may form a Band of Hope unaided by either union, minister, or committee.[14]

Increasingly, as time passed, there were calls for a better organised and better controlled movement. A number of religious men were leaders of a faction that wanted to keep a closer check on the activities of the individual bands. Complaints that there was an 'absence of religious tone and spirit' among some of the leaders of local groups were common.[15] Also common was the criticism that meetings were held too late in the day and that the 'semi-theatrical entertainment' provided was unsuitable.[16] The matter of entertainment was also a source of much friction between the northern and southern parts of the movement. The southerners were wont to object to the local dialect used and local pride fostered in the recitations of the local bands.[17] But discord between north and south over northern speech and cultural patterns was not new, nor was it restricted to the Band of Hope movement.[18]

If there seems to be a similarity between the Band of Hope and many Sunday Schools in organisation and attitudes, this is only a reflection of how closely the two movements worked together. Besides serving the same class of children, these organisations also shared the services of many of the same workers; Sunday School teachers were frequently Band of Hope organisers. Both movements shared the belief that there would have to be a reformation of manners if the working classes were to live more comfortably. But not all Sunday School officials were convinced that drink should be made the scapegoat for all the evils of society, and some felt the teetotallers placed too much emphasis on material gains and not enough on religious values.[19] Nevertheless, there was a great deal of cooperation at the local level; many children heard their first temperance lecture in Sunday School, and some even signed the teetotal pledge there.[20] Juvenile temperance organisations could help turn a 'whole army of Sunday Scholars' into home missionaries, believed the Rev. Charles G. Garrett, the Methodist leader who saw temperance as a bridge between the church and the masses.[21]

A major change in the relationship between the Sunday School movement and the non-sectarian Band of Hope came as both movements developed along different lines. With the coming of Gospel Temperance in the 1870s and its joining together of religion and temperance in a popular movement, many churches set up their own Bands of Hope.[22] The Wesleyans, in particular, formed a large and effective Band of Hope organisation which was established and controlled by church officials.

In order to give the Band of Hope child a cultural setting in which he could find a place, a temperance 'world-view' had to be created out of the industrial civilisation of which the child was a part. There was a need for a temperance history, a set of traditions and values that placed the temperance movement and its believers squarely in the middle of important historical developments. Focusing on total abstinence and anti-drink activities in both Biblical and modern times, the two eras important to nineteenth-century temperance reformers, temperance history and temperance heroes were created that fitted in with the cultural forms and heroes to which the child was exposed at home and school. Joseph Livesey, as the founder of the modern teetotal movement,[23] was the first figure in the temperance hagiology. The Rechabites, a teetotal tribe of water drinkers mentioned in the Bible, were moved from the obscure position they occupied in Christian culture generally to one of prominence in the teetotal world. All the stories – biblical or historical – taught to the children in the Band of Hope reinforced the teetotallers' world-view.

Central to the work of the Band of Hope was the teetotal catechism, which was in direct imitation of the Christian catechism so popular in nineteenth-century churches. Fifty-two questions, one for every week of the year, were memorised along with their ritual answers. Each week the Band of Hope child was to memorise one question and answer, and in the weekly meeting the leader would expound its meaning. 'What do we mean when we say we are teetotallers?' was the first question in one of these catechisms, and one entire weekly lesson would be devoted to teaching the children the official view of what it meant to be a teetotaller.[24] It was not deemed essential that the child have a true understanding of the drink problem. In fact, creative thinking was not encouraged. Instead, drink was simply the devil, to be shunned and rejected automatically by all children. They were taught to 'dread and avoid' all alcoholic beverages and that there is 'death in the cup'.[25] Drink, then, as the source of evil in the temperance culture was to be feared and was blamed for all misfortunes in any drinking man's life.

Personal involvement in a variety of activities was an important part of the Band of Hope method for winning the loyalties of their members. As part of their official assignments, the children marched in parades and performed at temperance concerts and other public functions. A strong group spirit was carefully fostered through the direct and indirect teachings of the movement: 'Temperance will also keep the children from bad companions and evil. Your people who live to drink will not be friendly to abstainers.' So wrote the Reverend Charles Garrett in the *National Temperance League Annual*.[26] The reformers tried to substitute temperance alternatives for proscribed drink-related activities, so that the children would not feel deprived of anything important because of their teetotal association. Deliberately the movement attempted to dislodge the child from the traditional drinking patterns that predominated in nineteenth-century life.

The Band of Hope mixed educational with recreational activities. Since attendance was purely voluntary, the organisation had to be attractive enough to draw the type of children it was prepared to help. Many bands found that their members were glad to study a variety of topics so long as they were presented in an attractive manner. Interesting addresses by dynamic speakers and eye-catching visual aids were invaluable in getting the movement's message across to the children.[27] Most of the speakers were chosen from the membership of temperance organisations in the vicinity; quite a few professional temperance workers were hired to do this work, either full time or part time. Such local reformers were a vital link in the chain that joined the juvenile abstainers to the larger temperance body of the town.

Most of the work of the movement was carried out in bands that met once a week for one hour in the evening, although some bands met once a fortnight or once a month. According to one spokesman, the ideal meeting would be as follows: first a prayer and a hymn, followed by a temperance lesson or a talk by an adult. Next, an opportunity for the children to sing and recite and finally another hymn and prayer.[28] Assemblies were kept short because it was found that most children could not be attentive for long, especially after working all day. Spokesmen for the movement emphasised the need to start and finish all meetings on time; punctuality would be taught by example as well as by precept.[29] It was considered desirable to have a well-planned programme for each meeting. Although it was not common practice, some bands printed the programmes for their regular meetings.[30]

The teetotal pledge played a prominent role in the Band of Hope movement. Fortunately for the public image of the movement, there was little controversy over the children's teetotal pledge. Many non-temperance adults who were inclined to be hostile towards the adult teetotal pledge saw only virtue in it when taken by children.[31] To prevent criticism, no child was permitted to make any personal commitment without the consent of the parents, written if possible.[32] The typical children's pledge combined an anti-drinking promise with an anti-tobacco one. Although there was a great deal of disagreement over the smoking habits of the adult workers of this juvenile organisation, there was very little difference of opinion over the use of tobacco by children.[33] All respectable people, inside and outside the temperance movement, condemned it. Anti-tobacco lectures were given the children along with the anti-drink talks.[34] Drink and tobacco were linked as twin evils to be shunned by all respectable children.

Of all its general activities the Band of Hope believed music to be among the most important. Wrote one Band of Hope worker:

> The influence for good of the cultivation of such music among the children could not be overrated. Was it not likely that a little girl singing a verse of some sweet melody in the hearing of her poor drunken father would melt his heart. And that the hymns that taught the worship of the Blessed God would sink into the little one's minds . . . their singing would be like the great shout of Jericho before the walls of intemperance.[35]

Music was introduced to all the children through the singing of temperance songs and religious hymns, but members were also encouraged to receive further instruction in either voice or instrumental music. Innumerable choirs were rehearsed for concerts and competitions, with great dedication on the part of both singers and the choir masters. Of the two agents in the employ of a certain Band of Hope Union, one did the general work of the organisation while the other was hired to establish and train choirs in the area.[36] Simple orchestras were also organised and the members given free lessons on the instruments they chose to play. For the majority of children, this was their first formal introduction to music.[37]

On the national scene, impressive formal concerts were held in London for the massed choirs of the Band of Hope movement. Starting in 1862, when the first of these concerts was given with a choir of 1000 singers, they became annual events, the size of the choirs increasing every year until by 1886 there were 15 000 singers divided into three choirs appearing on the same day on the stage of the Crystal Palace.[38] Such demonstrations of the influence of the movement not only gave pleasure to the singers and the audience, but also won valuable publicity for the temperance cause.

In the later part of the century, changes in society at large meant that the Band of Hope had to shift the emphasis of its work in order to retain its close relation with the children. The passing of the Education Act of 1870 brought increased attention by all involved in juvenile work to the state day schools. Temperance reformers were very much concerned about the effects of the improved educational opportunities on the children; the class from which the Band of Hope drew its greatest numbers was the one that would benefit the most from the extension of state-run education. The Band of Hope responded to this change by hiring educated men, former schoolteachers if possible, as school temperance lecturers. These men went from school to school lecturing on 'scientific temperance'.[39] Permission to visit the schools had to be gained from the local Boards of Education, but many boards were perfectly willing to allow them to teach so long as they were qualified to do the work.[40] Medical doctors in particular were popular lecturers on the physiological and scientific aspects of temperance, and the London Band of Hope Union felt itself very fortunate when it was able to hire the services of two medical men.[41] Because these programmes were very expensive, special funds were created by many Band of Hope unions to pay for them. The United Kingdom Band of Hope Union raised £10 000 in 1889 to pay for seven lecturers to give talks wherever schools would permit them.[42] By 1893 this London-based union had twenty-nine agents and lecturers, though not all were qualified to visit schools.[43] Other Band of Hope unions in the provinces hired their own school lecturers to work within the locality.

The amount of school work that could be done was limited only by the cost of the programme; there was no lack of qualified talent to fill the posts of school lecturers. When the United Kingdom Band of Hope Union advertised vacancies for such positions they received 200 replies; out of these replies seventy-five had adequate qualifications but only five were chosen. Of these five, four were teachers and one a medical doctor.[44]

Another important educational programme for the movement was the various competitions it sponsored for both children and teachers. Sunday School teachers and pupil teachers were the special targets for the propaganda of the movement because they had such great influence on so many children. One union held a competition for pupil teachers for the best lesson on one of the following topics: a glass of beer; the injurious effects of intoxicating drinks; or total abstinence.[45] Medals, books, certificates and other prizes were awarded to the winners at public ceremonies often attended by local dignitaries. Annual temperance examinations were held for all Band of Hope children and the winners received suitable prizes, usually books.

## BAND OF HOPE LITERATURE

The printed word, a tool much favoured by all segments of the temperance reformation, was well utilised by the children's organisation. Many Band of Hope Unions published books and journals that had nationwide circulation, extending the temperance message far beyond the direct personal work of union agents into numerous non-temperance homes. Most of these works had a strong moralistic tone, and all reflected the middle-class view of society and of the role of the lower classes. One of the earliest, a book published by the Band of Hope, was also the most direct in its teaching. Originally circulated under the title *Juvenile Abstainer*, it was expanded and republished in 1853 under the title *Morning Dewdrops*.[46] Its author, Mrs C. L. Balfour, had been closely connected with the temperance movement for several decades and wrote many essays and books on temperance topics for both adult and juvenile audiences. *Morning Dewdrops* was written specifically for Band of Hope children, to give the youthful mind 'a compendium view of the claims of the whole temperance question'.[47] Its tone emphasised self-improvement, with chapters entitled 'Essays on Self Denial', 'The Cost of Intemperance', 'Early Habits', 'The Force of Example', 'The Power of Customs' and 'Christian Courtesy and Benevolence'. In the introduction the author stated: 'Every sensible young person who desires to live wisely and usefully and to be a blessing to society, must be quite conscious that he or she has many *duties* to perform, and that what is called *good conduct* is the right performance of these duties.'

In order to encourage the creation of works suitable for their sponsorship, many Band of Hope Unions held essay competitions. One such Band of Hope prize-winner was the novel *Frank*

*Oldfield*,[48] which won for its author, a Church of England clergyman, £100 in 1869. In this book the Reverend T. P. Wilson, rector of Southcote, told the story of a teetotal boy living in a world of drink; his parents and friends all drank and, as a consequence, came to a sad end. As was true in most temperance stories, no one in this novel drank with impunity, not even in moderation. In contrast to the drinkers, all the teetotallers were materially successful, as well as being morally superior to the rest of the population. Indeed, in the early temperance novels especially, work played the central role. While in many middle-class stories for children, school life was the central theme, in the juvenile temperance stories success in the working world and in establishing a comfortable home and family were the main concerns. School was seen as a desirable and often a pleasant place for children, but not one that played a large role in the lives of the heroes. Of importance to many temperance writers was the period we now call adolescence – the time when the individual is starting to find his own way in life. It was a period that the Band of Hope saw as a crucial one, when a young adult was easily led astray by bad (that is, drinking) companions. Most of the readers of these temperance books were working before they reached their teens. Many had been half-timers since they were eight or nine years old, especially in the first decades of the movement, but, even in the later years of the century, most of the children over the age of eleven were working.

Another prize-winning novel that was very popular, both among lower-class and middle-class temperance families, was *Danesbury House*.[49] Written by Mrs Henry Wood, a popular mid-nineteenth-century writer and author of many non-temperance novels, this work won the Scottish Temperance League prize of £100 in 1860. Even though the central theme of *Danesbury House* was drinking – and there was no neutrality on this subject: once a character had started to drink the habit always became uncontrollable and disaster ensued – it was more than a temperance tale directed at a narrow nephalist audience. By 1892 over 304 000 copies had been sold in England alone, and other editions were published in the United States and other English-speaking countries. So great was its popularity that editions continued to be issued into the twentieth century, more than forty years after its first appearance.

*Danesbury House* was the story of a prosperous manufacturing family with its own family business. Of the four sons, three became drunkards and died early. Only the eldest, a lifelong teetotaller and a role model for the reader, was in the end successful both in business and in marriage. A sister, also a total abstainer, married a reformed drunkard from a noble family. The introduction of this character, Viscount Temple, 'an idle nobleman', gave the author the opportunity to castigate the upper classes for their bad habits. Their idleness, thriftlessness and irresponsibility were roundly condemned along with their drinking and gambling.[50] Mrs Wood used her novel to censure slatternly wives as well as drunken husbands; linked together, they were portrayed as belonging to the same reprehensible stratum of society.[51]

Following one of the popular beliefs of the period, all the children in this novel were seen to be the products of their environment. 'Train up a child in the way he should go and when he is old he will not depart from it', was not only quoted[52] but formed the basic tenet upon which the author based her view of juveniles. For example, the brother who was a teetotaller was the son of a teetotal mother who insisted that her son and daughter drink only water. When she died, and the husband married again, the second wife was no abstainer and it was her sons who drank and came to an early end. The husband himself was a moderate drinker, but he had very little influence on the dietary habits of his offspring – that was the mother's responsibility.

Whenever London intruded into this story, it was shown to be an evil place where ambitious men had their hopes and talents ruined. 'The evil indulgences of London life' were blamed for the misfortunes of many, with the gambling houses and gaudy gin palaces that abounded in the capital city held up as the major culprits.[53] The metropolitan area was also charged with being the source of 'cheap and low publications' that 'demoralized the minds of the lower classes'.[54] Altogether, *Danesbury House* was a very respectable and readable work, aimed at the lower middle and upper working classes in the provinces.

Along with anti-drink novels, the Band of Hope organisers constantly emphasised the value to the movement of the many juvenile temperance journals and weekly papers published by various Unions. Up to the 1860s there was little call for reading matter for working-class children but, with increased schooling and the related emphasis on literacy, there was a rapid rise in the number of working-class children who could read and who wanted suitable literature. Many local Band of Hope Unions sought to meet this need by publishing their own magazines, but most of them were short-lived. Two publications, however, came to dominate the field of juvenile temperance literature, the *Band of Hope Review* in the south and *Onward* in the north.[55] The former, begun in 1851, was the official publication of the London-based United Kingdom Band of Hope Union, while the latter, launched in 1865, was the journal of the Manchester-based Lancashire and Cheshire Band of Hope Union. A third magazine, the *Temperance Lighthouse*, was started in 1871 by the Yorkshire Band of Hope Union, but it lasted only a few years.

All these papers were specifically for children and contained stories and poems of interest to the class of child they wanted to reach. In addition to temperance, the *Band of Hope Review* supported many causes that were popular among the English lower classes. It was very patriotic as well as strongly anti-slavery. It was also a promoter of the self-help principle, printing stories about poor children who managed to find work to support themselves, albeit very marginally, and sprinkling its pages with such mottoes as, 'It is better to work than to beg'. The editors of this review were much concerned about the 'ragged schools'[56] and supported the emigration schemes adopted by various ragged schools in the 1850s. An article called 'The Young Emigrants' told about a father who loved England but was forced to emigrate in order to get food for his children.[57] Many of the children reading the story must have known of similar real-life tales.

Success stories about teetotal heroes who made good in both economic and religious life were very popular with the journals' readers. Such biographies of self-made men played an important part in the training of Band of Hope children. A story about the industrialist Titus Salt in the *Temperance Lighthouse* concluded: 'Heroes like him are those we should study, and in our own little spheres reflect, conscious that names like those of Crossley and Salt will live when warriors are forgotten, and that to such God will say "Well done!" '[58] None of these heroes was eccentric or went against the prevailing notions of 'respectable' behaviour. By trying to emulate these figures, the child learned that self-control, thrift, hard work, cleanliness and punctuality bring material rewards, which in turn lead to spiritual success. Early training and preparing for the future were stressed: it was never too early to plan for one's working career.

Often the hero was to be emulated in that he dared to take a 'right' stand when others would not or dared not do so. The opening line of a popular song exhorted the children to 'Dare to be a Daniel, dare to stand alone'; the teetotallers knew what it was like to stand alone, and wanted to prepare the children for their role as temperance reformers in a drinking world. As in this song, biblical heroes, in particular, were often discussed in Band of Hope meetings – the Bible was not a controversial book among the class of people who ran the Band of Hope.

Other publications were issued not for the children but to guide the adult workers in their activities. The United Kingdom Band of Hope Union, for instance, published such a journal, the *Band of Hope Chronicle*. Originally started as a quarterly in 1878, it was so popular, unlike many other temperance journals, that it was made a monthly two years later. Band of Hope workers could also refer to a handbook called the *Band of Hope Blue Book: A Manual of Instruction and Training*,[59] which dealt with every aspect of organising and running a band and included outlines for talks against drinking and gambling.

The Band of Hope movement made a great effort to price its publications so that they would reach the maximum number of people. The printers themselves were usually teetotallers and members of the movement who put more value on spreading temperance principles than on reaping great profits. Not only did children's magazines have to be within the financial reach of all children: it was not uncommon for Band of Hope papers to be distributed free to members as an inducement to attend the weekly meetings. Often wealthy supporters would defray the costs of such free distribution.[60]

## THE MEMBERSHIP

The Band of Hope movement recruited the majority of its members from the 'operative' class. Many children in this class came from stable families with steady incomes, whose economic margin was nevertheless too small to give them any great degree of security. Even small adversities could have a catastrophic effect.

The slums and workhouses were an ever-present reminder of what these people's fate could be if they overindulged in such leisure-time activities as drinking and gambling. Conversely, even a small step upward, economically and socially, took a great deal of effort and necessitated the use of every available resource.

The children of teetotal families were enrolled in the Band of Hope as a matter of course, but they made up only part of its membership. Many children of drinking families which had not been touched by prior temperance efforts joined the Band of Hope. Drinking parents were generally quite willing to allow their children to attend weekly meetings of the Band of Hope. With so few alternatives for recreational activity, parents and offspring were delighted to have such an organisation available in their neighbourhood. The Band of Hope was careful not to upset the parents or other members of the community if it could be avoided. No child, for example, was allowed to join the movement unless he had the express permission of at least one parent.[61] Neither politics nor sectarian matters were allowed to intrude into the official life of the movement.[62] However, depending on local circumstances, they could not always be avoided. For instance, the Band of Hope movement was active in the great licensing demonstrations that engulfed the whole of the temperance movement in the late nineteenth century,[63] and it was in the forefront of the fight that culminated in the enactment of the Child Messenger Act of 1908.[64] Whenever any matter dealing with the issue of children and drink was being agitated, the Band of Hope was in the forefront. But, apart from temperance issues, the movement tried to avoid taking any controversial position.

The Band of Hope was not so successful in enrolling children in the very poor slums, whose life-style was very different from that deemed desirable by the organisers of the movement. 'Delayed gratification', for instance, had very little meaning for people who had little or no chance of collecting on the promises for tomorrow. The lowest classes saw no reason to spend any of their meagre resources on educating children for a future that might never materialise. Thrift banks likewise had no significance for children who never had surplus pennies to invest in them; and public speaking, a subject of great importance in the educational activities of the Band of Hope, was only relevant to children who had at least a minimal degree of public presence. Few street urchins could have felt comfortable amongst such an upward-aspiring group as the Band of Hope children were encouraged to be.

A major problem in establishing bands in the poorest sections was the complete lack of discipline among very poor children, most of whom had no schooling at all. In order to establish juvenile temperance associations, a certain degree of personal organisation was required of the children. They had to come regularly, on time, and be clean and alert. Furthermore, help from the adults of the community, which often made the difference between success and failure for local bands, could not be expected from inhabitants of the slums, who could barely keep themselves going. Among the poorest sections of the population, then, no bands were established, and the very class of children whose futures were most likely to be filled with drink and intemperance was excluded from the movement.[65]

Another sector of the community in which the Band of Hope exerted little influence was the middle classes. Among this group the children's temperance movement was thought to be a strictly working-class organisation. Certain temperance reformers, unhappy with this situation and attempting to overcome the movement's lower-class image, set up a special association for middle-class children which they called the Young Abstainers.[66] When the Church of England Temperance Society was organising juvenile groups in the last decades of the century, it also set up a separate society to work among middle-class children. Most of the meetings of this Juvenile Union, as it was called, were held in public and grammar schools. As with its non-sectarian counterpart, progress was very limited.[67]

A great deal of the success of the movement among the working classes must be ascribed to the quality of the adult members of the organisation. Coming from backgrounds similar to those of the children they were working with, almost all the workers were themselves products of the Band of Hope. Even in later years, when more professional agents and workers were utilised, a large percentage of these paid officials were former Band of Hope children.[68] The Band played an important role in the lives of many of the adults. It was never just an odd hour a week granted to the local children, but a whole way of life, with weekends and evenings almost completely devoted to work with the children. When there were no meetings, choir rehearsals, entertainments or whatever, there were always families of potential or lapsed members to be visited. If these adult members were active in the larger temperance world, and most of them were, their lives were filled with the multifaceted roster of activities sponsored by local temperance communities.[69] For these adults temperance was a superior way of life, and the Band of Hope a means of introducing children to a better and more productive future. Many of the workers in other branches of the anti-drink movement were former Band of Hope children retaining an active interest in it long after they had 'graduated' from its ranks. Whereas many citizens might hesitate before giving their personal support to the greater teetotal movement, few would deny aid to the children. Local officials, society figures, and even the Queen were willing to link their names with the juvenile teetotal organisation. Particularly in the northern industrial centres, association with the juvenile groups could prove a political asset: it showed the local voters that one was concerned with the future of the community.

## A CHANGING MOVEMENT

By the end of the century, the Band of Hope movement was slowly changing its goals. It became oriented towards training children who would be easily integrated into the community rather than leaders who would carve their own empires in the economic world. There was less emphasis on individual heroic exploits and more on social adjustment. This was a reflection of some of the economic and social changes occurring in England at this time. Economically, the old free-wheeling days of commercial adventuring were ending and being replaced by a more rigid structure. The call was less for entrepreneurs to pioneer new modes of operation than for clerks and other white-collar workers to serve the industrial empires already created. These workers needed to be literate, self-disciplined and content – the very type that the Band of Hope aimed to produce by the end of the century. These were the new aristocrats of the working classes, or so they thought. Their children too believed themselves to be superior to other working-class children; were they not learning to sing and recite, as well as to study 'scientific' temperance lessons at their Band of Hope meetings?[70] Furthermore, they were quite sure they were respectable; they had been told so over and over again by many prominent adults.[71] Commenting on the role of the Band of Hope movement in the lives of working-class children, one life-long northern worker wrote:

> Who can tell the numbers who have been saved from the drink curse? . . . To how many had the Band of Hope meeting been the starting point of success, prosperity, position and influence in commerce, as well as in the church. What joy to hearth and home have our songs and melodies been. What lessons in good manners, thrift, economy, kindness to animals, in physiology, in chemistry, etc. have been disseminated . . .[72]

The temperance movement was not a static one. Changes and fashions within the society as a whole, new ideas and new interests often resulted in modification of the movement's goals. In the early days, when self-help was very popular among the working classes, the teetotal movement – including the early Band of Hope movement – was involved in a myriad of self-improvement schemes. Later, when there was a growing belief at all social levels in the necessity for change in society before the individual could be changed, the temperance movement absorbed these new thoughts and translated them into prohibitionist doctrines, believing that, if society was made free of drink, people would learn to live without it. Consequently, a great many anti-drink efforts of the later decades of the nineteenth century were focused on effecting changes through governmental action, and both local and national governments became the targets of great temperance pressure.[73]

The Band of Hope did not remain untouched by this new political agitation and found itself increasingly involved in both local and national politics, working particularly for bills that would restrict or forbid the selling or giving of alcoholic beverages to children.[74] With these new activities came a change in the philosophy of the movement. No longer were the children kept apart from political action; instead they were treated as weapons in the anti-drink fight, active agents of change who could be controlled and manipulated by the organisers of the movement. The children played an important role in the demonstrations against drink that took place in many northern towns in the last decades of the nineteenth century and the first decades of the twentieth century.[75]

This change in the role of children in the movement can be seen in Band of Hope songs. The first temperance song for the movement was written by its founder, Jabez Tunnicliff, in the 1840s and its first verse went as follows:

> Come, all ye children, sing a song, join with us heart and hand
> Come make our little party strong, a happy temperance band.
> We cannot sing of many things, for we are young we know,
> But we have signed the temperance pledge a short time ago.[76]

In the next and subsequent verses the children ask their fathers and their companions to come and join 'our happy band'. Fifty years later, a Jubilee Ode was officially adopted by the movement. Called 'The Might of the Child', its middle verse proclaimed:

> While the wise and mighty are planning
> Evil and Good to unite
> The youth of the nation is learning
> that Evil and Good must fight:
> The fawning and titles to Mammon
> Are things to be bought and sold,
> But the lives and souls of the children
> Are these not better than gold.[77]

The tone of this later work is much more militant than the founder's song, with the 'might' of the child replacing the gentle pleas of the 'happy band'.

The Band of Hope movement was also affected by fundamental social changes taking place in England in the late nineteenth century. A new community spirit had evolved around the non-conformist chapels and Gospel Temperance halls, especially in the northern manufacturing towns.[78] These communities gave rise to a chapel ethic that quickly permeated northern society. The ideal of a 'cheerful, happy and unambitious society' was replacing the old competitive one in which God says 'well done' to the commercially successful. Self-help was giving way to self-satisfaction, and personal ambitions were discouraged. Methodists in particular were taught not to strive after 'the brilliant, the remarkable, or the outstanding',[79] and Methodists made up the largest sect among the non-conformists of nineteenth-century England. Likewise, the children of the Band of

Hope were discouraged from aggressive individual competition. 'The undesirable element of unfriendly competition is not present. The competitors are encouraged to regard themselves as a team representing their own Society',[80] wrote the official historian of the movement in the twentieth century. The individualism of Titus Salt and other self-made men of the mid-century period was no longer to be imitated, though their personal characteristics, especially if they were teetotal, were still admired.

The new chapel-oriented society made a sharp distinction between right and wrong; no middle ground was allowed. Many such communities separated themselves into two groups, 'chapel' and 'pub', and anyone visiting a licensed premise was automatically placed in the unrespectable 'pub' category, at least by the chapel-goers. For this latter group, the religious institution became the centre and source of social as well as religious activities. Throughout the week they would attend a variety of events, many social and some educational, sponsored by their chapels. For the pub-goer, the chapel represented something else again. It was a hostile place where even moderate drinkers were condemned as sinners. In many communities, because of the rather uncompromising attitudes that developed in the final years of the century, there was little mixing between the two groups.[81]

The Band of Hope was very much affected by this division. It was firmly a part of the 'chapel' world, especially where the churches themselves sponsored their own bands. Many ministers of religion were hired as non-sectarian Band of Hope agents and they were the movement's spokesmen at conferences organised by the non-sectarian temperance organisations. There were many advantages to hiring men of the cloth, not the least of which was their established position in English society. Few questioned their respectability or their right to act as teachers and leaders of young children.

In terms of numbers, no one could deny the success of the Band of Hope. Like the rest of the temperance movement, the Band of Hope experienced great growth in the last three decades of the century. The increased support for temperance by churches and chapels of all denominations gave the children's organisation a great impetus to expand, particularly in the 1870s. During this decade the Yorkshire Union increased fourfold, and the Lancashire and Cheshire Union reported a similar growth.[82] By the end of the century the movement claimed a total of over three million members in the United Kingdom.[83]

But, though the growth of the movement was rapid and its place in respectable working-class society undisputed, not all temperance reformers were happy with its work. From the beginning doubts were expressed as to the effectiveness of the movement in spreading teetotal principles. When the children grew up they often forgot their temperance training and their pledges, and were then not only lost to the movement but harmful to it; they were living testimony to the failure of their training every time they took a drink.[84] Furthermore, as one temperance worker complained, they utilised the very weapons the movement gave them to help the enemy; the caution and self-control they learned at their Band of Hope meetings was used to make them successful moderate drinkers, which, in the eyes of many temperance reformers, was the greatest of all evils.[85]

The habits learned in youth were not necessarily continued into adulthood, contrary to the beliefs of the earlier temperance workers. Neither was the influence of the children proving effective in changing the drinking patterns of their parents. Joseph Livesey, the pioneer temperance reformer, believed the movement's priorities were all wrong, that a change in the habits of the parents was necessary before the children would learn different ways. 'Make the tree good and the fruit will be good', was the way he expressed it.[86] But many temperance leaders disagreed with Livesey, whose position reflected the older values of the movement that had prevailed when it was focused on individual character-building and self-improvement.

However, even the many former Band of Hope members who did not join the temperance movement when they became adults were not a complete loss to the movement. They could often be counted on to give support to temperance reformers when they organised mass public meetings and demonstrations. Even though they were drinkers, former teetotallers helped to make up a public opinion that insisted on the better regulation of public drinking facilities. The 'demon drink' was still the devil in the minds of many lapsed Band of Hope members.

Though there were many failures among the children of the movement, we must not ignore its successes. As we have seen, many of the children of the Band of Hope became firmly attached to teetotalism and developed such a love of the movement that it enveloped their lives. Running temperance hotels, working for temperance organisations and other drink-free activities, many former Band of Hope children were life-long teetotallers, firmly wedded to a life-style that was completely drink free.[87] They were a race uncontaminated by intoxicants and, through their living example, doctors, insurance companies, and even society in general radically changed their attitude towards the necessity of alcoholic drink for a good, healthy life.

# 7 'A Wave of Blue' – The Temperance Army

The upsurge of temperance sentiment that spread throughout the country in the last quarter of the nineteenth century made the issue of drink one that could not be ignored. The anti-drink agitations of the 1880s and 1890s deliberately fostered by many of the extreme teetotallers who wanted a clear-cut issue, led to an increasing polarisation in the attitudes of the country's population on the issue of drink: one was either for drink or against it, but not in between. Many citizens who did not want to take an extreme position found themselves regarded as defenders of the devil. 'The teetotalers have cornered the market on virtue', wrote one non-abstainer, lamenting the difficult position of the moderate drinker.[1] The Bishop of Reading's wife recognised this polarisation when she commented at a meeting: 'it is such a sad pity that the world has been divided into teetotalism and anti-teetotalism, for that is what it has come to, as if it were war to the knife' between the two.[2]

Along with this developing dichotomy between the temperance and the non-temperance world, teetotallers formed an increasingly intense attachment to the movement, which led to the development of a life-style that was completely drink-free. Apart from their work (and few abstainers were fortunate enough to get jobs in teetotal firms[3]), abstainers became increasingly isolated from the rest of the population. They began to form spiritual as well as physical temperance 'villages' in the midst of the larger urban setting, creating a drink-free world where they not only could freely practise their total abstinence principles, but where they were psychologically as well as physically 'at home'.

Personal contacts among the members were important in creating a cohesive temperance community. This was particularly true in the industrial areas where large numbers of immigrant workers had congregated, seeking jobs and opportunities that they could not find in their former life. But, though many found the economic openings they wanted, they discovered that their new situation offered only impoverished social conditions. If there was any traditional life still flourishing, they were not part of it and were regarded as intruders by the older inhabitants. Therefore, to give their lives a framework that was compatible with their temperance value system, that encompassed not only teetotalism but also 'respectability', the teetotallers found it necessary to create their own temperance communities, usually centred around a local temperance hall. Thus temperance reformers came to spend their entire lives among their fellow teetotallers, keeping their contacts with the drinking world to a minimum.

More and more temperance societies were formed to draw teetotallers of like religion, occupation and interests together. Separate associations were set up for specific occupations: doctors, laywers, postmen, commercial travellers, caterers and railway workers were among the groups with their own societies. There were organisations for every religious denomination, and societies divided by sex. The temperance reformers, as a consequence, became a very exclusive group, separating themselves from the rest of the population and eventually forming themselves into a sect. As one temperance historian wrote:

> . . . each Temperance society should be an essential part of the pattern of a family Temperance Movement. The father belongs to his Adult Society, the mother to the British Women and the children to the Band of Hope and all are insured members of a Friendly Society. A child can enter the movement at birth and can find a place in it throughout his life . . .[4]

This specialisation of temperance, however, did not mean its fragmentation. On the contrary, it had the effect of integrating teetotallers more fully into the movement. Membership in one association did not preclude joining another, so there was generally an interlocking relationship among the various temperance groups in one area. By the end of the century nearly every temperance reformer belonged to more than one anti-drink organisation, very few of which were concerned with reclaiming drunkards.

## A TOTAL TEMPERANCE COMMUNITY

For many teetotallers the ideal living conditions were those to be found in the many prohibition villages organised in the nineteenth century. These were comprised of private residential quarters built without any licensed premises. Legal contracts drawn up by the owners prevented any drink shop from being established within the boundaries. The idea grew in popularity in drink-conscious England. In 1868 the Committee on Intemperance for the Lower House of Convocation in the Province of Canterbury listed 1325 parishes, townships and hamlets in its province in which there were no licensed houses or beershops.[5] But not all the inhabitants of these areas were teetotallers and they had little or no say in their prohibition status. The majority, if not all, had drinking facilities forbidden by proprietary fiat. The inhabitants had no control over the issue; sometimes they could decide whether to live there or not, but even that was often impossible because they had no alternative accommodation.

This was true for the workers of Bessbrook, a well-known Irish prohibition village owned by a Quaker linen manufacturer, J. G. Richardson, who believed 'intoxicating drink was the cause of serious injury in his mills'.[6] It was a company town for the workers in Richardson's mills. Built in 1857, it soon had a population of 10 000.[7] Work was found within the community for all those inhabitants who needed it, and all the children had to go to a 'national' school set up by the owner. Parents paid one penny a week for the school whether they sent their children there or not, so there was a good incentive to comply with the owner's rule.[8] Because the town was geographically isolated, with no place nearby where its inhabitants could easily get drink, it was very much a teetotal area.

Quite different was a company town built in the West Riding of Yorkshire by Titus Salt, also a textile manufacturer. Saltaire, as this drink-free area was called, was close to the temperance strongholds of Leeds and Bradford. Here 700 houses were erected in which 3000 persons dwelt. Not all Salt's workpeople had to live in this teetotal village; many preferred to reside in a more normal situation and so lived in the surrounding areas.[9] By the rule laid down by Salt, no licensed premises could be opened within the boundaries of the village, but, as the village was small and was in the middle of an urban area, the effectiveness of the anti-drink measures was nullified somewhat by the appearance of many licensed premises on the edge of Saltaire. No inhabitant of this estate was more than a short walk away from a public drinking place.[10]

There was a similar situation in Liverpool. The area called

Toxteth Park was said to be the largest prohibition area in England, with a population of 50 000, none living more than a few steps from a neighbouring drinking place. The population of the estate was drawn mostly from the artisan class and the motive for prohibition was not so much the love of temperance as the commercial benefits that accrued from the absence of drinking establishments.[11] Teetotallers boasted, as with other estates also, that most rents were promptly paid and that very few of the estate shops were ever vacated or re-let, thus indicating to a limited extent the prosperity and stability of the area.[12] But, as one student of prohibition pointed out, the people who chose to live in such areas were generally sober citizens to start with and were happy to have their own streets unencumbered with public drinking houses while having some conveniently close at hand. Many Toxteth Park residents were not teetotallers and used the neighbouring licensed premises.[13]

Unfortunately for them, the majority of teetotallers did not have the option of living in a drink-free area. Instead, they had to create their own teetotal environment with the temperance hall as the prime focus of their lives. In the early days of the temperance movement, in the 1830s, a number of temperance halls had been opened up and down the country. When Bradford built the first temperance hall, costing £1400 in 1838, a wave of hall-buying was set off that left many temperance societies with costly establishments to support, and was the cause, according to one veteran teetotaller, of an indebtedness that led to the early demise of many a temperance society.[14] Some communities were lucky enough to have a wealthy sympathiser or member who bought a hall and gave it to the local temperance society, as happened at Leighton Buzzard.[15] But usually the money had to be raised through the selling of shares for one pound each to anyone willing to buy them, and very few temperance halls in the nineteenth century were without substantial mortgages. Money for these mortgages was often borrowed from local philanthropists: for example, John Priestman, a Bradford Quaker, lent the money for the Bradford Working Men's Hall.[16] Many of the early temperance halls came to be used for other purposes during the decline of interest in temperance in the late 1840s and 1850s. Some were rented out to businesses or societies that had no connection whatever with the temperance movement,[17] while others passed completely into non-temperance hands.

Of course not all societies in the first decades of the temperance reformation had the money or the desire to own or lease a large building that would require a great deal of care and attention.[18] Many local societies were content to continue using public rooms and schoolrooms for their activities.[19] Temperance societies in Halifax, Batley and Birstall were in this category and, until the revival of temperance activity in the last decades of the century, were happy not to have any such encumbrance as a hall. This attitude changed with the arrival in the 1870s of Gospel Temperance with its new attention to regular meetings, as much religious as temperance in character.[20]

Changing patterns of housing throughout the century also affected temperance halls. In Leeds the local temperance society bought a stone chapel in 1857 for use as a temperance hall. By the end of the century, however, abstainers found that the area around the hall had deteriorated so much that many of them did not like to visit it at night.[21] Furthermore, because in the later part of the century many members of the movement were much more affluent and living in more desirable areas than the earlier teetotallers (or than they themselves had been earlier), their homes in many cases were far from the old hall. Consequently, attendance at activities held in the temperance hall in Leeds was small,[22] and the Leeds reformers had to utilise other facilities if they wanted to attract a larger audience.

In the sister town of Bradford, the old temperance hall was still in a central location but for many years was not identified with the movement.[23] The Bradford Temperance Society actually rented rooms in another part of the town for their meetings; they could not afford to use the hall.[24] With the coming of Gospel Temperance and the renewed interest in anti-drink activities, the hall was drawn back into the centre of the temperance movement. To reflect its new-found importance, over £1200, almost as much as it originally cost, was spent on renovations and structural alterations. After the changes were completed there were opening ceremonies comparable to those held when it was first built.[25] A second temperance hall was bought by the Bradford Workingmen's Teetotal Association and thus the town had the honour of having two permanent temperance halls.[26]

The reformers in Huddersfield, after struggling to raise money for a hall in the early days, were successful in the 1870s. But it was not long before the Huddersfield teetotallers could not afford to use the building, which was let out to non-temperance users while the reformers acquired rooms elsewhere.[27] Nearby Keighley acquired an old Independent chapel, which had been a Mechanics Institute,[28] and close by the Skipton Temperance Society started a building fund to raise the money for a hall.[29]

It was rare to find a town in the West Riding and some parts of Lancashire that did not have its own temperance hall. Most of these buildings were solidly but plainly built, architecturally very similar to the Methodist chapels, being erected at the same time and in the same areas. Often financed by local people who wanted the most building for the least amount of money and insisted on a functional design, with beauty of little concern, their structures were solid and durable. The interior usually consisted simply of a large hall, with a balcony where there was enough money to pay for one; in some cases wealthy patrons would help pay for stained glass windows or other luxuries.[30] Occasionally a suitable building in the town that the reformers could buy became vacant. Thus in the 1870s the Dewsbury Temperance Society bought an old warehouse, which served them well for many decades.[31]

These temperance halls usually became the social centres, as well as the anti-drink headquarters, of the local teetotal communities. This was particularly true in the small towns of the North, where there were very few public places of amusement independent of the drink trade. During the latter part of the nineteenth century, many non-conformist chapels as well as temperance halls were built in the mushrooming industrial towns, and both served the social as well as the religious needs of their members. In the eyes of the strict, narrow-minded non-conformist world of the time, the 'respectable' did not visit public houses.[32]

## THE BIRSTALL TEMPERANCE COMMUNITY[33]

One typical example of a small industrial community where the temperance hall was the centre of a highly integrated temperance sect was Birstall, a small woollen town in the West Riding of Yorkshire. The Birstall Temperance Society first met in the local schoolrooms. The schoolmaster was an enthusiastic member of the society and so there was no problem with the use of his school. However, in 1872 he resigned and went to Manchester to work for a teetotal organisation, and his successor being no temperance supporter, the society found itself homeless in a village with no public buildings. Consequently, the teetotallers had to build their own hall. Starting very modestly, they bought 840 square yards of land for the sum of £175. To build their first structure – a one-room hall 9 yards by 6 yards – they used only volunteer labour.[34] The hall's trustees were men of humble background; in contrast to some of the other towns of the West Riding and elsewhere, there was no separation between the temperance society and the temperance hall. The Birstall Temperance Society owned the hall and controlled it.

From the moment it was raised, the structure proved to be inadequate for the needs of the society, and in the following year the hall was lengthened and improvements were made. But the Birstall Temperance Society continued to expand; as the hall attracted more attention and activities, so did its membership increase. By 1882 it was again decided that the hall was not large enough for the needs of the temperance community and so another hall was built on the original site, at a cost of £800. This hall served the Birstall teetotallers for two decades, until replaced by an even bigger building.[35]

Although comparatively large sums were spent on these buildings, the Birstall Temperance Society did not go into crippling debt to pay them, as so many other societies had done.[36] Because theirs was the only public hall in the village, the teetotallers were able to rent out their hall, to both temperance and non-temperance groups. The County Council was a steady client, paying five shillings a week for the regular use of the hall for its weights and measures department. Another weekly user was the Rechabites, who paid two pounds a year for their meetings. A local debating team also rented space for its activities.[37]

The acquisition of the hall wrought great changes within the Birstall Temperance Society and, even though there were some debts and continuing financial obligations from such ownership, there was never a thought that the hall was anything but an important asset to the teetotal community. Within a few months such worthies as Thomas Whittaker, Dr F. R. Lees, W. B. Affleck and William Gregson, all well-known temperance figures, gave lectures in the new building.[38] The Birstall teetotal calendar was based on events held at the hall and it became an increasingly important centre for many of its members. Much of their free time was spent within its walls on organised or unorganised activities.

Monday afternoons there was a 'Bright Hour' for the women; on Wednesdays the Band of Hope met at 7.30 and at 8.30; when the juveniles had finished, the Temperance Society held its committee meetings.[39] Sometimes the choir practised three times a week, held concerts on Saturdays and sang at the Sunday meetings.[40] Birstall had few commercial recreational facilities and so the people had to make their own entertainment. Amateur concerts, at which local talent was encouraged, were very popular, as well as cheap to produce. Sunday afternoons the men had a PSA meeting[41] at the hall; the Sunday evening meetings, with hymn-singing and temperance lectures, were open to anyone who wished to attend.

Along with these regular events, the temperance community planned and looked forward to many special events during the year. The annual meeting of the Birstall Temperance Society was the occasion for a great celebration lasting the whole weekend. Central to this weekend was the business meeting, when the financial report of the society was read and discussed. After the business meeting there was a tea. Concerts and temperance lectures filled the rest of the weekend.[42]

Every March the Band of Hope Union held their weekend celebration, which provided entertainment and education not only for the children of the union but for their families as well. Outsiders were welcome so they could see the work of this movement. The Saturdays of the Band of Hope weekend were devoted to recreational activities, while the Sundays were reserved for more serious matters; talks were given by invited speakers on topics concerning both temperance and children. Children often attended, but the speeches were aimed at their parents and much self-control had to be exercised by the children in sitting through the proceedings.[43]

A temperance event of great popularity in Birstall was the joint picnic held every summer by the member societies of the Heavy Woollen District Temperance Union. A popular park or picnic area was chosen, where the children could romp while their parents socialised with other teetotallers. Singing *The Messiah* was a traditional event at these picnics and was done as much for the pleasure of the singers as for that of the audience.[44] The emphasis of this outing was on recreation and fellowship.

Nevertheless, these joint meetings of the district temperance societies were more than pleasant gatherings; they were an integral part of the fabric that united the members. They were the means for bringing teetotal families of the district together and were instrumental in promoting alliances and marriages among them. Knowledge of jobs, births, weddings and many other developments in the temperance world gave the reformers a sense of community and also prevented the isolation of the individual temperance organisations. Through these intersociety events, teetotallers learned to identify fellow abstainers in the neighbouring towns and villages.

One of the major problems for the local temperance societies was to reach and to maintain a balance between their parochial interests and their wider temperance associations. Particularly in such small towns and villages as Birstall, where the teetotallers were committed to building up a community that would be able to take care of the wants of its members, did local conditions and needs predominate. Even so, the teetotallers recognised that they also belonged to a larger temperance world that was important in providing them with intellectual sustenance as well as in preventing them from becoming completely parochial. Here speakers and agents of the national societies played an important role in keeping in touch with the local societies and bringing them news of national developments in the movement. The northern-based British Temperance League sent speakers and agents all over the country to give public lectures and sell subscriptions to the league and its publications. The Band of Hope Union hired agents who performed the same functions for the juvenile group. Birstall was fortunate in that the local United Kingdom Alliance agent was resident in nearby Bradford and willing to come to their village periodically to talk on political developments that affected teetotallers.[45] This agent also helped organise demonstrations and petitions in the area, working through existing temperance organisations to get support for political action against the drink trade. In 1882 the Birstall Temperance Society formally affiliated with the United Kingdom Alliance and began to pay it an annual fee. Many individual members of the Birstall Temperance Community were also members of other temperance social and fraternal orders and friendly societies.

Associations with outside bodies were also reinforced through the temperance journals which were read by teetotallers all over the country. The Birstall teetotallers did not publish any journal of their own, nor did they buy a journal from a printer and have their name put on the masthead, as did the temperance society in Keighley, a neighbouring town.[46] The most popular journal in the north was the *British Temperance Advocate*, a monthly publication of the British Temperance League. In the south the *Weekly Record* predominated. It was the organ of the National Temperance League, having been acquired by the league from a private temperance publisher in 1864.[47] News of local communities played a prominent part in these journals, particularly in the *Advocate* which was less establishment oriented than its southern counterpart. Another popular temperance journal sold throughout the British Isles was the *Alliance News*, published by the United Kingdom Alliance. In its early decades this journal was mostly concerned with the prohibition movement but later in the century, when it was trying to act as a spokesman for the whole temperance movement,[48] it became a family journal, emphasising what was going on in the local communities and publishing articles that would appeal to its modestly educated readers.[49] Thus it became less of a political journal and more a family paper.

As we have already seen,[50] the Band of Hope also published children's magazines and journals that were circulated all over the country, wherever teetotal families were to be found. The most famous were *Onward*, published by the Lancashire and Cheshire Band of Hope Union, which had its headquarters at Manchester, and the *Band of Hope Review*, sponsored by the United Kingdom Band of Hope Union centred in London. Many copies of *Onward* doubtless circulated amongst the Birstall teetotallers; copies of the *Review* probably also found their way to the Yorkshire village.

When the Gospel Temperance movement appeared in England, Birstall was strongly influenced by the new trends it introduced. Not only did it cause the membership to increase very rapidly, many inhabitants of the village being influenced to join by the exhortations of Gospel Temperance speakers in the village square,[51] but it caused the Birstall Temperance Society to take a new direction, one that would have great consequences for the future of the society. Gospel Temperance missions were held in the hall at irregular times, sometimes led by a visiting missionary and sometimes by a local enthusiast.[52] In 1890, influenced by this new 'wave of blue', a Sunday School was inaugurated at the local temperance hall. It was felt that a more careful training of the children in temperance ways than they were receiving in the Band of Hope recreational meetings was needed. Sunday School was to be an educational and religious institution where the children would be taught the principles of evangelical religion mixed with the teachings of teetotalism.[53] In neighbouring Wyke the local temperance hall had started a Sunday School because the children at the existing church-connected Sunday School were given alcoholic drink on their outings.[54]

Very soon the teetotallers decided to hold a permanent Gospel Temperance mission in their hall, to which they could come every Sunday for regular services. The Birstall teetotallers who wanted a closer identification with the temperance community allowed their connection with other churches and chapels to lapse and thus broke the last major non-economic tie they had with the non-temperance world. Some members of the Birstall Temperance Society were not willing to commit themselves so fully to the movement. They retained their affiliation with their own churches but sought their temperance activities elsewhere. Most of the local chapels had their own Bands of Hope and some even had their own temperance societies. Although there was no official policy in the Birstall society to force members to renounce outside ties, the informal pressures to do so were often very strong.

There was some criticism from other local temperance societies over this change at Birstall.[55] Not all teetotallers were happy to have the temperance movement become a sect. The idea of becoming a mission hall as well as a temperance centre was raised in neighbouring Batley's temperance society but was rejected. Too many of the Batley teetotallers were happy with their existing temperance affiliation. Unlike Birstall, where the parish church had traditionally been antagonistic towards the teetotallers, [56] Batley had a vicar who was a good supporter of the temperance movement and very helpful to the local teetotal communities.[57]

For the teetotallers in Birstall who supported the change there were many benefits from the new situation. Most of all, their loyalties were no longer divided and the temperance hall became the one centre of their lives. Realising that the existing hall would soon be inadequate for the new needs of the society, the Birstall reformers started a building fund in 1893. Both temperance and non-temperance sympathisers proved to be very generous and by 1902 it was possible to build a new temperance hall on the same site. This, the third temperance hall for Birstall, had a large major hall, a smaller minor hall and a spacious balcony. The handsome edifice and its allied expenses cost the society £2500.[58] The opening of the new hall was the occasion of a great celebration for the Birstall teetotallers and Mrs Harrison Lee Cowie, 'Australia's Temperance Queen', was engaged for the opening ceremonies.[59]

The PSAs continued in the new centre and were a very important part of temperance activities. Supplementing the Sunday morning services, the PSA-sponsored temperance talks and discussions that stressed the evils, both material and spiritual, that sprang from drinking. The children in their Band of Hope were taught to sing prohibition songs. Music continued to be a significant part of the temperance society's activities and by the time the new hall was built the society had bought an organ and hired an organist to play it. The choir also continued to flourish under the leadership of a paid, part-time leader, giving concerts at every opportunity. As the amount of leisure time of the membership increased, so did the need for recreational activities. Part of this need was fulfilled by amateur concerts and lantern lectures held in the hall. Competitions were organised with the choirs of neighbouring temperance societies and a rose bowl was donated as a trophy to be competed for every year.[60]

However, the true strength of the Birstall Temperance Society lay not so much in its timetable of activities as in the quality of its membership. Many individuals and families, ordinary members and leaders, worked hard and faithfully for the society. Such fidelity was encouraged by the internal status structure of the society, which gave prestige and responsibility to many talented men and women who otherwise would have had little chance to exercise their organisational and leadership skills. Within the society, poorly educated working-class teetotallers were as active as the more prosperous members, and loyalty to the temperance community was often retained even when material success had raised the teetotaller out of his original class. James I. Nussey, for example, was a powerloom weaver of humble circumstances when he first joined the temperance society, but became a wealthy factory owner and a Justice of the Peace in the neighbourhood.[61] Throughout his life he maintained a close connection with the temperance community and served as president of the society for over twenty years. When he died in 1914, he left £100 annually for the support of a temperance missionary at Birstall.[62] Nussey also joined the teetotal friendly society when he was in humble circumstances and when he made his fortune he generously gave this society a house so they would have their own meeting-place.[63]

William Mann and David Spivey were also pillars of the
Birstall Temperance Society. Mann was secretary of the
organisation for thirty years and Spivey a member for fifty,
seventeen of which were spent as choirmaster. When Spivey died,
one of his sons succeeded him as choirmaster, while another son
became the organist.[64] The stability of the society was assured by
the many sons and daughters who succeeded their parents. (Even
in the 1970s, there were members of the Birstall Temperance
Society whose parents and grandparents had been active in the
same society in the late nineteenth century, almost 100 years
ago.)[65]

Although most of the members were as loyal to the society as
Nussey, few were as financially successful. In fact, the majority
were of steady but modest means and could not support their
temperance activities without outside help. The continued
generosity of individual members were not enough. Support also
came from manufacturers and tradesmen who were not
necessarily themselves teetotallers. George Hirst, a mayor of
Batley and a prominent manufacturer in the Spen Valley, was a
firm supporter of the temperance movement in his area. Frank
Crosfield, a Leeds schoolmaster, was a trustee of the Birstall
Temperance Hall and took a personal interest in the progress of
the teetotallers there.[66] In 1882, when the Birstall Temperance
Society was raising money for a new hall, F. R. Priestman, a
well-known Bradford philanthropist, gave handsomely to the
building fund.[67] There were other factory owners and men of
commerce who gave liberally to the temperance movement, as
they did to other causes.

Further down the economic and social scale, and more locally
based, many Birstall tradesmen gave financial support to
temperance causes. Some of these gifts were prompted by the
publication of lists of contributions to the local society, but many
were gratuitous acts of support for the temperance movement in
the village.[68] The teetotallers were valuable customers, thrifty and
reliable, who generally paid their bills on time; their life-style
emphasised the importance of financial responsibility.

By the end of the century the Birstall organisation, like many
other temperance societies, had begun to hire professional help for
many of its activities. Besides a paid organist and choirmaster, a
missionary was engaged. The first of these workers was a woman,

hired in 1893 to work among the women and children of the temperance community.[69] Then, after a succession of male missionaries who lasted from one to two years each, the society hired a Salvation Army Captain who had been on the staff of the Leeds City Mission for over twenty years. He stayed as the Birstall missionary for eighteen years,[70] running the services at the Temperance Hall and organising outdoor meetings using the talents of the members. There was little house-to-house visitation of non-temperance families. In fact, there was little contact between the temperance and the non-temperance parts of the village. Though relations between the teetotallers and the rest of Birstall were generally cordial, they were not close. Two separate worlds existed for the Birstall teetotallers by the end of the century; the teetotal world centred around the Temperance Hall, and a non-temperance world that was little known to the young teetotallers.[71] Whole families, including children from birth, were members of the teetotal community; from the age of six all could be fully enrolled by signing the pledge.[72]

Some of the cohesion of the Birstall teetotallers was due to the fact that there were no branches there of either the Independent Order of Good Templars or the British Women's Temperance Association. Both these organisations were highly controversial.[73] Although their difficulties were not the reason that they did not have branches in Birstall, their absence prevented the formation of factions among the village teetotallers over the disputes that surrounded them. Nearby Batley had branches of both the Good Templars and the British Women (as they were often called), so that, if any Birstall teetotaller wanted to join either of these groups, they were not far away.

## AGENTS AND SOCIETIES

It was not only in Birstall that volunteer labour was replaced by professional efforts. As institutionalisation of the movement increased, with more and more societies created to cater to every type of anti-drink supporter, a class of paid professional workers developed. From its beginnings, the temperance movement had relied on agents, both paid and unpaid, to carry the message of the reformation to all parts of England. But in the early days of teetotalism, when the movement was not so completely organised, the majority of teetotal advocates were unattached to any organisation and worked completely on their own.[74] As the movement progressed and settled down to a long, protracted fight against entrenched drinking customs, the groups that employed agents tried to set some standards for these agents' work. But the movement continued to suffer from the circulation of stories about the exploits of self-proclaimed temperance advocates.[75] Setting professional standards acceptable to all temperance organisations was an issue throughout the nineteenth century.

Calling oneself a temperance agent signified very little unless one had some connection with a temperance society or similar organisation. There were various types of agencies in the temperance movement but the most prestigious were those representing the national societies, especially the Lancashire-based and northern-supported British Temperance League and the London-centred and more establishment-oriented National Temperance League, which were the two temperance organisations best known for their aggressive missionary work. Other specialised groups such as the Band of Hope (children) and the United Kingdom Alliance (political) also employed agents to further their goals. One of the great advantages in working for a national society was the security of tenure. Hired by the central office, most of the agents of such a group as the British Temperance League retained their positions until they retired through ill-health or died in harness.[76]

In the days before the great upsurge of Gospel Temperance, the number of full-time agents employed by temperance organisations was not large. In 1863 the British Temperance League, which was known for its large and active staff, had only seven full-time agents in its service,[77] but, because they were hired out to different temperance groups throughout the country, the effect of their work was felt by many geographically diverse groups. All British Temperance League agents had to be willing to travel anywhere in England. This was a hardship for those with families as it usually meant that they would be away for months at a time, specially if they were from the north and working in such faraway places as Cornwall and Devon. Sometimes they had to travel on foot from Lancashire to all parts of the country, holding meetings on the way. No British Temperance League agent lived anywhere but in the north of England but they had to be willing to work anywhere.[78]

This northern-based organisation did not set up auxiliaries but instead tried to establish local groups operated and controlled by local teetotallers.[79] It did try to get these groups, once organised, to affiliate with the league, an act which committed both sides to very little. Affiliates paid a small fee and were given the right to have the services of agents at reduced rates. The agents of the British Temperance League, like agents employed by other societies and missions, did not generally make large salaries: twenty to thirty shillings a week was the average pay in the 1860s and 1870s.[80] It was the wage of a workman, which was what many of them were.

One of the most important jobs of the agents was to help the small local groups, which were not able to support themselves on their own, to form unions. Large city groups could hire expensive orators to activate local sentiment, but the small societies could only pay fees by pooling their resources. Speakers' plans were drawn up so that lecturers could be exchanged between members of a union and thus allow new ideas and talent to be infused into the smaller local societies.[81] An active union could keep temperance sentiment strong over a wide area, inspiring a new spirit of dedication among the more committed teetotallers after the initial excitement generated by an agent's visit had subsided. The unions were usually one of two types. The first was a union of societies of a similar interest, often spread over a large geographical area. For example, many local Bands of Hope were established independently. Eventually, Band of Hope Unions were formed at different levels of the movement: first, there was the local union, limited usually to the many Bands of Hope in the town and district; then came the county union, joining the unions of the different towns; and finally, at the top, the national group joining all the county unions. The second type of union was one in which the geographical location of the members was the determining feature. Such unions were often formed in an active temperance town and included all the anti-drink organisations of that town that wanted to join, such as the town temperance societies, local Bands of Hope, Church of England Temperance

Societies, temperance friendly societies, and so on. Bradford, Leeds and Halifax, for example, all at one time or another had their temperance societies united in a union.

One rung below the agents of the national societies in prestige were the town agents, especially those employed by the large, active organisations that some towns maintained. Some agents preferred working for a town organisation rather than a national one, as a town agent did not have to leave his family for protracted periods. The work of these town agents usually fell into a standard pattern: giving lectures, collecting subscriptions, visiting families that needed help, and seeing that the movement was kept alive in the town.[82] Sometimes an agent (or missionary as some were called) was paid by an individual reformer. Members of the Society of Friends, for instance, often undertook responsibility for the support of the local temperance agent. More frequently, however, the agent himself was expected to collect at least enough money through subscriptions and donations to pay for his own support.[83]

The quantity and quality of the activities of the local temperance society were largely dependent on the ability and enthusiasm of the agent. One good man could galvanise a sluggish temperance society into action.[84] He could plan parades and galas, and make home visits either to try to acquire new members or to raise the spirits of those already committed to the cause. Active agents were also regarded as the official representatives of the temperance movement in the area, especially if the local societies were themselves not very active. Getting the right man for the job was the greatest problem for a town society. It was much harder to find a suitable agent than it was to raise the money for his support.[85]

As indicated above, the town agents could stay closer to their families than the national agents; but there were also disadvantages in being employed by a town society. There was no security of tenure for town agents; they rarely stayed in one position for any great length of time. The successful ones went into a national society or a regional group, while the unsuccessful were dismissed. When the movement in a town was in one of its periodic spells of decline, as so often happened, the town agent was immediately dismissed. Rarely did town societies seek alternative work to tide their employees over the slack period, as did the national groups.[86]

At the bottom of the scale of temperance agents were the uneducated, 'self-employed', itinerant advocates, who took up the banner of temperance on their own initiative. Completely dependent on their own talents and energies for their livelihood, they travelled around the country on their own, living on the money they collected from whatever audience they could attract. Sometimes one was hired for a limited period by individuals or societies to do a particular job,[87] but when the job ended, he had to find something else. At best it was a precarious way to live; at worst they and their families starved.[88] A very few built up a national reputation, enabling them to secure a comfortable standard of living.[89] Such support, however, was not easily gained and the majority of self-employed advocates aspired to permanent positions in a temperance organisation.

Among those temperance advocates who could be counted among the most successful were men such as James Gough (1817–86). Born in England, he emigrated at an early age to the United States, where he eventually became a drunkard. He worked for a time as an actor, and his training in that profession was to stand him in good stead in his later years as a temperance orator. Eventually, after a long period of insolvency due to his intemperance, Gough joined the temperance movement and applied his acting talents to the temperance platform. He became the best-known orator on temperance in both England and America. Altogether he made three tours of England, in 1853, 1857 and 1878. These tours provided him with large sums of money. His fee for one lecture was twelve guineas,[90] a large amount but one which temperance societies were willing to pay because they were assured by his presence of a large audience prepared to pay a substantial admission fee.[91]

To help less successful independent temperance agents and to show appreciation for their work, benefits were held in temperance halls up and down the country. But so numerous did these become that there were complaints within the movement about them; members of the temperance community were pressured into giving money even if they did not know the man for whom the benefit was held.[92] Sometimes the sums raised were paltry, but it was not uncommon for substantial amounts to be collected. One such benefit, held for Dr Frederic Lees in the Leeds town hall, raised 1000 guineas;[93] another for James Teare produced a total of £788.[94] But most of these benefits occurred in the earlier days of the teetotal movement, when independent agents were more numerous and had an acknowledged role in spreading the principles of the movement. Later, when the movement did most of its work through organised groups, a tighter control was kept on the activities of individual advocates who claimed official status.

By the end of the 1870s the temperance societies in England employed 150 full-time workers.[95] Twenty years later, at the end of the century, the number had increased to more than 400.[96] They were a highly-trained group of professionals, whose whole world was the movement and who organised their own professional groups. There was a National Association of Official Temperance Advocates and an association for Band of Hope workers.[97] The London-based National Temperance League promoted these groups, recognising that the free exchange of ideas and experiences was advantageous both to the individual agents and to the movement as a whole.[98] The North of England Temperance League set up its own Northern Association of Temperance Advocates, 'to promote mutual help between Secretaries and Agents of the various temperance organisations in the North'.[99]

## BENEFIT SOCIETIES AND FRATERNAL ORDERS

In the mid-nineteenth century many English working men were joining together to form friendly societies, especially in the northern industrial towns of England.[100] Those associations had two basic functions that grew out of the needs and desires of immigrant working men trying to adapt themselves to the new life in an industrial society. The first was to provide an opportunity for building social relationships with others of the area in similar circumstances; and the second was to extend help in times of need (sickness and death) by providing sickness and burial benefits to its members, since at this time the state offered no help in these matters. These friendly societies were another example of the self-help institutions the workers organised themselves, learning by trial and error. Unfortunately for teetotal working men, all the social and business activities of these societies centred around drinking houses: meetings were held on licensed premises, with the rent for the meeting room assessed in drinks to be bought during meetings, or 'wet rent'.

In 1835 a group of teetotallers got together to establish a new type of friendly society that was to be drink free.[101] They felt that social intercourse could be enjoyed without alcoholic beverages. This society also hoped to be more stable financially, because its assets would not be wasted on drink, the greatest cause of insolvency among friendly societies.[102] They took the name of an abstaining group mentioned in the Bible and, following the form of the non-temperance societies, called themselves the Independent Order of the Rechabites. Their local branches were called tents and the members of each tent had to be pledged abstainers. The Rechabites did not attempt to diverge from the practices of the other friendly societies except in the matter of drink, and each week contributed sums of money to sickness and funeral funds to be withdrawn in times of need. They utilised the techniques of the drinking societies as long as they were consistent with their teetotalism. They had secret passwords, regalia and social activities. But, as the regular friendly societies discovered when the government forced them to decrease their drinking,[103] meetings of men without alcoholic beverages and without other purposes were not very stimulating or convivial: 'The societies grew rather into mutual insurance societies; the main business of club night became the collection of contributions.'[104]

Paralleling the experiences of many other working-class organisations, the first years of the Rechabites were marked by instability. The early tents were composed of reformed drunkards, whose reformation was not always complete. There were so many relapses that in its early years the order became notorious for the number of broken pledges among its membership, which caused the breakup of numerous tents.[105] Starting in 1835 with forty-five members, the Rechabites by 1844 had 28 000 adult and 1323 juvenile members, but this was the high point of the early movement; from then on the numbers fell. By 1857 the order, like the rest of the temperance movement, was in a state of decline and could count fewer than 6000 members.[106]

Besides a high rate of pledge-breaking, the Rechabites in their first decade were troubled by a proliferation of local and regional teetotal benefit societies all calling themselves 'Rechabites'. Once the idea of a teetotal friendly society was conceived and implemented by one group, others rushed to imitate them. As a result, there were many orders of the Rechabites and there were fights in temperance circles and outside as to which was the 'real' Rechabite organisation.[107] This situation was finally brought under control with the passing of the Friendly Societies Act of 1855. By this act all friendly societies had to register with the government and comply with strict legal regulations. As a result many of the small local groups joined with large ones, and eventually one, the Salford Unity, emerged as the largest and most important Rechabite organisation in England.[108] Even so, other Rechabite groups persisted, and one Order of the Rechabites, with headquarters at Bath, had over 1000 members in the 1880s.[109]

Paralleling trends in the rest of the temperance movement, a new spirit infused the teetotal benefit society in the late 1860s, leading the board of directors of the Salford Unity to launch a membership drive.[110] This started the Rechabites on an upward path that continued for the rest of the century and on into the next. By 1885 the Salford Unity had 59 097 members; by 1897 this figure had more than doubled to a total of 142 395.[111] Rechabite principles were attracting more and more working-class people – and their money – and by the end of the century the order claimed a capital of £1 million.[112]

The revived order, however, had a different reputation from the original one. No longer were Rechabites known as pledge-breakers; instead, they boasted of their loyalty to teetotal principles. In 1882 they claimed that only 1 per cent of their members had broken the pledge, which was, as they pointed out, a much lower proportion than for the rest of the movement.[113] Much of this change was the result of the different type of members the later order attracted. Reformed drunkards, who had made up a large part of the early order, were generally unstable individuals, as reflected in the rise and fall of so many tents. For these first Rechabites, teetotalism was what they aspired to, not what they had attained. In contrast, most of the later Rechabites were already fully committed to the temperance movement before they joined the benefit society. They were also more firmly rooted in their communities than were the workers of the early period, who were mostly recent immigrants to the towns. By the end of the century, being a Rechabite was part of being a teetotaller – in many teetotal families it was assumed that all would belong to this temperance organisation.[114] Like the rest of the temperance movement, the Rechabites of the late nineteenth century came from a segment of the population that had never drunk anything alcoholic in their lives, or not without pangs of guilt.

Undoubtedly much of the Rechabites' rising popularity was related to the changes occurring within the working class during these decades. In the early years of the century it was common practice for workers to wander around the country seeking work. Stopping when they found it, they stayed only as long as the work lasted. Then they moved on. Later, however, when industrial conditions demanded a reliable labour force, large numbers of workers were established in one place. They were no longer immigrants to the towns but settled members of a community, willing and able to form lasting associations with other members of that community. With this fixed way of life came a desire to plan for the future. It was a common belief among ambitious men of the nineteenth century that they could control their own destiny if they adhered to certain principles: hard work, ambition and thrift were the keys to success. Savings banks, building societies and provident societies sprang up in the second half of the century as embodiments of thrift and the Rechabites were the teetotal manifestation of this working-class thrift. By putting aside small sums of money every week, members were preparing for eventualities in the future; everyone died and needed a funeral and most people at some time or other fell sick. Furthermore, the attractiveness of the Rechabites increased when the 1857 Friendly Societies Act was passed. This legal control increased the stability of societies and protected their funds, a not inconsequential matter in a period when many working-class organisations were bankrupted by mismanagement or by outright theft.[115]

If we examine the rise and development of one Rechabite tent in a small industrial town in the West Riding of Yorkshire, we will see what was occurring in many other areas as well. Founded in 1868, by 1878 it had seventy-two members: fifty-nine men, four women and nine juveniles. By 1893 this number had grown to 216 members with an average age of 32.4 years, and the society was an important part of the local temperance community. The average age was greatly lowered by the inclusion of juveniles in the society, but, aside from this, it was a very young group and could not have retained very many of its original members of twenty-five years previously. This tent, like the other tents of the order, had experienced a revival in the last years of the century and, in a fifteen-year period, had tripled its membership.[116]

Besides the Rechabites, there were other teetotal benefit societies in England. The largest of these was the Sons of Temperance, originally started in the United States and brought to England in 1846. In 1879 it had 15 000 members and by 1905[117] that number had risen to 105 000.[118] Open to men, women and children, it collected a small sum from each member for sickness and funeral benefits at monthly meetings. Another teetotal benefit society, the United Order of the Total Abstaining Sons of the Phoenix, was founded in 1862 and mostly confined to London. It was similar to the other teetotal benefit societies, with the added distinction of supporting its own orphanage.[119]

Fraternal societies, unlike friendly societies, were mainly concerned with the social life of their members. They appeared on the temperance scene much later than the benefit societies, having no part in the early movement. The most popular of these orders for teetotallers was the Independent Order of the Good Templars. The Good Templars, as they were sometimes called, was an American organisation brought to England in 1868. From the beginning there was controversy surrounding the establishment of this order, and it was not received with open arms by all parts of the temperance movement.[120] There were many complaints, both in temperance circles and out, about its use of religious forms and appurtenances for its own purposes.[121] Although such a group would not have disturbed many temperance reformers in the early days, in the 1870s, when the movement was very concerned with having a 'respectable' image, it was viewed with suspicion. The rituals of the Good Templars offended some people, including Quakers, who refused to have anything to do with them.[122] Charles Garrett, the well-known teetotal Methodist leader, was a prominent member of the order until he resigned because of the 'ritual, regalia, titles and degrees'.[123]

Originally the Good Templars included a large number of reformed drunkards, but later they were only rarely to be found in its ranks. Like the rest of the temperance movement, the Good Templars became less concerned with rescuing the intemperate than with providing fellowship for members of the temperance community. A national officer of the order reported in 1883: 'Many who would otherwise have been brought into our ranks have been led to take the Blue Ribbon', and also that 'others when disposed to further promote temperance work have been led to do so in connection with their respective Christian churches rather than in our Order'.[124]

One topic of controversy among both outsiders and insiders of the order was the role of Joseph Malins, its English founder. He was president of the national organisation from its inception in 1868 until he retired in 1913. Some of his critics claimed he was a despotic ruler who controlled the widely spread movement through spies sent out to watch the activities of the individual temples.[125] Another criticism concerned finances. Membership in the order was not cheap. Besides a regular subscription, the individual member had to pay an initiation fee and an extra payment each time he was promoted within the order. A specified percentage of all these monies collected by the local temples was sent to the order's headquarters in Birmingham, and it was the handling of these funds that caused further criticism of Malins' rule. Although large sums of money were paid to the central offices, no comprehensive financial statement was issued.[126] It was estimated that the income of the order, excluding initiation and other fees, was between £10 000 and £20 000 per year.[127] Malins himself had an annual salary of £500, a large sum for a man who was self-educated and unable to earn a decent living outside the movement.[128]

Joseph Malins' life was the success story *par excellence* of a temperance family. Starting with a drunken father and a very poor home life, he had to emigrate to America to search for work (by trade he was a watchkey-maker), and it was while he was in the United States that he became acquainted with the Good Templars. On his return to England he started a Good Templar Lodge. After only two years he gave up his normal occupation and started to work full time for the order. Eventually he raised four sons, all of whom were well placed in the middle classes: one became a wealthy dentist, another a London University MA and headmaster of a school, a third a Methodist minister, and the fourth a sanitary engineer.[129]

The secrecy surrounding the activities of the Good Templars and their elaborate ceremonies were also responsible for a good deal of the criticism directed against them. These proceedings attracted the less educated, many of whom affected high-sounding titles and sometimes paraded their Templar status in non-Templar situations, which also caused much criticism.[130]

Regardless of all these objections, the movement proved to be a popular one among teetotallers. In 1874, only six years after it was first introduced to England, it had over 200 000 members in both senior and juvenile lodges.[131] However, two years later the order was split by what has been called the 'Negro Question'. Malins' group, which supported secession from the American mother group, claimed the Americans were not allowing Negroes in the Southern States to become full members of the order. The group that refused to secede, headed by William Hoyle and Frederic Lees, believed the issue of the Negroes was a false one and that the real reason for secession was that Malins and his followers were afraid that the American hierarchy might set up rival groups in England which would challenge the power and position of the original lodge.[132] This the Americans had the right to do. The English Grand Lodge, as the country's ruling body was called, was subordinate to the central authorities across the Atlantic, who also had the right to replace Malins himself if they so desired.

The 'loyalist' group claimed that the seceders were acting without the support of the membership, the majority of whom were unaware of the controversy until the secession had already taken place. This was also the opinion the judges handed down when the matter was later taken to court. They found that Malins 'kept the facts from the membership and the disruption was deliberately prepared, studied and brought about by him', according to his opponents.[133] Altogether 145 000 members split off and only 12 000 stayed with the original order.[134]

The issue was more than a personal one; a great deal of property and large financial holdings were involved. The smaller loyalist group went to court to prevent the Malins group from taking the assets of the original Grand Lodge for their seceded organisation. Nothing came of the case; neither side was awarded the charter which allowed the holder to claim legal authority of the order. Before the case came to court the Quakers had tried to arbitrate, but the Malins group refused to submit the dispute to arbitration.[135] The cost of the case was high, and, although the American central bureau helped to pay some of the loyalist costs, Frederick Lees, who brought the suit on behalf of the minority, used up most of his own resources in the fight.[136]

The split lasted ten years altogether, after which time the two sides were reunited. In 1886, the American headquarters sent emissaries to treat with Malins and offered terms acceptable to the seceders; the Negro question had been settled and was no longer a problem. Malins was confirmed as head of the order in England and it was agreed that his Grand Lodge would be the only one established in England.[137] Quickly the differences between the groups were covered over and the Good Templars became one. The lawsuit was allowed to lapse and the whole matter was forgotten as quickly as possible, but the settlement did credit neither to the order nor to the temperance movement as a whole, and was responsible for a decline in the membership of the Good Templars. By 1894 the Independent Order of the Good Templars in England had a total membership of only 50 000 adults and 50 000 juveniles, half of the peak figures of 1874.[138]

Many potential recruits were turned away by the Templars' extreme political stand on the subject of licensing legislation. The Good Templars saw themselves as the Israelites doing battle against the Philistine drinkers of intoxicants. Their David was the United Kingdom Alliance president, Sir Wilfrid Lawson, their Goliath the drink traffic, and the sling and stone of David were the Permissive Bills and Total Prohibition. In accordance with this biblical analogy for their anti-drink fight, the Templars reserved for themselves the role of God's 'Chosen People'.[139] Members of the order were told by their hierarchy not to vote for anyone who was not a prohibition candidate. Even if a candidate was 'of the highest character and desirable in all else' the Good Templars were not to compromise but should abstain from voting.[140] 'To vote for any candidate who will not vote for Local Option is to vote for the perpetuation of existing evils', explained their Grand Electoral Superintendent.[141] Malins himself was a leader in forming the National Temperance Federation, of which he was made secretary.[142] The Good Templar leadership was also personally involved in many of the fights over licensing and was particularly identified with the no-compensation campaigns that flourished in the 1880s and 1890s.[143]

Besides carrying on political work, the Good Templars were generous in supporting many charities. In 1881 they raised £2800 to open an orphanage and in 1885 £1000 for the Temperance Hospital in London.[144] In 1891 they held a National Bazaar which earned £500 for a temperance mission van. Also of great value to the entire temperance movement was the order's printing press at its head office in Birmingham. Many temperance books and leaflets were printed here, for the Good Templars and also for other temperance organisations.

By the end of the nineteenth century, the controversies surrounding the order had died down and the Good Templars were accepted as one more temperance social organisation, even if one a little more zealous and extremist than some teetotallers would have liked. With a total membership of 100 000 in the last decade of the century, the Independent Order of the Good Templars could claim to represent a large segment of the temperance reformation.[145]

## WOMEN'S WORK FOR TEMPERANCE

From the beginning of the temperance reformation in England, women were to be found in the ranks of its most active workers. Their contributions to the temperance cause were invaluable; Mrs Wightman,[146] Mrs Carlile[147] and Mrs Balfour[148] exemplify the many women who fought against intemperance. However, all these women worked either as individuals or as members of mixed societies; before the 1870s, female temperance organisations were not unknown, but they were the exception rather than the rule. There were many Ladies Committees attached to the male-dominated town societies; their functions were what current society accepted as purely female activities: teas, bazaars, children's work, and so on. In none of the major temperance organisations did women have important policy-making roles. It was not until the late 1860s, with the advent of the Independent Order of the Good Templars, that women were admitted to a national temperance association on an equal basis with men:[149] women Templars were eligible for election to all offices within the order. By the end of the century other groups had also admitted women to executive positions, but they were still exceptions to the general rule.

Small female temperance groups began to appear in the 1870s, when the temperance movement experienced a renewal. Most of these groups were concerned with local matters, had no connection with other women's organisations and were spontaneously organised locally by female teetotallers. The first attempt at a more than local women's organisation was the

Christian Workers Temperance Union, formed in 1875. Unfortunately for its members, it never attracted the support of more than a handful of women and disappeared after a decade of work.[150]

In 1876 the first female temperance organisation of national significance appeared. Much of the stimulation for a greater role for women in the temperance movement came from the United States, where female teetotallers had waged a 'Whisky War' with great energy. Their leader, Mrs E. D. Stewart, generally known as 'Mother' Stewart, came to England in 1876 and travelled all over the country telling of her experiences and those of her followers in this fight.[151] At the same time Mrs Margaret Parker, an active English teetotaller, visited the United States and, impressed with the public work the American women were doing, returned to England determined to organise her female compatriots in similar work.[152] A conference was called that same year to discuss the matter of women's work for the cause; Mrs Parker talked about her American trip and the work that was being done by women there. It was at this conference that the decision was taken to form the British Women's Temperance Association (usually referred to as the British Women), with Mrs Parker as its first president.[153]

Another prominent Englishwoman much influenced by the work of American women was Margaret Bright Lucas, sister of John Bright. Mrs Lucas had become an abstainer during a trip to the United States in 1870.[154] Active in the women's suffrage movement, the Women's Peace and Arbitration Society, the Women's Liberal Federation and many other women's groups, Mrs Lucas was anxious for all women to have a larger share in the running of the country. She was present at the founding conference of the British Women, and became its third president.[155] A firm member of the Society of Friends, Mrs Lucas drew many female Quakers into the British Women's Temperance Association and encouraged the association to take up work of a wider focus rather than limiting its attention to anti-drink matters.[156]

Mrs Lucas remained president of the association until her death in 1890, a tenure of thirteen years. Her successor, Lady Henry Somerset, held similar views with regard to a larger role for the British Women's Temperance Association. Prior to her work for the association, Lady Henry Somerset had made a name for herself as a social reformers of sorts. She had established her own mission hall in the town of Ledbury, to the dismay of church officials and the 'better' citizens of the area.[157] She was thus no stranger to controversy over the public role of women.

The British Women recognised that its real strength resided in local groups, which were proliferating throughout the country. These associations were set up by women whose major interest was in their own areas and not in national organisations. Therefore, to get the maximum cooperation with a minimum of interference, the association established itself as a loosely organised federation of county associations and local units. The aim was to create an interlocking network of women's temperance groups, covering the country.[158] Because of their primary attachment to their own neighbourhood, the small individual units varied according to local conditions, but on one matter they were all agreed: the basis of the movement was Christian. All meetings opened and closed with a prayer. Commenting on the reports submitted by its branches, the executive of the British Women noted with satisfaction that 'the Christian basis of the BWTA remains firm and that the ultimate aim of its work is to bring the erring ones into the safety of Christian life'.[159] Encompassing many different groups, the association would not support one denomination above the rest. Instead, it insisted that all religious activities be non-denominational, so that all Christians could belong. Many member organisations of the association sponsored Gospel Temperance missions,[160] hired the missionaries and personally helped with the work. (Some of these missions lasted for a week to ten days or even longer.) Such activities helped to combine temperance and Christian ideals and were fully acceptable in polite circles of the late nineteenth century. A number of female associations employed women to work as missionaries among the poor of the slums. Naturally female intemperance was a particular concern of the women's groups.

On the political scene, the British Women were not idle. They sponsored many memorials and petitions, particularly in support of eliminating grocers' licences. It was commonly believed by teetotallers that female drunkenness had increased owing to the sale of intoxicants by grocers, although the evidence presented by both sides was unclear and inconclusive.[161] These licences were first issued in 1861 by Gladstone as a method of reducing attendance at public houses, and in the hope that the English population would substitute the light French wines they could obtain at the grocers, which were believed to be less intoxicating, for the heavier and more potent beer that was popularly consumed.[162] Much to the consternation of the teetotallers, this method of selling intoxicants enabled women to get them with their grocery order and to disguise their purchases by having them billed as groceries.[163] Teetotallers also believed that many women who had never entered a public house or any other licensed premises had been encouraged to start drinking by the availability of alcoholic beverages at the respectable grocer's shop. To exert pressure against licensed merchants, the British Women asked its members and sympathisers to refuse to patronise any trader who had a licence.[164]

The British Women's Temperance Association grew steadily in its first years, until by 1892 it had 577 affiliated branches, with a total of 45 000 members.[165] Unions of societies as well as individual organisations could join. The Yorkshire Women's Christian Temperance Union, originally instituted at York in 1877 to draw together the women's temperance groups throughout the county, federated with the British Women's Temperance Association in 1878.[166]

Although much of the work of the association was of the usual temperance sort, some of its other activities were much more controversial. Lady Henry promoted a 'Do Everything' policy that encouraged members to be active in a wide variety of social causes, including women's suffrage.[167] Visiting the Women's Christian Temperance Union Convention in the United States in 1891, Lady Henry, like some of her predecessors, was much impressed by the wide range of work the female abstainers in America were doing, and she returned home full of enthusiasm to encourage similar work in her own association.[168] Not all the membership agreed. Lady Henry, aristocratic in outlook and holding advanced ideas on the role of women, clashed with those holding more plebeian views with the result that the association split into two camps. Her opponents wanted to limit the efforts of the association to working only and directly for temperance. In 1892 the narrower view prevailed among the executive; it voted to restrict the association to work considered suitable to temperance reformers: visiting homes to talk of teetotalism and holding drawing-room and cottage meetings for temperance talks.[169] The dissidents were also worried that the 'Do Everything' policy was attracting all kinds of strange characters to their movement, as even their president came to admit.[170] But the issue of policy was not settled so clearly. In 1893 the supporters of the president dominated the Annual Council Meeting. After a fight that lasted for twelve hours the 'Do Everything' policy was reinstated. The losers left the organisation to form their own national women's group, which was to be more closely linked with temperance.[171] The large Yorkshire Union, with its membership of 4700, severed its connection with the British Women and joined the new union.[172] The loss of such an important affiliate was a blow to the British Women.

Lady Henry continued to lead her organisation but was becoming a problem for her membership because of her views on drink. Before the Royal Commission on Licensing she claimed she was not against all drinking and saw nothing wrong in a glass of wine or in moderate drinking.[173] Such a statement from the head of an organisation that insisted that all its members be pledged teetotallers was difficult to ignore. There was mounting displeasure with Lady Henry and in 1903 she resigned the presidency.[174] This did not change the policy of the association, nor did it heal the split between the two women's organisations. It was not until the fiftieth anniversary, in 1926, of the founding of the first national women's temperance association that a merger between its two offspring was effected. They then combined names as well as membership and called themselves the National British Women's Total Abstinence Union.[175]

The women's temperance groups, like any other pioneering associations, ran up against the established social patterns of the day. Apart from a few talented and energetic females who were independent enough to fight for what they believed regardless of social consequences, the majority of women were reluctant to be involved in what might be considered unladylike activities. They were by training and cultural pressure ill equipped for an active role in public life. At a conference held by the British Women's Temperance Association in 1886, a prominent worker discussed this problem:

> If we are to be successful workers . . . we must be delivered from that miserable cowardice, born of unbelief which so often makes us shrink back from undertaking any offered work . . . with the words 'Oh I could not possibly do that'. We like to call this sort

of thing by nice names, 'shyness', 'timidity', almost a feminine grace, and our gentlemen relatives take care to foster the delusion.[176]

Aside from their missionary activities, individual women did their most effective temperance work on paper. Many of the best-known temperance works were written by women and unsigned temperance tracts and short tales also came from their pens. Such activity was fully acceptable even to the most proper members of contemporary society. But no one could make a living by their temperance writings; the sums they earned were quite small, except in the case of essay competitions where substantial prize money went to the winner.

Although women teetotallers continued to be active in all areas of the local and national anti-drink campaigns, the women's organisations never became really important in the nineteenth-century temperance movement. The whole weight of the male-dominated society of the time was against females having any independent role in the public affairs of their communities. The British Women attempted to involve its members in causes it thought worthy of their attention, but many of these members came from teetotal families that emphasised 'acceptance' and 'respectability' rather than rebellion and innovation. Women's suffrage and 'social purity' were not causes of which the hardheaded northern teetotallers could approve.[177] The many temperance reformers who were ambitious for public office were unwilling to have their womenfolk indulge in activities that might diminish support for their own candidacies; but without help from masculine sympathisers, the British Women could not survive. They were dependent on them to finance their activities; too few interested women had enough independent wealth to support their own organisation.[178]

The British Women suffered from a further disability caused mainly by the social situation of the teetotallers. The world as seen by working-class and lower middle-class families at the end of the nineteenth century was a very limited one. Establishing themselves permanently in the industrial centres of England, formerly itinerant and immigrant families were more interested in the problems of their own communities than in those of the larger world. London was a long way away, both physically and psychologically, for many provincial teetotallers; and even metropolitan abstainers, unless they were of the upper classes, were more inclined to be working in their own neighbourhoods than in the more cosmopolitan parts of the capital. For the majority of teetotallers the local temperance hall, and not Essex Hall, was the temperance centre. Similarly, the local town hall played a greater role in their political lives than did Parliament. Their womenfolk also worked much more in the local halls and groups than in national activities. They helped run the temperance halls, were active in the operation of the local children's societies, and organised cooking and sewing classes and general mothers' meetings. Their world was a long way from the sophisticated and cosmopolitan national headquarters of the British Women's Temperance Association.

# 8 The Temperance Party

When the Gospel Temperance fever abated in the second half of the 1880s, it might have appeared to the casual observer that temperance had once again failed and that the years of work and excitement had been in vain. But this was not so. The link between church and temperance forged by the Gospel Temperance movement was a lasting one and an important element in the new thrust of temperance. Turning away from religious missions and a moral suasion position,[1] dedicated teetotallers focused their attention once again on the political arena and sought to bring about changes in the drinking customs of England by means of legislative action. If the people would not, or could not on their own volition, become free of drink, then society, through its regulating agency, the government, would impose a drink-free life-style on the people. Fighting both for prohibition and for the curtailment of licensing hours and houses, the political temperance movement, like its predecessor the Gospel Temperance movement, swept through the country and put such pressure on the political parties that the Liberal Party made local prohibition an official part of its programme.

When examining the activities of the political anti-drink forces one must be careful to differentiate between the prohibition and the temperance parties. They were not the same. It was not until the 1870s that the term Temperance Party was used.[2] Prior to that decade, anti-drink political activity was organised mainly by the United Kingdom Alliance, the prohibition party. At first the so-called Temperance Party consisted only of informal groupings of all local anti-drink forces, including the United Kingdom Alliance. These individual associations worked together on the local scene for a variety of temperance reforms – by applying pressure to the licensing magistrates or organising local demonstrations. The latter were sometimes in support of local matters, such as a municipal drink ordinance; at other times they were organised as encouragement to the temperance reformers working in Parliament. The Temperance Party also included individual temperance reformers who were active in the local political arena, both as teetotallers and under other affiliations.

These men could be relied upon to further the temperance reformation whenever possible.

## NATIONAL TEMPERANCE FEDERATION

The start of the new direction for temperance reform came in 1883, at the height of the Gospel Temperance movement, when the chairman of the British Temperance League, Alderman Clegg of Sheffield, suggested that all the temperance organisations in Great Britain and Ireland should join together to form a federation.[3] Out of this suggestion came the idea of a conference of delegates from all interested temperance organisations; it was held in Exeter Hall, London, on 8 November 1883. The suggestion for a federation was approved and on 6 February 1884 the National Temperance Federation was inaugurated.

The federation was founded to 'Promote temperance by moral suasion and legal enactment'.[4] Harmonising the individual efforts of many diverse anti-drink bodies, it acted as a pressure group on Parliament and government. It also took up all matters that were of interest, both nationally and locally, and alerted temperance reformers throughout the country to pertinent developments. The federation did not adopt a specific programme, because all its member organisations had to agree on all official policies, and this was not easy to achieve. The major role of the federation was to encourage cooperation among its members whenever required by the temperance movement. Affiliated organisations might be national or local societies, the only requirement for membership being a determination to fight the traffic in drink. Most of the denominational temperance societies joined the federation,[5] although the Church of England Temperance Society and the Roman Catholic Temperance Society did not.[6] Joseph Malins, the head of the Independent Order of the Good Templars,[7] was instrumental in setting up the federation[8] and was appointed its first secretary. W. S. Caine, the teetotal MP, who was well known in many temperance and radical circles, was its first president.

The United Kingdom Alliance continued to play an important role on the national scene. Its agents, scattered throughout England and Wales, were in a good position to activate local groups against specific policies of the government of the day. In

1893 the Alliance had thirty paid agents who were directed from the headquarters at Manchester, as well as a number of auxiliary groups who received direct grants from Manchester and hired their own agents.[9] Most of the Alliance agents were teetotallers and, because they were permanent residents in one locality (unlike the peripatetic British Temperance League agents), they could become important members of the temperance community. Many of these agents ran their own missions, mixing gospel temperance with prohibitionist principles, but, more often than not, they were also part of a larger local effort, working as long-standing associates of other teetotallers in the town.[10] Henry Hibbert, for example, was the Alliance agent in Bradford, and was not only active in his Alliance work but also promoted many other temperance causes. Being a teetotaller and a native of the area where he worked, he was a very solid member of the local temperance community and could be found writing letters to local politicians, organising meetings in neighbouring towns and acting as spokesman for the anti-drink forces of his town.[11]

One of the main functions of Alliance agents was to organise electoral committees 'to promote petitions and in every legitimate way seek to create and extend an enlightened public opinion hostile to the liquor trade'.[12] When a special issue came to the fore, new associations were sometimes formed to deal with it. For example, in the late 1870s there was great excitement over the Permissive Bill, an Alliance-sponsored Bill that would allow prohibition in local communities if the inhabitants voted for it. Permissive Bill meetings organised by Alliance agents were held all over the country; in some places the agents set up Permissive Bill Associations.[13] Prominent local figures were persuaded to chair the meetings, even some – such as Lord Randolph Churchill – who were not teetotallers.[14] From the point of view of the prohibitionists, linking their names with the Permissive Bill was good politics.

In Hull in 1876 a monster parade was held to support the Permissive Bill as well as to protest intemperance in general. It was typical of many such demonstrations in the north of England. Organised mainly by the local auxiliary of the United Kingdom Alliance, it was a colourful and impressive parade. At its head was a mounted chief marshal followed by other horsemen. They were followed by a series of carriages, filled with delegates, religious ministers and the various speakers. These vehicles were followed by another mounted marshall, who led the British Workmen Brass Band. Behind the band came the first division, made up of trade societies, a second division of friendly societies, and the Good Templars Brass Band. The friendly societies represented were: the National Order of Oddfellows, Free Gardeners, the Order of the Druids and the Ancient Order of Druids. Another mounted marshal followed with another temperance band in the rear. Behind this third band marched the local political societies of Hull, including the Central Liberal Association, the North Myton Liberal Association, the United Kingdom Alliance, the Tichburn and Magna Carta Association, and the Hull Republican Club. This rich mixture of political groups was followed by the fourth band, the Leeds Irish Brass Band, and the Irish societies with a section to themselves, including Branch No. 1 and Branch No. 2 of the Home Rule Association. The next division was made up of members of the local temperance societies. Headed by another Good Templars Brass Band, they consisted of groups from the Saturday Evenings for the People, the Sons of Temperance, Lodges of the Good Templars, Rechabites, the Ham Temperance Society, the Temperance Coffee Cart Company, the Mason Street Adult School, the Friends Temperance Society, the United Temperance Association and the Church of England Temperance Society. At the end of the procession came well-wishers in carriages and those not connected with any society. All marching members wore the regalia of their associations and carried banners and flags, making a colourful sight which would catch the attention of many citizens of Hull.[15]

The procession marched through the town to an open field where four platforms had been set up, each of which had its own meeting with its own speaker. Four separate resolutions were passed, one by each of these meetings. The first resolution requested that a petition be sent to the government asking for a Bill against intemperance. Another petition was the subject of the second resolution, this one to Parliament in favour of the Licensing Board Bill and the Permissive Bill. The third resolution authorised another petition to Parliament to give support to the Sunday Closing Bill. Finally, the fourth resolution called upon the Town Council of Hull to appoint inspectors for public houses.[16]

In the evening of the same day an indoor meeting was held at which the same resolutions were again passed.[17] Admission to this evening meeting was by ticket only, but tickets were free except those for boxes and reserved seats. They had to be obtained from the participating societies prior to the meeting. Restricting admission to ticket-holders kept out a rowdy element that was the bane of most public meetings. (Publicans were known to bribe drunkards to attend temperance meetings to cause trouble.)[18] To secure a large attendance at the meetings, both indoor and out, Sir Wilfrid Lawson, the president of the United Kingdom Alliance and a very witty MP,[19] had been asked to speak. He was the anti-drink forces' best drawing card at such events, and his presence at the demonstrations and meetings had been advertised well in advance of the appointed day. Officially the demonstration was 'in favour of the suppression of intemperance', an objective to which few could object. However, there were complaints that, although fifty ministers had promised to come, the clergy did not show much interest.[20] This event took place before Gospel Temperance had taken hold and made anti-drink work popular in religious circles.

## LOCAL TEMPERANCE PARTIES

The establishment of the National Temperance Federation encouraged many town groups to form unions. There was a growing desire for greater cooperation among anti-drink associations for their work at the Brewster Sessions,[21] at demonstrations and also at the anti-compensation rallies[22] in the provincial towns. The last two decades of the century, therefore, saw the formation of many local anti-drink alliances. Like the National Federation, these alliances were not exclusive; quantity not quality was the dominant principle in organising political support and therefore these unions included such disparate groups as the Church of England Temperance Society and the Good Templars, working together for a common cause.

In Bradford, for example, where there was a long temperance tradition, six anti-drink groups organised a temperance confederation in 1889. It was the formal acknowledgement of a cooperation that had been in effect for some time. The eight official aims proclaimed by the group included working together at the Brewster Session, seeking publicity for their cause in the local press and trying to win the support of local groups not yet identified with the temperance cause.[23] Although the CETS joined at first, it eventually had to withdraw as many of the aims of the union were in conflict with the official policy of the established church's temperance organisation.[24] But members of the CETS could belong to other groups affiliated with the confederation if their personal views were not in conflict. The union held outdoor meetings, a revival of the original teetotal method of communicating with an indifferent public.[25]

In the town of Hull, a Hull and East Yorkshire Prohibition League was formed in 1887 'to unite all temperance reformers in a straight and solid vote for the Prohibition of the Liquor Traffic either nationally or locally'.[26] The local temperance agent, Guy Hayler, who was also an ardent prohibitionist, was elected its first president. All its members had to pledge to vote only for candidates who 'above and before all things support Direct Veto'.[27] The League supplied speakers to speak on Direct Veto to both temperance and non-temperance meetings.

At the other end of the country, in Dover, anti-drink reformers were active in trying to get the magistrates to close a number of licensed houses,[28] while in Liverpool a Vigilance Committee was set up in 1890 to try to get the city council 'purged of its predominant liquor making and selling element'.[29] This committee publicised all the doings of a questionable nature by the Council and presented memorials and held public meetings in their fight against the drink trade.[30] Strong pressure was brought to bear on the licensing magistrates of Liverpool at the Brewster Sessions by crowding the sessions with anti-drink supporters who opposed the issuance of licences.[31]

In Newcastle a very effective Temperance Council was formed that was active in all the anti-compensation demonstrations. The Countess of Carlisle, a noted abstaining temperance supporter and president of the North of England Temperance League,[32] also centred in Newcastle, gave active support to local, as well as national, efforts.[33] At the Veto Bill conference and demonstration in Newcastle in January 1894, veto songs, specially composed for the occasion, were sung.[34] Anti-drink enthusiasm was so strong throughout the north that there were few towns there without a temperance council agitating for a reduction of licences both in the newspapers and at the Brewster Sessions. There were also such organisations in many parts of the south of England coordinating their anti-drink efforts and focusing on work in Brewster Sessions.

Although the official licensing policy for the country was legislated by Parliament, temperance reformers realised that local authorities had a great deal of freedom in interpreting the licensing laws. It was at the Brewster Sessions, held once a year in autumn, that all licences for the sale of intoxicating beverages were issued or renewed. Originally these Brewster Sessions were private but, under pressure from the reformers, they were made public.[35] The temperance societies first sought to influence the licensing magistrates at these sessions by sending them memorials. But they soon discovered that these petitions were not particularly effective. Some licensing magistrates even evaded this mild form of pressure by claiming to have a regulation forbidding the acceptance of memorials from any group whatsoever.[36]

The great importance of the Brewster Sessions lay in the fact that all licences were issued for only one year and technically had to be renewed annually. Practically, however, renewal was a routine matter with refusals occurring only when certain regulations had not been complied with. Only after the effects of temperance pressure began to be felt in the 1870s was there a noticeable decrease in the number of licences issued. Increasingly the magistrates viewed the applications for new or renewed licences more critically. Under pressure from the Temperance Party the local authorities were scrutinising more carefully the applicant, his premises and the needs of his locality for drink facilities.[37] However, some licences the magistrates had no power to refuse. Off licences, for example, had to be issued if the applicant could present two character references to the licensing magistrates.[38]

When the teetotallers became aware of the importance of licences in the fight against intemperance, they made the Brewster Sessions a major target of their activities. As early as the 1840s temperance reformers had sent memorials to Brewster Sessions in the hope of persuading them to issue fewer licences,[39] but as the century progressed, more and more teetotallers came to believe that a reduction in the number of licensed premises would lead to an equivalent decrease in the amount of drinking. This argument was supported to some extent by the results of the Beer Act of 1830, which allowed the sale of beer by anyone who would pay a small fee. No restrictions were made on the number of licences or the conditions of the premises used for the sale of beer. The result was a beer-drinking orgy so shocking to many Englishmen that the government was forced to reimpose restrictions on the sale of beer.[40]

A more localised, but similar, example occurred in the 1860s. The city of Liverpool sought to staunch its high rate of intemperance by allowing free trade in beer. Anyone in the city could get a beer licence. The results were quite the opposite of those expected, but similar to the earlier national ones: drunkenness increased, and the city council, like the national government when faced with a similar situation, reimposed restrictions.[41]

With the new upsurge of interest in anti-drink activities in the 1870s there came a renewed interest in limiting the granting of liquor licences. The temperance reformers, in attempts to influence the licensing magistrates, attended personally the Brewster Sessions in towns where they had some support. But the reformers soon found that they accomplished little because they were unfamiliar with the intricacies of the licensing laws; they needed professional advice. Many town anti-drink groups therefore amalgamated to hire a solicitor to represent them at the Brewster Sessions. This legal watch was such a success that it became a common practice for local anti-drink organisations collectively to support the Brewster work of one solicitor.[42]

Not all the work concerning the issuing of licences was carried out by the solicitor. Teetotallers personally helped investigate new applications as well as examine all the renewals. By checking the background of the prospective licensee and his premises, they were often able to present evidence at the Brewster Sessions that caused the application to be denied.[43] Sometimes the magistrates actually asked the teetotallers to help them. One such magistrate told the temperance reformers in his town that he would have refused more licences if evidence of 'wrongdoing' had been submitted.[44] 'He hoped that some of our practical reformers before the return of another year would have armed the magistrates with power to deal with these licences.'[45] However, not all magistrates were so anxious to encourage the reformers. One in Huddersfield complained that temperance societies had been writing him and his fellow magistrates that they were not doing their duty. This led a temperance journal to comment:

No the magistrates are not policemen. These temperance men should look about the public houses themselves. Let *them* bring before the magistrate the innkeeper who is guilty of allowing drunkenness in his house and we'll let them see if the magistrates won't do their duty.[46]

The success or failure of the efforts of local temperance reformers depended a great deal on the goodwill of local officials. The chief of police, in particular, could be a great help if he wished, giving the reformers statistics and other information pertaining to the sale and consumption of drink in the town. In Bradford, for example, a reforming police chief took office in the second half of the century.[47] He kept the temperance and other interested groups supplied with significant figures relating to the number of licences per inhabitant, the number of arrests and convictions for drunkenness, and the number of licensees charged with offences against the licensing laws. All this information was utilised by local temperance organisations to make their case before the public. The diocesan branch of the CETS collected these figures from chief constables throughout the West Riding of Yorkshire and compiled tables showing comparative figures for the various towns. These tables were published in their annual reports.[48]

Traditionally the police were closely associated with the publicans, relying on them for bits of information that might be useful in apprehending criminals.[49] Licensed premises were important centres for gossip and meetings, of both a legal and an illegal nature, and so policemen were anxious to retain the good will of the publicans.[50] This meant that sometimes the police and town officials were unsympathetic to the aims of the teetotallers. The latter then had to find new ways of forcing the officials to cooperate. In some towns this was done by setting up Vigilance Committees to watch over the licensing actions of local officials. Such committees were to be found in towns as scattered as Dover, Hull and, as we have already seen, Liverpool. The Dover Temperance Council checked on all matters of local government, not just licensing problems, seeing to it that the letter of the law was adhered to and that the police did their job properly.[51] In Liverpool such a committee was set up because of the city's excessive drunkenness.[52] Even the abandonment of free licensing had not altered the situation very much. One magistrate tried to reduce intemperance in Liverpool by publishing the names of those convicted of it, along with the names of their employers,[53] but this had little effect. Then, in January 1890, some prominent citizens formed a Vigilance Committee, which became a prototype for reformers in other towns.[54] Bradford considered such a committee but rejected the idea, deciding to leave such matters in the hands of local police officials.[55] No doubt this decision was largely due to the good relations enjoyed with the chief constable.

With all this local activity, temperance reformers had to learn not to apply their weight too heavily. They soon realised that, if they antagonised local officials, very little would be done. In 1875 the secretary of the Good Templars lodges wrote to his fellow reformers in Bradford to tell them that the local bench was then favourable to temperance. He advised them to decrease their pressure on the magistrates lest they become hostile to the temperance cause. With regard to the suggestion that the anti-drink forces set up a Vigilance Committee, he wrote:

> If it is intended that the Committee shall take upon themselves to prosecute such offenders on their own responsibility, we should decidedly disagree with any such proposal, as we think it would bring contempt upon the Temperance Cause.[56]

This advice was accepted; no committee was formed, but men were hired to collect evidence of wrongdoing at licensed premises to be sent to the chief constable for his use.[57]

Sometimes the temperance reformers tried to rally more support for their work than that of their fellow abstainers. They felt that their watch on the work of the licensing bench was just as important to other members of the community as it was to themselves, and that working men in particular should be alerted to the dangers of an increased number of licensed premises. Working closely with other organisations on this matter, the Hull Temperance Society, for example, got permission to read a memorial to the Hull Brewster Session that was said to be supported by '93 trade, political, Friendly and Temperance Societies'. But, even with all this support, it met with little success and the magistrates granted all the licences requested.[58]

## ANTI-DRINK REFORMERS WITHIN LOCAL GOVERNMENT

In the last quarter of the nineteenth century many temperance reformers came to realise that the best way to influence municipal matters, especially licensing, was for active teetotallers to be elected to local government office. As early as 1837, an election for chief constable of Wilsden was fought between the teetotallers and their opponents and, when the temperance reformers won, it was regarded as a victory for the movement.[59] But this was a rare event in the early days. It was not until municipal government had been reformed in the mid-nineteenth century by Parliament that the teetotallers found themselves in a position to make their wishes known, for many of their supporters were small householders who acquired the right to vote in local and national elections only in the last decades of the century.[60]

Along with a growing teetotal electorate, the reformers were favoured by their growing reputation in civic matters. Over the years temperance workers had come into contact with many individuals and groups concerned with municipal affairs. Through their duties at the Brewster Sessions, their work in the Sunday Closing Movement[61] and other civic efforts they were in touch with members of the local government establishment. So closely did the teetotallers work with the political structure that, by the end of the century, there were very few active temperance reformers who had no political ambitions. Councillors, aldermen and mayors were soon to be found among the ranks of teetotallers. In a single year the Bradford Temperance Society listed one mayor, five Justices of the Peace, one alderman, four councillors and two Members of Parliament among its subscribers.[62] Not all these people were teetotallers, but they were all willing to be publicly linked with the temperance reformation.

It is not surprising to find so many teetotallers with political ambitions, especially in the northern industrial areas. By the 1870s many of the early teetotallers had achieved a great measure of personal economic success. They were a new class of self-made men, who had worked hard and had succeeded according to the prevailing standards of individual self-help. Said one eminent self-made shipowner: 'I would advise any man who wanted to be really successful to be a teetotaler, an early riser and to go early to bed. If you want to be successful you must be ahead of your neighbours everywhere and you can only do this by enthusiasm and activity.'[63] With the attainment of their economic goals, it was natural for these men to turn to public service for further personal satisfaction. Political success, both local and national, would bring social acceptance much more quickly than would any other means. Town councillors, aldermen and mayors, regardless of their origins, had status and could count on a great deal of respect from their fellow citizens.[64]

Besides valuing the prestige that accrued to one in public office, the late nineteenth-century teetotaller often felt that public office could be used to further the temperance reformation. From the point of view of the conservatively minded town councils of this period, the teetotallers made 'safe' officials. They had achieved their goals within the existing social, economic and political system and had no desire to make drastic changes. They were reformers rather than revolutionaries, especially in the last decades of the century.[65]

Teetotallers were also personally acceptable to many voters not because of their temperance views but because they had proved themselves to have the qualities of which the electorate of this period approved. Many citizens agreed with William Forster, the Member of Parliament for Bradford, when he said: 'Any man who takes your pledge and keeps it must be a man of very considerable self-denial, which will not apply merely to that particular temptation, but will apply to many others.'[66]

A few successful teetotallers looked farther afield than the local town council and became Members of Parliament. Sir Titus Salt, the Yorkshire manufacturer, owner of the prohibition village Saltaire and a financial supporter of innumerable temperance causes in the West Riding, was elected to Parliament; but he was not comfortable at Westminster and did not seek reelection when his term ended.[67] The local reformers were usually quite provincial, with little interest in going to Parliament.

Even professional temperance agents were attracted to the idea of holding public office. Both Henry Hibbert, the United Kingdom Alliance agent, and the British Temperance League agent William Gregson were successful candidates for the office of councillor. Thomas Whittaker, a former British Temperance League agent, was elected mayor of Scarborough and Joseph Malins, the head of the Good Templars, was also a councillor.[68]

Not all teetotallers were pleased with the direct participation of their fellow reformers in politics, especially if it interfered with their temperance work. The British Temperance League, when informed that one of its agents had been elected councillor, recorded in its minutes the resolution, 'That in the opinion of this Committttee Mr Gregson's connection with the Blackburn Town Council is not compatible with his duties to the British Temperance League.'[69] The League was concerned with the immediate practical problems of the agent's carrying out his duties. This agent did in fact have to ask for special consideration, as his work with the council often took up the time he should have used for his temperance duties.[70]

By 1880 there were twenty-seven teetotal mayors in England;[71] ten years later this number had grown to forty-five for England and Wales.[72] The importance of these abstaining local officials to the temperance movement was not overlooked. In 1883, under the sponsorship of the National Temperance League, the Lord Mayor of London invited all the teetotal mayors of England to a meeting at the Guildhall. Six years later there was another gathering of abstaining mayors, this time at Mansion House. A report by the National Temperance League after the Mansion House meeting stated:

> The popular notion of civic life has hitherto been associated with an unlimited amount of festivity; but of late the impression is gaining ground that corporations are intended, not merely to preserve ancient privileges, but to benefit the communities in which they are established. A meeting of Teetotal Mayors in the Mansion House is apt to dispel the first impression and to emphasize the second.[73]

In 1892 the National Temperance League took these meetings to the provinces, where most of the teetotal mayors were. Manchester and Rochdale were chosen as sites for these gatherings, both towns being traditional strongholds of temperance sentiments.[74]

One objection to a large-scale invasion of municipal government by teetotallers was the fear that the non-temperance public would feel they were being pressured by a minority. In one town a licensing magistrate had lectured his fellow magistrates on 'the evils of the liquor traffic' and told them that their conduct on the bench was 'immoral and unjust'. These words aroused the hostility of the moderate magistrates, who might otherwise have been favourable to temperance arguments.[75] In this case, having a temperance man on the bench worked to the detriment of the cause.

Nevertheless, in many northern communities where temperance was strong, ties between the town hall and the temperance hall grew quite close. Public celebrations organised by temperance reformers were often attended by civic officials. At Band of Hope prize-givings it was often a mayor or alderman who sat on the platform and presented the prizes. In 1900, when the Huddersfield Temperance Society built a new hall, the opening procession included the mayor, the mayoress, the mayor's chaplain, the town clerk and the chief constable. The mayor himself was a temperance man closely identified with the Band of Hope movement.[76] In Leeds two leading teetotallers were very influential in the town's political life: George Tatham, who became mayor in 1880, was also chairman of the Leeds Temperance Society as well as a pioneer worker in the cause;[77] Edward Baines was a Member of Parliament as well as owner of the Liberal newspaper the *Leeds Mercury*. In the nearby town of Sheffield the reformers were so well represented on the bench that the non-temperance public was unhappy about it: the teetotal magistrates insisted on a strict interpretation of the licensing laws.[78]

Without doubt the temperance reformation benefited greatly from its close association with local government. There were many ways in which local officials could help the reformers if they wished. In the town of Bradford teetotal advocates for years enjoyed preferential treatment in the matter of open air meetings: the town council allowed them to hold such gatherings on public land in a central location. When a local labour group, during a period of labour agitation, asked the council for the use of the same site it was denied. Unfortunately for the teetotallers, the council then had to deny them the use of the site to avoid political repercussions and the reformers had to hold their meetings at a less desirable location.[79]

On the other hand, if the town authorities were hostile to the temperance movement, they could often prevent the reformers from holding outdoor meetings or demonstrations on the grounds that such activities were obstructing traffic or creating a public nuisance. More than one temperance advocate found himself in court after a policeman had objected to his addressing an outdoor meeting.[80] Some of those arrested fought to uphold the right to organise such meetings, many with considerable success.[81] Those reformers who had friends in important town positions were less liable to be subjected to such harrassment. The chief of police would not allow his men to persecute local temperance speakers if the mayor or some other prominent citizen was known to support the movement.

Teetotal town officials were anxious to reduce drinking at official celebrations.[82] Drinking customs were a traditional part of civic life, as in so many other sections of the community. Mayors were frequently called upon to supply alcoholic beverages to citizens at special events, and intoxicants were served at many official civic dinners. Civic customs varied from town to town, but the majority of them involved drink. In Barnsley, the Yorkshire mining town, the Territorial Army paraded once a year on the 'Mayor's Day' and in appreciation the mayor was expected to supply the soldiers with beer. Against much opposition, teetotal mayors refused to do this.[83] In many towns it was traditional for the mayor to give a dinner upon leaving office: it was not unknown for civic officials to leave the table in a state of inebriation.[84] When George Tatham was first elected mayor by his fellow council members he refused the honour, believing that the duties of a mayor and those of a teetotaller were incompatible. But later, when re-elected, and being assured that his abstaining principles would be respected, he accepted the position and was a popular and successful holder of that office.[85]

Temperance reformers thought municipal governments could help reduce intemperance by supporting counter-attractions to licensed premises. Municipally-run parks, libraries and recreational facilities that were drink free would provide an attractive alternative to the public house when working men went in search of entertainment.[86] Because such activities were not profit-making, private sponsors were hard to find. Therefore some citizens felt that this public service was a legitimate sphere of activity for the municipalities.[87]

Another development that brought teetotallers closer to local authorities in the last decades of the nineteenth century was the growth of town-run schools. Set up as a result of the Education Act of 1870, they became a growing influence in the lives of the town's children. The teetotallers, always anxious to disseminate anti-drink information to children, recognised that the local schools provided the best opportunity for doing this. The children were gathered together in the schools and prepared to listen to any instruction given. But permission had to be gained from the local school boards. The decision of the board would often reflect the standing of the temperance movement in the community. If it was well respected, there would be little opposition to the introduction of temperance teachings into the schools. Thus in many northern towns the temperance reformers quickly gained authorisation to conduct temperance classes for board school pupils.[88] Once the reformers had established their teachings in the state schools, it was easier to get the church-related and other private schools to agree to include them. And again, the greater the influence the reformers had in local circles, the easier it was to get the admission of temperance materials into children's groups. Sunday Schools, for example, would listen more readily to the appeals of the mayor or some citizen of substance than to those of an ordinary working-class advocate.

No one, however, entered local politics with only one issue to fight, and so the teetotallers in local government could not restrict their interests to temperance matters. The majority were voted into office because of other associations. Many were elected in spite of their connection with temperance reform. Teetotallers were always in the minority in any community; therefore no one could be elected with their votes alone. Many abstainers were members of the Liberal Party and their dual loyalty could pose problems, as Joseph Livesey noted: 'Teetotalers have their party politics and many are vexed when they see the Temperance cause made use of in opposition to the party to which they belong.'[89] A good example of this occurred in Sheffield, where the temperance movement was split for more than four years.[90] The major temperance personality involved was the mayor, William Clegg, who was also head of the British Temperance League, the Sheffield Sunday Closing Association, the Sheffield auxiliary of the United Kingdom Alliance, and a member of a prominent temperance family. The trouble started in February 1885, when the Sheffield auxiliary of the Alliance passed a resolution stating that they would support only candidates who favoured the local form of prohibition called Direct Veto. The following month the auxiliary called a conference for all temperance voters at which the teetotallers agreed to work for one Direct Veto candidate. It was also suggested that a branch of the Direct Popular Veto Party be set up in every electoral district, the main function of which would be to question candidates of all parties as to their position regarding the Direct Veto. The auxiliary also wanted to set up a local temperance party to select candidates who would vote for immediate temperance legislation. A great struggle among the teetotallers ensued and the motion to organise a local temperance party was passed only after three meetings. The Good Templars of Sheffield officially entered the conflict when they called a conference of all temperance voters to take action on political matters. At this conference a Sheffield Temperance Electoral Association was created. Not every abstainer in Sheffield was happy with this turn of events. At one of the meetings of the Sheffield Temperance Electoral Association a well-known teetotaller said publicly that the idea of a separate temperance party was 'politically immoral'.[91] To the many teetotallers who needed the regular political parties to further their own ambitions it was also political suicide. Mayor Clegg, for instance, was disturbed by this attempt to polarise the political community on the issue of drink. Mr Mundella, a candidate for Parliament, was asked by the Sheffield Temperance Electoral Committee whether if he became a member of the Liberal Government and the Cabinet opposed Direct Veto, he would resign his seat. The mayor was distressed by this questioning and thought it impertinent, but he was unable to stop the extremists. At the next election it appeared that the Conservative candidate supported Direct Veto and the Liberal candidate did not. Consequently, the Sheffield Temperance Electoral Committee inserted an advertisement in the local newspapers asking all those sympathetic to temperance to vote for the Conservative candidate. Clegg, as a locally prominent member of the Liberal Party, could not be associated with this advertisement without offending his own supporters and so had publicly to dissociate himself from the action of his fellow teetotallers.

The next major instance of discord occurred in 1887, when the Sheffield auxiliary of the United Kingdom Alliance agreed to set up a Popular Veto Association for the Sheffield constituency. The members of this association had to sign the following pledge: 'Because of the awful evils caused directly and indirectly by the sale of intoxicating liquors, I promise that I will not vote for, or support any candidate for Parliament who will not vote for the

Direct Popular Veto.'[92] Although compulsory membership in this new group was defeated by the auxiliary it was decided to make the pledge obligatory for the auxiliary's members. This again put Mayor Clegg in an awkward position. If, for instance, a candidate supported Sunday Closing but not Direct Veto, what should he do? As head of the Sunday Closing Association he was obliged to vote for anyone who furthered its aims; but he was also a member of the United Kingdom Alliance Auxiliary, which now demanded the signing of the new pledge. This was not just a hypothetical problem: in some communities candidates who favoured Sunday Closing but not Direct Veto had stood for office.

The mayor called a meeting to clarify the situation. He believed that his personal enemies in the United Kingdom Alliance Auxiliary were responsible for this development and that they were trying to oust him.[93] The meeting was very heated; strong personal attacks were made by both sides. In the end the mayor won the overwhelming victory, and he told the Sheffield Temperance Electoral Association to set up a separate organisation and never again to use the funds of the Alliance Auxiliary.[94] The temperance movement in Sheffield was fragmented by these events, and for years the fight was carried on in the local newspapers,[95] bringing the movement much unfavourable publicity, and confirming many citizens in their belief that the teetotallers were a bellicose group.[96] The Alliance was very unhappy with the situation and sent agents from its Manchester headquarters to see what could be done. They accomplished little. Personal hostilities overrode any appeals for a compromise for the good of the movement.

This Sheffield controversy was a particularly deep and violent one even for the temperance cause, which was no stranger to open enmities. What made it more damaging to the movement than many other splits was that it occurred between temperance men in the same community and day-to-day activities ensured that there would be constant contact between the protagonists which would keep the antagonisms alive.

But, even with such parochial jealousies and petty divisions, temperance reformers were successful in many local elections. In some smaller towns there were so many teetotallers in the municipal government that there were complaints that the temperance hall was running the town hall.[97] But the teetotallers did not have everything their own way. The swiftly rising labour movement of the late nineteenth century felt it had a better claim to the role of leader of the working class than did the temperance reformers.

## TEMPERANCE AND LABOUR

The increasing involvement of teetotallers in local politics brought them more and more into contact with the growing labour movement. At first the temperance reformers had hoped to attract the support of working men, as they had done in a limited way in the early years of teetotalism. But, from the 1870s on, it became increasingly clear that the labour movement would have its own political programme which would not always be in agreement with that of the temperance movement. The lower-class working man, in particular, had not changed his view of the teetotallers; he still felt they were in league with the employers, and that the old iron law of wages still held.[98] If the workers could live on less, or appear able to do so, their wages would immediately be reduced. Teetotalism, by this argument, was a way of living on less.[99]

Nevertheless, there were many socially conscious working men in the 1870s and 1880s who joined the temperance movement. They were mostly found in the ranks of the benevolent and social orders, the Rechabites, Sons of Temperance, Good Templars, and the like.[100] But by 1890 these men realised that the temperance reformers were unwilling to support the radical changes that the labour movement felt were necessary to solve the dreadful problems of unemployment and poverty which were prevalent at this time. 'One characteristic of the present day is the discussion of the economics of the Temperance Question. Socialism in various forms is asserting itself boldly', reported the British Temperance League in its *Annual Report*.[101] The temperance movement was only against the use of alcohol. It was not against the economic system.

For decades the teetotal-dominated temperance movement had served as a means of helping individual workers up the economic and social ladder;[102] it was an important part of the self-help movement of the mid-nineteenth century. Now, in the latter part of the century, this role was being assumed by the socialists and other parts of the labour movement. The type of worker the

temperance reformers had traditionally tried to enrol in their
ranks was the same as that sought by the labour and socialist
groups, and it was therefore not unusual to find socialist workers
with teetotal backgrounds. Many labour leaders were the
offspring of temperance reformers. Thomas Burt, the miners'
leader, was the son of a Rechabite,[103] and the father of Charles
Muse, an active north country Fabian, was a member of the
United Kingdom Alliance.[104] Both Burt and Muse remained
teetotallers, though the temperance movement itself was not their
first loyalty.

   Throughout the nineteenth century it was not uncommon to
find labour unions encouraging teetotalism among their
members. As early as 1840 at least one trade group had recognised
the negative effect of drinking on its association and had changed
its meeting place from a licensed to an unlicensed place.[105] In
1871 the general secretary of the Boiler Makers and Iron
Shipbuilders Union calculated that over 5 per cent of its funds
were spent 'for the good of the house' – that is, for drink at
meetings. The union decided to stop this and give the money
saved to a Widows and Orphans Fund.[106] By the end of the
century the majority of socialist labour clubs did not allow
alcoholic beverages on their premises and many other trade
unions were searching for alternatives to the public houses for
their meetings.[107]

   But, while labour leaders could agree with the suasionist
temperance reformers that excessive drinking was bad for the
workers, they did not agree on much else. For the temperance
advocate the only way to improve the lot of the poorer classes was
for them to stop drinking. 'Self reformation is the best
reformation', proclaimed one teetotaller when trying to persuade
the workers that it was up to the individual, not society, to make
changes.[108] The teetotallers quoted Charles Booth's writings,
especially passages in which he declared drink to be the cause of a
large share of the poverty of the lower classes. To the temperance
reformers, the poor were poor because they drank. In a public
debate in 1894, the Alliance agent, Henry Hibbert, said:

   The labour market is glutted with *ne'er do wells, loafers, hangers on,
   or incapable* craftsmen, surely the cause is very largely to be
   attributed to drink . . . , The sensual, coarse, brutal, incapable
   men and women (the drunkards) are continually recruiting the

ranks of the unemployed and are largely the *spawn* of the liquor shops, always living from hand to mouth on the very verge of poverty.[109]

Refusing to admit that anything could be wrong with the *laissez-faire* economic system, the teetotallers even found in drink the cause of trade depressions. This was the point of a paper entitled *Why is Trade Depressed?*[110] Blaming drink was a simple way of solving the great problem of the second half of the century: why there was so much poverty in the midst of so much prosperity. Why did some people rise to a condition of affluence while others sank to squalor? For the temperance reformer the answer was simple: individual failure. Every drunkard had a flaw in his character that caused him to drink.[111] Society itself could not be charged with the responsibility for his condition; it was the weakness of the man.

To refute the arguments of the teetotallers, the socialists also used the findings of Charles Booth's research. They pointed out that Booth himself did not believe that the prime cause of poverty was drink. Instead he wrote that capitalism as it existed in the late nineteenth century needed a large pool of unemployed from which it could draw workers when needed. This meant that there would always be unemployment and poverty unless basic changes were made.[112] James Whyte, the secretary of the United Kingdom Alliance, would not accept this view. The unemployed, he wrote, are as a rule the unfit. Those most in want are the most unfit.[113]

A common method used by temperance reformers to show that drink caused most of the workers' troubles was to point out individual teetotallers, many of them reformed drunkards, who had successfully made their way in life. The socialists answered this by quoting Henry George; 'Industry, frugality and intelligence can only avail the individuals in so far as they are superior to the general level.'[114] The socialist H. Russell Smart took George's position and interpreted it for the workers by means of an analogy. If one man in a crowd of sightseers, he wrote, had a stool to stand on he has a great advantage over those who do not have such an aid. But if everyone had a stool no one would have an advantage. If all were to abstain, wages would go down or prices would go up.[115] Contradicting the teetotallers, the socialists claimed that drink was not the cause of poverty, it was its consequence. The poor drank more because they were trying to escape their physical surroundings; getting drunk was the easiest and quickest way of forgetting the misery in which they lived. Intemperance, believed the socialist, could only be eliminated by improvement in the total environment of the poorer classes. This view forced many thoughtful Englishmen to reject the oversimplified explanation of poverty put forth by the teetotallers and to seek a deeper understanding.[116]

One of the major difficulties facing the socialists in trying to explain how poverty caused drinking was the indisputable fact that the periods of greatest prosperity were also times of high consumption of alcoholic beverages. When working men had money in their pockets, a large proportion of it was spent on drink. Therefore, as the nineteenth century progressed and wages rose, so did the amount of drinking. As one teetotaller pointed out to a conference of working men, the year 1876 was a year both of great prosperity and of high consumption of alcoholic drinks.[117] John Burns believed that this was so because the poor were so unused to extra money that, when they had it, they spent it unwisely. He also noted that Saturday night, when most workers had just received their wages, was the night of the greatest number of arrests for drunkenness.[118]

With such a great difference between the positions of the temperance reformers and the socialists, there was little chance of cooperation between them. Some teetotallers saw the socialists as their enemies. 'The War Between Socialism and Teetotalism' was the title of a pamphlet written in 1888 to defend the position of the temperance reformers. Socialism and teetotalism cannot mix, wrote the author, because they are like 'oil and water'. The author also believed that if workers purchased only necessities, poverty would vanish in ten years.[119]

Debates were arranged between the two competitors for the workingman's vote. United Kingdom Alliance agents became expert at debating with local socialists, especially at election time. In some instances these agents were themselves standing for office, but in others they debated for the sake of the cause. In the 1890s in particular, we find the two groups clashing at the polls in the northern industrial areas. The debates were often quite heated with each side trying to blacken the other. The socialists portrayed the temperance reformers as allies of the industrialists,[120] while the teetotallers attempted to show that the socialists were defenders of the liquor trade.[121] Both sides openly resented the insinuations of the other.

Not all teetotallers, however, were hostile to the socialists. W. S. Caine, a prominent temperance Member of Parliament and head of the National Temperance Federation, asked the socialists to work for the spread of teetotalism while working for a change in the system. He did not see why there should be so much antagonism when the two groups had so much in common; both were concerned with their fellow men, he wrote, and should be anxious to improve their condition in any way possible. He pointed out that many labour leaders had been teetotallers before they became socialists and had found abstaining beneficial.[122] The Bradford Temperance Society also attempted to draw the labour movement closer to the temperance reformation. In 1895 the society arranged a conference on 'Liquour and Labour', inviting all the labour clubs in the area. Unfortunately for the teetotallers, the working men were not interested and very few came.[123]

In the 1880s and early 1890s, when the issue of Direct Veto was a prominent part of the Liberal Party's platform, many labour leaders supported it. Russell Smart claimed that the prohibitionists and the socialists supported the same principle but that the former did not go far enough. Whereas the anti-drink supporters believed that 'private interest must give way to public welfare' in the matter of drink, the socialists wanted the same principle extended to the entire industrial system. All sections of the community that acted against the interests of the majority should be made to desist from their activities, not just the drink industry.[124]

In 1893, a manifesto supporting Local Option, which blamed the licensing system for the 'poverty, debasement and weakness of the poor', was signed by more than 150 labour leaders.[125] Five years later, however, there was a shift in the attitude of the workers towards Direct Veto. No longer was it seen as an extension of the democratic principle, allowing the majority of people to decide the role drink should have in their own communities; the Fabians had pointed out that a middle-class majority could use the Direct Veto to get rid of a working-class minority from their community. Working people were more dependent on licensed premises than were the more comfortable classes, who had private alternatives to public houses for relaxation and social intercourse. If licences were abolished, it would be the poorer citizens who would suffer.[126] The Fabians also disputed the effectiveness of Local Option in remedying the evils in the lives of the lowest classes: 'Local Option is to social reform in the same relation as charity to social suffering.'[127]

Some socialists also disagreed with the teetotallers on the connection between the number of licensed premises and the amount of drunkenness.[128] Philip Snowden, an abstaining Independent Labour Party leader, felt the temperance reformers were wasting their time in concentrating on the reduction of licences. He pointed out that, while Oxfordshire had three times the number of public houses as Northumberland, the northerners had thirteen times more drunkenness than the Oxonians.[129] Another teetotaller also pointed out that, although there had been a decline in the number of licences issued in England and Wales during the period 1869 to 1896, drinking had increased.[130]

Agreeing with neither the prohibitionists nor the drink trade capitalists, the socialists supported a third programme for regulating the consumption of alcoholic beverages. Both Fabians and Independent Labour Party members wanted drinking facilities to be controlled by local government, a new type of municipal socialism that was very popular at the time among working men.[131] It was believed that if the local government ran the licensed premises, the profits could be used for the people; furthermore, strict control could be exercised over what was drunk, and the adulteration of beverages would no longer be a problem.[132] Variations on this thesis of municipal control of licensed premises were put forth by many divergent groups.[133]

Among some teetotallers, however, there was a growing suspicion that perhaps their traditional position on the relationship between poverty and drink was not correct. Maybe there were other reasons for poverty besides drink. Thomas Whittaker, the veteran teetotaller, expressed this changing view when he wrote: 'social and industrial problems are forcing themselves upon the attention of the nation in a way that cannot be ignored'. He admitted that the extremes of wealth and poverty revealed that something was wrong and that the problem was a complex one.[134] J. Crosfill went further and granted some validity to the socialists' environmental theory, admitting that 'many people live in the slums who could not get by even by total abstinence.'[135]

However, by the time the temperance movement had come round, and was willing to work with the labour movement, it was too late. The latter were just starting their climb to power, while temperance reform was on the decline. By the end of the century the two movements had come to represent two very diverse elements in the community. The teetotallers relied more and more on the artisans, who prized their independent success, and on the lower middle class, the poorer of the white-collar workers: small shopkeepers and clerks. The labour movement, on the other hand, was extending its appeal to a wider range of workers. By the 1890s and 1900s, the trade unions and the socialist parties were drawing into their folds the unskilled along with the skilled workers. To the lowest classes in England, the temperance experience had very little validity. They could not identify with the individual success stories on which the abstainers based their appeals. The temperance reformer, to many workers, was a 'narrow-minded individualist'.[136] By the end of the century, working men who had spent their youth in the temperance movement generally saw teetotalism as no more than a personal matter.

## THE GREAT COMPENSATION CAMPAIGNS OF 1888 AND 1890

Demonstrations and meetings such as the one at Hull[137] in 1876 became more frequent in the north of England in the 1880s and 1890s when the great compensation campaigns were organised throughout the country. In these last two decades of the century, the focus of anti-drink agitation was on the reduction of the number of licences issued at the Brewster Sessions. It was agreed by many diverse groups, including non-temperance ones, that too many licences were issued.[138] The problems then were how to extinguish these surplus licences, how to decide which ones should be refused renewal, and whether compensation should be paid for any licences that were eliminated when the licensee had committed no infringement of the law. In discussions on these issues, it was often pointed out that the slave owners in British possessions had been compensated when their slaves were freed.[139] Temperance ranks were severely divided on this matter. The Alliance, Good Templars and many others who were sometimes called 'extreme' Temperance Party members,[140] believed that, as the licence was issued for only one year with no guarantee that it would be renewed, there was no legal basis for compensation. On the pro-compensation side were the Church of England Temperance Society and the majority of Englishmen, who felt that Parliament had created a monopoly and had given the licensee good reason to believe that his licence was automatically renewable if he did not break any of the licensing laws. The country, pointed out the Archbishop of Canterbury, had a moral duty to pay compensation even if there was no legal right to it.

This issue was brought to a head in 1887 when the case of *Sharp* v. *Wakefield*[141] came before the courts. A public house worth £50 a year in rental had its licence extinguished in September 1887 when it was found that many of the inhabitants of the village where it was situated were against renewal. No real wrongdoing was charged, but it seemed that it was in the public interest to eliminate this public house. The owner of the house sued for compensation, claiming that the value of the house without a licence had dropped to £9 rental per annum. The case went through the courts until, in March 1891, it reached the House of Lords, where the judgement went against the plaintiff. No compensation was allowed.[142]

Meanwhile, before final judgement was given in *Sharp* v. *Wakefield*, Lord Salisbury's government decided to reform the licensing laws in the Local Government Bill of 1888, in which it was proposed to transfer authority for issuing liquor licences from the Justices of the Peace to committees of the County Councils. To clear up the existing confusion regarding compensation, the government put forth a scheme of compensation for all licence-holders who had their licences extinguished with no wrongdoing on their part. This compensation was to be based on the comparative value of the house with a similar house without a licence.

The temperance community was unhappy with both of these proposals. They were reasonably content to have the Justices continue to issue licences. They did not want the authority for licensing transferred to a body that was stronger than the existing Justices in Brewster Session. Already by the late 1880s, the temperance reformers had successfully infiltrated the ranks of the licensing justices, many of the reformers having themselves become Justices of the Peace, and had frequently been able to block the appointment to the Brewster Session of Justices favourable to the drink trade.[143] Furthermore, the new proposal would mean greater difficulties in getting Local Option implemented, the new committees being responsible to a much larger community than the old licensing magistrates.

But it was the compensation clauses that aroused the full ire of the Temperance Party and galvanised it into action. When the contents of the Bill were publicised, the United Kingdom Alliance called an executive meeting for 21 March 1888, and there resolved to fight the compensation clauses, calling upon 'all good citizens to assist in opposing these portions of the licensing clauses of the measure'.[144] The Alliance directed much of the campaign that ensued, encouraging its agents and auxiliaries to organise demonstrations in every town where they had any influence. The Alliance printed large numbers of anti-compensation petitions and offered to send them free to anyone who wanted to use them.[145] The National Temperance Federation was not idle either. It called a meeting at which delegates from twenty-four national temperance organisations attended. These delegates drew up a memorial to the Prime Minister, objecting to the transfer of authority and asking that Local Option be allowed. The Federation also protested the compensation clauses, claiming that they created a 'vested interest' in the licence that had previously not been allowed.[146]

The campaign focused on two activities. The first was to give the Bill the maximum publicity and to let the people know how much the payment of compensation would cost the country. Prominent men who supported the temperance reformers' stance were given favourable publicity in the temperance journals even if they were not in the anti-drink camp, while those who supported compensation were regarded as enemies even if they were otherwise temperance supporters.[147] Letters appeared in the local and national press on the issue, with Alliance agents spearheading the local letter-writing campaigns.[148]

The second and probably more important activity of the anti-compensation campaign, from the movement's point of view at least, was the organisation of mass demonstrations throughout the land. The Alliance directed its agents and auxiliaries to work for such demonstrations wherever they could. In Manchester and London monster demonstrations were held and the campaign was capped by a huge anti-compensation march to Hyde Park where a great rally was held on 2 June 1888,[149] attended by ten Members of Parliament.[150] After this agitation of 'unprecedented character', according to one temperance historian, 'which increased in force every day', the licensing clauses were withdrawn in June 1888.[151] The temperance reformers felt they had won the first round and girded themselves for bigger battles, which would, they hoped, lead to the adoption of Local Option.

> At no period in the history of the movement had the temperance party been so united and determined as in the conflict with the government on the licensing clauses of the Local Government Bill. With one voice and one heart they sank all small differences . . .[152]

So wrote one historian, giving a rather romantic view of the compensation fight. In fact, the movement did not sink its differences. The Church of England Temperance Society would not support anti-compensation activities, officially stating that licence owners had a moral, if not legal, right to just compensation for the loss of the licences.[153] Because of the CETS position, many reformers refused to recognise the society as being a full member of the temperance movement. Lists of temperance organisations would often include the United Kingdom Alliance, which was not really a temperance society, but exclude the Church of England Temperance Society, which certainly was.[154] But at this point many anti-drink workers felt they did not need the influence of the largest temperance organisation in the land. They took the position that those who would not support them completely should be treated as members of the opposition, and thus alienated potential allies; many moderates withheld their support of temperance measures because they did not want to be allied with 'fanatics'.[155]

Two years later, in 1890, another government bill was put forth to give compensation for extinguished licences and again the temperance movement mobilised its forces and successfully fought the enemy. At this point the Temperance Party was at the peak of its power, or so it seemed. It had managed to get the support of many local religious groups. Although the national denominational temperance bodies were not very active[156] and could not claim much power, the strength of denominational temperance, as with the rest of the movement, was in the local bodies. When the anti-compensation excitement had galvanised the town temperance societies into action, the chapel groups were an invaluable source of help. The non-conformist chapels, already seasoned veterans of pressure politics, having fought against their civic and religious disabilities, gave the fruits of their experience and their mass support to the anti-drink campaigns. Especially in the northern towns, where temperance was becoming an important part of chapel culture, the support of the chapel communities was of great importance in the crusade against drink.[157] Charles Garrett agitated in the *Methodist Times* against the compensation clauses, stimulating opposition among Methodists who were not normally closely identified with the anti-drink movement.[158] This national Methodist leader was the greatest ally the temperance movement had in the Methodist hierarchy. During the 1885 election he had appealed to his coreligionists to 'vote for a sober country' by supporting anti-drink candidates.[159]

The anti-compensation campaigns brought many temperance groups to the fore in the political agitation. The Good Templars, with branches in most towns, were leaders in local fights against the government's bills. This order was the most extreme politically of any of the national temperance societies. Their head, Joseph Malins, wrote and lectured against compensation and in support of prohibition. Devoted to teetotalism and to a society free from drink, the Good Templars were often called 'fanatics' by their opponents,[160] but they were a cohesive body that could command a great deal of loyalty among members of the temperance community if they chose to do so. Right after the first compensation fight, the Good Templars in Brighton proposed to set up 'Temperance Hundreds' for the parliamentary borough, 'to take cognisance of all matters, political and municipal, which concern that body and its aims and principles'. They wanted a Temperance Party that would put the temperance cause first and political affiliations second.[161]

It had frequently been suggested by many groups that a party devoted just to temperance should be set up, and the Alliance had talked of itself as a political party. But the many teetotallers who were experienced in the political life of the country realised that such a move would do more harm than good, and that temperance supporters, being in the minority, could exert far more influence by infiltrating the existing parties.[162] This was successfully done with the Liberal Party: in 1886 the National Liberal Federation, under great pressure from its temperance and chapel members, adopted Direct Veto as part of its programme, and for the next nine years temperance and liberalism were closely indentified. In 1891 the United Kingdom Alliance was officially recognised as an auxiliary of the Liberal Party.[163]

There had been abstainers in Parliament for decades but, until the political agitation over the licensing bills of the 1860s and early 1870s,[164] no one really cared who was a teetotaller and who was not – it was a personal matter. But with the increasing agitation, temperance and teetotalism became issues on the political scene. Prior to 1872, neither political party, Liberal or Conservative, could have been considered a particular friend of temperance. Although many of the temperance leaders in Parliament were radical members of the Liberal Party, there was also a substantial number of Conservative temperance supporters. Forbes Mackenzie, Selwin-Ibbetson, Wilson-Patten, all of whose names were attached to bills that favoured temperance, were Conservatives, while Bass and Whitbread, both from famous brewing families, were Liberal members. In 1862 a pro-temperance bill was supported by forty-eight Liberals and forty-seven Conservatives.[165] It was not until the United Kingdom Alliance decided to take direct action that a division along party lines began to take shape. At the election of 1872 candidates were asked by representatives of the Alliance whether or not they would support the Permissive Bill, and their answers were given wide publicity.[166] More and more, temperance supporters favoured the Liberals, while the liquor interests turned towards the Conservatives. This alignment was a boon to the Conservative Party, which was given large sums of money by the liquor trade.[167] By the mid-1890s, after the Liberal Party had adopted temperance goals, it could be said that the liquor interests were firmly established in the Conservative Party.[168]

In 1893, William V. Harcourt, the Liberal Chancellor of the Exchequer and a strong supporter of local prohibition, introduced into Parliament the Liquor Traffic (Local Control) Bill. This measure allowed for a poll to be taken on the prohibition of licences in a locality on the demand of one-tenth of the municipal electors. If a two-thirds majority of those voting favoured prohibition, then no licences would be issued after three years had elapsed. Exempt from this prohibition, however, were inns, hotels, restaurants and railway refreshment rooms. No compensation was to be paid for any licence thus extinguished. As can be expected, the Bill caused a national furore, with the anti-drink forces strongly supporting it, while the trade, as the drink industry was commonly called, was just as strongly opposed. A stalemate developed and the Bill was stalled in the Commons. Both Gladstone, the Prime Minister, and Harcourt assured the Bill's supporters that it would be reintroduced the following year, when they thought it would have a better chance of passing.

Meanwhile, in 1893, flush with the certainty of approaching victory, the Temperance Party held a series of national conferences which were called by the participants 'Temperance Parliaments'. The first one was organised and financed by Arnold F. Hills, a teetotaller who was also President of the Vegetarian Federation Union. Representatives came from national, county and local societies, as well as from the Church of England Temperance Society and non-conformist temperance societies.[169] At this gathering, which lasted two days, a standing committee was set up to deal with a series of anti-drink proposals and it was agreed to meet the following year to draw up a United Temperance Bill.[170]

Unfortunately for the anti-drink movement, these parliaments did more harm to the movement than good. By the time the fifth one met in 1896, feelings were running high on practically every issue and the reformers were proving to be just as contentious as their critics said they were. Everyone present agreed that changes were needed in the licensing laws, but that was the only point on which all were in accord. At one end of the spectrum of views was the Church of England Temperance Society, which supported only the mildest of measures. Even on the Liberal Liquor Control Bill that was before Parliament in 1893 the CETS remained neutral. Among its members there were both opponents and proponents of this Bill; the only way the society could avoid splitting asunder was by taking no position at all but leaving it to the individual members to make their own decisions on anti-drink matters.[171] At the other end of the spectrum were the representatives of the Good Templars and the UKA, the two prohibitionist organisations, for whom nothing less than total prohibition would be satisfactory. The UKA repeatedly announced that they were not interested in improving the licensing system but in destroying it,[172] although in 1894 their representative, James Raper, did agree to support the ameliorative efforts of the reformers while waiting for prohibition to be established.[173] There was constant conflict also over compensation, the CETS leading the group that favoured compensation, which included the organiser Hills himself, and the UKA and the Good Templars refusing to agree to payment for any licence. Because of this conflict T. P. Whittaker, a well-known temperance Member of Parliament and son of one of the first teetotallers, wanted to adjourn the conference in 1894 with the understanding that it never meet again.[174] He saw the negative effect it was having on the movement. But it was decided to carry on.

The end of these temperance parliaments finally came in 1896, after a bitter fight over a clause in the United Temperance Bill proposing to limit licences according to the number of inhabitants to be served. Opponents managed to get the clause removed from the Bill and, during the fight that ensued, Hills, among others, withdrew.[175] Thus, as these meetings ended, the reformers were further than ever from agreeing on a common platform for the whole anti-drink movement.

# 9 A World Free From Drink

After the anti-compensation demonstrations, the temperance movement continued its high pitch of political involvement. The reformers knew there was a great battle coming in the near future, one that would have a momentous effect on the anti-drink movement thoughout England. Interest in the issue of drink was kept alive by the introduction of a Local Option Bill in Parliament by Sir William Harcourt,[1] the Chancellor of the Exchequer, in 1893[2] and again in 1895. Special electoral associations were organised through the country by the United Kingdom Alliance to encourage local pressure for the Bill.[3] At a county conference held in Bradford in 1893, a resolution was passed reminding the Liberal Associations of the help the Temperance Party had given them at the previous election and claiming some share in their victory. The reformers presented their 'due bills' for payment by asking the Liberal Associations to support the Liquor Traffic (Control) Bill as presented by Harcourt. Many local Members of Parliament, as well as local government officials, were present at this meeting.[4] The British Temperance League, at its conference in York, also reminded the Liberal Party of its obligation to support temperance legislation.[5] But, even though the prohibitionists held demonstrations all over the country to support it, the Bill was stalled in the House of Commons each time it was introduced.[6]

Despite these failures the temperance reformers were optimistic, as is clear in the speech of Alderman Clegg of Sheffield at a meeting of the local auxiliary of the Alliance. Proudly he proclaimed that, despite the fact that little had been accomplished in temperance legislation, 'the Temperance Movement stood in a much better position than it had ever done before'.[7] W. S. Caine, the prohibitionist MP and head of the National Temperance Federation, proclaimed publicly that the Advanced Temperance Party in Parliament would accept nothing less than the Local Veto; no compromise would be made. 'We have given our lives to fifty years of agitation and spent hundreds of thousands of pounds in convincing the country that our proposals are reasonable, practical and possible and we have succeeded', he wrote.[8] The three major demands of the Advanced Temperance Party were Sunday Closing, Direct Veto and No Compensation.[9] Caine also wrote that the Advanced Temperance Party thought the 'trade in intoxicants is immoral and therefore they are not interested in licensing schemes of any sort; just the complete abolishment of licenses.'[10]

However, with all the publicity for Local Option, Direct Veto and Local Veto, there was much confusion in the public's mind as to what these terms meant. Even to various temperance reformers they meant different things. Sir William Harcourt, in a speech in the Free Trade Hall, Manchester, in 1888, admitted that there was concern by some over the difficulty of defining Local Option. He said:

> I am sometimes asked – what do you mean by Local Option. It is a vague term, it is said. I should not have imagined it very difficult to understand . . . I suppose it means this – that in each locality the proper authority should decide the question of the liquor traffic according to the wants, the sentiments, and the will of the people of the district controlling the liquor traffic.[11]

Later in this same speech he defined what he meant by controlling the liquor traffic: 'the locality should determine what houses should be licensed, whether any, or none at all, or how many'.[12] But Sir William did not clear up the confusion surrounding the meaning of Local Option and there were continuing demands in the non-temperance press for a more detailed definition. Eventually in the 1895 election, this lack of precision enabled the drink trade to propose its own version of Local Option, one that, naturally, was repugnant to most moderate drinking Englishmen.[13]

Local Option, for many people, came to mean the election by local voters of a neighbourhood board, which would introduce local prohibition or regulate the liquor traffic according to the wishes of the electorate. There were objections from many sides. Some people feared it would lead to the tyranny of a majority over the minority.[14] To escape some of this criticism the Liberal Local Veto Bill made a two-thirds vote necessary for the denial of any or all licences and a simple majority for a limit on the number of licences to be issued. But, besides the tyranny of the majority, other defects were pointed out. In communities where the majority of inhabitants were already quite temperate, prohibition would have a good chance of acceptance, whereas in a heavy drinking area, where it was truly needed, there would be little chance of the voters' approval.[15] Furthermore, there was always the possibility that some areas would vote for local prohibition so long as they could use neighbouring liquor facilities. This was not so fanciful as it might seem; it had frequently happened in the United States, where Local Option had been adopted by a number of states.[16] The Fabians feared Local Option could be used as a class weapon in districts where the middle class predominated – as a means of forcing the working men to live elsewhere. For not only was the worker dependent on the public houses for drink, entertainment and various types of meetings, but his meals were often supplied by the 'locals'.[17]

A problem related to Local Option could arise from popular election of the licensing board. A battle between the temperance groups on one side and the publicans on the other could create a situation in which the public interest would be crushed by the protagonists. This occurred in Aberdeen, where the two groups fought out every election of the town council, which issued licences. Those not directly concerned would stay away from the polls and the elections degenerated into battles between temperance reformers and publicans.[18]

Direct Veto was a variation of Local Option. Again it is very difficult to discover what it actually meant but, according to Peter Winskill, the temperance historian, it meant that local electors should vote directly on the drink question – in other words, a local referendum.[19] Direct Veto Associations fought unsuccessfully for its adoption. It may be that, defining their aims too carefully, they drastically limited their following. However, Local Option and Direct Veto came to be viewed by many people as the same thing. They were even used interchangeably by their supporters, including the Alliance in its publications.

Another variation of local action was called Local Veto. This, the Fabians claimed, meant a vote by the electors of a neighbourhood as to whether or not they wanted to reduce by one-quarter the number of licensed premises in their district.[20] Mr Gladstone said of this that 'the mere limitation of numbers – is, if pretending to the honour of a remedy, little better than an imposture';[21] in this view he was joined by the Alliance, who felt that a reduction of public houses would not lead to a reduction in drinking. Nevertheless, both political parties subscribed to the belief that fewer licences should be issued, which had also been the first recommendation of the Convocation of York when it investigated intemperance in 1874.[22]

The non-temperance press was also caught up in the licensing excitement. In the autumn of 1894 *The Times* sent a special correspondent to investigate the municipal control of drink by the Swedish city of Gothenburg. The resulting articles in the London paper were not at all favourable to the Swedish system.[23] This negative view called forth an angry letter to *The Times* from the Bishop of Chester, a great proponent of municipalisation of the English drink trade. He complained that their anonymous 'special correspondent' was really Arthur Shadwell, a popular journalist who had previously written a critical article about bishops and the drink trade.[24]

Despite all the excitement, not everyone believed that the temperance millennium had come. Many prominent politicians were uneasy at having Local Veto as a part of the Liberal Party programme. The *Westminster Gazette*, a well-known Liberal journal, questioned whether the Local Veto Bill was popular with all sections of the party.[25] Herbert Gladstone, the Grand Old Man's son and a nationally known politician in his own right, had been a long-time opponent of the Local Veto Bill, but had changed his position on the grounds that 'most of the party supported it'. However, he continued to call it a 'contentious measure' and dealt with it 'with a certain amount of apprehension'.[26] Herbert Gladstone, wrote the *Alliance News*, was never more than a 'candid friend' to Local Veto.

The opposition to temperance measures was strong. Many moderate drinkers were unhappy with these political developments. Arthur Shadwell, who had angered the Bishop of Chester with his articles in *The Times*, was again in print. He defended the publicans against the 'Hebraic wrath' of the reformers, noting that 'Christian forgiveness' was extended only to the buyer, who was treated as an 'erring brother' by the anti-drink movement.[27] In his article, 'The English Public House', Shadwell charged the extreme reformers with getting psychological satisfaction from stories of degradation due to drink; far from being shocked, the reformers 'gloat over a particular bad drunkard' and 'the more dreadful the details of his case the greater their satisfaction'.[28] The author also pointed out that the United Kingdom Alliance seemed little interested 'in promoting sobriety or improving the habits of the people'. Instead they focused all their hostility on the drink trade, making them the sole villains responsible for all drunkenness in the country; 'the means have become the end.'[29] Shadwell discussed the important role of the public house in the leisure-time activities of the working class, pointing out that the majority of patrons were regular customers, honest working-class people coming in for a glass of beer and to pass the time away from the factory.[30] The licensed house was an important centre in the lives of many urban working-class families. That there was drunkenness no one denied, claimed Shadwell, but he believed that everyone, including the publican, would like it eliminated. The public objected to the demand of temperance reformers that all drink be banned because a small minority were habitual drunkards.[31]

## THE CAMPAIGN OF 1895

When the government fell and a general election was called for July 1895, the anti-drink workers were ready. The moment they had been waiting for had finally arrived; an editorial entitled 'The Struggle at Hand' appeared in the *Alliance News*, organ of the United Kingdom Alliance. Local, national and sectarian newspapers contained election manifestos of all the various anti-drink organisations; very few ignored this opportunity to issue a grand call to action.[32] the *Alliance News*, the major prohibition publication, saw the election as a 'conflict between interest and patriotism such as had not been witnessed for the last fifty years. The forces of drink, lust and sobriety are in deadly conflict.'[33] The Temperance Committee of the Wesleyan Conference was more moderate in its language as it called on all Wesleyans to vote 'only for candidates who support Local Option'.[34] The Good Templars' Executive of the Grand Lodge of England adopted and publicised a resolution calling on all Good Templar electors and workers to put 'forth strenuous efforts in their various constituencies to secure the return of Members of Parliament who will support the passage of a Local Veto Bill uncomplicated by compensation'.[35] The electors of the north of England were asked by the North of England Temperance League to 'weigh well the issue; consider what defeat means, and what victory will give . . .'[36]

The Bishop of London, a long-time friend of temperance and president of the National Temperance League and also of the Church of England Temperance Society, asked members of the Established Church's temperance organisation to 'press on candidates for seats in parliament' the importance of legislation to promote the cause of temperance. He wanted them to work for Sunday Closing, regulation of clubs, the interdiction of the serving of alcoholic beverages to children, the abolition of grocers' licences and a reduction in the number of public houses.[37] Nothing was officially said about Local Option as proposed by the Liberal Party; the Church of England Temperance Society did not support confiscation of licences *without* compensation where there had been no infringement of the law.[38] Canon Basil Wilberforce, grandson of the anti-slave reformer and son of Bishop Wilberforce, was one of the most committed of the teetotal Anglican hierarchy. He made his own personal appeal to the electors, asking them not to vote for a Conservative–Unionist if they could not vote for a Liberal candidate.[39]

Canon Wilberforce, like many other members of the anti-drink movement at this time, was very much concerned with the power of the drink trade.[40] The trade was increasingly controlled by fewer and more powerful limited liability companies which regulated even the retail sale of their products through houses whose licences they controlled.[41] These 'tied houses' could sell only the beer of the brewery that controlled them and thus many small local breweries were forced out of business. This monopolistic trend was deplored by many Englishmen, not only because of its adverse commercial consequences, but also because of the potential political power such an industry could exercise. Lord Rosebery, leader of the Liberal Party at this time, although no staunch temperance reformer, publicly denounced this political power of the 'trade'.[42] In Leeds the members of the Off Licence Holders Protection Association also condemned the tied house system, but for different reasons. They saw it as a threat to their own businesses.[43]

Not all temperance supporters were happy with the election manifestos of the anti-drink organisations. The old problem that had plagued the Temperance Party for decades reasserted itself: should one vote for one's own party or should the temperance issue take precedence? The Advanced Temperance Party felt the temperance issue was the most crucial one, and that no reforms could be made without first eliminating drinking.[44] On the other hand, some prominent Englishmen agreed with Lord Morpeth when he resigned as vice president of the North of England Temperance League because he found its election manifesto offensive.[45] But such individual acts of disapproval could not affect the high spirits of the reformers, who were not going to be hampered by those who were not willing to give their support, 100 per cent, to this great fight.

The trade matched the efforts of the anti-drink forces, throwing itself into the campaign with 'volcanic energy'.[46] The London publicans in particular consolidated their efforts against all the temperance candidates in the metropolitan area,[47] and were in a good position to do so because of their close and intimate contact with many voters. Cards were placed in the windows of many licenced houses proclaiming that, 'This house will be closed if the Liberals are elected.' Many people still did not understand what Local Option meant and the drink trade took advantage of this ignorance; its own hostile interpretation claimed that all public houses would be closed and total prohibition imposed on the working classes.[48] The Yorkshire Victualler Defence League issued an appeal to its members to use their 'enormous power' in defence of their 'just rights and for the protection of their houses'.[49] The Trade Defence League, a co-ordinating association for all the individual trade defence orgnisations throughout the country, entered the fray with gusto; the League claimed to have spent only £5000 pounds on this campaign,[50] but the prohibitionists were sure they had spent a great deal more.[51]

With these two protagonists thus armed and ready for battle, the election was bitterly fought. During the days of polling and counting (which at that time took a number of days), the two sides were busy fighting all the time. The executive of the Alliance met daily in their Manchester headquarters.[52] Every return was scrutinised and either rejoiced over or bemoaned as appropriate. It was difficult to be indifferent to the issues; almost all Englishmen would be affected by the outcome of this election, not only for its temperance measures but also for the rest of the Liberal programme.

When the results of the election were finally computed and a clear picture of the new political establishment had emerged, the reformers were truly shattered. 'Drink swept the country more thoroughly than it had ever done before', lamented Sir Wilfrid Lawson, the head of the United Kingdom Alliance.[53] He himself had managed to be re-elected, but with a reduced majority. His prohibitionist colleague, W. S. Caine, who was head of the British Temperance League and the National Temperance Federation as well as a leader in the anti-compensation campaigns, went down in defeat, as did many prohibitionist candidates. Almost all the leading Liberals who had been identified with temperance reform lost their seats. Despite the boasted popularity of Sir William Harcourt, this Liberal leader was turned out of his seat at Derby.[54] John Morley, another Liberal who had spoken on the anti-drink platform, also lost. In London alone, fifty-one successful candidates were against Local Option and only eight supported it, a striking blow against the prohibitionists in the capital city.[55] Besides Lawson, the only national temperance figure who won his election was T. P. Whittaker of the Spen Valley in the West Riding of Yorkshire. Although his constituency was a very strong anti-drink one, he had not based his campaign on Local Option alone. He had made a broad appeal to all groups in his constituency and because of it had attracted many non-temperance votes; many Catholics, contrary to the wishes of their priests, had given him their votes.[56] According to the *Brewer's Almanack*, out of the 410 Unionist–Conservative candidates returned, 388 were favourable to the drink trade, 9 were against and 13 were openly committed to neither the trade nor temperance. Out of the 179 Liberals returned, 172 were against the drink trade, 5 supported it and 2 were unknown.[57] The working classes, this election showed, were neither anti-publican nor anti-drink.

After the initial shock had worn off, the prohibitionists reverted to their traditional rigidity and refused to accept the result as a defeat for their programme. In an open letter on the future of the prohibition party, Sir Wilfrid Lawson traced the history of the prohibition movement and insisted it not give up its principles. Claiming that past resolutions had garnered support in the House of Commons (though he failed to mention that such resolutions did not commit the supporter to any positive action) Sir Wilfrid now supposed that future support could perhaps be found in Conservative ranks. He agreed to support any 'bona fide efforts for checking the liquor trade from either side of the house', though he did not define what he meant by 'bona fide efforts'.[58]

The fledgling Independent Labour Party became the prohibitionists' scapegoat for the Liberal Party's defeat. The annual report of the Alliance claimed that this new party took away votes that would normally have gone to the Liberal Party.[59] Later, when the excitement had died down and a sober analysis of the election was made, few denied that the temperance issue had contributed to the defeat of the Liberal Party in the 1895 election.

## CONSEQUENCES OF DEFEAT: THE NATIONAL TEMPERANCE CONGRESS, CHESTER, 1895

The failure of the prohibitionists at the 1895 election reopened the split within the temperance movement between moral and legal suasion. For the former, it was a question of getting back to early temperance principles, following Joseph Livesey's belief that a drinking Parliament would not introduce prohibitionist legislation, that the people must first become convinced that drinking was wrong before they adhered to legislation against it.[60] Imposing prohibition on an unwilling population would not bring about the temperance reform that the movement had worked so hard to achieve.[61] In November 1895 a paper was read at St Bride Institute on 'How Best to Revive Interest and Effort on old Teetotal Lines'.[62] So much interest was aroused by this paper, and the discussion it stimulated, that a new organisation called the 'Old Guard' was set up, which, as its name implies, was dedicated to the furtherance of teetotal principles along the old lines. A new crusade against drink was planned but, instead of focusing on prohibition, Local Option, Direct Veto and other politically imposed restrictions, it emphasised individual work on moral suasion lines as its guiding principle.[63]

Similar plans were made for action by other groups. In the North of England, in Newcastle, a 'Forward' movement was organised both to draw in new recruits and to revive interest in moral suasion among the old members.[64] But the major national event of the temperance movement in the post-election period was the National Temperance Congress at Chester, held in September–October 1895, only a few months after the ill-fated election. The National Temperance League had traditionally been a moral suasion organisation, but it had usually supported the work of the legal suasionists at least unofficially. Many of its members were also members of the United Kingdom Alliance and other legal suasion groups; its president was the Bishop of London, Frederick Temple, who supported the Church of England Temperance Society's Temperance Bill for strong regulation of the drink trade.[65]

The President of the Congress at Chester, Sir Benjamin Ward Richardson, called for a more realistic approach to the temperance question than that taken by the prohibitionists. He urged the teetotallers to learn to be more moderate in their demands. To emphasise this point he quoted from a letter by a 'Primitive Methodist' which had been published in a popular newspaper. The writer complained that 'the intense spirit of teetotallers renders a fair discussion of the temperance question impracticable'.[66] Believing there was only one teetotaller out of every twenty adults, Sir Benjamin wanted the National Temperance League to focus its energies on educating this great majority of Englishmen who were drinkers and thus supporters of the drink-tainted world.[67] Also warning about 'sudden miracles of revivals', the president said 'they are illusory and in time do more mischief than good', and that the only solid gains the temperance movement could make would be through educating the public about the evils of drink. Moral suasion should be taught on scientific principles, 'that the body as an engine of life is a water engine and was never intended to be worked, at the temperature provided for it, by any other fluid than water'.[68] He concluded: 'We are permitted in some measure to learn His conceptions . . . Let us be wise in learning them, resolute in enforcing them as those of a Creator above the created, a Designer above the design.'[69]

The Reverend Hutton of Paisley expressed concern about the lack of personal commitment to the cause by many anti-drink workers. Unlike the president, who believed this to be due to the revivalist spirit which had led to 'bursts of action' but showed little lasting effect,[70] the Rev. Hutton saw the problem as stemming from the public outrage at the drink trade that had 'swept into the ranks of abstainers and temperance men, not a few ardent, some of them distinguished, friends of more mixed sentiments.'[71] These newcomers were less dedicated to temperance principles than the older, long-time members of the movement. Hutton also saw a general lack of understanding about the evils of drink and wanted the Temperance Movement to concentrate on instructing the public on this matter.[72]

Many other speakers at this conference emphasised the value of educating the individual. The Rev. E. L. Hicks, in speaking about the Band of Hope movement, deplored its lack of success in raising up a large number of abstaining citizens. 'We have not reaped a full harvest', he said. The lesson Canon Hicks drew from the recent election was that there was an amazing amount of ignorance and prejudice concerning the Temperance Movement', and that a more intensive effort should be made to keep Band of Hope members within the movement.[73]

Another speaker was Frederick Sherlock, a prominent and active member of the CETS and editor of *The Church Monthly*. He was concerned with the lack of interest shown by the temperance movement in enrolling young men and women eighteen to twenty-five years old. This group, falling between juvenile and adult organisations, was being overlooked by temperance workers and consequently was being lost to the movement. Only a very small proportion of this age group was represented in anti-drink organisations; this deficiency concerned Sherlock particularly because the veterans and the leaders of the movement had come up through the ranks, most of them having been active in their early adult years. Where will the veterans of tomorrow come from, he asked, if there are no young adult members today?[74]

Not all the papers read at the Chester Congress were concerned with moral suasion. In a section called 'Legislative Remedies for Intemperance', four papers offered various proposals for legal control of the drink trade. The chairman of this session was Alderman Snape, who in his opening remarks asked the supporters of the Local Veto Bill of 1895 to 'consider if there is not room for further additional options to the Bill'. He thought that the two-thirds majority 'required for the main proposal of the Bill' would have been achieved in very few cases and that the Bill would therefore have made little change in current conditions.[75] Calling for a more flexible approach by the prohibitionists, Alderman Snape asked them to consider methods of compensation and to give support to such payments; it would be worth the cost, he said, if it got rid of the 'drink evil'.[76] Among the papers presented in this section was one by the Bishop of Chester, who was again offering up his proposals for the municipalisation of the drink trade, and another by A. F. Hills in support of his brainchild, the United Temperance Bill.[77] J. J. Cockshott of Southport presented to the conference the position of the CETS on temperance legislation, while at the other extreme of the legislative picture, David Lewis of Scotland, the most prohibitionist of the four, put forth the traditional no-compensation prohibitionist view. Believing 'the evil is in the drink and not in the time, place or circumstances in which it is sold', Lewis spoke for the abolishment of the trade, not its regulation.[78] Lewis was the only one of the four speakers to receive the wholehearted support of the Alliance, which was made clear in the biased reporting of the conference in the pages of *Alliance News*. Lewis's views were given great prominence while those of the other speakers were dismissed as being of little worth.[79]

One of the consequences of the failure of the local prohibitionists in 1895 was a search for legislative alternatives to Local Option. Many schemes proposed in bygone years received renewed attention from those who wished to continue the fight for increased control of the trade. Various forms of municipalisation were explored and expounded in journals of the day. New attention was given to the Bishop of Chester's proposals, based on the Gothenburg system which operated in Sweden and Norway. It was admired and supported by many English reformers, including Joseph Chamberlain. As mayor of Birmingham, Chamberlain had managed to get the city council to agree to buy up local licensed houses whenever they were thought to be redundant.[80] However, little came of this experiment because Chamberlain left the local scene for national politics before much was accomplished.

In the Gothenburg system, all drink shops, except those selling beer, were owned and controlled by the municipality and run by salaried managers, who derived no personal gain from the sale of drink. All profits were used either for special public projects or to pay some of the expenses of local government and thus reduce the rates. The whole community would enjoy the profits of the trade, and it was this aspect of the system that caused such great hostility to the municipalisation of drink. On the matter of profits, many anti-drink reformers agreed with John Burns MP, when he said,

City ownership of public houses will elevate drinking into a civic virtue, boozing will be a test of local patriotism, and working people will drink their village into a free library, or a park, by a process that will land many into the hospital, some into gaol, a great number into asylums, all into misery, and send not a few to the cemetery.[81]

## THE NATIONAL PROHIBITION CONVENTION, NEWCASTLE, 1897

The Congress at Chester did not heal any wounds within the movement and even increased the despondency of the reformers, particularly the prohibitionists. Guy Hayler, an agent of the North of England Temperance League whose life had been dedicated to the cause, was anxious to do something to bring about changes. Writing to another temperance agent he said, 'both the London and Provincial Newspapers continually hold up the Temperance Party to ridicule and contempt and this will doubtlessly go on, while the Temperance Party are divided and disunited, the cards of every juggler and the pawns of every intriguer'.[82] Hayler, supported by George Tomlinson, the Newcastle agent of the United Kingdom Alliance, proposed that a prohibition convention be held that would be a 'favourable opportunity of determining the future aggressive action of Temperance reformers'.[83] Just as the first prohibition conference of 1862 had helped make the issue of prohibition a national one and had bound the anti-drink forces together, this new convention, it was hoped, would bring the scattered remnants of the iniquitous defeat of 1895 together and help create a substantial anti-drink thrust. It was to take place in Newcastle, where temperance sentiment was extremely strong and where the 'Forward' movement of the North of England Temperance League was active.

The National Prohibition Convention was held on 3–9 April 1897, and was attended by all the faithful old prohibitionists. They were there to show that the old cause was not dead, despite what many of its critics said.[84] Frederic Lees, though now an old man and unable to make the journey, sent a paper dealing with the history of the prohibition movement; Thomas Whittaker of Scarborough, that veteran from the early days of Preston, read it and was given an ovation. The cheers, no doubt, were meant for both Lees and Whittaker who were the last of the old breed.[85] In his opening address, the chairman, Sir Wilfrid Lawson, answered the statements of Sir Benjamin Richardson at Chester and others who had insisted on moral suasion as the only method of fighting drink. Lawson talked of the work of Father Mathew and, using the standard argument for prohibition, pointed out that although the Irish priest gave the teetotal pledge to millions of Irishmen who believed they would be able to avoid drink, the majority broke their promise at the nearest public house; they were unable to resist the temptation of the drink shops all around them. If there had been prohibition at that time, Lawson declared, many more of these pledged men would have kept their promise. Instead, Ireland was as drunken as if Father Mathew had never been.[86] Unable to boast of any great achievements, Lawson was proud of the negative accomplishments of the anti-drink forces: he pointed out that, largely because of the efforts of the United Kingdom Alliance, there had been no legislation favourable to the drink trade in the past twenty years.[87]

Contrary to the hopes of its organisers, the Prohibition Convention of 1897 did not bring the warring anti-drink factions together. Nor did it give the prohibitionists leadership for a new forward thrust. Instead it gave a public platform to those who wanted to vent their frustrations and unhappiness over the failure of their efforts of 1895. The *Newcastle Chronicle*, a paper favourable to the temperance cause, complained that the tone of the convention was 'objectionably high pitched'.[88] There was much talk about their 'righteous cause'. When James H. Raper, a well-known Alliance agent, made a positive remark about municipalisation,[89] the Rev. C. F. Aked answered him in the words of Isaiah, saying that the drink traffic was 'a league with hell and a covenant with death'.[90] He also suggested that some of those present at the convention were not genuine prohibitionists dedicated to the elimination of the sale of drink.[91] True prohibitionists, he insisted, were not interested in schemes for improving the licensing system; they were not reformers but destroyers of all licensing and all sales of drink.[92] The large numbers at this convention who agreed with the Rev. Aked caused such an outburst that, according to the official report, it 'threatened to disturb the harmony of the convention'.[93] Terryson Smith, who said he 'had been called a firebrand and he glories in it . . .' and continued to speak in this vein, was eventually 'made to sit down and be quiet'.[94]

There were many complaints over the lack of support the movement received from ministers of religion. James Winning of Paisley voiced his unhappiness over the continuing use of alcoholic wines for the sacraments and said he 'dare not' ask his two sons to become church members because they would get 'drink at the Lord's Table'.[95] An officer of the Salvation Army described his organisation's attitude towards prohibition. The Salvation Army was dedicated to the abolition of liquor-selling because it was demoralising to those who profited from it. The brewer and the publican had souls to save and it was the duty of the Salvation Army to do this work.[96] To them the publican was the victim, not the villain as he was in many prohibition circles.

This convention was unique in its treatment of women. They were given a large share in the general proceedings as well as a section of their own called 'Women's Help for Prohibition'. Although there were temperance reformers in England who were supporters of women's rights – especially their right to the franchise, which it was hoped would lead to greater support for anti-drink candidates[97] – the movement as a whole was still very much dominated by men. Very few of the national organisations had women in policy-making position, except of course those organisations that were distinctly female, such as the British Women's Temperance Association. But at Newcastle women for the first time were given, officially at least, 'full recognition as equal helpers'.[98] Over the last years of the century the women's temperance associations had increasingly focused on legislative restrictions on drink, which brought them into agreement with the Alliance on many issues relating to prohibition.

Frederic Lees, the veteran polemicist for the movement, in his paper 'The Last Decade of Temperance Work', showed his dissatisfaction with the public's attitude towards the prohibitionists. 'We have awakened the people to the dangers [of drink] but have received small thanks, insults and scorn in return.'[99] He decried the 'unholy Alliance of Beer and Church'[100] and thought that the clergy should be better educated on the dangers of drink. 'Our failure therefore is due to our ignorance or inattention to His methods.'[101] He wanted teetotallers to avoid '*Compromise* of principle' and called on the prohibitionists to reject any traditional allies who were now willing to compromise their former principles.[102]

The Newcastle convention intensified the schisms in the ranks of political temperance workers. Both old problems and new ones prevented a unified front. With emphasis on the reduction of licences there was a return of the compensation issue: should compensation be paid, and, if so, how should it be done?

## GOVERNMENT ACTION

Although the incoming government in 1895 was spared pressure from the anti-drink forces, especially the more extreme ones, it could not escape the demands of its allies. The drink trade wanted legislation that would give them security and regulate their operations, not by custom but by law. They wanted their right with regard to licensing made clear so that they would be protected from the continuing harassment of temperance reformers. The Earl of Wemyss introduced a bill in February 1896 designed to clarify the situation,[103] but nothing came of it. The government preferred to do nothing on the licensing question if it could avoid it. For the Conservatives as for the Liberal Party, the field of liquor licensing was 'a sea strewn with many wrecks',[104] where any action would lead only to trouble.

But the Church of England Temperance Society, which claimed that its members – despite Canon Wilberforce's plea[105] – had given support mostly to the Conservative–Unionist Party, would not allow the matter to drop.[106] A deputation to the new prime minister, Lord Salisbury, of eleven bishops under the leadership of Frederick Temple, Bishop of London, demanded changes in the existing system. Most of all they wanted Sunday Closing and a reduction in the number of licences issued.[107] A meeting was arranged between this delegation and the government in February 1896. Salisbury was blunt. He would not support any further legislation concerning Local Option. It was not politically wise. The opposition of the extreme temperance reformers to any moderate reform made it fruitless to spend one's time in sponsoring such legislation.[108] Balfour, who was also present at this meeting, took the same position. What the government was willing to do was to set up a Royal Commission to study changes in liquor licensing.[109] This committed the government to nothing, yet gave them an excuse for inaction in the matter of licensing legislation during the three years the Commission sat.

The Commission was made up of an equal number of drink trade supporters, temperance reformers and neutrals, known in some quarters as 'Christians at large'.[110] The chairman was Viscount Peel, a former speaker of the House of Commons, who had not previously been identified with either side on the liquor issue. The drink trade was happy with his appointment and the prohibitionists accepted him.[111] During the three years the Commission sat, Viscount Peel became increasingly identified with the temperance reformers, who were in the minority because the 'Christians at large' supported the position of the 'trade'.[112] Because they were thus outnumbered, the temperance reformers set up a Central Temperance Evidence Board to organise their efforts and to make sure that every temperance viewpoint and experience was presented to the Commission.[113]

Very little came of the Commission's work. The two sides could not agree. Lord Peel and the temperance reformers issued a minority report, which was called Lord Peel's report to give it the prestige of the chairman. A second report, passed by a majority of commissioners, was of course less of a temperance document than the first one.[114] There were some points of agreement. Both agreed that there should be some control of the drink trade; free trade in alcoholic beverages found very few supporters at the end of the nineteenth century. Both parties also wanted a reduction in the number of licences and agreed on the need for compensation for those who were dispossessed without any wrongdoing. The Commission declared: 'While from the point of view of strict justice, no claim to compensation can be urged by those who lose their licences, some allowance might be made, as a matter of grace and expediency, though not of right.[115] It was on the more specific proposals that there was disagreement: the exact numbers of public houses that should be licensed, for instance, and the method by which the money to pay compensation should be raised.[116]

Within the Liberal Party there was much criticism over the party's temperance programme and many members wanted changes. The temperance reformers, stated one critic, 'by their fanaticism and extreme, and I must confess, illiberal views . . . have put back the clock of temperance reform for at least another generation'.[117] Thomas Scanlon, in another article in the *Westminster Review*, claimed that Local Option was no longer a useful plan and that alternative temperance plans should be explored by the Liberal Party. He felt that whatever the programme, compensation would have to be paid.[118]

Compensation continued to be the thorniest of problems for the anti-drink reformers. W. S. Caine, an ardent prohibitionist and one who had resigned his seat from Parliament when his party had insisted on supporting compensation,[119] was now converted to the policy of limited compensation, as was T. P. Whittaker, another of the temperance commissioners. Both these men, along with many other reformers, felt that compromises would have to be made if anything was to be achieved. Even Sir Wilfrid Lawson, when he heard Prime Minister Salisbury's position on Local Option, was, in these post-election years, willing to compromise. When the pro-temperance report of the Royal Commission was issued favouring compensation and licensing reform, the Alliance took no official stand, allowing individual members to make their own choice on whether to support or fight it. They maintained this position even when the Liberal Party, unhappy with its commitment to Local Option, decided to adopt Lord Peel's minority report as its programme for licensing reform.[120]

Not all temperance reformers were willing to accept these modifications to their position and the Independent Order of the Good Templars led the fight against any changes, refusing to have anything to do with compensation, on the grounds that publicans should first compensate all the victims of drink before they themselves received one penny.[121] The Good Templars in 1899 set up a Prohibition Party which had very little success. They were willing to fight friend and foe alike if they tried to compromise the 'no compensation' stand. When W. S. Caine, the president of the National Temperance Federation as well as the British Temperance League, and one of the leaders of the Advanced Temperance Party, stood as a candidate in a constituency in Scotland, the Good Templars were so hostile and virulent in their attack against their former ally that Caine withdrew his candidacy. He felt that to continue to fight would bring further divisions and greater dishonour on the temperance movement.[122]

The true consequence of the defeat of 1895 was not just the fragmentation of the anti-drink movement, though that was serious, but also the shift in the focus of the movement from the prohibition of all drink, to the support for schemes to control more effectively the selling of alcoholic beverages, placing the emphasis on the reduction of the number of licences not on eliminating drink.

There was never to be another great national anti-drink campaign like those of the 1880s and 1890s. Instead, the efforts of the teetotallers were devoted to less ambitious and more personal work. On the political side, support was given to correcting specific abuses by the existing system. The Band of Hope, for example, gave a great deal of support to the Children's Messenger Bill of 1902, which forbade the selling of alcoholic beverages to young children. The Bill also eliminated the giving of sweets to young customers by the publican who did it to encourage the child to come to his public house for the drink of the family.[123] But probably the most significant work of the licensing reformers was the pressure they maintained on the local Brewster Sessions. In Birmingham, Arthur Chamberlain, brother of Joseph, formed a committee of drink sellers to buy up licences for extinction. They raised money to pay compensation from amongst themselves, knowing that each licence eliminated would mean greater sales for those that were left. By this method, 10 per cent of Birmingham's licences were extinguished and by 1903 the city of Birmingham boasted a ratio of one licence for every 243 persons,[124] which was still a lot more than the one per 750 persons recommended by the Royal Commission.

In the year 1903 a total of 639 licences throughout the country were refused, though 159 of these were reinstated on appeal.[125] Conditions for holding licences were in some cases so difficult that many licences were dropped voluntarily. In 1903 more than 300 beer houses and public house licences were dropped in this way.[126] This was considered the 'greatest blow the Trade ever had' and caused the trade to agitate against such decisions by local magistrates.[127] Questions were asked in Parliament about the 'wholesale elimination of licences'[128] and fresh bills were introduced to give the trade some protection.[129] Nothing was done. The government still preferred to ignore the issue as long as possible. But in 1904 pressure was so great for a clarification of the situation through parliamentary edict that a licensing bill was passed that set up compensation for those licences eliminated for no illegal act. Prime Minister Balfour, according to Lord Askwith, wanted to improve the conditions of the public house keeper so that men of better character would be attracted to the trade, which could only be done if some security was offered to the licence-holder.[130] In 1908, when for the first time since 1895 there was a Liberal government favourable to the anti-drink movement,[131] an attempt was made to eliminate the compensation clauses of the 1904 bill and impose stricter curbs on the trade. This failed when the House of Lords rejected the bill.[132]

## TEMPERANCE AT THE END OF THE CENTURY

After a period of high activity covering almost three decades the temperance movement was declining. The promises of the 1870s and 1880s had not been fulfilled: England was not free from drink and by the end of the century seemed just as far from that state as ever. 'Riotous drunkenness' was gone, according to James Whyte, secretary of the United Kingdom Alliance, testifying before the Royal Commission on Licensing in 1899. But he added that quiet 'soaking drinking' was on the increase.[133] According to statistics, Whyte was right; the consumption of alcoholic beverages was as high as ever.[134]

The teetotallers also suffered great disappointment with the religious institutions; Gospel Temperance had not made total abstinence an integral part of Christianity, as so many reformers had hoped. The majority of churches continued to use intoxicating wines in their ceremonies. While the Church of England had established a temperance society, it had not promoted the teetotal pledge to the extent that many temperance reformers had hoped it would: in fact, it had given moderation an improved standing in the temperance movement.[135] Not since the decline of the anti-spirit societies in the late 1830s and 1840s had moderation been considered any part of the reformation. The Church of England Temperance Society was never a fully integrated part of the temperance movement; it held its own demonstrations, temperance examination and other activities. It even had its own 'temperance Sunday', not celebrating the non-conformist and non-sectarian temperance Sunday.[136]

The other churches and chapels had done even worse. The denominational temperance societies had not been a success. Methodists, Baptist and Congregational churches had all set up their own temperance societies, but they were less important within their churches than was the CETS in the Church of

England. No doubt there were a few individual temperance societies attached to various chapels and churches which had influence within their local region, but in the central adminstration temperance had surprisingly little influence. Not until the end of the century did the Methodists allow teetotal societies as part of their denomination, and in the 1890s, when persistent attempts were made to forbid men connected to the drink trade, either makers or sellers of such drink, from holding office within the Wesleyan Methodist Church, it was defeated.[137] The Society of Friends had not been anxious to impose teetotalism on its members and instead preferred to 'advise' the adoption of temperance by individual Quakers.[138] The Congregational Union of England and Wales issued a report in 1877 suggesting that 'an organization be established in each Church to promote temperance'. Other recommendations were made, such as the establishment of Bands of Hope in every church, the preaching of a temperance sermon in every church once a year and meetings to be called to discuss the matter of temperance among the church members.[139] But little further was done. After the 1870s, the Congregational Union gave little support to the temperance movement. In the Baptist Church temperance was hardly more active. A Baptist Total Abstinence Association was founded in 1874 and, although it claimed over 1000 members, its total income for the year 1879 was only £28.[140]

The reaction of local temperance groups to the adversity of the 1890s was immediate. Because in the post-election debacle a large number of supporters left the temperance ranks altogether, many societies had to be disbanded. Other temperance organisations slowly faded away without any official notification of their demise. But for those individuals who stayed with the movement the local temperance community became increasingly important. Less interested than formerly in extending their teetotal principles, the reformers concentrated on protecting those already within the movement. The children in particular were the concern of much of the activity of the local temperance societies: it was essential that they be raised without drink. To separate themselves further from the drinking world, the reformers increased their activities at the temperance hall and set up children's recreational clubs to parallel those of the drinking world. Their children were to be given a full life within their own community. Many temperance churches were founded at this time and, as we have already seen in the case of Birstall, this intensified the relationship of the teetotaller with his temperance community.

With this increase in local identification there was a concomitant decline in the nationally-focused parts of the movement. By the end of the nineteenth century both the London-based National Temperance League and the Sheffield-based British Temperance League were in difficulties.[141] An amalgamation was proposed between the two to make one really national body.[142] But nothing came of it. It was an inopportune time to attempt to extend the loyalties of local reformers, who were more interested in narrowing them. As a result of this shift of focus, the agents of the national groups became less important. Few of the local societies, which were the centres of the movement now, were any longer interested in their services, for these agents were not identified with the area; they were not local men.[143]

The United Kingdom Alliance, on the other hand, the group that had earlier been rejected by many local temperance societies as not a true part of the temperance reformation,[144] became, at the end of the century, the most important national association in the temperance world. Part of this change was due to the fact that the Alliance was making an effort to improve its image with the moral suasion groups.[145] But more important was that each of its agents was permanently placed in one town and able to put down roots in the local temperance community, while the wandering agents of the British Temperance League and the National Temperance League did not have homes in the communities they served. It has also been suggested that the Alliance agents were popular because they were well financed and the local community receiving their services would not have to pay for them.[146]

By the end of the Victorian era there was a great rise in the number of local temperance agents in the movement, serving the teetotal communities in a multitude of ways.[147] But even the role of the agent had changed somewhat, and the focus had shifted from propagandising the cause to working only within the temperance community. Temperance missioners were frequently uninterested in, and sometimes even hostile to, the drinker and drunkard.[148] When an old vagrant charged with drunkenness told the magistrates 'he did not think his relations would do anything for him as they were all teetotal', the foremost anti-drink journal, the *Alliance News*, commented: 'Any intelligent teetotaler would know that doing anything for a drunkard who will persist in being such, and who will make no effort to abstain from what makes him drunk, can only be expenses and labour lost.'[149]

It is not surprising that there were complaints about the lack of charity among teetotallers.[150] Joseph Livesey and his followers, who had constantly stressed the need for close contact between the teetotallers and the drunkards and had wanted the reformers to visit the drunken poor and degraded every Sunday morning (believing the drunkard needs more sympathy and love than any others), were dead or old and ineffective in the movement of the early twentieth century. William Livesey, the son of Joseph, was distressed by what he called 'the Gospel of Despair' which pervaded the movement.[151] This gospel believed that it is useless to attempt to convert the drunkard and that all the efforts of the teetotallers should be concentrated on preventing the young 'from falling into habits of intemperance'.[152] This was an attitude closer to the old moderation movement than to that of the original teetotal reform.

The temperance movement in the early twentieth century continued to build these isolated teetotal communities set apart from the regular 'drinking' society, and managed to continue this way until the outbreak of war in 1914. Then the isolation of the abstainers was broken down. The young teetotal males were called to the army and there learned to live happily with non-temperance comrades. They discovered that those who drank were not necessarily evil and that drinking a glass or two of ale did not inevitably lead to chronic drunkenness and disaster. At the end of the war many young teetotallers found jobs elsewhere and did not return to their native temperance communities. Some married women in other parts of the country, many not from teetotal families.[153] More generally, the spirit of England in 1918 was so changed that when the war was over and moves were made to return to normal peacetime conditions, gospel missions and the temperance reformation no longer seemed relevant to many people. The year 1914 was, for most English temperance societies, the beginning of the end.

# Conclusion

We have followed the temperance reformation from its beginnings in England through its successes on to its decline. The situation when the Victorian era ended was very different with regard to drink than when it opened. The Webbs credited the temperance movement with much of this difference, finding it instrumental in reducing alcoholism among the lower classes.[1] The public during the Victorian era had slowly come to realise the social importance of controlling drink facilities. Never again were there to be experiments in free trade of alcoholic beverages. In the century separating 1870 from 1970 there were no serious proposals to do away with the licensing system altogether. By the time Queen Victoria passed away, drunkenness was no longer treated with the good-hearted tolerance of former times. Public drunkards were taken to jail, locked up until sober and then charged with the crime of drunkenness. Among the respectable public, boasts of two- and three-bottle men were a thing of the past. Increasingly all public drinking facilities at the end of the century were coming under scrutiny.

The temperance reformers had been successful in reforming many established customs with regard to the use of drink. An increasing number of Englishmen were accepting the teetotallers' contention that the use of alcoholic beverages was not essential for good health. On the contrary, statistics had been drawn up by the temperance insurance companies as well as teetotal benefit societies, to show that abstaining working men were healthier than their drinking colleagues.[2] It was also being accepted that the children of drunkards inherited a weaker constitution than did the offspring of abstainers and therefore, men and women owed a duty to their unborn children not to drink excessively.[3]

However, the temperance cause was more than a traditional reforming movement. It was not just a response to the drinking problem of the nineteenth century but to the whole difficulty of social dislocation. There was heavy drinking and a great deal of drunkenness in rural areas, as the evidence presented to the Church of England's Committees on Intemperance clearly showed,[4] but the temperance reform in England, unlike in America,[5] was not a rural movement and only in isolated cases did

244

it find any support in agricultural areas. Instead it got its strength in the same districts where other working-class self-help and protest movements were to be found. Chartism, Primitive Methodism and trade unionism, to name only a few, were active at the same time and in the same places as the early teetotal movement. Here traditional goals and values had to be replaced with new ones that were more in keeping with the changed circumstances of the English industrial worker. New emotional outlets were also required to relieve the tensions of lives dominated by a new 'work discipline' and urban living. For many workers the drinking houses provided such an outlet, but for the teetotallers the temperance halls came to serve this role. Like other causes, the temperance movement offered its adherents a new fraternity based on common needs and experiences. Leaders such as Joseph Livesey, Thomas Whittaker and John Cassell emerged to offer a teetotal interpretation of the past and present acceptable to the reformers. Drink for them was the prime cause of all troubles. Poverty, crime and violence could be blamed on drink and one need look no further to seek the causes of want, disease and failure than drink.[6]

These leaders also offered a formula for the future that gave significance and direction to the lives of their supporters. Hard work and a disciplined life would lead to success. A man's success, they believed, was only restricted by his own personal limitations. Teetotallers, wrote Thomas Whittaker, 'made me feel that a man's position did not after all, depend so much on his birth and parentage as on his own efforts and perseverance'.[7] The temperance movement at this period gave prestige and responsibility to many talented working-class men and women who otherwise would have had little chance to exercise their organisational and leadership skills. With little formal education and few personal connections, many teetotallers would have had a harder time making their way if the movement had not helped them. With this supportive framework for its members, it is not surprising to find that teetotallers active in the 1840s had become leaders in business and politics in the 1860s, 1870s and 1880s. At the end of the century prominent families in the industrial and commercial cities had been founded by men of modest means who in the 1840s and 1850s had been members of the temperance movement.

In the 1850s and 1860s the temperance reform lay dormant.

Only a few individual groups were still active and working for the cause. A great revival appeared in the late nineteenth century, but it was a changed movement. Many of the older temperance practices were no longer sanctioned. Eccentrically dressed advocates, lurid confessions of former drunkards and unlettered and untutored leaders were no longer prominent. The temperance men of the 1870s and 1880s were well established and economically secure. Even the older members from former times had now made their place in the world. Not everyone had gathered a large fortune like Thomas Cook,[8] Sir Titus Salt,[9] or John Cassell,[10] but many were 'comfortable' and ready to enter 'respectable Victorian society. They were now anxious to move up in the established status ladder – to have social and political power commensurate with their improved economic standing. The majority of them now no longer thought of themselves as 'working class', nor were they considered part of the traditional middle class. They had some education but not much: they were followers not leaders; trained to carry out the orders of others. Their ideal character would be one that was reliable, obedient and stable, not creative or aggressive. They were part of an emerging class created by the new industrial society, the 'white-collar' class, as it has been called.

With their economic position reasonably stable, many of the temperance supporters of the late nineteenth century were busy establishing themselves within their communities. They were no longer considered 'eccentric'. They had established themselves politically through the Liberal Party's adoption of the anti-drink programme, and religiously through the Gospel Temperance movement. They were no longer outside the mainstream of late Victorian society. They had made the drinking of alcoholic beverages and the use of public houses disreputable in the chapel culture of the northern towns and were foremost in the fight to make drink a symbol of domestic profligacy.

At the same time as the temperance movement changed direction the socialist movement took on new vigour. It competed with the anti-drink reformers for the loyalties of the same segment of the population, especially for its leaders and organisers. A consequence of this rivalry was the occurrence of socialist–temperance debates, both oral and printed. The temperance movement was always anxious to have successful labour leaders who supported teetotalism on its platform. But many of these socialists found temperance was not enough to change the position of workers in society. The socialists would be satisfied only with a revolution completely remaking society. The goal of temperance, on the other hand, was a reformation rather than a revolution; it sought to effect changes in established customs only by acceptable means. The system for them was fundamentally good – it was man that was the problem.

Changes came again to the temperance movement in the late 1890s. The double blow of the political defeat of prohibition and the religious rejection of teetotalism as an integral part of Christianity at the end of the nineteenth century devastated the morale of many temperance reformers. The temperance movement left the mainstream of English society and found itself once again going against popular beliefs. For the majority of Englishmen drink could not longer be blamed for the ills of society. Other causes were examined and declared guilty. Tensions appeared in the temperance reformation with this change. Many of the reformers wanted modifications in temperance principles to make it more compatible with the beliefs of the majority feeling that 'half a loaf was better than none'. There were counter-demands supporting established customs from reformers. For many of this latter group the temperance reformation had become both the means and the end. For them teetotalism could only be kept 'pure' by isolation from the predominant drinking culture. Thus the temperance movement evolved into a sect supporting a drink-free life-style that increasingly was cut off from the rest of society. These dedicated teetotallers saw themselves as keepers of the true principles of temperance and believed that one day the rest of society would come to acknowledge the truth of their position.

One question that always arises when discussing the temperance reformation, is how many reformers were there at any given time. Unfortunately this cannot be answered with any degree of accuracy. No one could ever discover how many teetotallers there were in England. The Royal Commission on Licensing in the 1890s tried to find this out but received a variety of answers – none of them satisfactory. Joseph Malins claimed there were a total of eight million teetotallers in the United Kingdom.[11] This was surely an inflated figure. Another prominent temperance reformer, W. S. Caine, believed there were one million teetotal families in England at the turn of the century.[12] Even this figure must be regarded with suspicion. Naturally the reformers were anxious to show how extensive was their movement and so were liable to issue very high estimates of their support. The CETS was able to give its membership numbers, but not all were teetotallers and, as its officials admitted on many occasions, they had difficulty in getting an accurate count of their members. One writer felt that a parliamentary survey of membership in teetotal organisations should be made.[13]

Temperance in the twentieth century was never the vital force that it was in the nineteenth. It had not made England free from drink and the great crusade had not dealt the death-blow to the liquor industry that the anti-drink supporters had expected. But temperance did not decline because it failed to reach its goals; it withered away because its frame of reference and its values were no longer valid in English life in the twentieth century. Just as the industrialisation and urbanisation of the early nineteenth century had provided a fertile soil for the establishment and growth of the temperance movement, so did further great changes alter the needs of the people. The First World War, in particular, had caused such a social and economic upheaval that new patterns of development and new life-styles were wanted. The arguments over whether drink leads to poverty or poverty to drink, so popular in the second half of the nineteenth century, were no longer seen as a valid issue. By 1918, young ambitious workers, who seventy-five years previously would have been the backbone of the teetotal movement, were joining the cause of Labour and giving their support to collective action. Individual effort, the keystone of the temperance reformation, was now believed to be inadequate to the needs of the times.

# Notes and References

## 1 The Temperance Reformation

1. John Edgar, *A Complete View of the Principles and Objects of Temperance Societies* (Bradford, 1831).
2. Ibid.
3. Ibid.
4. Ibid.
5. The moderation pledge bound the member to abstain from all distilled beverages and to drink others in moderation. One could take spirits if the doctor prescribed it for one's health.
6. William Collins, speech at the first public meeting of the Bradford Temperance Society printed as a tract in Bradford, 1830.
7. *Temperance Penny Magazine*, V, 54 (May 1840) p. 76.
8. Ibid.
9. Thomas Whittaker, *Life's Battles in Temperance Armour* (1892) p. 98.
10. Rev. D. S. Wayland, *Temperance Penny Magazine* (October 1840).
11. Leeds Temperance Society, *Minutes*, 9 March 1831.
12. Dawson Burns, *Temperance History*, vol. I, (London, circa 1889) p. 44.
13. Ibid., p. 54.
14. Samuel Couling, *History of the Temperance Movement* (London, 1862) p. 48.
15. Many of these merchants had themselves come from working-class backgrounds and knew the importance of not dissipating one's meagre resources on drink.
16. Doctors were often accused of leading women in particular to drink by prescribing spirits for any real or imaginary ailment.
17. Burns, *Temperance History*, p. 43.
18. Ibid., p. 54.
19. Couling, *History of the Temperance Movement*, pp. 44–5.
20. Burns, *Temperance History*, p. 60.
21. Ibid.
22. Jackson helped form twenty-three new societies and pledged over 1000 in this first year as the Bradford agent. Bradford Temperance Society, *Second Annual Report*, 29 June 1832.
23. Burns, *Temperance History*, p. 76.
24. Ibid., p. 60.
25. The loyalty and commitment to the temperance cause by many of its advocates were frequently commented on. For opponents it bordered on 'fanaticism'.
26. In the south of England the Quakers were often the only group supporting temperance. See *Life of William Gregson*, J. G. Shaw (Blackburn, 1891) for the story of a northern teetotaller hired by Quakers in Brighton for work among the poor.
27. Many Friends bought large numbers of temperance tracts and then hired a working-class man to distribute them. William Wilson of Bradford paid for

half a million tracts and hired Thomas Worsnop to distribute them (F. Butterfield, *The Life and Sayings of Thomas Worsnop the Great Apostle of Total Abstinence in the North of England* (Bingley, 1870) p. 17).

28. This money was all donated by individual Friends as an act of charity, not by any official Quaker body.

29. William Livesey, *The Earliest Days of the Teetotal Movement* (private circulation, 1900) p. 131.

30. See Brian Harrison, *Drink and the Victorians* (London, 1971) Chapter 3 for a full discussion of the Beer Act of 1830.

31. Ibid., p. 82.

32. The London newspaper *Echo* wrote more than a half century later 'Notwithstanding the persistent propaganda of the teetotallers, beer is still the national drink of Englishmen' (6 June 1885) clvii.

33. The British and Foreign Moderation Society kept going until 1848 but its last years were spent in obscurity. Couling, *History of the Temperance Movement*, p. 171.

34. See Couling, ibid., pp. 117–19 for a description of the 'most tumultuous meeting ever held' in Exeter Hall. This meeting was physically disrupted over the issue of moderation and teetotalism.

35. Englishmen were becoming notorious for their excessive drinking – to be 'as drunk as an Englishman' was a common expression in France. 'You English are a nation of drunkards' said one foreigner according to Henry Ellison, honorary chaplain to the Queen. (*The Temperance Reformation Movement in the Church of England*, Henry J. Ellison (London, 1878) p. 32.)

36. Joseph Livesey, *Staunch Teetotaler* (London, 1869) p. 10.

37. William Pickwell, *The Temperance Movement in the City of York* (York, 1886) pp. 10–11.

38. Ibid., p. 9.

## 2   The Teetotal Lifeboat

1. See page 10 above.

2. Sam Couling, *History of the Temperance Movement* (London, 1862) p. 54 disagreed with this usually accepted version of the birth of teetotalism. He believed the movement orginated in Scotland in the Dunfermline Temperance Society.

3. *Preston Temperance Advocate*, November 1836. The use of the lifeboat throughout the nineteenth century was popular. In parades there was often a float depicting a lifeboat with the crew of temperance men, ready 'to rescue those drowning in drink'. The Independent Order of the Good Templars (see below, Chapter 7), as a work of charity, bought a lifeboat and gave it to one of the fishing ports. At temperance entertainments, which became very popular in the last three decades of the century, temperance men would dress up as a lifeboat crew and sing songs about rescuing the intemperate. *Keighley Visitor*, December 1866.

4. *The Teetotaler*, 25 July 1840.

5. See Joseph Livesey or any other account of the early days of teetotalism for a description of these meetings.

6. J. Livesey, *Staunch Teetotaler*, p. 86.
7. 'Some Reminiscences of a Pioneer' in *The British Temperance Advocate* (1885) p. 55.
8. Ibid., p. 56.
9. William Pallister, *Essays, Chiefly on the Temperance Questions* (Leeds, 1849) p. 28.
10. Francis Butterfield, *The Life and Sayings of Thomas Worsnop* (Bingley, 1870) p. 14.
11. Mrs Charles Wightman, *Haste to the Rescue* (London, 1860) p. 22.
12. William Livesey, *The Earliest Days of the Teetotal Movement* (private circulation, 1900) p. 168.
13. *The Temperance Advocate*, 28 June 1862.
14. Livesey, *Staunch Teetotaler*, p. 70.
15. Wightman, *Haste to the Rescue*, p. 23.
16. *The Temperance Advocate*, 28 June 1862.
17. Whittaker, *Life's Battles in Temperance Armour*, p. 233.
18. George Lucas, *Reply to Charges Against Teetotalism* (Leeds, 1851).
19. T. E. Bridgett, *The Discipline of Drink* (London, 1876) p. 214.
20. Joseph Peter Draper, *Jubilee Sketch of the Fitzroy Teetotal Association* (London, 1889) p. 109.
21. Thomas Whittaker, *Brighter England and the Way to It* (London, 1891) p. 175.
22. Joseph Livesey, whenever he found himself in a public carriage or any other such situation where there was a captive audience, always found a way to introduce the topic of temperance to his fellow travellers. *Staunch Teetotaler*, p. 167.
23. Ibid., p. 86.
24. In 1844 there was a debate raging in one of the temperance journals as to which class was the most important to the cause of teetotalism; the working class or the middle class. *Metropolitan Temperance Intelligencer and Journal*, 23 March 1844.
25. Whittaker, *Brighter England*, p. 175.
26. Butterfield, *Thomas Worsnop*, p. 39.
27. Ibid., p. 24.
28. *Lees v Gough*: speech by Edward Grubb, 15 July 1858, printed as a tract in 1858.
29. In 1839 at the British Temperance Association's conference in Liverpool a resolution was passed stating that the movement should be careful about whom they hired for their work and that personal testimonials were not worth much and only accredited agents of larger societies of general associations should be employed. *The Teetotaler*, 24 April 1841.
30. *Keighley Visitor*, July 1861.
31. Collins speech.
32. *Preston Temperance Advocate*, March 1837.
33. Pallister, *Essays*, p. 124.
34. When the temperance societies held their processions it was a common practice to have a special section of the parade reserved for reformed drunkards, who marched together proud of their particular status.
35. *British Temperance Advocate and Journal*, 15 January 1839.
36. W. Livesey, *Earliest Days*, p. 146.

37. *The Teetotal Times*, April 1846.
38. W. Livesey, *Earliest Days*, p. 50.
39. *The Temperance Advocate*, 3 May 1862.
40. *Keighley Visitor*, 1 July 1867.
41. Lucas, *Reply to Charges*.
42. John Swindon, *Teetotalism Unmasked* (Leeds, 1864).
43. Ibid.
44. Brian Harrison, 'The Temperance Question in England, 1829–1869' (unpublished Oxford DPhil thesis, 1966) p. 179.
45. The Rev. William Hudswell, 'The Great Discussion, Moderation v. Total Abstinence' report of meeting held at Music Hall, 21 June 1836, printed as a tract.
46. Ibid., speech by B. Crossley.
47. Wightman, *Haste*, p. 4.
48. See William Pickwell, *The Temperance Movement in the City of York* (York, 1886) for a discussion of the two societies and the *Northern Temperance Witness* (1845) for a description of the Bradford working class temperance group. See also Shiman, *Crusade Against Drink in Victorian England* (unpublished PhD thesis, Wisconsin, 1970) ch. III.
49. Peter Winskill, *The Temperance Movement*, vol. 3, p. 14.
50. D. S. Wayland, 'Reasons for Not Supporting Total Abstinence Societies as at present Constituted', *Temperance Penny Magazine*, October 1840, p. 156.
51. *British Temperance Advocate*, March 1885, p. 38.
52. Whittaker, *Life's Battles in Temperance Armour*, p. 98.
53. *The Teetotaler*, 28 August 1841.
54. Winskill, *Temperance Movement*, vol. 1, p. 183.
55. Couling, *History of the Temperance Movement*, p. 267; *Minutes*, Leeds Temperance Society, 24 August 1848.
56. *Preston Temperance Advocate*, Supplement, July 1836, p. 7.
57. *Band of Hope Chronicle*, April 1896.
58. M. E. Docwra, 'Woman's Work in the Victorian Era' paper read at the Women's Total Abstinence Union meeting in 1897, reprinted as a tract.
59. Ervine, St John, *God's Soldier* (New York, 1935) p. 27.
60. Whittaker, *Life's Battles in Temperance Armour*, p. 98.
61. W. Livesey, *Earliest Days*, p. 124.
62. Butterfield, *Thomas Worsnop*, p. 14.
63. William Farish, *Autobiography of William Farish* (Chester, 1889).
64. J. Livesey, *Staunch Teetotaler*, p. 238.
65. *Northern Temperance Witness*, 1845.
66. Unpublished note in minute book of the Bradford Long Pledge Association.
67. Minutes of the Educational Institute of the Bradford Long Pledge Association (unpublished).
68. Ibid.
69. Minutes of the Bradford Long Pledge Association (unpublished).
70. Ibid.
71. *Preston Temperance Advocate*, September 1834.
72. Lucas, *Reply to Charges*.
73. *Keighley Visitor*, October 1861.

74. *Temperance Advocate*, 12 July 1862.
75. *Temperance Advocate*, 9 August 1862.
76. *The Teetotaler*, 10 April 1841.
77. John F. C. Harrison, 'Chartism in Leeds' in Asa Briggs (ed.), *Chartist Studies* (New York, 1967), p. 81.
78. *Northern Temperance Witness*, 1845.
79. *The Teetotaler*, 26 September 1840.
80. Ibid.
81. Ibid.
82. Ibid.
83. *The Teetotaler*, 3 October 1840.
84. *The Teetotaler*, 18 November 1840.
85. Pallister, *Essays*.
86. Wightman, *Haste*, p. 4.
87. John Burns, *Labour and Drink*, Manchester lecture reprinted as tract, 1904, p. 19.
88. Ibid., p. 18.
89. Ibid., p. 18.
90. *Spectator*, 20 January 1872, p. 75.
91. *The Teetotal Times*, November 1846.
92. J. Livesey, *Staunch Teetotaler*, p. 54.
93. J. D. Hilton, *James Hayes Raper* (London, 1898) pp. 52–3.
94. W. Livesey, *Earliest Days*, p. 146.
95. 'Lady Brooke's Fund for the Relief of the Distress of Influenza distributed 2,000 bottles of brandy.' *Alliance News*, 5 February 1892, p. 87. For cholera see Burns, *History*, vol. I, p. 63.
96. *Keighley Visitor*, December 1866.
97. The Rev. E. Paxton Hood gave up teetotalism on doctor's advice. *Alliance News*, 11 July 1885.
98. *The Teetotal Times*, 2 December 1846.
99. William Gourlay, *National Temperance* (London, 1906) p. 155.
100. *Good Templar Watchword*, 15 December 1890.
101. Frederick R. Lees, 'Teetotalers or Tipplers. Who Live Longest and Best?', tract 1888.
102. *Keighley Visitor*, December 1866.
103. *British Temperance Advocate*, 1 December 1852.
104. Harrison, 'The Temperance Question', p. 208.
105. *The Teetotal Times and Essayist*, August 1847.
106. *The Temperance Advocate*, 26 April 1862.
107. *The Teetotaler*, 14 November 1840.
108. *The British Temperance Advocate*, 1 February 1859.
109. J. Livesey, *Staunch Teetotaler*, p. 158.
110. Ibid., p. 158.
111. *The Teetotal Times and Essays*, August 1847.
112. Harrison, 'The Temperance Question', p. 184.
113. *The British League of Total Abstainers Magazine*, January 1847.
114. *Keighley Visitor*, 1 December 1866.
115. Swinden, *Teetotalism Unmasked*.
116. *The Teetotaler*, 17 July 1841.

117. J. Livesey, *Staunch Teetotaler*, p. 551.
118. J. Wesley Bready, *Lord Shaftesbury and Social Industrial Progress* (London, 1926) p. 366.
119. *Preston Temperance Advocate*, December 1834.
120. *Keighley Visitor*, December 1866.
121. *British Temperance Advocate and Journal*, 15 May 1839.
122. J. Crossfill, *The Temperance Movement as a Business Proposition*, paper to the National Commercial Temperance League, 4 December 1915, printed as a tract.
123. *British Temperance Advocate and Journal*, 15 January 1839.
124. Whittaker, *Life's Battles*, p. 71; J. G. Shaw, *Life of William Gregson* (Blackburn, 1891) p. 7.
125. Dawson Burns, *Temperance History*, vol. I, p. 144.
126. Whittaker, *Life's Battles*, p. 69.
127. Advertisement in *The Teetotal Times*, July 1846 for apprentices.
128. Shaw, *William Gregson*, p. 150.
129. J. Livesey, *Staunch Teetotaler*, pp. 337–40.
130. There were many references to 'rich' publicans and 'poor' drinkers in temperance journals. Teetotal agents told stories about the lack of hospitality by innkeepers when the customer's money had run out.
131. *The Teetotaler*, 19 September 1840.
132. Fred. Atkin, *Reminiscences of a Temperance Advocate* (London, 1899).
133. *British Temperance Advocate*, vol. 24 (1857) p. 66.
134. *The Teetotal Times*, September 1847.

## 3 So Many Christian Icebergs to Melt

1. J. Livesey, *Staunch Teetotaler*, p. 236.
2. See pp. 68–73.
3. E. C. Urwin, *Methodism and Sobriety* (London, 1943) p. 32.
4. Ibid., p. 32.
5. Archdeacon Jeffreys, 'The Religious Objection to Teetotalism' (London, 1840) p. 30.
6. Burns, Jabez, *A Retrospect of Forty-Five Years Christian Ministry* (London, 1875) p. 157.
7. *British Temperance Advocate*, 15 July 1839.
8. Ibid., April 26, 1862.
9. Urwin, *Methodism and Sobriety*, p. 13.
10. Chapter 1 above.
11. See pp. 12–13.
12. Many early teetotallers had harsh and unkind things to say about the churches and their attitude towards teetotalism. See George Wilson McCree, *Old Friends and New Faces* (London, 1883).
13. *The Teetotaler*, 3 July 1841.
14. Jabez Burns, *Retrospect*, p. 162.
15. Urwin, *Methodism and Sobriety*, p. 37.
16. *Proceedings of the Opening of the Bradford Temperance Hall* (Bradford, 1838).

17. *Preston Temperance Advocate*, 25 March 1835.
18. William Cudworth, *Round About Bradford* (Bradford, 1876) p. 231.
19. Ibid.
20. *Alliance News*, 29 May 1886.
21. This was a movement to get the factory working day limited to ten hours.
22. J. C. Gill, *The Ten Hours Parson* (London, 1959) p. 30; Wm. Keighley, *Keighley Past and Present* (Keighley, 1879).
23. Gill, *Ten Hours Parson*, p. 2.
24. Burns, *Temperance History*, vol. I, p. 126.
25. *The British Temperance Advocate*, 15 July 1840.
26. Ibid.
27. Ibid.
28. *Preston Temperance Advocate*, March 1835.
29. Ibid., February 1835.
30. Ibid., March 1835.
31. See below pp. 81–6.
32. Winskill, *Temperance Movement*, vol. 3, pp. 146–7.
33. Ibid.
34. Ibid.
35. Ibid., vol. 2, p. 31.
36. Burns, *History*, vol. I, pp. 179–80.
37. Ibid., p. 198.
38. *Alliance News*, 4 August 1877.
39. Burns, *History*, vol. I, pp. 179–80.
40. See below pp. 99–109.
41. Winskill, *Temperance Movement*, vol. 3, p. 284.
42. Archdeacon Jeffreys, 'The Religious Objection', p. 7.
43. Wightman, *Haste*, p. 8.
44. Ibid., p. 211.
45. Gourlay, *National Temperance*, p. 120.
46. Ibid., pp. 108–9.
47. Joseph Eaton, 'Address to the Society of Friends on Temperance Reformation' (London, 1839) p. 6.
48. G. W. Olsen, 'Pub and Parish: The Beginnings of Temperance Reform in the Church of England 1835–75' (unpublished thesis, University of Western Ontario, London, Canada, 1971) p. 250.
49. George Lucas, 'Reply to Charges Against Teetotalism' (Leeds, 1851).
50. Ibid.
51. Ibid.
52. *British Temperance Advocate*, 15 April 1840.
53. Martin Field, *Bradford Temperance Society History* (Bradford, n.d.).
54. When the Church of England later established its own temperance society, this independence was recognised. All branches of the Church of England Temperance Society were to be formed only under the direct authority of the local clergyman and he was to be president of the branch.
55. CETS, Ripon Diocese, *Minutes*, 6 June 1894.
56. Urwin, *Methodism and Sobriety*, p. 12.
57. Ibid.

58. John Wesley, tract 1747, published Bristol, quoted *Church Quarterly Review*, vol. 9 (1879–80) p. 373.
59. Burns, *Temperance History*, vol. I, p. 199.
60. Urwin, *Methodism and Sobriety*, p. 34.
61. Michael S. Edwards, 'The Teetotal Wesleyan Methodists', *Proceedings of the Wesley Historical Society*, xxxiii (1961–2) p. 64.
62. Ibid., p. 63.
63. Urwin, *Methodism and Sobriety*, p. 34.
64. Whittaker, *Brighter England*, p. 71.
65. Urwin, *Methodism and Sobriety*, p. 66.
66. E. C. Urwin, *Henry Carter, CBE* (London, 1955) p. 28.
67. Ibid.
68. Robert Currie, *Methodism Divided* (London, 1968) p. 70.
69. Urwin, *Methodism*, p. 33.
70. Owen Chadwick, *The Victorian Church* (London, 1966) p. 378.
71. Ibid.
72. Edwards, 'Teetotal Wesleyan Methodists', p. 70. Edwards sees the issue in Cornwall not so much as a battle over teetotalism as a question of the Pastoral Office 'with its ominous power of converting differences into divisions', p. 70.
73. Ibid., p. 70.
74. *British Temperance Advocate*, July 1849.
75. Ibid.
76. Pickwell, *Temperance Movement in the City of York*, p. 39.
77. Shaw, *The Life of William Gregson*, p. 79.
78. Ibid., p. 79.
79. *Preston Temperance Advocate*, 25 February 1835.
80. H. B. Kendal, *History of the Primitive Methodist Church* (London, 1919) p. 80.
81. Urwin, *Methodism*, p. 37.
82. Ibid., p. 36.
83. In Great Horton it was claimed that teetotallers alone built the Primitive Methodist chapel (*Temperance Advocate*, 8 February 1862) and in Halifax the Primitive Methodists held a series of meetings with the object of getting people to sign the total abstinence pledge (*Temperance Advocate*, 3 August 1861).
84. See below, Chapter 6.
85. Many of the temperance societies were also 'self-improvement' associations and classes on many topics were held. See the *Minutes* of the Long Pledge Association of Bradford for a description of one of their educational institutes which ran from 1855 to 1863.
86. Ethel Wood, 'Sixty Years of Temperance Effort', paper read at IOGT meeting, no date. Also D. Burns, *Temperance History*, vol. I, 144. The Hull circuit was noted for the close control it exercised over its ministers in all matters, not just temperance. Chadwick, *Victorian Church*, p. 390.
87. Joseph Wilson, *Joseph Wilson His Life and Work* (Bradford, n.d.) p. 46.
88. Thomas Shaw, *The Bible Christians 1815–1907* (London, 1965) p. 53.
89. Ibid., p. 54.
90. Pallister, 'Reminiscences No. 3', *British Temperance Advocate*, 1885, p. 69.
91. Elizabeth Isichei, *Quakers* (London, 1970) p. 235.

92. Ibid., p. 238.
93. Burns, *Temperance History*, vol. I, p. 127.
94. 'Address to the Society of Friends on Temperance', 1837, signed by 50 members.
95. Joseph Eaton's will, 26 May 1858. This sum came at an important time to the national teetotal societies – they were both in financial trouble because of declining support for the movement. See below p. 74.
96. Isichei, *Quakers*, p. 238.
97. Ibid., p. 240.
98. Sam Bowly, Address to the Friends Temperance Union in 1865, p. 9.
99. In 1895 it had only an alloted budget of £174. Isichei, *Quakers*.
100. Ibid., p. 239.
101. Burns, *History*, vol. I, p. 200.
102. Peter Winskill and Joseph Thomas, *History of the Temperance Movement in Liverpool and District* (Liverpool, 1887) p. 55.
103. Isichei, *Quakers*, p. 240.
104. Ibid.
105. *The Teetotaler*, 17 October 1840.
106. John G. Woolley and Wm. E. Johnson, *Temperance Progress of the Century* (London, 1905) p. 290.
107. *British Temperance Advocate*, 15 February 1842.
108. T. E. Bridgett, *The Discipline of Drink* (London, 1876). Introduction by Manning, pp. XVIII–XIX.
109. Ibid., p. XV.
110. A. E. Dingle and B. Harrison, 'Cardinal Manning as Temperance Reformer', *Historical Journal* (1969) gives a good account of the temperance work of the Cardinal.
111. Rev. J. Keating, *The Drink Question* (London, 1914) p. 55.
112. Ibid., p. 54.
113. Ibid., p. 48.
114. Father Mathew's work is always cited as an example of what happens when no organisations are set up to work with the newly pledged.
115. *British Temperance Advocate*, 16 March 1840.
116. *The Teetotaler*, 30 January 1842.
117. *British Temperance Advocate*, December 1839.
118. *Alliance News*, 22 July 1892.
119. *Alliance News*, 12 January 1878.
120. Burns, *History*, vol. I, p. 127.
121. Ibid., vol. I, p. 161, *British Temperance Advocate*, 15 November 1839.
122. Wood, 'Sixty Years', p. 7.
123. Burns, *History*, vol. I, p. 444.
124. *The Teetotal Times*, August 1846.
125. Burns, *History*, vol. I, p. 286.
126. John Calvert, 'The Relation of the Church to the Temperance Movement' (London, 1872).
127. Burns, *History*, vol. I, p. 303.
128. These declarations not only committed the signer to support the reformation but also then could be used to publicise the cause among the uncommitted.

129. Burns, *History*, vol. I, p. 303.
130. Ibid.
131. Chadwick, *Victorian Church*, p. 365.
132. Ibid.
133. Ibid.
134. The old Independents at this period were being drawn into a Congregational Organisation and the situation was still rather fluid; it being difficult to see who was and who was not Congregational. Chadwick, ibid., p. 400.
135. Leeds Temperance Society, *Minutes*, 20 April 1847.
136. Ibid., 28 October 1847.
137. *Report*, Leeds Temperance Society Minutes, 1848.
138. Ibid.
139. See above pp. 51–2.
140. Eaton, 'Address', p. 4.
141. *The Teetotaler*, 1 May 1841.
142. Ibid.
143. *Temperance Advocate*, 26 July 1862.
144. *The Teetotaler*, 1 May 1841.
145. Pickwell, *Temperance Movement in the City of York*, p. 18.
146. *Leeds Temperance Herald*, March 1837.
147. *The Teetotal Times*, October 1847.
148. Schools, with only a few exceptions, were still controlled by the religious establishment with both Church of England and non-conformists having their own network of elementary schools throughout the country.
149. *The Teetotal Times*, September 1847.
150. Ibid., October 1847.
151. Ibid.
152. George Field, 'Historical Survey of the Bradford Temperance Society . . . 1830–1897' (Bradford, 1897) p. 15.
153. John Unwin, *Minutes*, Sheffield Temperance Society, 26 March 1863, unpublished.
154. J. Livesey, *Staunch Teetotaler*, p. 242.
155. *British Temperance Advocate*, December 1839.
156. Whittaker, *Brighter England*, p. 284.
157. McCree, *Old Friends and New Faces*, p. 26.
158. John Edgar, *Complete View of the Principles and Objectives of Temperance Societies*.
159. Burns, *History*, vol. I, p. 127.
160. There were a variety of different pledges, rather than a standard one for the whole movement. In the 1830s and 1840s there were many battles about what was to be excluded and what allowed in the pledge.
161. F. R. Lees, *The Marriage at Cana*, tract (London, 1883).
162. Ibid.
163. Ibid.
164. Ibid.
165. Ibid.
166. Ibid.
167. Mr Pyper was also an agent of the Irish Temperance League and in 1868 circulated among ministers of the Irish Presbyterian Church 1000 copies of

a tract dealing with non-alcoholic wines in the Bible. Burns, *History*, vol. II, p. 105.

168. John Pyper, *Bible Temperance and Infidelity*, tract (Belfast, 1891).
169. *British Temperance Advocate*, 1 October 1859.
170. Ibid.
171. Benjamin Parsons, *Anti-Bacchus*, American Edn (New York, 1840) p. 283.
172. W. J. Shrewsbury, 'Alcohol Against the Bible and the Bible Against Alcohol' (Bradford, 1840).
173. *Preston Temperance Advocate*, May 1837.
174. Ibid., July 1836.
175. *British Temperance Advocate*, 1 March 1852.
176. Norman Kerr, *Wines Scriptural and Ecclesiastical* (London, 1887), p. 98.
177. *Methodist Temperance Magazine*, vol. VII (1874).
178. W. E. Moss, *The Life of Mrs Lewis* (London, 1926) p. 159.
179. Ibid., pp. 159–60.
180. Ibid.
181. 'Temperance Fanaticism in Regard to Sacramental Wine', A Churchman, February 1885.
182. Ibid.
183. Gourlay, *National Temperance*, p. 367.
184. M. E. Docwra, *BWTA. What it is, What it has done and What it has still to do*, Printed copy of speech issued as tract.
185. Kerr, *Wines*, p. 143.
186. 'Temperance Fanaticism . . .'
187. Ibid.
188. Burns, *History*, vol. II, pp. 244–5.
189. Urwin, *Methodism and Sobriety*, p. 33.
190. The majority of teetotallers had no difficulty on this issue, but for those most dedicated to teetotal principles, it was a major problem.

# 4 Legal Suasion

1. Joseph Livesey, *Staunch Teetotaler*, p. 83.
2. Burns, *History*, vol. I, p. 338.
3. *British Temperance Register*, 1863.
4. Bradford Temperance Society, *Annual Report*, 1860.
5. *Report of the Royal Commission on Liquor Licensing*, 1899, p. 51.
6. James Harrison, letter to the *Huddersfield and Holmfirth Examiner*, July 1853.
7. Ibid.
8. Brian Harrison, p. 197.
9. Leeds Temperance Society, *Annual Report*, 1854.
10. Ibid.
11. British Temperance League, Minutes of the General Purposes Committee, 5 May 1859.
12. Gourlay, *National Temperance*, p. 257.
13. Ibid., p. 257.
14. Ibid.

15. Harrison, *Huddersfield and Holmfirth Examiner*, July 1853.
16. *Huddersfield Parkin Almanack*, Huddersfield.
17. Huddersfield Centenary.
18. *British Temperance Advocate*, 1 February 1860.
19. Ibid.
20. Frederick Lees, *Dr F. R. Lees* (London, 1904) p. 167.
21. Bradford United Temperance Society, *Annual Report*, 1863.
22. Gough v. Lees, Correspondence published in the *Weekly Record* and republished as a tract, 1858.
23. His son and biographer wrote of Lees' 'stormy life', Lees, *Dr F. R. Lees*, p. 90.
24. Gough v. Lees, correspondence.
25. The case was widely publicised in non-temperance newspapers, seen as another of the interminable disputes of the 'ridiculous fanatical' teetotallers. Responsible temperance men saw what damage was being done and remained neutral, taking no sides. See British Association *Minutes* of the General Purposes Committee, 14 April 1858.
26. Livesey's lack of support for prohibition upset many men of the anti-drink movement who repeatedly tried to get the founder to endorse prohibition.
27. *British Temperance Register*, 1857–8.
28. Ibid.
29. For a detailed description of the movement and an analysis of its policies see Brian Harrison, *Drink and the Victorians* (London, 1971).
30. John S. Mill, *On Liberty* (London, 1947) p. 91.
31. Brian Harrison, 'The Sunday Trading Riots of 1855', *The Historical Journal*, vol. VIII, no. 2 (1965).
32. James Sterling, *Failure of the Forbes Mackenzie Act* (London, 1859).
33. W. S. Jevons, *Methods of Social Reform* (London, 1883) p. 241.
34. Ibid., p. 242.
35. Ibid., p. 247.
36. H. B. Harrop, *The Direct Veto* (London, 1893) p. 4.
37. Eventually the Alliance abandoned any thought of national prohibition, causing a small group of extremists to set up a new National Prohibition Party in the late 1880s. Winskill, *The Temperance Movement*, vol. 4, p. 145.
38. All licences in the country were issued only for one year at a time.
39. George W. E. Russell, *Sir Wilfred Lawson* (London, 1909) p. 62.
40. Henry Carter, *The English Temperance Movement*, vol. I (London, 1933) p. 196.
41. Hayler scrapbook, newspaper clipping, no name, no date.
42. Gourlay, *National Temperance*, p. 293.
43. Brian Harrison, 'The Temperance Question in England, 1829–1869' (unpublished Oxford DPhil thesis, 1966) p. 458.
44. Speech made at Oxford on 31 December 1871 and printed as a tract.
45. Interview Cecil Heath, President, United Kingdom Alliance, August 1969.
46. When he died his wife took over his position as agent.
47. Henry Carter and Thomas Whittaker both were critical of the Alliance.
48. Jevons, *Methods of Social Reform*, p. 247.
49. Brian Harrison, 'The Temperance Question', p. 313.
50. Interview with Cecil Heath.

51. *Our Legislative Policy 1864–1908*, CETS (1908).
52. Bradford United Temperance Society, *Annual Report*, 1867.
53. Bradford Temperance Society, *Annual Report*, 1878.
54. Ibid., 1862.
55. Burns, *History*, vol. I, p. 245.
56. Ibid., vol. I, p. 274.
57. *The Teetotal Times*, January 1847.
58. *British Temperance League Register*, 1857–8.
59. British Temperance League General Purposes Committee, *Minutes*, 22 June 1853.
60. Winskill, *Temperance Movement*, vol. 3, p. 132.
61. Ibid.
62. Ibid., p. 134.
63. Ibid., Burns, *History*, vol. 2, p. 21.
64. Ibid., p. 69.
65. Ibid., vol. II, p. 79.
66. British Temperance League, General Purposes Committee, *Minutes*, 27 January 1867.
67. Letter head in the Sunday Closing collection (W. S. Nichols) in the Bradford Public Library.
68. *Burns, History*, vol. II, p. 79.
69. List of donations in Bradford Library.
70. British Temperance League, General Purposes Committee, *Minutes*, June 1865.
71. Ibid., June 1865.
72. Printed letter in Bradford Library.
73. Ibid.
74. Notice in Sunday Closing collection of Bradford Library.
75. Ibid.
76. Ibid.
77. Letter dated 19 November 1875 from Shephard and Nichols in Sunday Closing collection in Bradford Library.
78. Ibid.
79. Huddersfield Parkin Almanack.

# Part Two: Introduction

1. David Owens in his book *English Philanthroopy 1660–1960* (Cambridge, 1964) states that he did not think Mayhew's writings had such a great influence on his contemporaries (p. 21).
2. George Melly, MP, 'The Uneducated Children In Our Large Towns' speech to the House of Commons, 12 March 1869, published as a pamphlet, London, 1869, p. 10.
3. William Booth, *In Darkest England and The Way Out* (London, 1890) p. 12.
4. Ibid., p. 24.
5. For a discussion of drink by Booth see *Life and Labour of the People in London*, final volume, Part II, Section 4, pp. 59–75 (AMS Press Edition, 1970).

6. William Hoyle, 'Why is Trade Depressed?', published as tract Manchester, 1879.
7. John Burns, 'Labour and Drink' (Manchester, 1904).
8. There was a dearth of drink-free recreational facilities in the nineteenth century. The second half of the century saw many organisations and individuals working for the development of free municipal parks, drink-free music halls and drink-free recreational facilities in social and mission halls.
9. John Burns, 'Labour and Drink'.
10. Joseph Livesey, *Staunch Teetotaler*, p. 44.
11. This was a common claim made throughout the nineteenth century. In 1893, at a public meeting on licensing reform, the Rev. Dr Goodrich said that Judge Coleridge had claimed that if the country was sober 90 per cent of crime would not exist. *Report of the Proceedings at a Public Meeting*, 26 January 1893. The Manchester Scheme of Licensing Law Reform. Printed as a tract.
12. British Temperance League, *Annual Report*, 1882, p. 10.

# 5   To The Rescue

1. K. S. Inglis, *Churches and the Working Classes* (London, 1963) p. 15.
2. *Alliance News*, 9 September 1882.
3. For a detailed description of the founding and development of the Church of England Temperance Society, see Gerald W. Olsen, 'Pub and Parish, The Beginnings of Temperance Reform in the Church of England 1835–1875'.
4. All ran their own parish missions, which were teetotal.
5. Gourlay, *National Temperance*, p. 120.
6. H. J. Ellison, *Temperance Reformation Movement*, p. 11.
7. Olson, 'Pub and Parish', p. 254.
8. Ibid., p. 190.
9. Ellison, *Temperance Reformation Movement*, p. 10.
10. *Church of England Temperance Chronicle*, 1 August 1866, p. 255.
11. Ibid.
12. Ibid., p. 288.
13. There was much truth to this, as teetotallers have testified. Gregson, a teetotal agent, was originally a member of the established church and left it to become a non-conformist. The change was caused by his temperance work among the non-conformists. Shaw, *William Gregson*, p. 15.
14. Ellison, *Temperance Reformation Movement*, pp. 42–3.
15. Ibid.
16. Ibid.
17. Ibid., p. 17.
18. *Report of the Convocation of Canterbury, Committee on Intemperance* (London, 1869) p. 1.
19. Ibid., p. 5.
20. Ibid., p. 6.
21. Hearing evidence from parish clergy was an important part of the work of the Committee.

22. Herman Ausubel, *In Hard Times* (New York, 1960) p. 47.
23. Canon Wilberforce, *The Place, the Power and the Claims of the Gospel Total Abstinence*, speech given Edinburgh, circa 1880s, published as tract.
24. *A Plea for the Pledge*, CETS leaflet no. 76.
25. Ellison, *Temperance Reformation Movement*, p. 66.
26. Mrs Wightman told of the care she took to see that she did not infringe on the authority of any other parish when working in that of her husband (see *Haste to the Rescue*, pp. 51–2).
27. CETS, Ripon Diocese, *Annual Report*, 1882.
28. CETS, Ripon Diocese, *Minutes*, 1887 (unpublished).
29. Ibid., 1887.
30. See Women's Union, *Annual Reports*, 1889, 1882.
31. Keeping them in their own parish so as not to cause problems with the hierarchy of the parish and diocese was always important in church activities.
32. CETS, *Jubilee Book* (1887) p. 34.
33. John Isabell, *A Speakers and Workers Vade-Mecum* (CETS, 1900).
34. CETS, *Annual Report*, 1887.
35. Isabell, *Vade-Mecum*, p. 69.
36. Yet the public offered drinks to the engine driver.
37. W. E. Moss, *Book of Memories* (Blackburn, 1951) p. 151.
38. Women's Union, *Annual Report*, 1889.
39. CETS, *Annual Report*, 1881.
40. CETS, *Jubilee Book*.
41. See below, Chapter 6.
42. CETS, *Annual Report*, 1892.
43. Isabell, *Vade-Mecum*, Preface.
44. Chadwick, *Victorian Church*, p. 368.
45. Ibid., p. 365.
46. CETS, *Annual Report*, 1881.
47. Ibid., 1887.
48. Ibid., 1889.
49. Ibid., 1886.
50. Royal Commission on Liquor Licensing, *Report*, v. 34, p. 25.
51. See above, Chapter 2.
52. Temple signed the pledge in the 1880s as a help to others in their fight against intemperance. E. G. Sandford (ed.), *Memoirs of Archbishop Temple* (London, 1906) vol. II, p. 137.
53. *Daily Chronicle*, 1900, clipping in Hayler Collection, no month.
54. British Temperance League, *Annual Report*, 1897, p. 11.
55. See below, Chapter 8.
56. The United Kingdom Alliance did not list the CETS when it compiled lists of temperance organisations.
57. See p. 10.
58. See p. 72.
59. James Winning refused to let his sons become church members because they would get drink at the Lord's Table. *The Prohibition Movement Papers and Proceedings of the National Convention for the Prohibition of the Liquor Traffic* (Newcastle upon Tyne, 1897). See p. 235.

60. J. J. Cockshott, 'The CETS and Temperance Legislation', National Temperance Congress, 1889.

61. *Report*, Royal Commission on Liquor Licensing, v. 34, p. 2.

62. See pp. 231–2.

63. *Daily Chronicle*, 1900.

64. Ibid.

65. Ernest Blackwell, *Richard T. Booth of the Blue Ribbon Movement* (London, 1883) p. 119.

66. Ibid.

67. The Salvation Army attempted the same in England but failed. See p. 132.

68. Blackwell, *Booth*, pp. 119–20.

69. *Standard Encyclopedia of the Alcohol Problem*, E. H. Cherrington (Ohio, 1928) vol. IV, pp. 1838–40.

70. Ibid.

71. Blackwell, *Booth*, p. 143.

72. This is similar to the policy of the Salvation Army. See p. 235.

73. *Gospel Temperance Traveller*, April 1883.

74. *Temperance World*, 1 March 1888.

75. Ibid.

76. See p. 115.

77. In the late nineteenth century there was great interest in 'respectable' working-class entertainment. In 1880 the Royal Victoria Hall was opened as a temperance answer to the public house. No smoking was allowed but the cheap entertainment every Saturday night was so attractive that the hall was crowded with working-class people (*Temperance World*, 5 November 1890). A group of the Victoria Hall supporters wanted to buy the hall as a memorial to Samuel Morley, who had been a very generous benefactor to it (*Church of England Temperance Chronicle*, 14 April 1888).

78. *Blue Ribbon Gazette*, 1883.

79. *Temperance World*, 15 March 1888.

80. A. and Z. B. Gustafson, *Foundation of Death: A Study of the Drink Question*, 5th edn (London, 1888) pp. 450–2.

81. *Blue Ribbon Chronicle*, 18 November 1882; *Alliance News*, 17 May 1889. Lady Howard, a future leader of the Northern temperance community, was converted by a Blue Ribbon Mission. Dorothy Henley, *Rosalind Howard, Countess of Carlisle* (London, 1958) p. 109.

82. *Alliance News*, 27 July 1882.

83. *Alliance News*, 2 December 1882.

84. It was even suggested that a violet Ribbon Army be formed 'to stop taking nips' by people in commerce. *Gospel Temperance Traveller* no. 1 (1 March 1883) p. 9.

85. For a discussion of revivalist techniques see *Modern Revivalism* by W. G. McLoughlin (New York, 1959).

86. Booth in 1886 emigrated to New Zealand where he became an insurance agent, *Signal*, 27 February 1889.

87. Blackwell, *Booth*, p. 168.

88. Ibid., p. 179.

89. Ibid., p. 248.

90. See below, Chapter 8, 'Anti-Drink Reformers in the Local Government'.
91. *British Temperance Advocate* (1882) p. 700.
92. Ibid.
93. Blackwell, *Booth*, p. 248.
94. *British Temperance Advocate* (1882) p. 700.
95. Church of England started holding missions in school rooms or mission rooms. *Church of England Temperance Chronicle*, 14 July 1888. Reported the Bishop of Liverpool approving such a move to 'get the biggest audience', p. 447.
96. *Blue Ribbon Chronicle*, 30 December 1882.
97. *Weekly Record*, 7 April 1881. *Blue Ribbon Chronicle*, 30 December 1882.
98. Blackwell, *Booth*, pp. 253–6; This is the same method the Rev. Billy Graham uses in his 'Crusades for Christ' in the mid-twentieth century.
99. *Gospel Temperance Traveller*, June 1883, p. 7.
100. Blackwell, *Booth*, p. 251.
101. Ibid., p. 205.
102. *Temperance World*, 26 January 1888.
103. *Alliance News*, 15 October 1881.
104. This was an article in the *Echo* which was commented on by the *Blue Ribbon Official Gazette*, 2 December 1882.
105. Ibid.
106. Complaints came from both inside and outside the movement. See Winskill, *Temperance Movement*, vol. IV, p. 34, letter of advocate Atkins in the *Alliance News*, 2 July 1881.
107. Ministers of all types invited – to make mission nonsectarian (*Weekly Record*, 7 April 1881).
108. Blackwell, *Booth*, p. 181.
109. This issue was often raised. *The Church of England Temperance Chronicle* discusses this matter when describing the career of Noble in its issue of 9 December 1882.
110. Blackwell, *Booth*, pp. 248–9.
111. See pp. 19–21.
112. Burns, *History*, vol. II, p. 325.
113. *Church of England Temperance Chronicle*, 9 December 1882, p. 118.
114. Editor Rev. M. Baxter was a cleric of the established church but most of his members and readers were dissenters. The Rev. M. Baxter also edited the *Christian Herald*, the largest religious penny weekly, or so it claimed.
115. *The Signal*, 3 November 1886.
116. *Blue Ribbon Gazette*, 3 May 1883, p. 170.
117. At this conference Thomas Whittaker, one of the founders of the teetotal movement, was opposed to having Hoxton Hall as a Central Board of Control for the movement. Ibid.
118. Ibid.
119. *Temperance Record*, 7 April 1881.
120. Ibid.
121. *Alliance News*, 25 November 1882.
122. Blackwell, *Booth*, p. 315.
123. *Weekly Record*, 21 April 1881.
124. Winskill, *Temperance Movement*, vol. IV, p. 34.

125. Joseph Livesey, *Life and Teachings of Joseph Livesey* (London, 1885) pp. 83–7.
126. Frederic Smith, *Band of Hope Jubilee Volume*, p. 260.
127. George Wilson McCree, *Old Friends and New Faces*, p. 16.
128. *Church of England Temperance Chronicle*, 8 July 1882.
129. Whittaker, *Brighter England*, 1891.
130. *British Temperance Advocate*, September 1884, p. 1143.
131. *Alliance News*, 14 July 1888, in its report of the conference.
132. *British Temperance Advocate* (1882) p. 744.
133. *Onward* (1883) p. 26.
134. Ibid., p. 11.
135. British Temperance League Meeting of 1888, reported in *Alliance News*, 14 July 1888.
136. This was particularly true in many rural areas where temperance only penetrated when allied with religion. For the influence of Gospel Temperance in one small town see Rev. T. Lumbs scrapbook – local preacher of Glasshouses in private hands (Joanna Dawson).
137. See below, Chapter 9.
138. See below, Chapters 6 and 7.
139. In 1886 the *Gospel Temperance Herald* changed its name to *Signal*, to act as 'a signal hoisted to rally help all who are fighting against the tyrant alcohol', 24 February 1886, p. 60.
140. By 1888 Hoxton Hall had become a local mission hall again and the Blue Ribbon Army had 'faded away', *Temperance World*, 3 August 1888.
141. *Church of England Chronicle*, 1 July 1882.
142. Booth never talked of drunkards but of 'drinking men'. Booth, Noble and Murphy, leaders in the Gospel Temperance Movement, were all former drunkards.
143. *Blue Ribbon Gospel Temperance Chronicle*, 23 December 1882.
144. *Weekly Record*, 21 April 1881. Writing about another successful Gospel Temperance missionary, the *Alliance News* reported 'as the quality of his nightly address has become known, crowds have flocked to hear him', 7 October 1892.
145. W. H. Burnette, *Sunlight in the Slums* (Manchester, 1888).
146. Moss, *Mrs Lewis*, p. 202.
147. Wm. E. A. Axon, 'The Social Results of Temperance in Blackburn', reprinted from *Manchester Guardian*, 1886.
148. Ibid.
149. Moss, *Mrs Lewis*, p. 112.
150. Ibid., pp. 89–91; *Alliance News*, 11 April 1890.
151. *Alliance News*, 25 April 1890.
152. *Alliance News*, 21 November 1890.
153. The movement was criticised whether its workers left much money (J. G. Shaw, *The Life of William Gregson*, p. 14) or too little. If the latter it showed that the movement did not appreciate its workers. (W. Livesey, *Earliest Days*, p. 89.)
154. Burnette, *Sunlight in the Slums*, p. 8.
155. Moss, *Mrs Lewis*, p. 135.
156. *Alliance News*, 27 March 1886.
157. Burnette, *Sunlight in the Slums*, p. 22.

158. Ibid.
159. Moss, *Mrs Lewis*, p. 200.
160. *Alliance News*, 4 August 1888.
161. Guy Thorne, *A Great Acceptance, The Life and Story of F. N. Charrington* (1913) p. 28.
162. Ibid., p. 146.
163. *The Templar*, vol. IX (July–December 1876) p. 318.
164. *The Temperance World*, May 1892.
165. *Alliance News*, 7 July 1883, pp. 424–5.
166. Ibid., 21 July 1883.
167. Ibid., 7 July 1883.
168. *Alliance News*, 7 March 1885.
169. Thorne, p. 143.
170. Ibid., p. 121.
171. *Alliance News*, 17 November 1883.
172. Thorne, *A Great Acceptance*, p. 218.
173. Clipping – obituary – Hayler Collection, no name, no date.
174. *Alliance News*, 1 December 1888.
175. Thorne, *A Great Acceptance*, p. 241.
176. *Alliance News*, 2 January 1888.
177. *Alliance News*, 16 August 1889.
178. *Alliance News*, 2 June 1888.
179. *Alliance News* 16 March 1889.
180. Ibid.
181. *Alliance News*, 10 February 1887.
182. Doris Gulliver, *Dame Agnes Weston* (London, 1971) p. 31.
183. See *My Life Among the Blue Jackets* by Agnes Weston, Supplement to *Alliance News*, 18 December 1891.
184. William Gourlay, *'National Temperance'. A Jubilee Biograph of The National Temperance League* (London, 1906) p. 217.
185. See General Havelock's remarks in the *Temperance Record*, 21 June 1877.
186. J. M. J. Fletcher, *Mrs Wightman of Shrewsbury* (London, 1906) p. 140.
187. Ibid., p. 139.
188. Ibid., p. 272.
189. Ibid., p. 228.
190. The Salvation Army was also against smoking but did not prohibit it. It did not promote those who smoked. *Alliance News*, 8 August 1890.
191. See below p. 55.
192. *Standard Encyclopedia of the Alcohol Problem*, vol. I, p. 369.
193. Thorne, *A Great Acceptance*, p. 81.
194. Crusaders, *Alliance News* 1 December 1888. White Ribbon Army, *Alliance News*, 2 December 1882, 24 February 1883.
195. P. Cassell, *The History of the Year Oct. 1, 1881–Sept. 30, 1882* (London, 1882) p. 448.
196. K. S. Inglis, *Churches and the Working Classes* (London, 1963) p. 193, *Alliance News*, 2 December 1882.
197. A change in the public attitude came in 1889: *Standard Encyclopedia of the Alcohol Problem*, vol. I, p. 369.
198. *Alliance News*, 8 October 1881.

199. T. H. Huxley, *Social Diseases and Worse Remedies* (London, 1891).
200. *Church of England Chronicle*, 26 August 1882.
201. *Standard Encyclopedia of the Alcohol Problem*, vol. I, p. 369.
202. *Alliance News*, 9 January 1891.
203. See below, Chapter 9.
204. See below, Chapter 7.

# 6   Come All Ye Children

1. Dawson Burns, 'Juvenile Temperance Work Prior to the Band of Hope Era', *The Jubilee of the Band of Hope Movement*, edited by Frederic Smith (London, 1897) pp. 18, 23.
2. Rev. T. Holme, 'Suggestions on Band of Hope Unions', paper given at the International Temperance and Prohibition Convention, London, 1862 and published in the *Proceedings*, p. 160. See also *Extending the Borders*, United Kingdom Band of Hope Union Conference in Bradford 1869, proceedings printed as Bradford Tract.
3. There was some controversy over the founding of the Band of Hope but the movement itself accepts this version as its official history. See the *Temperance Record*, 11 March 1897 and 20 August 1893 for parts of the controversy.
4. Winskill, *Temperance Movement*, vol. IV, p. 211; *Jubilee Volume*, p. 130.
5. *Band of Hope Review*, November 1852.
6. J. F. C. Harrison, *Learning and Living, 1790–1960* (London, 1961) p. 177 and D. G. Wright, 'A Radical Borough: Parliamentary Politics in Bradford 1832–41', *Northern History*, IV (1969) p. 134.
7. See the *Minutes* of the Leeds Temperance Society, July–October, 1847.
8. This might have been due to the fact that the Catholics in the manufacturing areas were much poorer than the Protestants, being mostly from Irish immigrant families who could not afford the luxury of keeping their women secluded in the home.
9. Robert Tayler, *The Hope of the Race* (London, 1946) p. 38.
10. Martin Field, *Historical Sketch of the Band of Hope Union* (Bradford, 1886) p. 6.
11. Bradford Band of Hope Union, *Annual Report*, 1895.
12. Rowland Hill, 'The Story and Work of the United Kingdom Band of Hope Union', *Jubilee Volume*, p. 78.
13. The rules of the Sunday School Union, published in their annual reports, state that the control of their schools should be in the hands of 'gentlemen'.
14. Joseph Livesey, *Temperance Lighthouse*, I (April, 1871) p. 10.
15. George W. McCree, 'The History, Design and Progress of the Band of Hope Union', paper given at the International Temperance and Prohibition Convention, 1862, published in the *Proceedings*, p. 158.
16. Ibid., p. 158.
17. Ibid., p. 158.
18. Edward Baines, Jr, *The Social, Educational and Religious State of the Manufacturing Districts, Two Letters to Robert Peel* (London, 1843) Letter II.
19. A complaint made about the temperance movement in general. See pp. 38–9.

20. *Jubilee Volume*, p. 269.
21. 'Juvenile Temperance Organizations', *National Temperance League Annual* (London, 1881). In Sheffield a Sunday School Band of Hope Union was formed in 1855 to unite all the Bands of Hope connected with Sunday Schools. *Proceedings*, p. 172.
22. See Chapter 5 above.
23. See p. 18 above.
24. There does not appear to have been any one 'official' catechism, but many, often published by the authors who were mostly ministers of religion. A handwritten copy of a Band of Hope catechism was given to the author by an old Band of Hope worker.
25. Mrs C. L. Balfour, 'Our Bands of Hope and Some Causes that Prevent their Efficiency', paper given at the International Temperance and Prohibition Convention, 1862, published in the *Proceedings*, p. 167; and Bowman tract.
26. Rev. Charles Garrett, 'Juvenile Temperance Organisations', *National Temperance League Annual 1881* (London, 1881) p. 161.
27. Tayler, *Hope of the Race*, p. 41.
28. Peter Sinclair, 'The Temperance Movement among the Young in Edinburgh, the U.S. and Canada', paper read at the International Temperance and Prohibition Convention 1862, published in the *Proceedings*, p. 148, and C. J. Whitehead, 'Our Work and How to Do it', paper read at a conference held 4 December 1875, and published as a tract.
29. 'Extending the Borders', p. 13.
30. J. D. Hilton, *James Hayes Raper* (London, 1898).
31. See above p. 20.
32. J. F. Chown, *The Band of Hope and Sunday Schools*, speech given to a special meeting of Sunday School teachers, organised by the Bradford Temperance Society in St George's Hall, Bradford in 1873. This speech was printed as a tract.
33. *Barnsley Times and South Yorks Gazette*, October 1876.
34. *Texts, Topics and Truths for Band of Hope Workers* (London, 1892).
35. 'Extending the Borders', p. 13.
36. Bradford Band of Hope Union, *Annual Report*, 1886.
37. Interview with Mrs Elizabeth Rastrick in 1969, a member of the Band of Hope at Wyke at the turn of the century.
38. Hill, *Jubilee Volume*, p. 99.
39. Bradford Band of Hope Union, *Annual Report*, 1886.
40. This led to an increase in the numbers of teachers hired as Band of Hope agents.
41. Tayler, *Hope of the Race*, p. 47.
42. Hill, *Jubilee Volume*, p. 116.
43. Frederic Smith, 'The Juvenile Temperance Organisations in Great Britain and Ireland', *Temperance in All Nations*, edited by J. N. Stearns (New York, 1893) vol. I, p. 216.
44. Hill, *Jubilee Volume*, p. 117.
45. Bradford Band of Hope Union, *Annual Report*, 1877.
46. *Morning Dewdrops* (London, 1853). Even at the end of the century this book was still a 'standard textbook' for the movement. See *Jubilee Volume*, p. 250.

47. Balfour, *Morning Dewdrops*, Preface.
48. T. P. Wilson, *Frank Oldfield* (London, 1871).
49. Mrs Henry Wood, *Danesbury House* (New York, 1893). All citations in this chapter refer to the 1893 edition published in the United States. When representatives of the Scottish Temperance League visited Mrs Wood to discuss her prize-winning book, they were shocked because she offered them a glass of wine for refreshment, a common practice at the time. Commented a temperance journal, 'it seemed opposite in spirit to her book', *Alliance News*, 26 March 1887, p. 204.
50. Wood, *Danesbury House*, p. 154.
51. Ibid., p. 74.
52. Ibid., p. 193.
53. Ibid., p. 191.
54. Ibid., p. 184.
55. See Harriet L. W. Schupf, 'Ragged Schools: Education for the Neglected in 19th Century England', *Higher Education Quarterly* (Winter 1971).
56. Thomas Bywater Smithies, founder of the publishing house S. W. Partridge and Co. started the *Band of Hope Review* (*Jubilee Volume*, p. 268). William Hoyle, noted for his temperance songs, was the one most closely connected with *Onward*. Its pages were full of songs and poems, many written by Hoyle himself.
57. Much of the fiction of this magazine focused on disadvantaged children: blind boys and girls, orphans, etc.
58. *Temperance Lighthouse*, vol. II (October 1872) p. 110.
59. *Band of Hope Blue Book: A Manual of Instruction and Training*. No place and no date of publication given. Probably privately printed for local use.
60. Joseph Livesey, among others, was continually calling upon individual temperance reformers to pay for the free distribution of temperance journals and tracts to children and adults. Some teetotallers, however, felt that if they cost a little they would be more valued. Shaw, *William Gregson*, p. 176.
61. W. P. Ingham, 'How to Form a Town or District Band of Hope Union', paper given 1894 and published as a tract.
62. This was not true for the denominational bands. They were under the direct authority of their churches.
63. See below, Chapters 8 and 9.
64. *Standard Encyclopedia of the Alcohol Problem* (Westerville, 1925) vol. I, p. 265.
65. *Jubilee Volume*, p. 310.
66. United Kingdom Band of Hope Union Conference, Bradford, 1893, proceedings published as a tract.
67. Church of England Temperance Society, *Annual Report*, 1884.
68. Tayler, *Hope of the Race*, p. 39.
69. Interview with Miss Peel, veteran organiser of the Band of Hope in Birstall, in 1969. Her father and mother had also been completely absorbed in the local temperance activities.
70. Interview with Mrs Elizabeth Rastrick, 1969.
71. For criticism of Band of Hope 'superior airs' see Arthur Shadwell, *Drink, Temperance and Legislation* (London, 1915) p. 100 and James A. Newbold, *The Nonconformist Conscience as a Persecuting Force* (Manchester, 1908) p. 212.

72. Field, 'Historical Survey', p. 7.
73. See below, Chapter 8.
74. *Standard Encylopedia*, vol. I, p. 265.
75. See below pp. 215–17.
76. Burns, *Jubilee Volume*, p. 49.
77. *Jubilee Volume*, p. 4.
78. Robert Currie, *Methodism Divided* (London, 1968) pp. 138–40.
79. Ibid., pp. 138–40.
80. Tayler, *Hope of the Race*, p. 39.
81. Interview with G. H. Walker, Barnsley Temperance Society, 1969. Mr Walker's father had not only been the head of the Barnsley Temperance Society, but also the first teetotal mayor of Barnsley. See also *The Gin Shop*, a well-known rhyme illustrated by George Cruikshank and reproduced in the *Band of Hope Review*, March, April and May issues, 1868. In this tale the pastor rescues the drunkard, who 'crosses over' from the drinking world to the teetotal chapel community.
82. For the Lancashire and Cheshire figures see the *Barnsley Times and South Yorks Gazette*, October 1876, and for the Yorkshire figures see 'Juvenile Temperance Organizations', *National Temperance League Annual* (London, 1881).
83. Tayler, *Hope of the Race*, p. 55.
84. Mrs C. L. Balfour, 'On Bands of Hope, and Some Causes that Prevent Their Efficiency', *Proceedings of the International Temperance and Prohibition Convention* (1862) pp. 167–70. Winskill, *Temperance Movement*, vol. IV, p. 35.
85. Balfour, 'On Bands', p. 169.
86. Livesey, *Staunch Teetotaler*.
87. See below, Chapter 7.

# 7 'A Wave of Blue' – The Temperance Army

1. H. B. Harrop, *The Direct Veto: An Exposure of a Falsehood* (Liberty Property Defence League, 1893) p. 4.
2. *Alliance News*, 18 December 1880, p. 814.
3. There were some business that would employ only teetotallers, but they were few. See Hertz Bird Food letter in Hayler Collection.
4. Tayler, *Hope of the Race*, p. 85.
5. Winskill, *Temperance Movement*, vol. III, p. 111.
6. A. and Z. B. Gustafson, *Foundation of Death: A Study of the Drink Question* (London, 1888) pp. 439–41.
7. Ibid.
8. Winskill, *Temperance Movement*, vol. III, pp. 111–12.
9. Ibid., p. 112.
10. Salt fought the issue of licences for premises close to Saltaire, but the local Justices were not sympathetic and issued them. See Balgarnie, *Sir Titus Salt, Bart. His Life and Its Lessons* (London, 1877).
11. Edward Jones, 'Prohibition in England', tract, *BWT Journal* reprint, circa 1890.
12. Ibid.

13. See Joseph Rowntree and Arthur Sherwell, *The Temperance Problem* (London, 1899) for a full discussion of these prohibition towns from the point of view of social scientists.

14. See T. Whittaker's letter *British Temperance Advocate*, (1857) p. 66, and Whittaker's book, *Life's Battles in Temperance Armour* (London, 1892) p. 337.

15. Burns, *History*, vol. I, p. 258.

16. The Priestmans were a prominent Quaker family noted for their philanthropy. Originally farmers and corn millers, they grew wealthy in the textile industry having parlayed one spare room with handlooms into a large mill. John Priestman started the first ragged school in Bradford and his sons continued his work both in temperance and in other charities. (See Alice Priestman, *Recollections of Henry Brady Priestman* (Bradford, circa 1918) privately printed. Author examined a copy in the hands of the Priestman family.)

17. Bradford United Temperance Society, *Annual Report*, 1863.

18. The Rechabites, who were called the oldest and wealthiest temperance society in the world, by the end of the nineteenth century had accumulated over a million pounds and were sometimes willing to lend it to local temperance societies for mortgages on temperance halls. A National Temperance Land and Building Co. was set up to help with temperance mortgages but it did not do so well. See the British Temperance League Minutes for a discussion of this company with regards to shares in it that were left to the League in a bequest from George Ling. (*Minutes* of the Executive Meetings, 15 June 1895.)

19. Brighouse Temperance Society, *Annual Report*, 1873.

20. Francis Murphy at a Gospel Temperance meeting suggested that more temperance halls were needed, which prompted a supporter to write to the *Blue Ribbon Chronicle* a letter in support of this position (2 December 1882, p. 110).

21. '. . . the Hall is not in the most inviting part of town' reported the *Leeds Temperance Society*, in its Annual Report, 1854.

22. Leeds still had this problem thirty years later. See Leeds Temperance Society, *Annual Report*, 1887.

23. Temperance was in a bad way in Bradford at this time. In the *Minutes of the General Purposes Committee* of the British Temperance League it is reported 'that the state of the Temperance cause in Bradford and the neighbourhood is such as to demand the attention of this Committee.' (27 November 1860).

24. Bradford Temperance Society, *Annual Report*, 1852.

25. Ibid., *Annual Report*, 1879.

26. Joseph Wilson, *Joseph Wilson, His Life and Work*.

27. Peggy Rastrick, 'The Bradford Temperance Movement' (unpublished essay, 1969).

28. Keighley, *Keighley Past & Present*.

29. Skipton, a market town, was late in acquiring its temperance hall – 1891 (*Alliance News*, 15 May 1891).

30. Rastrick, *The Bradford Temperance Movement*.

31. Newspaper clipping, Dewsbury newspaper, July 1939.

32. Interview with G. H. Walker, Barnsley Temperance Society, September 1969.

33. For a fuller discussion of this society see the author's article 'The Birstall Temperance Society', *Yorkshire Archaeological Journal*, vol. 46 (1974).

34. *Birstall Gospel Temperance Society*, Souvenir and Brief History of the Society, Birstall, no date.

35. Birstall Temperance Society records (unpublished).

36. The Rechabites in Birstall gave the morgage on the Birstall Temperance Hall. See records of the Star of Birstall tent, Birstall.

37. Birstall Temperance records.

38. Ibid.

39. Interview, Miss Peel, longtime member of the Birstall Temperance Society, former choirmistress and leader of the Band of Hope, daughter of previous choirmaster, in 1969.

40. Ibid.

41. The PSA meetings were a popular development of the late nineteenth century. The initials stood for 'Pleasant Sunday Afternoon'. The movement was started in Manchester by a Yorkshire minister and quickly spread throughout Lancashire and Yorkshire. It was hoped that the PSAs would prove to be an association by which 'the moral, intellectual, social and material prosperity of the masses may be combined with the religious' (*Yorkshire County Magazine*, vol. IV, p. 131). Meetings were usually held at chapels and churches at 3 p.m. on Sunday afternoons. There, with elevating and semi-religious talks, and community hymn-singing, the PSA fulfilled a recreational need that was an important problem for the churches. Without any alternative, many men spent the Sabbath afternoon in the public houses getting drunk. Claims were made about the great changes wrought by the promotion of PSAs. One in Manchester, said to have over 3000 members, was credited with changing the whole character of the neighbourhood it served. 'P.S.A.', *Yorkshire County Magazine*, vol. IV, ed. J. H. Turner (1891) pp. 131–2.

42. Interview Miss Peel. Birstall Temperance Society Records.

43. These Band of Hope festivals were held, at different times, all over England, wherever Band of Hope Unions were to be found. Mixing parochial patriotism with temperance principles, they often found much favour among the local non-temperance public, who were invited to attend, as well as among their own teetotallers.

44. Miss Peel.

45. Birstall Temperance Society records, Miss Peel.

46. '*Keighley Visitor* published in London'. *Keighley Visitor*, October 1861. Printer Samuel Jarrold published the *Monthly Temperance Visitor* which he claimed to sell to 150 societies and large employers of labour as their own organ. Their name, local heading and notices were printed on it (advertisement leaflet for Jarrold).

47. William Gourlay, '*National Temperance*': *A Jubilee Biograph* (London, 1906) p. 350.

48. See below, Chapter 9.

49. *Alliance News*, 4 March 1892.

50. Chapter 6, above.

51. Miss Dickinson, long-time member of the Birstall Temperance Society interview, 1969. Her family joined the temperance movement after her

brother and father heard a Gospel Temperance missionary at an outdoor mission in the village centre in the 1880s.

52. Miss Dickinson's father became a part-time unpaid missionary, preaching Gospel Temperance in the village and neighbouring communities. Interview, 1969.

53. Souvenir history, Birstall.

54. Rastrick, *The Bradford Temperance Movement*, p. 45.

55. Interview with Mr Mawson, former president of the Batley Temperance Society, in 1969.

56. The Birstall incumbent from 1801 to 1836 was the son of a maltster and his successor (1836–75) was his son, the grandson of a maltster. (H. C. Craddock, *A History of the Ancient Parish of Birstall, Yorkshire* (London, 1933) pp. 268–9.) It was also common practice for the parish churchgoers to adjourn to a nearby public house for a sociable time after all church events. Newspaper clipping in Alderman Stone's scrapbook, no name, no date.

57. Canon Davies of Batley was a noted temperance supporter (*Alliance News*, 23 May 1885).

58. Birstall Temperance Society Records.

59. Souvenir history, Birstall.

60. Interview Miss Peel.

61. *Cleckheaton Guardian*, 1 September 1910.

62. This bequest in the 1970s is still helping pay part of the salary of the leader of the Birstall Gospel Temperance Hall (name changed in the twentieth century).

63. *Cleckheaton Guardian*, 1 September 1910.

64. Souvenir history, Birstall.

65. The Birstall Gospel Temperance Hall is still in existence and has a minister and an active congregation. But the temperance activities of its members are no longer very important. The missionary is now a man of religion and wears a clerical collar. The hall is now affiliated with the Federation of Independent Evangelical Churches. It has no affiliation with any temperance organisation.

66. Miss Peel.

67. Birstall Temperance Society Records.

68. Interview with Miss Dickinson.

69. Souvenir history, Birstall.

70. Ibid.

71. Miss Dickinson. This lady, now in her eighties, has grown up in the temperance world. Her conversations betray a strong separation in her mind between 'us' and 'them' though not in any antagonistic way.

72. Miss Peel.

73. See below pp. 178–9, 185–6.

74. See above, Chapter 2 p. 25.

75. *Keighley Visitor*, August 1861 and the *Alliance News*, 6 January 1883, are just two of the journals which, at different times, have complained about the actions of men claiming to be temperance advocates.

76. British Temperance League *Minutes*, 13 October 1858. Also minutes for 16 September 1858 for discussion of health and old age insurance for the League's agents.

77. *Minutes*, British Temperance League, General Purposes Committee, 6 October 1863.

78. This sometimes caused trouble. Agents of the British Association (the early name of the British Temperance League) were sent to areas for a whole winter and were expected to work in whole countries. The agent in Cornwall wanted to leave, but on account of difficulty in sending substitute to Cornwall he was told to stay' (Minutes of the British Association, 21 November 1851). Ten years later there were problems about agents not wanting to go where assigned. Minutes of the General Purposes Committee of the British Temperance League, 18 June 1861.

79. 'The Committee had always left agents to run own meetings in own fashion. They are completely free as to manner of their temperance advocacy.' Minutes of the General Purposes Committee, 5 February 1861.

80. Ibid., 21 January 1858 Salaries of agents of the British Temperance League were £95 per annum. By 1903 this had risen to £130 per annum (minutes for 3 February 1903).

81. *National Temperance Advocate*, 1 August 1849.

82. Many tried to supplement their salaries or whatever they earned by running a temperance hotel. W. Farish, *Autobiography and Other Writings* (Chester, 1889) p. 94, tells of his experience but there were few temperance men who at one time or another did not run a temperance hotel, Thomas Whittaker, Joseph Livesey (a mission hotel) Guy Hayler, John Andrews, etc.

83. T. W. P. Taylder, *The History of the Rise and Progress of Teetotalism* (Newcastle upon Tyne, 1886) p. 24 tells of an early agent who had to collect his salary – if he collected in excess of his remuneration he had to turn the surplus over to the Temperance Society, but if he did not collect enough he went short. The early agents of the British Association were asked to collect enough to equal their salaries (minutes of the British Association, 2 December 1853). Later this organisation charged the individual societies for the services of their agents.

84. *Temperance Advocate*, 25 January 1862.

85. *National Temperance Advocate*, 1 Sept. 1850.

86. See minutes of the British Temperance League for efforts to find work for agents in slow periods.

87. Thomas Whittaker, *Brighter England and the Way to It*, p. 37.

88. Francis Butterfield, *Life and Sayings of Thomas Worsnop* (Bingley, 1870) p. 70, for a description of the difficulties of some of these non-affiliated advocates.

89. 'Lees v. Gough' speech by Edward Grubb, 15 July 1858, p. 15.

90. Brian Harrison, private letter, 1969. Gough was said to have made £5000 in three years.

91. In 1879 Gough gave an oration in Bradford which cost the local temperance society £56 for Gough's expenses but they made £81 from admissions. (Bradford Temperance Society, *Annual Report*, 1879.)

92. Joseph Livesey was against individual testimonials, believing that it creates jealousy and dissatisfaction (*Staunch Teetotaler*, p. 112).

93. Burns, *History*, vol. I, p. 443.

94. Ibid.

95. Guy Hayler, 'Proposed Provident Fund', paper read at the annual conference of the National Association of Official Temperance Advocates, 15 August 1898 and reprinted as a leaflet.
96. Ibid.
97. National Fraternal Association of Secretaries and Agents of the Band of Hope Union (NFASABHU).
98. NFASABHU Annual Report, 1894.
99. Printed Circular of the North of England Temperance League.
100. For a detailed history of the Friendly Society movement see P. H. J. H. Gosden, *The Friendly Societies in England, 1815–1875* (Manchester, 1961).
101. Burns, *History*, vol. I, p. 96.
102. Gosden, *Friendly Societies*, p. 117.
103. Ibid., pp. 123–4.
104. Ibid., pp. 214–15.
105. Dawson Burns, *Temperance in the Victorian Age* (London, 1897) p. 129.
106. Ibid., p. 130.
107. For an example of these arguments on this topic see *The Teetotaler*, 12 June 1841, 19 June 1841, and 3 July 1841.
108. Councillor Cunliff, 'Temperance Orders and Benefit Societies', *National Temperance League Annual for 1882* (London, 1882) p. 109.
109. Ibid.
110. Ibid.
111. *The Annual Report of the Board of Directors of the Rechabites, 1896* (Hayler Collection).
112. Printed Circular, Rechabites (Hayler Collection).
113. Cunliff, 'Temperance Orders', p. 110.
114. When Peter Winksill in his *Temperance Standard Bearers of the Nineteenth Century* (Liverpool, 1898) lists the activities of various temperance workers, after their names he lists 'organizations' abbreviated as such 'IOR, IOGT, etc.'
115. Nearly all working-class organisations faced the problem of the protection of their funds, especially as they were usually in the keeping of one man who had control of them (see minutes, General Purposes Committee, British Temperance League, 9 August 1864).
116. Minutes of the Star of Birstall, Rechabite tent in Birstall.
117. Cunliff, 'Temperance Orders', p. 113.
118. Newspaper clipping, Hayler Collection, no name no date.
119. Cunliff, 'Temperance Orders', p. 113.
120. Charles Bell, 'Good Templars', paper given before the North of England Temperance League on 16 September 1873.
121. *Good Templarism Denounced as a Temperance and a Religious Organization*, anonymous (Patley Bridge, 1873).
122. Charles Bell, 'Good Templars'.
123. 'Good Templarism', a series of articles reprinted from the *Liverpool Leader*, circa 1872, p. 5.
124. Tom Honeyman, *Good Templary in Scotland* (Glasgow, 1894) p. 30.
125. 'Good Templarism', p. 9.
126. Ibid., p. 22.

127. Ibid., p. 30.
128. Ibid.
129. *Paterson Evening News*, 10 February 1915.
130. 'Good Templarism', p. 31.
131. Woolley and Johnson, *Temperance Progress of the Century*, p. 106.
132. *A Plain Statement About the Good Templars and the Subordinate Secessionists*, IOGT.
133. *Watchword*, 19 and 20 March 1883, quoted 'Secession Seeking Compromise', *British Loyal Templar*, March 1885.
134. Newspaper clipping, Hayler Collection (no name, no date).
135. 'Secession', p. 3.
136. In 1889 Frederic Lees wrote a letter to the British Temperance League, informing them that his wife had left £50 to the League payable when her husband died. Lees writes that the bequest will be paid 'unless the IOGT leaves me to pay the law costs of the suits, which will absorb the means left by my dear one'. Minutes of the Executive Meeting of the British Temperance League, June 1889.
137. Woolley and Johnson, *Temperance Progress*, p. 107.
138. Newspaper clipping, Hayler Collection.
139. Charles Bell, 'Good Templars'.
140. John Kempster, 'Good Templars' speech by the Grand Electoral Superintendent of the Grand Lodge of England, 17 November 1884.
141. Ibid.
142. See pp. 190–3.
143. Chapter 8 below.
144. In 1874 a Temperance Hospital in London was established for treatment of patients with the minimum of alcohol.
145. Honeyman, *Good Templary*, p. 250.
146. See p. 100.
147. See p. 135.
148. See p. 143.
149. Burns, *Temperance in the Victorian Age*, p. 121.
150. Ibid., p. 122.
151. Ibid.
152. K. FitzPatrick, *Lady Henry Somerset* (Boston, 1923) p. 151.
153. Louisa Stewart, *Memoirs of Margaret Bright Lucas* (London, 1890) p. 30.
154. Ibid.
155. After Mrs Balfour had spent one year in office.
156. FitzPatrick, *Lady Henry Somerset*, p. 150.
157. Ibid., p. 147.
158. British Women's Temperance Association (BWTA), booklet.
159. BWTA Annual Report 1886–7, p. 35.
160. Miss Forsaith, 'The Work done by our Association', 1886, p. 41.
161. *Evidence*, Royal Commission on Liquor Licensing, V. 34, p. 184, L. Tait's Evidence.
162. Brian Harrison, 'The Temperance Question', p. 396.
163. Gustafson, *Foundation of Death*, p. 365.
164. Forsaith, 'The Work', p. 6.

165. Docwra, 'BWTA', p. 9.
166. M. E. Docwra, 'Women's Work for Temperance during the Victorian Era', 1897. Paper read at the WTAU meeting and published as a tract.
167. Fitzpatrick, *Lady Henry Somerset*, p. 186.
168. For details of trip, ibid., pp. 164–81.
169. Ibid., p. 188.
170. Ibid., p. 191.
171. Ibid., p. 189. For a fuller discussion of this split, as well as women's role in nineteenth-century temperance, see Lilian Lewis Shiman, '"Changes Are Dangerous", Women and Temperance in the Nineteenth Century', *Religion in the Lives of English Women, 1760–1930*, ed. Gail Malmgreen (London, 1986).
172. Docwra, 'Women's Work for Temperance'.
173. FitzPatrick, *Lady Henry Somerset*, p. 208.
174. Ibid., p. 191.
175. Mrs Cecil Heath, 'A Far Reaching Movement', *White Ribboner*, March 1969, p. 20.
176. Forsaith, 'The Work', p. 7.
177. Josephine Butler, leader of the Purity movement, was a teetotaller and a supporter of the movement. (Peter Winskill, *Temperance Standard Bearers of the Nineteenth Century*, p. 180.)
178. Docwra, 'BWTA'.

# 8 The Temperance Party

1. See above, Chapter 5.
2. It was a loose term used to denote any individual, group or organisation, either inside or outside Parliament, who was willing to support some or all political anti-drink measures.
3. Newspaper clipping, Hayler Collection, no name, no date.
4. Printed circular, Hayler Collection.
5. Royal Commission on Liquor Licensing, *Report*, p. 202, Joseph Malins' testimony.
6. The Roman Catholic League of the Cross, and the Church of England Temperance Society did not join. John Newton, *W. S. Caine, MP* (London, 1907) p. 106.
7. See above, Chapter 7, p. 179.
8. Joseph Malins, *Joseph Malins* (Birmingham, 1932) p. 42.
9. *Alliance News*, 5 August 1892.
10. *Alliance News*, 12 November 1887.
11. When he died his wife took his place as the alliance agent (P. Rastrick).
12. United Kingdom Alliance, *Annual Report*, 1888–9.
13. *Alliance News*, 9 February 1878.
14. Ibid. In 1890 Churchill had his own bill for reforming the licensing system – have elected licensing commissions. (*Alliance News*, 7 March 1890.)
15. *Hull Express*, 14 August 1876.
16. Ibid.
17. Ibid.

18. See Shaw or Whittaker for examples of these happenings.
19. Lawson was noted for his wit and was a strong, popular speaker for the anti-drink cause. See *Gay Wisdom* (Liverpool, 1877) for a collection of his witty statements.
20. *Hull Express*, 14 August 1876.
21. See pp. 213–15.
22. pp. 215–17.
23. Bradford Temperance Confederation, *1st Annual Report*, 1889–90.
24. Ibid.
25. Ibid.
26. Printed circular, Hayler Collection.
27. Ibid.
28. *Alliance News*, 9 September 1892.
29. 'Drunkenness in Liverpool' paper read by George Lignes to the Newcastle Temperance Council on 25 January 1895.
30. Ibid.
31. *Alliance News*, 16 September 1892.
32. The first woman to head an English general temperance organisation of national importance.
33. The North of England Temperance League under the guidance of Guy Hayler, one of the most dedicated of temperance advocates, was an active organisation right into the twentieth century.
34. See the Hayler Collection for many of these souvenirs of temperance conferences.
35. *Brampton Home Messenger*, 16 September 1897.
36. Newspaper clipping, Hayler Collection, no name, no date.
37. Report of the Magistrates, W. S. Nichols papers, Bradford Library.
38. Annual Licensing Meeting, August 1875, Bradford.
39. *British Temperance Advocate*, 1849, p. 11.
40. Whether free licensing did cause increased drinking or not was not so important as the fact that people believed it did.
41. Lignes. Free trade in Liverpool was operative 1862–5.
42. In 1892 the *Alliance News* suggested organising groups all over England to pay for barristers at Brewster Sessions. *Alliance News*, 23 September 1892.
43. W. S. Nichols papers, Bradford Library.
44. Bradford Temperance Society, *Annual Report*, 1890.
45. Ibid.
46. *British Temperance Advocate*, 1 February 1860.
47. Bradford Temperance Society, *Annual Report*, 1857.
48. CETS, *Annual Report*, 1886.
49. Wightman, *Haste*, p. 244.
50. The Report of the Committee on Intemperance at Canterbury, 1869, had clerical testimony: 'The Publicans in too many cases buy over the police who afterwards are afraid to inform against them' (54) and it was reported in the *Alliance News* that the chief of Metropolitan Police issued an order threatening severe punishment for policemen found in public houses unless on official business (11 January 1895).
51. Newspaper clipping, Hayler Collection dated 7 August 1891, no name.
52. Lignes, 'Drunkenness in Liverpool'.

53. Ibid.
54. Ibid.
55. Bradford Temperance Confederation, *Annual Report*, 1890.
56. Letter from J. Y. Gilyard, Secretary of the IOGT Mount of Olives, Bradford, November 1875, in W. S. Nichols papers, Bradford.
57. In the Nichols papers there are reports from these watchers.
58. Newspaper clipping, Hayler Collection, no name, no date.
59. *Leeds Temperance Herald*, 21 January 1837.
60. *Alliance News*, 25 August 1888. The 1888 Reform Bills was seen as having enfranchised many potential temperance supporters.
61. See Chapter 4.
62. Bradford Temperance Society, *Annual Report*, 1889.
63. Sir Alfred Lewis Jones, *Daily News* (London), 14 December 1909.
64. One successful teetotaller, when discussing his appointment as a JP, wrote 'Thus attaining to an ambition always esteemed laudable' (Farish, *Autobiography*, p. 190).
65. In 1892 the *Manchester Guardian* claimed more than one-sixth of the chief magistrates of English boroughs belonged to the Temperance Party. *Alliance News*, 15 April 1892, p. 242.
66. William Forster, report of his speech at Temperance Hall, 1 February 1879.
67. Balgarnie, *Sir Titus Salt, Bart.*
68. He was made a JP in 1907 and a County Alderman in 1911.
69. British Temperance League General Purposes Committee, *Minutes*, November 1866.
70. Ibid. They were right. He did have to ask for special schedules,
71. Gourlay, '*National Temperance*', p. 291.
72. Ibid., p. 295.
73. Ibid., p. 294.
74. Ibid.
75. *Hull and East Riding Critic*, 22 September 1883.
76. *Huddersfield Centenary History*, p. 24.
77. Tatham, a Quaker, was re-elected mayor. He invited the teetotal mayors of other towns to dinner at Leeds. Ten came out of 27 invited (*Alliance News*, 26 March 1881).
78. Mary Walton, *Sheffield – Its Story and Achievements* (Sheffield, 1949), p. 214.
79. Bradford Temperance Confederation, *Annual Report*, 1890–1.
80. J. G. Shaw, *Gregson*, p. 83.
81. Ibid., pp. 124–6.
82. Joseph Livesey, *Staunch Teetotaler*, p. 4. The problem of official hospitality for teetotaller mayors was called the 'social difficulty'. Drinking customs had been regarded as an 'essential element of civic hospitality' discussed at a National Temperance League meeting reported in the *Alliance News*, 4 May 1878. Some teetotal mayors turned over the responsibility for civic hospitality to a committee.
83. G. W. Walker, interview 1969. Mr Walker is the son of this mayor and also is himself still active in the Barnsley temperance movement.
84. 1164 bottles of champagne were consumed at the Mayor's Grand Ball,

Liverpool 1867. Livesey, *Staunch Teetotaler*, p. 237. Many civic dinners consisted of drinking toast after toast all evening.

85. *Alliance News*, 16 April 1881.
86. John Burns, 'Labour and Drink', p. 9.
87. Ibid., p. 25.
88. Teetotallers contested many School Board elections. Of fifteen members elected to the Sheffield School Board, ten were teetotallers and three were 'sympathetic'. *Alliance News*, 1 December 1888.
89. Joseph Livesey, quoted in *Forward*, 19 August 1933.
90. 'Temperance Electoral Controversy in Sheffield, 1885–1889', published Sheffield. This is an extensive treatment of the controversy.
91. Ibid.
92. Ibid.
93. Ibid.
94. Ibid.
95. *Alliance News*, 13 September 1889, p. 730.
96. The Bishop of Chester said 'the greatest obstacle lies in the dissention and internecine hostilities of the Temperance Reformers themselves', quoted in Gourlay, *'National Temperance'*, p. 253.
97. Interview with Mawson, Batley. A letter in *The Sportsman* warned: 'Beware of the Temperance Party candidates at the municipal elections' and stated that many citizens 'are becoming alive to the fact that there is too much of the go-to-chapel element in our town councils ... The vagaries of obstructive cliques of the "Little Bethel" rushlights posing in town council chambers are duly chronicled in the local newspapers'. Quoted in *Alliance News*, 3 November 1888.
98. J. Crosfill, *The Temperance Movement as a Business Proposition*.
99. Ibid.
100. *Alliance News*, November 1891.
101. British Temperance League, *Annual Report*, 1894.
102. See above, Chapter 2.
103. Obituary, 13 April 1922, newspaper clipping Hayler Collection.
104. 'Is Drink the Greatest Cause of Poverty?', debate, Robert Watson (UKA) v. Charles Muse (Fabian).
105. Guy Hayler, 'Labour and the Temperance Reformation', 1927.
106. Ibid.
107. H. Russell Smart, *Socialism and Drink* (Manchester, n.d.).
108. Joseph Howes, *Freedom or Bondage* (Manchester, circa 1880s).
109. Henry Hibbert v. H. Russell Smart, public debate, 10 November 1894.
110. William Hoyle, *Why is Trade Depressed?* (Manchester, 1879, 3rd edn).
111. Peter Mathias, *The Brewing Industry in England 1700–1830 (Cambridge, 1959)* p. 108.
112. Hibbert v. Smart debate.
113. James Whyte, *The Socialist Propaganda and the Drink Difficulty* (UKA, 1894).
114. Henry George, *Progress and Poverty* (New York, 1942 edition) p. 215, quoted by Smart, 'Socialism and Drink'.
115. Ibid.
116. See Joseph Rowntree and Arthur Sherwell, *The Temperance Problem and Social*

*Reform* (London, 1899). This is an example of the search for a better understanding of the problem of intemperance by those who are of the 'temperance group'.

117. 'Thought for Working Men', paper read at a conference of Working Men at Norwich, 1889.

118. John Burns, 'Labour and Drink', p. 16.

119. Thomas Beckwith, 'The War Between Socialism and Teetotalism' (Newcastle upon Tyne, 1888). Beckwith was the agent of the Newcastle Temperance Society.

120. Hibbert v. Smart debate. James Whyte in 'The Socialist Propaganda' argued that drinking made rent collecting very difficult and took the employers' standpoint. Whyte was an official of the UKA.

121. Hibbert v. Smart debate.

122. W. S. Caine, 'Socialists and Teetotalers', British Temperance League Pictorial Tract, n.d.

123. Bradford Temperance Society, *Annual Report*, 1895.

124. Smart, 'Socialism and Drink'.

125. J. Crosfill, *The Temperance Movement* . . .

126. 'Municipal Drink Traffic', Fabian Tract no. 86 (London, 1898).

127. Ibid.

128. See pp. 223–4.

129. Philip Snowden, *Socialism and Teetotalism* (ILP, London 1909), pp. 10–11.

130. Henry Carter, *The English Temperance Movement* (London, 1933) p. 231.

131. Snowden, p. 13.

132. One argument for the co-op to sell drink was so that beverages of good quality could be sold. See *The Temperance Record*, 2 June 1898, for a report of the Rochdale District Co-op Association, quarterly meeting, where it was discussed.

133. *Report of the Royal Commission on Liquor Licensing*, p. 183.

134. T. P. Whittaker, 'The Drinking System and Social and Industrial Problems' (1894).

135. J. Crosfill, *The Temperance Movement* . . .

136. The teetotallers were well aware that they were unpopular and that many personal abstainers did not want to be identified with the temperance movement. *Alliance News*, 15 November 1889, and 22 September 1888.

137. See pp. 191–3.

138. It was one of the first recommendations of the Canterbury Convocation on Intemperance and continued to be an aim of the CETS throughout the nineteenth century – see evidence of the CETS spokesman before Royal Commission on Liquor Licensing, p. 3 of evidence. The Bruce Bill also aimed to reduce licences as a temperance measure.

139. One writer on the subject of compensation raised the point that slave owners were compensated for slaves bought for life service while licences were bought for only one year. (D. S. Govett, *Strong Drink and Its Results* (National Temp. Publication Depot) p. 19.)

140. W. S. Caine called it the Advanced Temperance Party – all parties for abstinence for individuals and/or prohibition for the state ('The Attitude of the Advanced Temperance Party', *Contemporary Review*, July 1893).

141. D. Burns, *Temperance in the Victorian Age*, p. 185.

142. Ibid.
143. British Temperance League, *Annual Report*, 1891; Bradford Band of Hope Union, *Annual Report*, 1896.
144. P. Winskill, *The Temperance Movement*, vol. IV, p. 222.
145. *Alliance News*, 7 April 1888.
146. Winskill, *The Temperance Movement*, vol. IV, p. 221.
147. The 'fanatical' IOGT were at the forefront of the anti-compensation fights – Malins wrote tracts and lectured up and down the country on platforms against compensation.
148. *Alliance News*, 24 March 1888.
149. John Newton, *W. S. Caine, MP*, p. 195; *Alliance News*, 9 June 1888.
150. Lloyd George, a member of the Congregational Total Abstinence Association (*Alliance News*, 2 May 1891), gave his maiden speech in Parliament on the question of compensation. (George W. E. Russell, *Sir Wilfrid Lawson* (London, 1909) p. 202.)
151. Winskill, *The Temperance Movement*, vol. IV, p. 224.
152. Ibid.
153. Letter of Henry J. Ellison to *The Times*, 18 February 1888, p. 15. See CETS evidence, Royal Commission on Liquor Licensing, House of Commons 1899, v. 34–5. Some individuals like Canon Wilberforce were against compensation (*Alliance News*, 30 May 1890).
154. The differences between the CETS and the UKA were commented on by the editors of the *CETS Chronicle*, 12 May 1888, p. 304.
155. When called 'extreme' W. S. Caine, leader of the National Temperance Federation, said 'the evil was so extreme that they could not help being extreme in the remedies for which they pressed . . .' Reported in *Alliance News*, 31 October 1890.
156. In 1888 all the denominations had temperance associations but they were not very large or important in their central administrations. In 1888 the Catholic League of the Cross had 50 000 and the important support of Cardinal Manning. The Baptist Total Abstinence Association had only 14 000 members, the Wesleyan Methodist adult society 27 087 members and the New Connection Methodists had 32 837 members. Their budgets were all rather small – the Congregational TAA, for example, in 1892 had a total income of £400 (*Alliance News*, 14 January 1888, 14 October 1892).
157. This shift to chapel support can be seen in the pages of the *Alliance News*, which gives increasingly less space to the establishment and more to non-denominational activities.
158. The strength of the Methodists was in the Band of Hope and local temperance organisations. Not until 1892 were adult total abstinence societies officially permitted. Before that date all societies had to be on the dual basis like the CETS (Urwin, *Methodism and Sobriety*).
159. Carter, *The English Temperance Movement*, p. 214. Garrett was a long-time teetotaller, having signed the pledge when he was in his teens.
160. The Grand Electoral Superintendent of the movement said 'A vote for one who does not support Local Option is a vote for evil . . .' Kempster, 'Good Templars', speech made 21 November 1884, published as a tract by Good Templars.
161. *Alliance News*, 25 August 1888.

162. See John Morley's remarks at the National Liberal Federation Conference of 1891, reported in *The Times*, 1 October 1891.
163. Harold J. Hanham, *Elections and Party Management: Politics in the Time of Disraeli and Gladstone* (London, 1959) p. 122.
164. Carter, *The English Temperance Movement*, p. 128.
165. Carter, p. 188.
166. Ibid., p. 186.
167. Peter Mathias, 'The Brewing Industry, Temperance and Politics', *Historical Journal*, vol. 1, no. 2 (1958) p. 24.
168. Rowntree and Sherwell, *Temperance Problem*, p. 101.
169. United Temperance Conference, London 1893. 1st Temperance Parliament. All the proceedings of this and subsequent 'parliaments' were printed as leaflets. Hayler Collection.
170. United Temperance Conference, 2nd Parliament, London 1894, with United Temperance Bill.
171. Ibid.
172. Ibid.
173. Ibid.
174. Ibid.
175. United Temperance Conference, 4th Parliament, London 1896.

# 9  A World Free From Drink

1. William Harcourt was one of the most important converts the Temperance Party made. He was against the prohibitionists in 1872 but changed his position so that in 1893 he introduced a prohibitionist bill into Parliament.
2. In 1893 there was the largest political meeting ever held organised in Hyde Park by the anti-drink forces. (Basil Long Crapster, 'Our Trade, Our Politics', unpublished thesis, Harvard University, 1949, p. 348.)
3. Almost all the temperance groups were drawn into the anti-drink cause. Complained a brewer, they had 'extreme energy, fanatical enthusiasm and splendid organization'. Charles Walker, 'The Veto Bill from the Trade Point of View', *Fortnightly Review*, May 1893, p. 741.
4. British Temperance League, *Annual Report*, 1893.
5. British Temperance League, *Annual Report*, 1893.
6. The bills were shelved because of problems over Ireland which took precedence. (Woolley and Johnson, *Temperance Progress*, p. 301.)
7. *Alliance News*, 1 February 1895.
8. Caine, 'The Attitude of the Advanced Temperance Party', p. 52.
9. Ibid.
10. Ibid., p. 54.
11. William Harcourt, 'Local Option and the Liquor Traffic', speech published by the UKA.
12. Ibid.
13. See p. 236.
14. Arthur Shadwell, *Drink, Temperance and Legislation* (London, 1915) p. 182. Shadwell claims that the electorate was only 15 per cent of the population.

15. Philip Snowden, *Socialism and Teetotalism* (ILP, London, 1909) p. 12.

16. Rowntree and Sherwell, *Temperance Problem*, p. 156.

17. Most working-class men in the nineteenth century took food to work and ate at a public house or in a dingy coffee house (*Daily News and Leader*, 31 October 1912). It is often forgotten how recent are cheap, clean eating facilities without drink. The coffee tavern movement was popular in the 1870s but such taverns were mainly to replace the recreational role of the pub. See E. Hepple Hall, 'Coffee Taverns, Cocoa Houses and Coffee Palaces' (1878), and Thomas Hogben, 'The Coffee House Movement' in *The Handbook of Temperance History* (National Temperance League, London, 1880). Many papers were read at temperance conferences on the need for good cheap eating places for workers.

18. See the evidence of M. W. Johnson, Secretary of the Aberdeen United Trades Council before the Royal Commission on Liquor Licensing, House of Commons, 1899, v. 34, p. 157.

19. There was continual confusion about these prohibition terms. Even the temperance supporters themselves were not clear what many of them really meant. Leif Jones, an official and soon to be president of the UKA in a speech in 1898 said Local Veto meant to vote to reduce the number of houses to be licensed while Local Option meant local prohibition. (Leif Jones, 'The Local Veto on the Liquor Traffic and the Liberal Party' (UKA, 1898).) The biographer of Sir Wilfrid Lawson claimed the Permissive Bill was the same as Local Option which was the same as Local Veto (Russell, *Sir Wilfrid Lawson*, p. 76). In 1897 the situation was no better in regard to understanding these terms. *The Newcastle Daily News* on 5 April 1897 demanded that the temperance people give some 'intelligible definition of what is meant by Local Veto or Prohibition. . . . The public do not know what these things mean, and there is also a somewhat reasonable suspicion that the temperance advocates do not know either.'

20. 'Municipal Drink Traffic', Fabian Tract no. 86 (London, 1898).

21. Quoted in James Whyte, *The UKA Review of Fifty Years* (Manchester, 1908) p. 21. Gladstone never made clear his feeling about temperance reform. At one meeting of the National Liberal Federation when the Prime Minister had to address the participants on temperance he said 'We are so much agreed in regard to it that it doesn't require detailed discussion . . .', reported in *The Times*, 2 October 1891.

22. Report by the committee on Intemperance for the Lower House of Convocation of the Province of York, 1874.

23. *The Times*, 26, 27 and 31 December 1894.

24. *The Times*, 29 December 1894, p. 11.

25. Reported in the *Alliance News*, 31 May 1895.

26. *Alliance News*, 11 June 1895.

27. Arthur Shadwell, 'The English Public House', *The National Review* (May 1895) p. 375.

28. Ibid.

29. Ibid. Sir Wilfrid Lawson, according to the *Alliance News*, was not interested in drunkards or the treatment of habitual drunkards. 'He says his business is to stop the sale of drink, not to take care of drunkards' (9 October 1891).

30. Shadwell, 'The English Public House', p. 383.

31. Ibid.
32. *Alliance News*, 13 July 1895.
33. Ibid. Sir Wilfrid Lawson was so confident of the attitude of the people that he wrote a letter to *The Times* in which he said 'I have no manner of doubt that vast numbers of the people are eager to obtain this power to abolish drink. A few weeks or months will show whether the present Parliament is ready to meet their wishes' (31 December 1894, p. 14).
34. *Alliance News*, 19 July 1895.
35. *Alliance News*, 5 July 1895.
36. *Alliance News*, 13 July 1895.
37. *Alliance News*, 13 July 1895.
38. This was the official position of the CETS but there were individual members such as Canon Wilberforce who were against compensation.
39. *Alliance News*, 19 July 1895, p. 464.
40. Ibid.
41. It was claimed by one writer on the subject that by 1890 75 per cent of all public houses were tied in some way to a brewer. Brewers controlled the drink trade (Lord Askwith, *British Taverns, Their History and Laws* (London, 1928) p. 133).
42. *Alliance News*, 28 June 1895; *Alliance News*, 13 July 1895.
43. *Alliance News*, 13 July 1895, p. 441. There was no love lost between the publican and the grocer–licensee. The former agreed with the temperance party that off-licences should be eliminated (no doubt because they took away business from the publican) (*Alliance News*, 10 December 1887). The off-licence grocers did not trust the brewers, who often had their own tied houses for the retail sale of their wares.
44. Clipping, Hayler Collection, speech by W. S. Caine, reported by the press Feb. 1893, no name.
45. *Alliance News*, 19 July 1895, p. 458.
46. Basil L. Crapster, 'Our Trade Our Politics A Study of the Political Activity of the British Liquor Industry 1808–1880' (Harvard University unpublished PhD thesis, 1949) p. 353. The drink trade only came together under pressure of the temperance reformers' threats.
47. Ibid.
48. Seymour Williams, 'Another Cause of the Collapse', *Westminster Review* (November 1895).
49. *Alliance News*, 13 July 1895, p. 441.
50. Letter to *The Times* reproduced in *Alliance News*, 16 August 1895, p. 50.
51. *Alliance News*, 16 August 1895, 2 August 1895.
52. *Alliance News*, 28 June 1895.
53. Russell, *Sir Wilfrid Lawson*, p. 229.
54. The defeat of Harcourt was a great blow particularly as before the election the anti-drink reformers boasted that Harcourt had for fifteen years had good relations with his constituents and now he is supporting the anti-drink side nothing had changed: 'his popularity has in no way declined' (*Alliance News*, 1 February 1895). Years later the Secretary of the UKA admitted that Harcourt was defeated because of his Local Option support. (Whyte, *Review of the Work of Fifty Years* (London, 1908), p. 11.)
55. *Alliance News*, 26 July 1895.

56. Ibid.

57. Rowntree and Sherwell, *Temperance Problem*, p. 98.

58. *Alliance News*, 16 August 1895.

59. Reported in the *Alliance News*, 18 October 1895.

60. Joseph Livesey wrote that the legislators and their families are drinkers, so cannot be expected to pass prohibitionist measures. *Staunch Teetotaler*, p. 379.

61. Regulation of drink selling was not so important if the individual himself was unwilling to buy was an old moral suasion argument.

62. Gourlay, p. 342.

63. Ibid.

64. *United Temperance Gazette*, no date, Hayler Collection.

65. The CETS had its own official bill for the regulation of the drink trade, but some of its members had their own bills. The Bishop of Chester sponsored a bill for municipal control while some clerics supported the UKA bill (Wilberforce, 'The Established Church and the Liquor Traffic').

66. *National Temperance Congress*, Chester 1895, the President's Address, p. 10 (London).

67. Ibid., p. 13.

68. Ibid., pp. 30–1.

69. Ibid., p. 31.

70. Ibid., p. 14.

71. Rev. Hutton, 'The Primary Requisite: Intelligent and Conscientious Conviction', p. 39.

72. Ibid.

73. Rev. E. L. Hicks, 'The Educational Element in Band of Hope Work', p. 122.

74. Frederick Sherlock, 'The Place of Young Men and Young Women in Temperance Work', p. 127.

75. Ibid, p. 172.

76. Ibid., p. 174.

77. See p. 219. A. F. Hills, 'Proposed Temperance Legislation'.

78. David Lewis, 'Liquor Legislation in Scotland and its Lessons', p. 215.

79. See the report in *Alliance News*, 9 April 1897.

80. Chamberlain maintained his support for municipal control of the trade and spoke for it to a House of Lords Committee on Intemperance in 1877. He had also introduced a resolution into the House of Commons supporting municipal control of the drink trade in 1876 (Russell, *Sir Wilfrid Lawson*, p. 129).

81. John Burns, *Labour and Drink*, p. 29.

82. (Personal letter in the Hayler Collection.) From Guy Hayler to Francis Smith, agent, Plymouth Total Abstinence Society, dated 11 February 1896.

83. *United Temperance Gazette*, Hayler Collection, no date.

84. The published proceedings were 'a manifesto from a determined party, which knows, with perfect clearness, its own political aims, and will follow them out inflexibly'. *The Prohibition Movement*, Papers and Proceedings of the National Convention for the Prohibition of the Liquor Traffic, Newcastle upon Tyne, 3 to 9 April 1897. Introduction, p. 16.

85. Joseph Livesey died in 1884, Thomas Whittaker, the old colleague of Livesey, lived until 1899, Frederic Lees was dying at the time of the convention in 1897 and William J. Clegg died in 1895. These were the giants of northern teetotalism.

86. Presidential Address, p. 36.

87. *Alliance News*, 9 April 1897.

88. Ibid. The *Newcastle Chronicle* was owned by a teetotaller, Joseph Cowen.

89. He said that it was only natural for those that were making the fortunes of great men to want to have a share which was the basis of municipal socialism. Guy Hadler (ed.), *The Prohibition Movement* (Newcastle upon Tyne, 1897), p. 167.

90. Ibid., p. 168.

91. Ibid.

92. The temperance movement was continually torn by arguments over who was a true teetotaller and who was not, who was a true prohibitionist and who was not, etc.

93. *Alliance News*, 16 April 1897.

94. Ibid.

95. James Winning, in G. Hayler (ed.), *The Prohibition Movement*, p. 254.

96. G. Hayler (ed.), *The Prohibition Movement*, p. 250.

97. It was believed, rightly or wrongly, that women as protectors of the home would be more anxious to curb that wrecker of homes – drink – as the American experience was showing.

98. Proceedings of the Convention, p. 29, in G. Hayler (ed.), *The Prohibition Movement*.

99. Ibid., p. 50.

100. Ibid., p. 51.

101. Ibid.

102. Ibid., p. 52.

103. This bill wanted justices who refuse to grant licences to put their reasons in writing, and would allow denial of licences only on specified grounds. It also wanted it recognised that the publican had a vested interest in his licence. The problem here is that though a licence was officially granted for only one year, when the licensee died his estate tax was assessed as though the licence was a permanent thing; he was taxed on the value of his business with a licence. Any premises with a licence was far more valuable than the equivalent without one, which was a sore point with the temperance reformers who felt that the licensee got his licence for nothing and therefore should not claim to have a vested interest in it.

104. When Sir William Harcourt introduced his Local Option Bill he said 'they were navigating an ocean which is covered by many wrecks'. Frederick Dolman, 'The Liberal Party and Local Veto', *Fortnightly Review* (February 1899).

105. See p. 226.

106. Crapster, p. 359.

107. Schofield, *Temperance Politics*, p. 25.

108. Ibid., p. 60.

109. Balfour also said that he regretted that the extreme party had not been willing to compromise and 'by their strenuous and persistent agitations the

one serious attempt to deal with this question during the last twenty-five years was defeated'. Ibid., p. 65.

110. Russell, *Sir Wilfrid Lawson*, p. 234.
111. Crapster, p. 360.
112. Crapster, p. 361.
113. *Minutes*, Executive Committee, British Temperance League, August 1899.
114. See David M. Fahey's article 'Temperance and the Liberal Party – Lord Peel's Report, 1899' for a full description of the politics that were involved in the work of this commission. (*Journal of British Studies*, vol. X, no. 2 (May 1971).)
115. Royal Commission on Licensing Laws, *Report*, p. 289.
116. Fahey, 'Temperance', pp. 136–7.
117. Hugh H. L. Bellot, 'The Moral of the General Election', *Westminster Review*, vol. 144, no. 2 (August 1895).
118. Thomas Scanlon, 'Wanted – a New Liberal Programme', *Westminster Review*, vol. 144, no. 4 (October, 1895). See also Seymour Williams, 'Another Cause of the Collapse', *Westminster Review*, vol. 144, no. 5 (November 1895).
119. It seems to have been a poor move. Caine lost the by-election caused by his resignation and was out of Parliament for a while. *Alliance News*, 4 July 1890.
120. Fahey, 'Temperance', p. 152.
121. Joseph Malins, 'No Compensation', paper read February 1886 and printed by the IOGT press.
122. Fahey, 'Temperance', p. 155.
123. One argument against this prohibition was that if the child was sucking a sweet while taking the drink home he would not be trying to drink some of the beverage. (Arthur Shadwell, *Drink, Temperance and Legislation* (1876) pp. 152–3).
124. Arthur Chamberlain, 'The Birmingham Scheme of Surrender', *National Review* (May 1903).
125. The reduction in licences caused great anxiety in the trade. In 1876 there were 98 944 full licences for a total population of 32 700 000, while in 1893 there were 91 473 full licences for a total population of 39 000 000. ('Lord Wemyss' Licensing Bill: A Rejoinder to the UKA', tract published by the Federated Brewers' Association, Manchester, 1895, p. 14.)
126. Crapster, p. 370.
127. Ibid.
128. 4 *Hansard* 119, 16 March 1903.
129. Crapster, p. 373.
130. Askwith, *British Taverns*, p. 181.
131. Campbell-Bannerman, the Liberal Prime Minister, was a Scottish non-conformist not at all favourable to the drink interest.
132. Crapster p. 393. As Crapster pointed out, there was apathy and hostility to the Liberal Bill on the part of the electorate.
133. Royal Commission, *Report*, vol. 34, p. 45.
134. *Report of the Royal Commission on Liquor Licensing*, ch. II, p. 7.
135. The Dean of Rochester was advertised as giving a 'temperance sermon' and

when the teetotallers came to hear it they were horrified when the Dean proclaimed 'the individual who partook moderately was more manly and more noble than he who, owing to a lack of moral strength, abstained altogether' (*Alliance News*, 8 December 1888).

136. Temperance Sunday was held once a year and was a day when the churches and chapels were supposed to focus their services and activities for that day on temperance subjects. Collections were often taken then for temperance causes and the Band of Hope sang temperance songs.

137. Urwin, *Methodism and Sobriety*, pp. 50–1.

138. Isichei, *Quakers*, p. 238.

139. Sir R. Murray Hyslop, *The Centenary of the Temperance Movement* (London, 1931) p. 48.

140. Newspaper clipping, no name, no date, Hayler Collection.

141. The sad state of affairs at the National Temperance League caused one group of dissidents to publish their own unsigned tract 'exposing' the conditions at that organisation. The tract states that there was a decline in membership and in subscriptions, that the organisation was badly run and most members were unaware of what was happening at the headquarters. The Executive Committee of the League was co-opted and no new members had been elected in years. 'National Temperance League and Its Members' (no date, circa 1895–6).

The finances of the British Temperance League were in a bad way. Also it was felt by the executive committee of the League that the work and influence of the League were declining in importance. See the *Minutes* of the British Temperance League Executive Meeting, 15 November 1899.

142. Ibid., Memorandum of Resolution – meeting between British Temperance League and the National Temperance League, no date circa 1897, marked 'Private and Confidential'.

143. The North of England Temperance League in September 1899 wanted agents to live in communities to do continuing temperance work in the villages (speech by Guy Hayler, Secretary of the NETL, Hayler Collection).

144. See pp. 77–9.

145. Whyte, *Review of the Work of Fifty Years* (London, 1908), p. 15.

146. Thomas Whittaker, *Brighter England*, p. 117.

147. See Guy Hayler's paper 'Proposed Provident Fund', read at the Annual Conference of the National Association of Official Temperance Advocates. In it he estimated that there were 150 official agents employed by temperance organisations in the decade 1869 to 1878, 300 between 1879 and 1888 and 400 between 1889 and 1898. The fact that such an insurance scheme could be proposed is a further sign of the professionalism of temperance agents.

148. In Birstall there was no home visitation of non-temperance families by the hall's missionary.

149. *Alliance News*, 4 November 1892.

150. For just one example of a common complaint see 'Drink and Industrial Unrest', by Judge Parry (True Temperance Monograph no. 8, 1919) p. 5. Judge Parry believed that the founder of teetotalism may have been pure

and self-sacrificing but the later movement had many people with the attitude 'Stand by, I am holier than thou.'

151. William Livesey, *Earliest Days*, p. 10.
152. Ibid.
153. Interview, Mrs Holmes, Birstall, 1969.

# Conclusion

1. Sidney and Beatrice Webb, *The History of Liquor Licensing in England Principally from 1700 to 1830* (New York, 1903).
2. F. R. Lees, 'Teetotalers or Tipplers. Who Live Longest and Best?', p. 17.
3. John Burns, 'Labour and Drink', p. 20.
4. Convocation of Canterbury, Committee on Intemperance, *Report*, 1869, and Convocation of York, Committee on Intemperance, *Report*, 1872.
5. See Whitney Cross, *The Burned-Over District* (Ithaca, New York, 1950).
6. Joseph Livesey even believed *all* the troubles in nineteenth-century Ireland were caused by drink. 'Drain Ireland of whiskey, and persuade the Irish in America from drinking it and you will not be much troubled about Fenians' (*Staunch Teetotaler*, p. 255).
7. Thomas Whittaker, *Life's Battles in Temperance Armour*, p. 68.
8. Cook ran his first travel excursion under temperance auspices – it was to a temperance festival.
9. Sir Titus Salt started life as a working man and made a fortune in alpaca and wool textiles.
10. John Cassell was extremely poor as a young man but eventually founded the Cassell publishing house.
11. Evidence before the Royal Commission on Liquor Licensing.
12. *Alliance News*, 29 March 1895.
13. Shadwell, *Drink, Temperance and Legislation*, p. 99.

# Bibliography

## MINUTES AND MANUSCRIPTS

Bradford Long Pledge Association, Conveyance of Teetotal Hall, 15 August 1850

Bradford Long Pledge Association, Minutes of the Trustees of the Long Pledge Hall, 1843–63

Bradford Long Pledge Association, Treasurer's Report, Educational Institute, 1855–63

Bradford Temperance Hall, Conveyance, Declaration of Trusts, 27 March 1848

British Temperance Association, Minutes of the Executive Committee, September 1847–October 1859

British Temperance League, Minutes of the General Purposes Committee, 1 March 1859–16 July 1861, December 1863–October 1877, February 1898–September 1908

British Temperance League, Minutes of the Executive Committee, June 1886–November 1899

British Women's Temperance Association, Minutes of the Executive Committee, 1876–8, 1879–80, 1882–4, 1885–90

British Women's Temperance Association, Minutes Annual Council Meetings, 1885–92

British Women's Temperance Association, Sub-committee Minute Book, 1920–4

Church of England Temperance Society, Ripon Diocese, Minutes of the Executive Committee, 1882–1900

National British Total Abstinence Union, Sub-committee Minute Book, 1924–8

Rechabite Tent, Birstall, miscellaneous papers

Sheffield Temperance Association, Minutes of the Executive Committee, 1856–January 1861

Sam Sims Personal Minute Book, 1850

Women's Total Abstinence Union, Minutes of the Executive Committee, 1894–6, 1896–8, 1898–1900, 1901–4, 1904–6

Women's Total Abstinence Union, Minutes of the General Committee, 1898–1900, 1900–4, 1905–10

## ANNUAL REPORTS

Bradford Band of Hope Union, *Annual Reports*, 1857–1900

Bradford Temperance Society, *Annual Reports*, 1832, 1848, 1855–8, 1860–9, 1871–83, 1889, 1890, 1894, 1895

Bradford Women's Society for the Suppression of Intemperance, *Annual Report*, 1895

British Temperance League, *Annual Reports*, 1886–1900

British Women's Temperance Association, *Annual Reports*, 1881–1900
Church of England Temperance Society, *Annual Reports*, 1881–1900
Church of England Temperance Society, Ripon Diocese, *Annual Reports*, 1880–1900
Church of England Temperance Society, York Diocese, *Annual Report*, 1884
Huddersfield Temperance Society, *Annual Report*, 1843
Leeds Temperance Society, *Annual Reports*, 1845–7, 1854, 1870, 1880, 1882, 1888
United Kingdom Alliance, *Annual Reports*, 1855–80


## PERIODICALS

*Alliance News*, 1878–1900
*The British League or Total Abstainer's Magazine*, vol. I, January 1847
*British Temperance Advocate*, 1841, 1850, 1851, 1852, 1857–9, 1860–1, 1885
*British Temperance Advocate and Journal*, 15 January 1838–September 1840
*British Women's Temperance Journal*, 1883–92
*The Church of England Temperance Magazine*, 1866
*The Keighley Visitor*, March 1854–December 1867
*National Temperance Advocate*, January 1842–August 1843, March–December 1849
*Preston Temperance Advocate*, January 1834–February 1835
*The Teetotal Times*, April 1846–December 1847
*The Teetotaler*, July 1840–September 1841
*Temperance Advocate*, 6 July 1861–October 1862
*Wings*, October 1892–1910


## CONTEMPORARY WORKS

Arlie, James, 'Social Recreation and Other Aids to Temperance', paper to the National Temperance Congress, 1889
Baines, Edward, 'The Experiences of Ed Baines', Ipswich Temperance Tract no. 196, 9 November 1852
Balfour, Clara Lucas, *Morning Dewdrops* (London, 1853)
——, 'Our Bands of Hope and Some Causes that Prevent their Efficiency', paper given at the International Temperance Convention, 1862
Barker, T. H., 'Glance at the World's Convention of 1846, and Subsequent Progress', *Proceedings of the International Temperance and Prohibition Convention*, 1862
*Band of Hope Blue Book, A Manual of Instruction and Training* (n.d., n.p.)
Baxter, Andrew, 'The Wines of the Word. A Critical Study', tract (Edinburgh, n.d.)
Beckwith, T., 'The War Between Socialism and Teetotalism', tract (Newcastle upon Tyne, 1888)
Bellot, Hugh H. L., 'The Moral of the General Election', *Westminster Review*, vol. 144, no. 12 (August 1895)

Bennett, Edward T., 'Arguments of Trade: Four Fallacies of the Liquor Traffickers', tract (n.d., n.p.)

Bently, Joseph, 'Temperance Restaurant and Coffee Houses', paper read at World Temperance Congress 1893, printed *Temperance In All Nations*, ed. Stearns (New York, 1893)

'Bible Temperance and Infidelity', three essays: 'The Bible–Wine Question & Infidelity', Rev. John Pyper, 'Free Thinking Bible Criticisms', F. R. Lees; and 'Controversy on the Bible Wine Question Between a Christian and an Infidel' (n.a.) (Bible Temperance Association, Ireland, Belfast, 1891)

Biddulph, Lady Elizabeth, 'What Women Have Done for Prohibition', Paper read at National Prohibition Convention 1897, *The Prohibition Movement*, ed. G. Hayler (Newcastle upon Tyne, 1897)

Blaikie, Mrs, 'Women's Help for Prohibition', National Prohibition Convention 1897, *The Prohibition Movement*

Blaiklock, George, *The Alcohol Factor in Social Conditions* (London, 1914)

Bowly, Samuel, *Address to the Friends Temperance Union*, tract (n.p., 1865)

Bowman, Fred H., *Philosophy of the Band of Hope Movement*, tract (London, 1877)

*Proceedings of the Opening of the Bradford Temperance Hall*, tract (Bradford Temperance Society, Bradford, 1838)

Bridgett, T. E., *The Discipline of Drink* (London, 1876)

*British Temperance League Annual*, 1857–8

*British Temperance Register*, 1857–8

Bromley, James, 'Observations on Totalism', tract (Sheffield, 1840)

Brown, Samuel, 'Physical Puritanism', *Westminster Review*, vol. 57, no. 112 (April 1852)

Buckingham, J. S., *Temperance and Peace* (London, n.d.)

Burns, John, *Labour and Drink*, lecture 31 October 1904, Manchester, published by United Kingdom Alliance (Manchester, 1904)

Caine, W. Rev., 'Drinking in Schools and Colleges', *International Temperance and Prohibition Convention*, ed. Street, Lees and Burns (London, 1862)

Caine, W. S., 'The Attitude of the Advanced Temperance Party', *Contemporary Review* (July 1893) reprinted as tract

Caine, W. S., Hoyle, Wm and Burns, D., *Local Option* (London, 1885)

Calvert, John, *The Relation of the Church of England to the Temperance Movement*, paper read before Congregational Union Autumnal meeting, October 1872, printed as tract (London, 1872)

Carpenter, Philip, 'The Cup of the Lord, and the Cup of the Devil', printed at request of Bradford Total Abstinence Society (n.d.)

Causer, J. Woodford, 'Sunday Closing for England', *The Prohibition Movement* (Newcastle, 1897)

Chown, Rev. J. P., *Band of Hope and Sunday Schools*, paper read at Conference of Sunday School teachers, 8 April 1873, Bradford, printed as tract

Church of England Temperance Society, 'Our Legislative Policy 1864–1908' (London, 1908)

A Churchman, 'Temperance Fanaticism in Regard to Sacramental Wine', tract (n.p., February 1885)

Cockshott, J. J., 'The CETS and Temperance Legislation', paper read at National Temperance Congress 1889, reprinted as tract

*Trouble at Colne Temperance Society August 8, 9, 10, 1836*, tract (n.p., n.d.)

Convocation of York, *Report on Intemperance* Manchester, 1874)

Crosfill, J., *The Temperance Movement as a Business Proposition*, paper read to National Commercial Temperance League, 4 December 1915, printed as tract

——, *Historical Survey of the Temperance Question: A Statement of the Problem. The Case for Effective Legislation*, rev. edn (London, 1922)

Cumming, A. N., *Public House Reform* (London, 1901)

Cunliffe, Councillor, 'Temperance Orders and Benefit Societies', *The National Temperance League's Annual for 1882* (London, 1882)

Docwra, M. E., *BWTA. What It Is, What It Has Done and What it Has Still to Do*, tract (BWTA, n.d.)

——, 'Women's Work for Temperance During the Victorian Era', paper published by Women's Total Abstinence Union (London, 1897)

Dolman, Frederick 'The Liberal Party and the Local Veto', *Fortnightly Review* (February 1899)

Dowman, J., 'Failures in English Temperance Reform', *Arena*, vol. 24, no. 118 (August 1900)

Dowty, Rev. John, 'The Force of Habit: A Plea for Christian Churches to Support the Band of Hope', *International Prohibition and Temperance Convention*, ed. Street, Lees and Burns (London, 1862)

Draper, Joseph Peter, *Jubilee Sketch of the Fitzroy Teetotal Association* (London, 1889)

Dunlop, John, *The Philosophy of Artificial and Compulsory Drinking Usage in Great Britain and Ireland*, 6th edn (London, 1839)

Eaton, Joseph, 'Address to the Society of Friends on Temperance Reformation', tract (London, 1839)

'Economics of Drink in Halifax', public speech given by P. S. A. Halifax, 31 March 1895, reprinted as tract

'The Liquor Problem', *The Economist*, 26 October 1895, p. 1396

Edgar, John, 'Complete View of the Principles and Objects of Temperance Societies', tract (Bradford, 1831)

Ellison, Rev. Canon Henry J., 'Church of England Temperance Society', paper published in *Temperance in All Nations*, ed. Stearns (New York, 1893)

Ellison, James, *Dawn of Teetotalism* (Preston, 1932; privately published)

'Municipal Drink Traffic', Fabian Tract no. 86 (1898)

*Falmouth Tee-Total Advocate and Cornwall Moral Reformer*, 2 July 1838

Finnemore, William, *The Addison Temperance Reader* (London, n.d.)

Forsaith, Miss, 'The Work Done by our Association', paper given London 1886 to the BWTA, printed as tract

*The Fraserburgh Beacon and Northern Temperance Guide*, June 1843

'Address to the Society of Friends on the Temperance Reformation' (signed by many Quakers) (London, 1840)

Gale, Henry, 'How the Church can Save the Nation', tract (London, 1877)

Garrett, Rev. Charles, 'Juvenile Temperance Organizations', *National Temperance League Annual 1881* (London, 1881)

Gibson, Edmund, Bishop of London, 'An Earnest Dissuasive from Intemperance in Meats and Drinks: with a more Particular View to the Point of Spirituous Liquors' (London, 1818 edn; original from eighteenth century)

'Good Templarism', articles reprinted from the *Liverpool Leader*, circa 1872 (n.n., n.d.)

'Good Templarism Denounced as a Temperance and a Religious Organization', anon (Pateley Bridge, 1873)

Gough v. Lees correspondence published in *The Weekly Record*, 26 June 1858, reprinted as tract

Govett, D. S., *Strong Drink and its Results* National Temperance Publication Depot (London, n.d.) tract

Grubb, Edward, *Lees v Gough*, speech 15 July 1858, printed as tract

Hall, E. Hepple, 'Coffee Taverns, Cocoa Houses and Coffee Palaces' (London, 1878)

Harrison, James, Letter to *Huddersfield and Holmfirth Examiner*, reprinted as leaflet, July 1853

Harrop, H. B., *The Direct Veto. An Exposure of a Falsehood*, Liberty and Property Defence League (London, 1893)

Hayler, Guy, 'Proposed Provident Fund', paper read at Annual Conference of the National Association of Official Temperance Advocates, 15 August 1898, tract

——, 'Labour and the Temperance Reformation' (1927)

Public Debate, Henry Hibbert v. H. Russell Smart, 10 November 1894, tract

Hicks, E. L., 'Present Phase of Temperance', *Contemporary Review*, vol. 76, no. 51 (July 1899)

Holme, Rev. T., 'Suggestions on Band of Hope Unions', *International Prohibition and Temperance Convention*, ed. Street, Lees and Burns (London, 1862)

Howard, E., *Tomorrow: A Peaceful Path to Real Reform* (London, 1898)

Hoyle, William, *Our National Resources and How They are Wasted*, People's Edition (Manchester, 1873)

'The Alliance. Its Supercilious Treatment of the Newspaper Press', reprinted from the *Huddersfield and Holmfirth Examiner* (n.d.)

Hudson, Thomas, 'Temperance Literature as a Means of Consolidating and Extending the Temperance Reformation', *National Temperance League Annual* (1889) reprinted as tract

Ingham, W. P., *How to Form a Town or District Band of Hope Union*, paper given 1894, reprinted as tract

Ingle, Joseph, *A Moral Indictment of Teetotalism* (London, 1908)

Isabell, John, *A Speakers and Workers Vade-Mecum* (CETS, London, 1900)

Jeffreys, Archdeacon, 'The Religious Objection to Teetotalism' (London, 1840)

Jones, Leif, *The Local Veto on the Liquor Traffic and the Liberal Party*, speech given 1898, printed as tract

Jones, W., *Education and Temperance*, address to Band of Hope 1877 at Sion Hall, tract (n.d., n.p.)

'Juvenile Temperance Organizations', *National Temperance League Annual* (1881)

Keating, Rev. Joseph S. J., *The Drink Question* (Catholic Studies in Social Reform, London, 1914)

Kerr, Norman, *Wines Scriptural and Ecclesiastical* (London, 1887)

Knight, Robert J. P., 'Drinking and Gambling' paper by Secretary Boilermakers and Iron Ship Builders Society, *The Prohibition Movement*, ed. G. Hayler (Newcastle upon Tyne, 1897)

'Report of a Leeds Temperance Society Visitation of All the Religious Ministers and Clergy in Leeds 1848', inserted in Leeds Temperance Society Papers

*The Great Discussion, Moderation v. Total Abstinence 1836 debate in the Leeds Temperance Society*, tract (Leeds, 1836)

Lees, F. R., *Teetotalers or Tipplers. Who Live Longest and Best?*; tract (Leeds, 1888)
——, *An Exposure on the Tract entitled Observations on Teetotalism by James Bromley, Wesleyan Minister, 1840* (Leeds, 1841)
——, *The Marriage at Cana and Reply to Clerical World Appendix to Volume 3*, tract (London, 1883)
——, *Wines Ancient and Modern*
——, *An Argument for the Legislative Prohibition of the Liquor Traffic*, tract 2nd revised edn (London, 1856)
——, *Essays on the Moral and Scientific Aspects of the Temperance Question* (London, 1854)
——, 'The Last Decade of Temperance Work', *The Prohibition Movement*, ed. G. Hayler (Newcastle upon Tyne, 1897)
——, and Dawson Burns, *The Temperance Bible Commentary* (London, 1872)
Lewis, David, 'Civil Government and the Drink Trade', National Temperance League Publication (London, 1894)
——, *The Drink Problem and Its Solution* (London, 1883)
*The Liberal Platform Historic Facts and Current Problems* (London, 1895)
*The Liberal Programme Temperance Reform*, Liberal Leaflet no. 1575
Lignes, George, 'Drunkenness in Liverpool', paper read Newcastle Temperance Council, 25 January (Newcastle, 1895)
Livesey, Joseph, *Reminiscences of Early Teetotalism* (Preston, 1867)
——, *The Staunch Teetotaler* (Preston, 1868; also London, 1869)
Livesey, William, *The Earliest Days of the Teetotal Movement* (private publication and circulation, 1900)
Lucas, George, *Reply to Charges Against Teetotalism* (Leeds, 1851)
McCree, G. W., 'The History, Design and Progress of the Band of Hope Union', *Proceedings of the International Prohibition and Temperance Convention* (London, 1862)
——, *Old Friends and New Faces*, tract (London, 1883)
McKenzie, F. A., *Sober by Act of Parliament* (London, 1896)
Malins, Joseph, 'The Gothenburg System and the Municipalization of the Liquor Traffic', Good Templar publication (Birmingham, n.d.)
Mitchell, James, *Texts, Topics and Truths for Band of Hope Workers*, National Temperance League (London, 1895)
Mitchell, Dr Kate, *The Drink Question: Its Social and Medical Aspects* (London, 1880)
*The Northern Temperance Almanack* (1839)
*Northern Temperance Witness* (December 1845)
*Texts Topics and Truths for Band of Hope Workers*, National Temperance League (London, 1892)
Pallister, W. R., *Essays, Chiefly on the Temperance Question* (Leeds, 1849)
Parson, Rev. B., *Anti-Bacchus*, American edn (New York, 1840)
Pease, Edward R., 'Liquor Licensing at Home and Abroad', Fabian Tract no. 85
Peel, Sidney, *Practical Licensing Reform* (London, 1901)
Pereira, Henry Horace, Bishop of Croydon, *Intemperance* (London, 1905)
Phillips, Isaac, 'The Bands of Hope and Their Results', paper given before Annual Conference of the National Temperance League in 1880, printed as tract (London, 1880)
'The Pledge', anon. (London, 1873)
Powell, Frederick, *Bacchus Dethroned* (New York, 1875)

Pyper, John, 'Bible Temperance and Infidelity', tract (Belfast, 1891) tract

Quelch, H. and J. H. Roberts, 'Would Universal Total Abstinence Reduce Wages? A Verbatim Report of a Public Debate', Carlisle, 29 November 1904, printed 1905

Rae, John T., 'The Blue Ribbon Gospel Temperance Movement, and Other Aggressive Agencies', *Temperance in All Nations*, vol. I, ed. J. N. Stearns (New York, 1893)

'Reply to an Infidel Tract on Bible Wines', by a London member of the BWTA (London, n.d.: after 1890)

Roberts, James, 'The Financial Dangers of Open Air Demonstrations and Galas', tract (n.d., n.p.)

Rooke, Rev. Thomas, *Parochial Temperance Associations*, paper read before Conference of Church of England and Ireland Temperance Reform Society, 4 May 1866, printed as tract

Russell, T. W., 'Compensation or Confiscation', *Nineteenth Century*, vol. 28, no. 23 (July 1890)

Scanlon, Thomas, 'Wanted – a New Liberal Programme', *Westminster Review*, vol. 144, no. 4 (October 1895)

Scott, Abraham, 'Teetotalism and the Bible', tract (London, 1839)

'Temperance Electoral Controversy in Sheffield 1885–1889', tract (Sheffield, n.d.)

Sherlock, Frederick, 'The Press in its Relation to the Temperance Movement', *A Handbook of Temperance History* (n.d., n.p.)

Shrewsbury, W. J., 'Alcohol Against the Bible and the Bible Against Alcohol', lecture given in Bradford Temperance Hall, 29 September 1840, issued as tract (Bradford, n.d.)

Skinner, J. Martin, 'Socialistic Theories and the Drink Traffic', *The Prohibition Movement*, ed. G. Hayler (Newcastle upon Tyne, 1897)

Smart, H. Russel, 'The Economics of Temperance' (Glasgow, 1894)

——, 'Socialism and Drink', Labour Press Society (Manchester, n.d.)

Snowden, Philip, *Socialism and Teetotalism*, tract, Independent Labour Party (London, 1909)

——, 'Socialism and the Drink Question', Independent Labour Party (1908)

Somerset, Lady Henry (Isabel), 'Practical Temperance Legislation', *Contemporary Review*, vol. 76, no. 51 (October 1899)

Sowden, Rev. George, *The Good and Evil of Temperance Societies*, sermon by vicar at Hebden Bridge, printed as tract (1837)

Sterling, James, *Failure of the Forbes Mackenzie Act*, pamphlet (London, 1859)

Stewart, Mrs Louisa, 'What do We Gain by Affiliation', BWTA leaflet no. 6 (London, 1887)

*International Temperance and Prohibition Convention Proceedings 1862*, ed. Rev. J. C. Street, Dr F. R. Lees and Rev. D. Burns (London, 1862)

'The Case for Sunday Closing' (London, 1899) (National Temperance Publication Depot)

Swindon, John, *Teetotalism Unmasked* (Leeds, 1864)

Sykes, D. F. E., *Drink* (Huddersfield, 1897)

'Temperance Terrorism' editorial, *The Spectator*, vol. 66, no. 437 (28 March 1891)

Thompson, Sir Henry, B. W. Richardson, Rev. Canon Farrar, Ed. Baines, Sir James Sullivan and Rev. H. Sinclair Paterson, *Moderate Drinking*, speeches given Exeter Hall meeting 1877, National Temperance League (London, 1877)

Thompson, Rev. Peter, 'Total Abstinence as an Essential Element in Successful Home Mission Work', World Temperance Congress, 1900, printed as tract

United Kingdom Alliance, 'Methodism and the Liquor Traffic' (Manchester, n.d.)

——, 'Local Option and the Liquor Traffic' (Manchester, n.d.)

——, 'Nationalization of the Drink Traffic. Ought Temperance Reformers Support It?' (Manchester, 1915)

——, *United Kingdom Alliance Jubilee 1853–1903*, anon (Manchester, 1903)

United Temperance Conferences London 1893–6, printed proceedings

Walker, Charles, 'The Veto Bill from the Trade Point of View', *Fortnightly Review* (May 1893)

Ward, George, 'E. A. Leatham Esq. M.P. for Huddersfield, on the Permissive Bill. A Reply to Some of His Fallacies', tract (n.d., n.p.)

Ward, Robert, *The Fallacies of Teetotalism* (London, 1872)

Watson, Robert v. Charles Muse, 'Is Drink the Greatest Cause of Poverty?' debate published as tract (n.d., n.p.)

Wayland, Rev. D. S., 'Reasons for Not Supporting Total Abstinence Societies as at Present Constituted', *Temperance Penny Magazine* (October and November 1840)

Wheeler, Rev. Henry, *Methodism and the Temperance Reformation* (Cincinnati, 1882)

Whittaker, Thomas, 'The Drinking System and Social and Industrial Problems', (n.p., 1894)

Whittaker, Sir T. P. and G. P. Gooch, 'The Temperance Question in Relation to Sociology and Economics' (1906)

Whyte, James, *The Socialist Propaganda and the Drink Difficulty*, United Kingdom Alliance (Manchester, 1894)

Wilberforce, Canon B., *The Place, the Power and the Claims of Gospel Total Abstinence*, speech given to Church of Scotland Young Men's Guild, tract (Edinburgh, n.d.; circa 1880s)

——, 'The Established Church and the Liquor Traffic' (Manchester, 1882)

Willard, Francis, *Do Everything: A Handbook for White Ribboners* (Chicago, 1895)

Williams, Seymour, 'Another Cause of the Collapse', *Westminster Review*, vol. 144, no. 5 (November 1895)

Willis, J. R. and Rev. W. B. Affleck, 'Temperance v. Moderation and Liberty v. Licence', two debates, Dewsbury, 3 and 4 September 1873, tract

Winskill, P. T., *Temperance Standard Bearers of the Nineteenth Century*, 2 vols. (Liverpool 1898)

Wright, Colonel, 'The Salvation Army and the Liquor Traffic', *The Prohibition Movement*, ed. G. Hayler (Newcastle upon Tyne, 1897)

'Woman's Work in the Temperance Reformation', paper given at conference, London, 26 May 1868 (London, 1868)

Wightman, Julia, *Haste to the Rescue* (London, 1860)

Wyndham, G., 'Deadlock in Temperance Reform', *Contemporary Review*, vol. 63, no. 61 (January 1893)

## SECONDARY SOURCES

Askwith, Lord, George Ranken, *British Taverns, Their History and Laws* (London, 1928)

Atkin, Fred, *Reminiscences of a Temperance Advocate* (London, 1899)

Balgarnie, Robert, *Sir Titus Salt, Bart. His Life and Its Lessons* (London, 1877)

Balmer, J. S., *John Clegg Booth* (London, 1874)

Bell, Lady, *At the Works* (London, 1907)

Berridge, Virginia (ed.), *British Journal of Addiction*, centenary historical (Spring 1984)

*The History of Birstall Gospel Temperance Society* (Birstall, n.d.)

Blackwell, Ernest, *Richard T. Booth of the Blue Ribbon Movement* (London, 1883)

'Temperance in Bradford. A Jubilee', *Bradford Observer* (4 September 1901)

Brown, James B., 'The Pig or the Stye: Drink and Poverty in Late Victorian England', *International Review of Social History*, 18, part 3 (1973)

Burns, Dawson, *Temperance History*, vols I and II (London, 1889)

——, *Temperance in the Victorian Age* (London, 1897)

——, *Pen Pictures of Some Temperance Notables* (London, 1895)

——, *The Basis of Temperance Reformation* (New York, 1873)

——, *Christendom and the Drink Curse* (London, 1875)

Burns, Jabez, *A Retrospect of Forty-Five Years Christian Ministry* (London, 1875)

Butler, Josephine E., *Personal Reminiscences of a Great Crusade* (London, 1898)

Butterfield, F., *The Life and Sayings of Thomas Worsnop the Great Apostle of Total Abstinence in the North of England* (Bingley, 1870)

Carter, Henry, *The Control of the Drink Trade in Britain* (London, 1919)

——, *The English Temperance Movement* (London, 1933)

Cherrington, Ernest H. (ed.), *Standard Encyclopedia of the Alcohol Problem*, 6 vols (Westerville, Ohio, 1925–30)

*Church of England Temperance Society Jubilee Book* (1887)

Clark, Peter A., *The English Alehouse: A Social History 1200–1830* (London, 1983)

Couling, Samuel, *History of the Temperance Movement* (London, 1862)

Crapster, Basil L. 'Our Trade Our Politics: A Study of the Political Activity of the British Liquor Industry 1868–1880' (Harvard University unpublished PhD thesis, 1949)

Dingle, A. E., 'Drink and Working Class Living Standards in Britain 1870–1914', *Economic History Review*, 2nd Ser. (1972) 608–22

——, 'The Rise and Fall of Temperance Economics', *Monash Papers in Economic History*, no. 3 (1977)

——, *The Campaign for Prohibition in Victorian England: The United Kingdom Alliance 1872–1895* (London, 1980)

Easton, George, *Autobiography of George Easton Agent of the Scottish Temperance League* (London, 1866)

Edwards, Michael S., 'The Teetotal Wesleyan Methodists', *Proceedings of the Wesley Historical Society*, vol. XXXIII (1961–2) 63–70

——, 'The Divisions of Cornish Methodism', Cornish Methodist Historical Association, Occasional Publication no. 7 (1964)

Ellison, H. J., *The Temperance Reformation Movement in the Church of England* (London, 1878)

Ervine, St John, *God's Soldier* (New York, 1935)

Fahey, David M., 'Drink and Temperance in the United Kingdom: Works Appearing in 1940–1980', *Alcohol and Temperance History Group Newsletter*, no. 3 (Spring 1981)

——, 'Brewers, Publicans and Working-class Drinkers: Pressure Group Politics in Late Victorian and Edwardian England', *Histoire Sociale – Social History* (13 May 1980) 85–103

——, 'The Politics of Drink: Pressure Groups and the British Liberal Party, 1883–1908', *Social Science*, vol. 54 (Spring 1979) 76–85

——, 'Drink and the Meaning of Reform in Late Victorian and Edwardian England', *Cithara* (13 May 1974) 46–56

——, 'Rosebery, "The Times" and the Newcastle Programme', *Bulletin of the Institute of Historical Research*, vol. XLV (May 1971)

——, 'Temperance and the Liberal Party – Lord Peel's Report, 1899', *The Journal of British Studies*, vol. X, no. 2 (May 1971)

Farish, Wm, *Autobiography of Wm. Farish* (Chester, 1889, privately circulated)

Field, George, 'Historical Survey of the Bradford Temperance Society during its First 67 Years of its Existence 1830–1897', lecture given 19 December 1897 (Bradford, 1897)

Field, Martin, 'Bradford Temperance Society History' (Bradford n.d.)

——, *Historical Sketch of the Band of Hope Union*, leaflet (Bradford, 1886)

FitzPatrick, Kathleen, *Lady Henry Somerset* (Boston, 1923)

Fletcher, J. M. J., *Mrs Wightman of Shrewsbury* (London, 1906)

French, R. V., *Nineteen Centuries of Drink in England* (London, 1884)

Gill, J. C., *The Ten Hours Parson* (London, 1959)

Gordon, Anna A., *The Beautiful Life of Frances E. Willard* (Chicago, 1898)

Gosden, P. H. J. H., *The Friendly Societies in England, 1815–1875* (Manchester, 1961)

Gourlay, William, *'National Temperance': A Jubilee Biograph of The National Temperance League* (London, 1906)

Greenaway, John R., 'Bishops, Brewers and the Liquor Question in England, 1890–1914', *Historical Magazine of the Protestant Episcopal Church*, 53 (March 1984)

Grindrod, R. B., 'Personal Reminiscences', *British Temperance Advocate* (January 1879)

Gulliver, Doris, *Dame Agnes Weston* (London, 1971)

Gustafson, A. and Z. B., *Foundation of Death: A Study of the Drink Question*, 5th edn (London, 1888)

Gutzke, David W., ' "The Cry of the Children": The Edwardian Campaign against Maternal Drinking', *British Journal of Addition*, vol. 79 (March 1984)

——, and David M. Fahey, 'Drink and Temperance in Britain', *Alcohol in History*, no. 9 (Spring 1984)

*Halifax and District Band of Hope Union Jubilee, 1908 Historical Record* (Halifax, 1908)

Hall, B. T., *Our Fifty Years* (London, 1912)

Hamer, D. A., *The Politics of Electoral Pressure* (Hassocks: Harvester; Atlantic Highlands: Humanities, 1977)

*Handbook of Temperance History* 1880 and 1881 Annuals of the National Temperance League (London, 1882)

Harrison, Brian, *Drink and the Victorians* (London, 1971)

——, 'Teetotal Chartism', *History*, vol. 58 (June 1973) 193–217

——, *Dictionary of British Temperance Biography* (Coventry and Sheffield, 1973: Society for the Study of Labour History)

——, 'The British Prohibitionists, 1853–72: a Biographical Analysis', *International Review of Social History*, vol. 15, pt 3 (1970) 375–467

——, 'A World of which we had no Conception. Liberalism and the English Temperance Press: 1830–1872', *Victorian Studies*, 13 (December 1967) 125–58

——, 'The Sunday Trading Riots of 1855', *Historical Journal*, vol. VIII, no. 2 (1965)

——, 'Drunkards and Reformers', *History Today*, vol. 13 (March 1963) 185

——, and A. E. Dingle, 'Cardinal Manning as Temperance Reformer', *Historical Journal*, vol. 12 (1969) 485–510

——, 'Underneath the Victorians', *Victorian Studies* (March 1967)

Harrison, John F. C., 'The Victorian Gospel of Success', *Victorian Studies*, vol. I (1957–8)

——, *Learning and Living* (London, 1961)

——, 'Chartism in Leeds', *Chartist Studies*, ed. Asa Briggs (New York, 1967)

Hayler, Guy, *Famous Fanatics* (London, 1910)

Hayler, Mark H. C., *Vision of a Century* (London, 1953)

Heath, H. Cecil, *The Control of a Dangerous Trade* (London, 1947)

Henley, Lady Dorothy, *Rosalind Howard, Countess of Carlisle* (London, 1958)

Hewitt, Margaret, *Mothers and Wives in Victorian Industry* (Rockcliffe, 1958)

Higgs, E. J., 'Research into the History of Alcohol Use and Control in England and Wales: The Available Sources in the Public Record Office', *British Journal of Addiction*, vol. 79 (March 1984)

Hilton, J. D., *A Brief Memoir of James Hayes Raper* (London, 1898)

Hodder, E., *Life of Samuel Morley* (London, 1887)

Hodder, E. and G. Williams, *The Life of Sir George Williams* (London, 1906)

Hogben, Thomas, 'The Coffee House Movement', *The Handbook of Temperance History* (London, 1880)

Holroyd, A., *Saltaire and its Founder, Sir Titus Salt, Bart.* (Bradford, 1873)

Honeyman, Tom, *Good Templary in Scotland, Its Work and its Workers* (Glasgow, 1894)

*Souvenir of the Centenary Celebration of the Huddersfield Temperance Society, 1832–1932* (Huddersfield, 1932)

Hyslop, Sir R. Murray, 'Lest We Forget', the Rae Memorial Lecture, London, 1932

Keighley, Wm, *Keighley Past and Present* (Keighley, 1879)

Lees, F., *Dr F. R. Lees* (London, 1904)

Levy, Hermann, *Drink: An Economic and Social Study* (London, 1951)

Longmate, Norman, *The Waterdrinkers: A History of Temperance* (London, 1968)

*Mass Observation: The Pub and the People; A Worktown Study* (London, 1943)

McCandless, Peter, ' "Curse of Civilization": Insanity and Drunkenness in Victorian Britain', *British Journal of Addiction*, vol. 79 (March 1984)

Mathias, Peter, *The Brewing Industry in England 1700–1830* (Cambridge, 1959)

——, 'The Brewing Industry, Temperance and Politics', *Historical Journal*, vol. 1, no. 2 (1958)

Moss, W. E., *Book of Memories* (Blackburn, 1951)

——, *The Life of Mrs Lewis* (London, 1926)

Newton, John, *W. S. Caine MP* (London, 1907)

Olsen, Gerald Wayne, '*The Church of England Temperance Magazine*, 1862–1873', *Victorian Periodicals Newsletter*, 11 (June 1978) 38–49

——, 'Pub and Parish: The Beginnings of Temperance Reform in the Church of England 1835–1875' (unpublished thesis, University of Western Ontario, London, Canada, 1971)

Parker, Rev. T. F., *History of the Independent Order of Good Templars* (New York, 1882)

Paulson, Ross, *Women's Suffrage and Prohibition: A Comparative Study of Equality and Social Control* (New York, 1973)

Pickwell, Wm, *The Temperance Movement in the City of York* (York, 1886)

Pike, G. Holden, *John Cassell* (London, 1894)

Price, Seymour J., *From Queen to Queen, Story of the Temperance Permanent Building Society* (London, 1954)

Priestman, H. B., *Recollections of Henry Brady Priestman* (Bradford, 1918, privately printed for private circulation)

Rastrick, Peggy 'The Bradford Temperance Movement', (unpublished paper, Margaret MacMillan Training College, Bradford, 1969)

Reid, Caroline 'Temperance, Teetotalism and Local Culture: the Early Temperance Movement in Sheffield', *Northern History* vol. 13, (1977) pp. 248–64.

Reid, G. Archdall, *Alcoholism. A Study in Heredity* (London, 1902)

Roberts, C., *The Radical Countess* (Carlisle, 1962)

Roberts, D., 'Tory Paternalism and Social Reform in Early Victorian England', *American Historical Review* vol. 63 (1957–8)

Rowntree, Joseph and Sherwell, Arthur, *The Temperance Problem* (London, 1899)

Russell, George W. E., *Sir Wilfrid Lawson* (London, 1909)

Salt, Titus and Sons, *Saltaire, Yorks England, A Jubilee Sketch History* (Saltaire, n.d.)

Schofield, A., *Temperance Politics* (London, 1896)

Shadwell, Arthur, *Drink, Temperance and Legislation* (London, 1915)

——, 'The English Public House', *National Review* (May 1895)

Shaw, James, *History of the Great Temperance Reforms* (Ohio, 1875)

Shaw, John G., *Life of William Gregson, Temperance Advocate* (Blackburn, 1891)

Shaw, Thomas, *The Bible Christians 1815–1907* (London, 1965)

——, *A History of Cornish Methodism* (Truro, 1967)

*Sheffield Sunday School Band of Hope Jubilee Booklet 1855–1905* (Sheffield, 1905)

Sherlock, Frederick, *Illustrious Abstainers* (London, 1880)

Shiman, Lilian Lewis, 'The Blue Ribbon Army: Gospel Temperance in England', *The Historical Magazine of the Protestant Episcopal Church*, vol. I, no. 4 (December 1981)

——, 'The Birstall Temperance Society', *The Yorkshire Archaeological Journal*, vol. 46 (1974)

——, 'The Band of Hope Movement: Respectable Recreation for Working Class Children', *Victorian Studies*, vol. XVII, no. 1 (September 1973)

——, 'The Church of England Temperance Society in the Nineteenth Century', *The Historical Magazine of the Protestant Episcopal Church*, vol. XLI, no. 2 (June 1972)

——, 'Temperance and Class in Bradford: 1830–1860', *The Yorkshire Archaeological Journal* (January 1986)

——, 'Changes Are Dangerous: Women and Temperance in Victorian

England', *Religion in the Lives of English Women, 1760–1930*, ed. Gail Malmgreen (London, 1986)

Smith, Edward, *The Jubilee of the Band of Hope Movement* (London, 1897)

Stewart, Louisa, *Memoirs of Margaret Bright Lucas* (London, 1890)

Talbot, Lady Edmond, 'Settlement Work', *Social Work for Catholic Layfolk* (London, 1911)

Taylder, T. W. P. 'The History of the Rise and Progress of Teetotalism in Newcastle upon Tyne', pamphlet (Newcastle upon Tyne, 1886)

Tayler, Robert, *The Hope of the Race* (London, 1946)

Thompson, E. P., *The Making of the English Working Class* (London, 1963)

Thornton, John G., 'Joseph Eaton and the Temperance Movement in the West of England', *International Temperance and Prohibition Convention Proceedings* (1862)

Tillyard, A. C. W., *Agnes Slack* (Cambridge, 1926)

Tomkinson, E. M., *Sarah Robinson, Agnes Weston, Mrs Meredith* (London, 1887)

Urwin, E. C., *Henry Carter CBE* (London, 1955)

Vernon, H. M., *The Alcohol Problem* (London, 1928)

Webb, Sidney and Beatrice, *The History of Liquor Licensing in England Principally from 1700 to 1830* (New York, 1903)

Weir, R. B., 'Obsessed with Moderation: The Drink Trades and the Drink Question 1870–1930', *British Journal of Addiction*, vol. 79 (March 1984)

Weston, Agnes, *My Life Among the Bluejackets*, 2nd edn (London, 1909)

Whittaker, Thomas, *Brighter England and the Way to It* (London, 1891)

——, *Life's Battles in Temperance Armour* (London, 1892)

Whyte, James, *Review of the Work of Fifty Years* (London, 1903)

Wilson, G. B., *Alcohol and the Nation* (London, 1940)

Wilson, Joseph, *Joseph Wilson His Life and Work* (Bradford, n.d.). Privately published

Winskill, Peter, *The Temperance Movement*, vols I–IV (London, 1892)

——, *Temperance Standard Bearers of the Nineteenth Century*, 2 vols (Liverpool, 1898)

Wood, Ethel, *Sixty Years of Temperance Effort*, paper read to IOGT, published as tract (n.d., n.p.)

Woolley, John G. and Johnson, William E., *Temperance Progress of the Century*, Nineteenth Century Series (London, 1905)

*A Century of Hope*, Yorkshire Band of Hope Union, Centenary Souvenir Handbook, 1865–1965

# Index

305